Impact Estimation of Exchange Rates on Exports and Annual Update of Competitiveness Analysis for 34 Greater China Economies

NUS National University of Singapore

Lee Kuan Yew School of Public Policy
ASIA COMPETITIVENESS INSTITUTE

In 2019, ACI was ranked 12th globally, 2nd in Asia, and 1st in Singapore amongst 94 think tanks worldwide under the "Best University Affiliated Think Tank" category by the Think Tanks and Civil Societies Program at the University of Pennsylvania, USA.

About ACI

The Asia Competitiveness Institute (ACI) was established in August 2006 as a Research Centre at the Lee Kuan Yew School of Public Policy (LKYSPP), National University of Singapore (NUS). It aims to build the intellectual leadership and network for understanding and developing competitiveness in the Asia region. ACI seeks to contribute to the enhancement of inclusive growth, living standards, and institutional governance through competitiveness research on sub-national economies in Asia. It identifies mitigating issues and challenges for potential public policy interventions through close collaboration with regional governments, business corporations, policy think-tanks, and academics. ACI's three key research pillars include (I) Sub-national economies level competitiveness analysis and city-level liveability analysis; (II) Firm-level competitiveness analysis in 16 Asia economies; and (III) Singapore's long-term growth strategies and public policy analysis.

ACI's value propositions may be encapsulated in its acronym:
Analytical inputs to initiate policies for policy-makers and business leaders in Asia
Capacity building to enable others through improvement in productivity and efficiency
Intellectual leadership to create pragmatic models of competitiveness and inclusive growth

The institute's core research competencies can also be encapsulated in this acronym describing our evidence-based assessments conducted on public policies for **A**SEAN in the context of the rise of **C**hina and **I**ndia.

Vision and Mission

- ACI's over-arching vision is to build up its research credibility with policy impact, contributing as a professional, world-class think-tank.
- ACI's mission is to establish our niche as a leading policy think-tank by identifying competitiveness trends, opportunities, and challenges, as well as promoting competition and synergizing complementarities amongst Asian economies and business corporations.
- ACI endeavours to articulate sound recommendations, entice discourse, and shape agenda in the arena of public policy amongst Asian governments.
- ACI undertakes evidence-based analysis of public policy issues and decisions, in order to provide assessment of their effectiveness as well as economic and societal impact.

Research Initiatives and Collaborations

I. Identify trends of competitiveness and policy analysis on trade and investment of ASEAN, within the regional context of competition and complementarities with China and India.
II. Identify competitive strengths and conduct policy analysis on Singapore within the context of regional economies with international benchmarking.
III. We are regularly releasing three indices on liveability ranking including 64 Global Cities, 100 Greater China Cities, and 17 Shandong Cities.
IV. We have established an Ease of Doing Business (EDB) Index on Attractiveness to Investors, Business Friendliness, and Competitive Policies for 21 sub-national economies of India and 33 sub-national economies of Indonesia.
V. We have signed Memoranda of Understanding (MoU) with The World Bank (2015), Enterprise Singapore formally known as SPRING Singapore (2014) and European Central Bank (2014). The MoU between The World Bank and National University of Singapore, coordinated through ACI, was signed in 2016.
VI. We have signed MoUs with various institutions in Greater China economies, including Institute of Economics at Shanghai Academy of Social Sciences (2019), Institute of World Economics at Shanghai Academy of Social Sciences (2016), Shandong Academy of Social Sciences (2015), Chongqing Municipal

People's Government (2015), China Institute for Reform and Development, Haikou (2015), Counsellors' Office of the People's Government of Guangdong Province (LOI, 2014), and Chung-Hua Institution for Economic Research, Taiwan (2015).

VII. We have signed MoUs with seven Chief Ministers' Offices in Uttarakhand (2019), Andhra Pradesh (2018, 2017 & 2015), Bihar (2015), Chhattisgarh (2015), Madhya Pradesh (2015), Odisha (2015), and Punjab (2015).

VIII. We have signed a MoU with Committee for Acceleration of Priority Infrastructure Delivery at Coordinating Ministry for Economic Affairs, Indonesia (2016), Indonesia Investment Coordinating Board (2014), Indonesian Agency for Agricultural Research and Development at Ministry of Agriculture (2014), Indonesian President's Delivery Unit for Developing Monitoring and Oversight (2013), and Employer's Association of Indonesia (2013).

IX. We have signed MoUs with Asian think-tanks and institutions, including Institute of Economic Growth, India (2018), Vietnam Chamber of Commerce and Industry, Vietnam (2016), Centre for Strategic and International Studies, Indonesia (2015), Institute of Strategic & International Studies, Malaysia (2015), Philippine Institute for Development Studies, the Philippines (2015), Thailand Development Research Institute, Thailand (2015), and Central Institute for Economic Management, Vietnam (2015).

About ACI's Research Pillars

ACI has consciously engaged in economic research that has significant relevance to Singapore and the Asian region. Over the years, ACI has focused on our expertise in quantitative competitiveness analysis and simulation, spinning off volumes of research output in the applications of our methodology and regional insight. At this stage, ACI has identified three core research pillars that will guide and define its research efforts moving forward. The three research pillars are as follows:

Pillar I. Sub-national Economies Competitiveness Analysis

ACI engages in systematic and methodical competitiveness analyses of the sub-national economies by using an evidence-based, empirical approach involving a comprehensive list of relevant indicators, which are categorised under multiple layers called the 'environments'. A number of our projects, including competitiveness analyses of Greater China, ASEAN-10, India, and Indonesia, as well as other thematic research projects, were conducted by adopting this common methodology, with potential variations in the specific environments and indicators. ACI's competitiveness analysis of Asian economies goes beyond the usual ranking to offer constructive policy recommendations on how individual member states can improve their rankings vis-à-vis their sub-national or regional peers through the application of the 'what-if' simulation, which provides the projected improvements of each state's ranking whereby the bottom one-fifth of its indicators are enhanced.

Pillar II. Micro-based Firm Level Competitiveness Analysis

Micro-based firm level competitiveness analysis is ACI's second research pillar that has been developed in view of the intrinsic importance of firm-level competitiveness in terms of productivity, efficiency, and governance. In the context of globalisation, mobility of economic activities, and blurring of borders, an understanding of the determinants and dynamics of firm-level competitiveness is paramount, in order for policy makers to adjust and prepare their industries for an increasingly competitive economic landscape. To this end, ACI has partnered with the European Central Bank to carry out research in this area, possessing a solid foundation in firm-level productivity research in the form of European Competitiveness Network database and methodology. ACI envisaged the expansion of Competitiveness Research Network (CompNet) into Asia, thereby pioneering the Asia's CompNet in encompassing 16 economies in Asia.

Pillar III. Singapore's Long-term Economic Growth Strategies and Public Policies Analysis

The third and imminent research pillar focuses on Singapore's long-term economic growth strategies in the context of changing circumstances, future trends, and emerging opportunities for Singapore in the decades ahead. In particular, ACI will take on the task of critically examining Singapore's public policy strengths and areas of improvement by assessing policy successes of the past, identifying new issues to address and the current policy gaps, through a systematic and evidence-based research inquiry using quantitative methodology and empirical data, leveraging on our network of policy experts.

Founding Patron and International Advisory Panel

Founding Patron

Mr George Yeo
Visiting Scholar, Lee Kuan Yew School of Public Policy, National University of Singapore & Former Minister of Foreign Affairs, Singapore

International Advisory Panel

Co-Chairs:

Professor Michael Porter (2006-2010)
Bishop William Lawrence University Professor

Ms Marjorie Yang (2006-2012)
Chairman, Esquel Group

Members:

Professor Kishore Mahbubani
Former Dean, Lee Kuan Yew School of Public Policy, National University of Singapore

Dr Kuntoro Mangkusubroto
Former Head, President's Delivery Unit for Developing Monitoring and Oversight (UKP4), Indonesia

Mr Narayana Murthy
Former Chairman, Infosys Technologies Limited

Mr Philip Yeo
Former Chairman, Enterprise Singapore

Mr Loh Khum Yean
Permanent Secretary, Ministry of Trade and Industry

Ms Yong Ying-I
Permanent Secretary, Public Service Division

Professor Chan Kam Leung Alan
Former Dean, College of Humanities, Arts and Social Sciences, Nanyang Technological University

Asia Competitiveness Institute

Co-Directors:

Associate Professor Tan Khee Giap (2011 till now)
Professor Tan Kong Yam (2011 till now)

Asia Competitiveness Institute - World Scientific Series

(ISSN: 2424-9912)

Series Editor: Tan Khee Giap (*Lee Kuan Yew School of Public Policy, NUS, Singapore*)

In the tradition of the Asia Competitiveness Institute (ACI) at the Lee Kuan Yew School of Public Policy, National University of Singapore (NUS), our research publications make a distinctive contribution to the understanding of economic development in Asia. These books, first published in 2013, in the Asia Competitiveness Institute - World Scientific Series evaluate and track competitiveness for the sub-national economies of China, India, Indonesia and ASEAN annually through combining leading-edge methodologies with an extensive dataset. The study covers four environments of competitiveness: (1) Macroeconomic Stability, (2) Government and Institutional Setting, (3) Financial, Businesses and Manpower Conditions, and (4) Quality of Life and Infrastructure Development. It also conducts "what-if" policy simulations to propose policy suggestions.

2018

Annual Competitiveness Analysis and Impact Estimation of Exchange Rates on Trade in Value-Added of ASEAN Economies
by Tan Khee Giap, Tan Kway Guan, Melissa Poh Wei Le & Doris Liew Wan Yin (Lee Kuan Yew School of Public Policy, NUS, Singapore)

Impact Estimation of Exchange Rates on Exports and Annual Update of Competitiveness Analysis for 34 Greater China Economies
by Tan Khee Giap, Zhang Xuyao & Mao Ke (Lee Kuan Yew School of Public Policy, NUS, Singapore)

Annual Competitiveness Analysis and Impact Estimation of Exchange Rates on Exports from Sub-National Economies of India
by Tan Khee Giap, Sasidaran Gopalan & Jigyasa Sharma (Lee Kuan Yew School of Public Policy, NUS, Singapore)

Annual Competitiveness Analysis and Impact Estimation of Exchange Rates on Exports from Sub-National Economies of Indonesia
by Tan Khee Giap, Nursyahida Ahmad, S Shalini Sivakrishnan & Doris Liew Wan Yin (Lee Kuan Yew School of Public Policy, NUS, Singapore)

2017

2017 Annual Competitiveness Analysis and Impact of Exchange Rates on Foreign Direct Investment Inflows to ASEAN Economies
by Tan Khee Giap, Luu Nguyen Trieu Duong, Chuah Hui Yin & Nguyen Duy (Lee Kuan Yew School of Public Policy, NUS, Singapore)

Balanced, Sustainable and Competitiveness Enhancement Study for Vietnam: A Critical Evaluation with Development Potentials
by Vu Tien Loc (Vietnam Chamber of Commerce and Industry, Vietnam), Tan Khee Giap, Luu Nguyen Trieu Duong & Nguyen Duy (Lee Kuan Yew School of Public Policy, NUS, Singapore)

*More information on this series can also be found at http://www.worldscientific.com/series/aciwss

(Continued at end of book)

Asia Competitiveness Institute - World Scientific Series

Impact Estimation of Exchange Rates on Exports and Annual Update of Competitiveness Analysis for 34 Greater China Economies

Tan Khee Giap

Co-Director, Asia Competitiveness Institute
Lee Kuan Yew School of Public Policy, National University of Singapore

Zhang Xuyao

Research Fellow, Asia Competitiveness Institute
Lee Kuan Yew School of Public Policy, National University of Singapore

Mao Ke

Research Assistant, Asia Competitiveness Institute
Lee Kuan Yew School of Public Policy, National University of Singapore

Special Remarks

Goh Chok Tong
Former Prime Minister and now Emeritus Senior Minister of Singapore

Reviewers

Professor Zheng Yongnian
Director of East Asian Institute
National University of Singapore

Dr Dániel Palotai
Chief Economist and Executive Director
The Central Bank of Hungary

Dr Fan Yubo
Associate Professor
Policy Research Office
Shandong Academy of Social Sciences

Dr Luo Hairong
Research Fellow
Institute of World Economy
Shanghai Academy of Social Sciences

Dr He Dongni
Deputy Director
China Institute for Reform and Development

Lee Kuan Yew School of Public Policy
Asia Competitiveness Institute

NUS National University of Singapore

World Scientific

Published by

World Scientific Publishing Co. Pte. Ltd.
5 Toh Tuck Link, Singapore 596224
USA office: 27 Warren Street, Suite 401-402, Hackensack, NJ 07601
UK office: 57 Shelton Street, Covent Garden, London WC2H 9HE

British Library Cataloguing-in-Publication Data
A catalogue record for this book is available from the British Library.

Asia Competitiveness Institute – World Scientific Series
IMPACT ESTIMATION OF EXCHANGE RATES ON EXPORTS AND ANNUAL UPDATE OF COMPETITIVENESS ANALYSIS FOR 34 GREATER CHINA ECONOMIES

ISBN 978-981-120-787-7

Desk Editor: Jiang Yulin

Typeset by Stallion Press
Email: enquiries@stallionpress.com

Printed in Singapore

Contents

*Based on the keynote address by Professor Zheng Yongnian, Director of East Asian Institute of National University of Singapore, at 2018 The World Bank Group — Asia Competitiveness Institute Annual Conference on 27 November 2018.

*Based on the opening address by Singapore's former Prime Minister and now Emeritus Senior Minister Goh Chok Tong at ANZ's Finance and Treasury Forum in Singapore.

Foreword

The US President Donald Trump has brought unprecedented disruptions to the global order. In the first two years of his presidency, he has accused the North Atlantic Treaty Organization members on imbalanced spending, pulled out from the Trans-Pacific Partnership, withdrew from the Intermediate-Range Nuclear Forces Treaty, among others. Among these political, economic and military policy changes, the US–China Trade War is of particular interest to the world, as its outcome holds major implications that could lead to another widespread economic crisis after the Global Financial Crisis in 2008.

Besides the accusations on China's discriminatory licensing practices and restricted investment in key technology sectors, the US government also imposed 25 percent of tariff on Chinese products worth of USD 50 billion. There is another round of 10 percent tariff on USD 200 billion worth of goods yet to be implemented, depending on the trade negotiation outcomes between the two countries. In response to the accusations and sanctions, China publicly announced that "we want no trade war with anyone, but if our hands are forced, we will not quail nor recoil from it" (Ministry of Foreign Affairs of the People's Republic of China) and retaliated with tariffs on U.S. products worth USD 110 billion.

The war has already brought enormous pressure on the US farmers and Chinese manufacturers. President Xi Jinping has spoken on various occasions that there will be no winner in the trade war. According to the 2019 Government Work Report, China's anticipation for GDP growth is 6–6.5 percent. China is also preparing for the worst outcome. President Xi brought up the term "self-reliance" several times, which had only appeared during Chairman Mao's era.

Will the fundamentals of China's economy be challenged? How will China mitigate the risks of trade war? Before addressing these questions, it is essential to understand the heterogeneity at the sub-national level in order for any policy discussion or economic strategy to be relevant. This is where the flagship competitiveness studies undertaken by Asia Competitiveness Institute (ACI) assume immense policy significance.

This book titled *Impact Estimation of Exchange Rates on Exports and Annual Update of Competitiveness Analysis for 34 Greater China Economies* takes an important step in deepening our understanding of some critical policy issues confronting Greater China at the sub-national level. Moreover, the book also features a timely piece of empirical research exploring the nexus between real effective exchange rate and exports in order for us to gain better understanding about impact of the US–China Trade War on Greater China economies.

To sum up, given the increasingly important role of Greater China in the global economy, this book attempts to tackle some relevant economic issues and policy concerns by studying competitiveness of Greater China at the sub-national level. I am confident that the insights derived in this book will contribute to figuring out the complex dynamics of Greater China economy pertaining to policymakers in not only Greater China but also worldwide.

Professor Zheng Yongnian
Director
East Asian Institute
National University of Singapore

Preface

This book is the sixth edition of the Greater China competitiveness research series conducted by Asia Competitiveness Institute (ACI) at Lee Kuan Yew School of Public Policy (LKYSPP), National University of Singapore (NUS). As one of ACI's flagship projects, the study not only adopts a comprehensive framework to measure competitiveness, but is also conducted at the sub-national level to account for considerable provincial disparities within Greater China.

ACI's approach differs from major international competitiveness indices in at least four ways. First, as noted, it focuses on sub-national-level competitiveness. Second, it deploys an objective weighting method, namely the Shapley weight method, in computing the index. Third, it provides policy recommendations based on the *What-if* simulation study. Fourth, it defines competitiveness in a holistic manner with a consistent set of indicators, allowing both a snapshot view and a cross-time comparison for economies.

The policy chapter of this book studies the impact of real effective exchange rate (REER) on exports for 31 Mainland China provinces. Since China's accession to the World Trade Organisation (WTO), based on data from the National Bureau of Statistics of China, the country's trade has been experiencing a strong upward trend, surging from USD 510 billion in 2001 to USD 3,700 billion in 2016, a more than seven-fold increase over 15 years. At the regional level, the Eastern Coastal Area still holds a dominant position, accounting for more than 80 percent of China's trade volume. There has also been a steady improvement in Western China because of the Belt and Road Initiative and the China Western Development Strategy.

In the era of escalating trade protectionism, price competitiveness has taken on added significance. To this end, the book's analysis of the impact of REER changes (levels and volatility) on China's provincial exports is especially timely. I am confident that this publication will help deepen our understandings of Greater China's competitiveness and policy directions at the sub-national level.

Ramkishen S. Rajan
Vice Dean (Research) and Professor
Lee Kuan Yew School of Public Policy
National University of Singapore

Acknowledgements

Asia Competitiveness Institute (ACI) at the Lee Kuan Yew School of Public Policy (LKYSPP), National University of Singapore (NUS) has been tracking the competitiveness profile of Greater China at the sub-national level since 2000. Analysing the strengths and weaknesses individually for large and diverse countries is best done when the policymaking process and outcomes are assessed effectively at the sub-national level.

In this book titled *Impact Estimation of Exchange Rates on Exports and Annual Update of Competitiveness Analysis for 34 Greater China Economies*, we update our previous sub-national and regional competitiveness studies with the latest available data. Our comprehensive approach to measuring competitiveness takes into account different factors that collectively shape the ability of a nation or region to achieve substantial and inclusive economic development over a sustained period of time. In addition, this year, we introduce a novel approach of weights assignment in the form of Shapley values to test the robustness of the findings. Furthermore, we analyse the impact of exchange rates on foreign direct investment inflows to Greater China at the sub-national level.

This book has benefitted immensely from our annual flagship events which include (a) 2017 The World Bank–Asia Competitiveness Institute Annual Conference on "Infrastructure Development for Economic Competitiveness" held on 23rd and 24th November, 2017 and (b) the 2018 Asia Economic Forum on "Economic Competitiveness, Welfare Spending and Budget Sustainability for ASEAN Economies" held on 29th August, 2018. We received tremendous support from various experts as well as regional policy think tanks. We appreciate the effort and time taken by the reviewers in evaluating our papers presented during these events whose constructive comments have helped us improve our study significantly. The valuable comments offered to us have also been included in this book as discussant notes to enrich the discussion. We therefore would like to thank the following experts and academic reviewers including:

Dr Dániel Palotai
Chief Economist and Executive Director, The Central Bank of Hungary
Dr Luo Hairong
Research Fellow, Institute of World Economy, Shanghai Academy of Social Sciences
Dr Fan Yubo
Associate Professor, Policy Research Office, Shandong Academy of Social Sciences
Dr He Dongni
Deputy Director, China Institute for Reform and Development

This book would not have been possible without the support of our research and administrative colleagues. In particular, we would like to extend our sincere thanks to an able and dedicated administrative team at ACI including Yap Xin Yi, Cai Jiao Tracy, Nurliyana Binte Yusoff and Dewi Jelina Ayu Binte Johari. We would also like to note with great appreciation the high team spirit and contributions from ACI research staff including Professor Tan Kong Yam, Dr Sasidaran Gopalan, Luu Nguyen Trieu Duong, Diamanta Vania Lavi, Leong Puey Ei, Lim Tao Oei, Nguyen Duy, Nursyahida Binte Ahmad, Melissa Poh Wei Le, Jigyasa Sharma, Sky Chua Jun Jie, Doris Liew Wan Yin, S Shalini Sivakrishnan, Tan Kway Guan, Isaac Tan, Zhang Yanjiang, Vardaan Chawala, Aloysius Kang Wen Tao, Lim Yee Wee, Luo Siwei, Sharen Shen Jing, Constance Siew Hui Hui, Tay Wei Xian, Tay Wei Yi, Jessica Ting Jia Hui, Wang Chongyang, Xie Teleixi, Zhang Hao and Jeremy Zhou Shida.

We place on record our appreciation for the encouragement from Acting Dean Danny Quah, Professor Ramkishen Rajan, Vice Dean (Research), Mr Donald Low, Associate Dean (Research and Executive Education) and other colleagues in LKYSPP for making this effort possible.

Tan Khee Giap
Zhang Xuyao
Mao Ke
Lee Kuan Yew School of Public Policy, National University of Singapore, Singapore

About the Authors

Tan Khee Giap is a Co-Director of the Asia Competitiveness Institute (ACI) and Associate Professor at the Lee Kuan Yew School of Public Policy, National University of Singapore. He is also the Chairman of the Singapore National Committee for Pacific Economic Cooperation. Upon graduating with a PhD from University of East Anglia, England, in 1987 under the Overseas Research Scheme awarded by the Committee of Vice-Chancellors and Principals of the Universities of the United Kingdom, he joined the banking sector as a treasury manager and served as secretary to the Assets and Liabilities Committee for three years, thereafter he taught at the Department of Economics and Statistics, National University of Singapore, 1990–1993. Dr Tan joined Nanyang Technological University in 1993 and was Associate Dean, Graduate Studies Office, 2007–2009.

Dr Tan has consulted extensively with the various government ministries, statutory boards and government-linked companies of Singapore government including Ministry of Finance, Ministry of Trade & Industry, Ministry of Manpower, Housing & Development Board, Civil Aviation Authority of Singapore, Singapore Tourism Board, Trade Development Board, Maritime Port Authority, Ministry of Information, Culture & Arts, Economic Development Board, Ministry of National Development, Media Development Authority, Ministry of Environment and Water Resources, Singapore Design Council, Ministry of Community Development, Youth & Sports, Singapore Press Holdings, Yayasan Mendaki, StarHub, CapitaLand and Great Eastern Life. He has also served as a consultant to international agencies such as the Asian Development Bank, Asian Development Bank Institute, United Nations Industrial Development Group, World Bank Group, World Gold Council, ASEAN Secretariat, Central Policy Unit of Hong Kong, Kerzner International, Las Vegas Sands and Marina Bay Sands.

Dr Tan is the lead author for more than 20 books, serving as journals editor and published widely in international refereed journals. He is the associate editor of the journal *Review of Pacific Basin Financial Markets and Policies* (US) and is on the editorial advisory board of the journal *Competitiveness Review* (UK). His current research interests include Cost of Living and Purchasing Power Index for World's 105 Cities, Global Liveable Cities Index, Ease of Doing Business Index and competitiveness analysis on sub-national economies of China, India, Indonesia and Association of South East Asian Nations.

Dr Tan was Deputy President of the Singapore Economic Society, 2004. He served in the 2002 Economic Review Committee (ERC), served as Chairman of the Task Force on Portable Medical Benefits (PMB), served as the Deputy Chairman of the IPS Forum for Economic Restructuring (IFER) in 2003 and served as a member of the Resource Panel of the Government Parliamentary Committee for Transport and Government Parliamentary Committee for Finance and Trade & Industry and Government Parliamentary Committee for Defence and Foreign Affairs since 2007. Dr Tan is currently an Independent Director of the publicly listed BreadTalk Group, Boustead

Singapore, TEE Land and Chengdu Rural Commercial Bank, and Senior Business Advisor to United Overseas Bank Limited, Singapore.

Zhang Xuyao is a Research Fellow at the Asia Competitiveness Institute (ACI) at the Lee Kuan Yew School of Public Policy, National University of Singapore (NUS). Dr Zhang received his PhD in Economics from NUS in 2016 and obtained his Bachelor (Honours) degree in Applied Mathematics from NUS as well in 2012. During the PhD candidature, he worked as teaching assistant in conducting undergraduate tutorials, such as Microeconomics, Macroeconomics and Managerial Economics. His research focuses on Industrial Organizations, Applied Game Theory, and Public Economics. In particular, he is interested in technology transfers and anti-trust policies. He studies the optimal environmental taxation on the pollution problems in the presence of corruption. He also works on the beneficiary of research joint ventures with technology transfer. He also studies the Qualcomm's anti-trust case in China.

At ACI, Dr Zhang is supervising all the Competitiveness Projects (ASEAN, China, India and Indonesia). He is the coordinator for the Welfare Spending and Budget Sustainability project and Shandong Urban Composite Development Index project. He is also the co-coordinator for the project studying the impact of exchange rate on trade at provincial level of Mainland China. Dr Zhang is also working on the methodology of applying the concept of Shapley values to index ranking analysis. This method will subsequently serve as a robustness check to all the competitiveness ranking studies in ACI. Additional projects he is working on include the construction of the Special Economic Development Area index, the construction of Infrastructure index and the Independent Review and Efficiency Monitoring (IREM) of Real Time Outcome Monitoring System (ROMS) for the Government of Andhra Pradesh (GoAP), India.

Mao Ke is a Research Assistant at the Asia Competitiveness Institute, Lee Kuan Yew School of Public Policy, National University of Singapore. He graduated from National University of Singapore with Bachelor of Business Administration with Honours (Distinction) and specialised in Finance and Operations & Supply Chain Management. At ACI, he works as the coordinator of the project on Annual Competitiveness Analysis for 34 Greater China Economies. He is deeply involved in the project: Independent Review and Efficiency Monitoring (IREM) of Real Time Outcome Monitoring System (ROMS) for the Government of Andhra Pradesh (GoAP), India, providing data insights for government authorities. He is also actively involved in several other projects such as Welfare Spending and Fiscal Sustainability Analysis and Cost of Living and Wages for Expatriates and Average Residents for 105 Cities. His research interests cover the fields of financial economics, macroeconomic policy and development economics.

List of Abbreviations

ACI	Asia Competitiveness Institute
ARDL	Autoregressive Distributed Lag
ASEAN	Association of Southeast Asian Nations
BAT	Baidu, Alibaba and Tencent
BIS	Bank for International Settlements
BRI	The Belt and Road Initiative
BTH	Beijing–Tianjin–Hebei
CPFTZ	China (Shanghai) Pilot Free Trade Zone
CPI	Consumer Price Index
CPTPP	Comprehensive and Progressive Agreement for Trans-Pacific Partnership
DSB	Dispute Settlement Body
DSM	Dispute Settlement Mechanism
DSS	Dispute Settlement System
DTF	Distance-to-Frontier
EU	European Union
FDI	Foreign Direct Investment
FRAND	Fair Reasonable and Non Discriminatory
FTA	Free Trade Agreement
G20	Group of Twenty
GATT	General Agreement on Trade and Tariffs
GBA	Guangdong–Hong Kong–Macau Greater Bay Area
GDP	Gross Domestic Product
GFC	Global Financial Crisis
GMM	Generalised Method of Moments
GPA	Government Procurement Agreement
GRDP	Gross Regional Domestic Product
GVC	Global Value Chain
HP Filter	Hodrick-Prescott Filter
ICT	Information and Communications Technology
ILO	International Labour Organization

IMF	International Monetary Fund
IP	Intellectual Property
IPR	Intellectual Property Rights
JV	Joint Venture
LDCs	Least Developed Countries
LKYSPP	Lee Kuan Yew School of Public Policy
MES	Market Economy Status
MFN	Most Favoured Nation
MIC2025	Made in China 2025 Initiative
MNC	Multinational Corporation
MOU	Memorandum of Understanding
NAFTA	North American Free Trade Agreement
NASS	National Agricultural Statistic Services
NATO	The North Atlantic Treaty Organization
NME	Non-Market Economy
NUS	National University of Singapore
OCC	Open Coastal City
OECD	Organisation for Economic Co-operation and Development
PPI	Produccr Price Index
PPP	Purchasing Power Parity
PRC	People’s Republic of China
R&D	Research and Development
REER	Real Effective Exchange Rates
RMB	Renminbi
RSVI	“Ranked” Standardised Value of Indicator
S&D	Special and Different
SD	Standard Deviation
SELS	Single E-Lock Scheme
SEP	Standard-Essential Patent
SEZ	Special Economic Zone
SPFTZ	China (Shanghai) Pilot Free Trade Zone
SOE	State-Owned Enterprises
SVI	Standardised Value of Indicator
TBT	Technical Barriers to Trade
TPP	Trans-Pacific Partnership

TRIPS	Trade-Related Aspects of Intellectual Property Rights
UK	United Kingdom
UN	United Nations
US	United States
USCBC	US–China Business Council
USD	United States Dollar
USDA	United States Department of Agriculture
USDOC	United States Department of Commerce
USTR	United States Trade Representative
WEF	World Economic Forum
WTO	World Trade Organisation
YRD	Yangtze River Delta

List of Economies

	Name of Economies in English	Name of Economies in Chinese
1	Anhui	安徽
2	Beijing	北京
3	Chongqing	重庆
4	Fujian	福建
5	Gansu	甘肃
6	Guangdong	广东
7	Guangxi	广西
8	Guizhou	贵州
9	Hainan	海南
10	Hebei	河北
11	Heilongjiang	黑龙江
12	Henan	河南
13	Hong Kong	香港
14	Hubei	湖北
15	Hunan	湖南
16	Inner Mongolia	内蒙古
17	Jiangsu	江苏
18	Jiangxi	江西
19	Jilin	吉林
20	Liaoning	辽宁
21	Macau	澳门
22	Ningxia	宁夏
23	Qinghai	青海
24	Shaanxi	陕西
25	Shandong	山东
26	Shanghai	上海
27	Shanxi	山西

(*Continued*)

(*Continued*)

	Name of Economies in English	Name of Economies in Chinese
28	Sichuan	四川
29	Taiwan	台湾
30	Tianjin	天津
31	Tibet	西藏
32	Xinjiang	新疆
33	Yunnan	云南
34	Zhejiang	浙江

List of Figures and Tables

Chapter 4

Chapter 5

Chapter 6

Chapter 1
Introduction

1.1 Background and Impact of the US–China Trade War

In March 2018, the US started the investigation of unfair trade policies and practices on its largest trading partner — China, marking the beginning of the US–China trade war. The trade volume between China and the US was USD 710.4 billion in 2017 (Office of the United States Trade Representative 2018a). According to the Department of Commerce, US exports of Goods and Services to China supported an estimated 911,000 jobs in 2015. These statistics not only corroborate the fact that China is a vital trade partner of the US, but also render the concern that this trade war may come at a high price.

As the exact outcome for this trade war is yet to be revealed, this section would set forth the context for further discussions, detailing the background and impacts of the US–China trade war. This section is organised as follows: Section 1.1.1 will focus on the global impact of the trade war; the brief history of the US–China relationship and the timeline of the trade war will be presented in Sections 1.1.2 and 1.1.3, respectively; Section 1.1.4 will discuss the impact of a trade war on both the US and China.

1.1.1 Why Is the Trade War so Critical to the Global Economy?

The trade tension between the US and China has been of global interest, as they are the World's top two economic powerhouses constituting almost 40 percent of the World GDP in 2017 (Figure 1.1). Since world economies have progressively integrated into the global value chain and the interdependence among countries continues to grow, the impacts of an economic shock in one country will spread to the other countries swiftly.

According to a study presented at the 2019 World Economic Forum Annual Meeting, if the trade war escalates further, the global GDP growth will shrink by 0.7 percentage points to 2.8 percent in 2019. The impact will be the highest for China, with a GDP growth slowdown of 0.9 percentage point, while Europe and the US will decelerate 0.8 and 0.4 percentage points respectively (Mario 2019).

Apart from the challenges, the trade war will also open new windows for other countries' development. The tariff imposed on the US goods will make China seek alternatives, promoting the export growth of Australasian, ASEAN and Latin American countries. For example, China may import more soybean from Brazil. According to the General Administration of Customs, in January 2019, the import of soybean from Brazil is 4.9 million tons, more than 36 times the amount from the US.

The direct competitors of Chinese products in the US market will also benefit. According to the UN Comtrade Database, between 2017 and 2018, US's third-quarter import of electronic products from China decreased by 5 percent, while that from Mexico and South Korea increased

Figure 1.1: US's and China's GDP as a Percentage of the World GDP

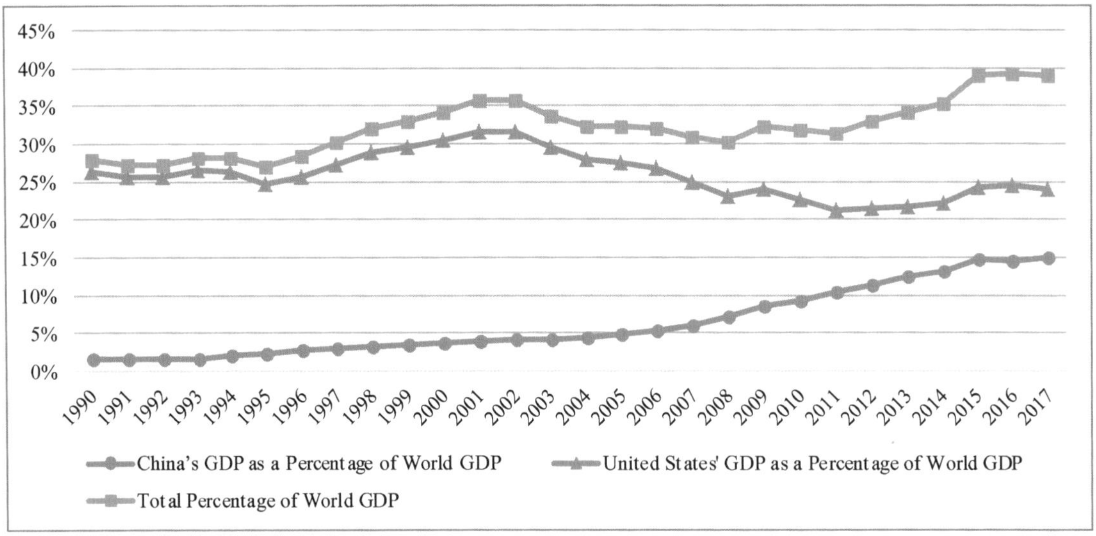

Source: Asia Competitiveness Institute based on information retrieved from the World Bank.

by 2.9 percent and 1.2 percent, respectively. Located at the centre of the trade war, how will China mitigate the risks and find new growth engines? The rest of the book will explore this topic in detail.

1.1.2 A Brief History on the US and China Relationship

Since the Reform and Opening-up in 1978, China has gradually increased trade and investment ties with the US. Disputes arose with these development opportunities. The most notable one was that the US urged China to introduce and develop the Intellectual Property (IP) rights protection policies (Peter 2000).

In 1988, the US placed China on the "Priority Watch List" as part of its Omnibus Trade and Competitiveness Act, an amendment enacted on Section 301 of the Trade Act of 1974. Under this act, the United State Trade Representative (USTR) will now be able to identify and impose sanctions on a list of "Priority Foreign Countries", which have inadequate intellectual property rights.

In 1989, the American business executives claimed to lose USD 100 million to USD 400 million revenue a year, due to China's violation of IP rights on computer software. Thus, they pressured USTR to place China on the watch list. In response to this, China adopted its Copyright Law of the People's Republic of China in 1990. The law essentially protects the copyrights of authors' work in areas such as Literature, Art, Natural Science and Engineering Technology. In 1991, China published its Computer Software Copyright Regulations. However, these laws are yet to meet the international standard.

In 1992, both countries signed a Memorandum of Understanding (MOU) on the IP rights protection, which requires China to accede to the Berne Convention, the Paris Convention and the Geneva Convention. In compliance with this, China amended its copyright law by implementing new regulations to protect computer software programs. While this MOU helped China to establish a new IP regime, it was not properly enforced.

In 1994, American businesses complained again about the lack of IP protection in China, as copyright infringement remained rampant. According to USTR, as of 1993, China exported approximately 50 million pirated compact and laser discs to Hong Kong, Southeast Asia, and Canada. Subsequently, the US and China reached an Intellectual Property Agreement, rectifying the copyright piracy, addressing the ineffective enforcement, and improving the market access (Patrick 1996). For example, in addressing the ineffective enforcement, the State Council Working Conference on Intellectual Property Right was set up, and Enforcement Task Forces were created. The council is responsible for the central organisation and coordination of protection and enforcement of the intellectual property law. China has since gradually improved its IP protection regime.

Despite the disputes on IP rights, in 2000, President Bill Clinton still signed the US–China Relationship Act, which grants China a permanent normal trade relationship with the US. This eventually helped to pave the road for China to join the World Trade Organisation (WTO) in 2001. The President saw the economic potentials in China's huge market, which could benefit the US in terms of exports and domestic employment. He believed that China's accession to WTO would lead to greater financial and market liberalisation, which will benefit the US economy.

Indeed, the accession to WTO made the US and China trade surge. China has become the US's largest trading partner, surpassing Mexico and Canada in 2006 and 2015, respectively. As shown in Figure 1.2, the total trade in merchandised goods reached USD 659.8 billion in 2018, almost 100 times higher than the value in 1985.

Figure 1.2: Total Value of US Trade in Goods with China from 1985 to 2018

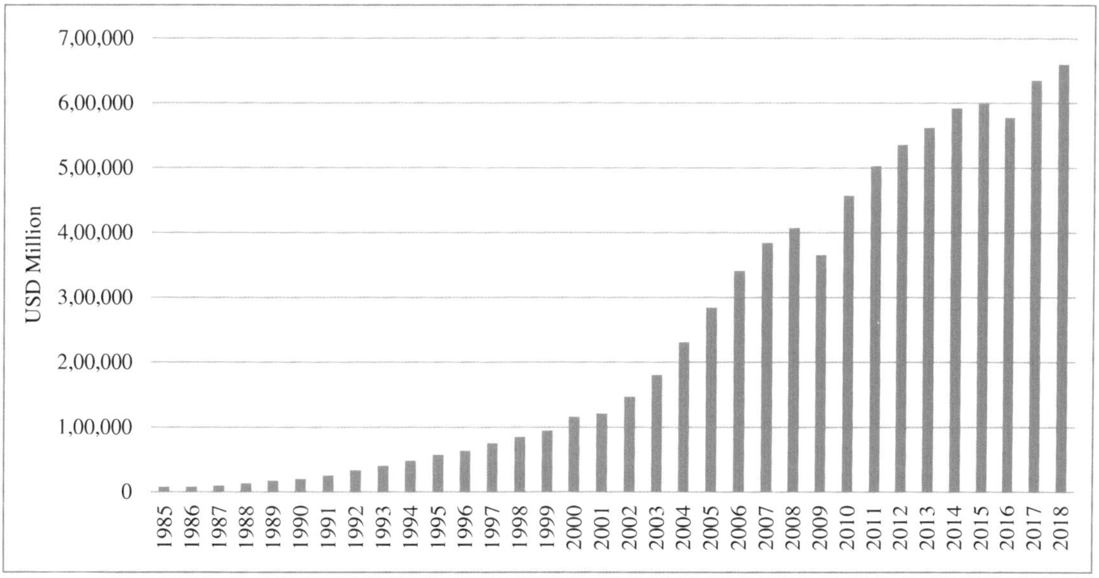

Source: Asia Competitiveness Institute based on information retrieved from the US Census Bureau.

The accession also contributed towards China's economic success and inclusive development. Data from The World Bank showed that China's GDP per capita grew almost 100-fold, from USD 89.5 in 1960 to USD 8,800 in 2017. China's poverty level fell drastically as well, from 66.6 percent of its population living below $1.90 per day in 1990 to below 1 percent in 2015.

1.1.3 A Brief Timeline on the Trade War

Since the inauguration on 20th January 2017, President Trump has highlighted his policy — "America First", which marked the US's foreign policy stance for the years to come. "Every decision on trade, on taxes, on immigration and on foreign affairs will be made to benefit American worker and American families. We must protect our border from the ravages of other countries making our products, stealing our companies, and destroying our jobs. Protection will lead to great prosperity and strength (Donald Trump 2017)."

Upon reviewing the multilateral trade agreements, which were not aligned with the US's interest, President Trump signed an executive order withdrawing the US from the Trans-Pacific Partnership (TPP), a free trade agreement between the US and 11 Pacific Rim nations. Following that, on 31st March 2017, he signed another executive order which seeks to review the trade deficit and investigates potential unfair trading terms.

President Trump also addresses China's unfair practices. On 18th August 2017, he instructed the USTR to initiate Section 301 to investigate China's laws, policies and practices that may be harming US intellectual property rights (Office of the United States Trade Representative 2018b).

On 23rd January 2018, Trump's administration announced the imposition of steep tariffs on imported washing machines and solar panels. A 20 percent tariff is imposed on large residential washers on the first 1.2 million imports and up to 50 percent for subsequent washers above the limit. The tariff will decline to 16 percent and 40 percent, respectively, from third the year onwards. As for the imported solar panel, a 30 percent tariff will be imposed in the first year and gradually decline to 15 percent by the fourth year. While the tariffs are applied to a wide spread of countries, the action can be seen as the prelude of the US–China trade war.

On 8th March 2018, President Trump signed an order to enact tariffs on imported steels and aluminium for all nations including China. A tariff of 25 percent on steel and 10 percent on aluminium came into effect on 23rd March 2018. On the same day, China's Ministry of Commerce, Head of Law Department made it public that "China does not want a trade war with anyone. But China is not afraid of and will not recoil from a trade war. China is confident and capable of facing any challenge. If the US initiated a trade war, China would fight to the end to defend its legitimate interest with all necessary measures." Subsequently, China unveiled plans to retaliate by introducing its tariff on USD three billion of US imports including fresh fruits, nuts, wine and pork (Ministry of Commerce People's Republic of China 2018). Under the escalating tensions, both countries started to engage in trade talks hoping to cease the tit-for-tat tariff.

Despite China's offer of cutting the bilateral trade deficits, the talk broke down after the US demanded China to curtail its support for high-technology industries. Under the PRC Foreign

Investment Catalogue, companies that intend to do business in China are required to form a joint venture with local partners, who have to be the controlling shareholders (FDI China 2017). While WTO does have regulations protecting IP rights, such a negotiation between companies is hard to detect. In 2017, the Commission on The Theft of American Intellectual Property showed an estimated annual loss of USD 600 billion, with China being its principal infringer (The Commission on the Theft of American Intellectual Property 2017).

The US proposed another round of tariffs on a list of imports of USD 50 billion, dominated by high-tech industrial products. The aim was to recoup the alleged losses that the US suffered from China's infringement of IP rights (Office of the United States Trade Representative 2018c). In response, China announced an additional tariff of 25 percent on imports of 106 US products, which include soybeans, automobiles and aircraft (Ministry of Commerce People's Republic of China 2018). The retaliation by China was not well received by President Trump. He labelled it "unfair retaliation" and announced his consideration on imposing additional USD 100 billion tariffs on Chinese products. The situation was made worse when US accused ZTE, a Chinese technology firm, of engaging in businesses with Iran and North Korea, and banned the firm from buying the US technology.

On 19th May, after constructive consultation in Washington, China and the US released a joint statement, which demonstrated the commitment of both countries to decelerate the ongoing trade war (The White House 2018a). Both countries reached an agreement to settle the ZTE dispute. China also announced to cut import duties for cars to 15 percent, from the existing 25 percent, and to remove the tariff on US farm products.

In June, the US announced plans to impose tariffs on USD 50 billion of imports from China, as well as to restrict the visas granted to Chinese citizens (The White House 2018b). Immediately, China responded by increasing the tariff to 25 percent for a list of 659 products.

In September, the US announced a 10 percent tariff on USD 200 billion of imports from China, which will be further increased to 25 percent at the start of 2019 (Office of the United States Trade Representative 2018d). In response, China retaliated with an additional tariff on USD 60 billion of American products.

Despite high tensions and numerous failed bilateral talks, President Trump and President Xi Jinping met up for a high-stakes talk in Argentina during the G20 Leaders' Summit on 1st December 2018. The two presidents managed to reach an agreement on postponing the proposed 25 percent tariff till 1st March 2019. The truce allowed both countries to continue negotiating the trade disputes. After several rounds of high-level talks, Trump Administration announced significant progress between the two countries, and the truce was further extended.

This announcement was critical for both countries. The few months of trade tension took a toll on both countries with significant political and economic impacts.

1.1.4 Impact of the Trade War on Both China and the US Today

Although the trade war just started, in less than one year, short-run impacts on both countries have already arisen. These effects will be briefly outlined in this section, while a detailed analysis will be conducted in Chapter 6.

Figure 1.3: China's Quarterly FDI Inflow

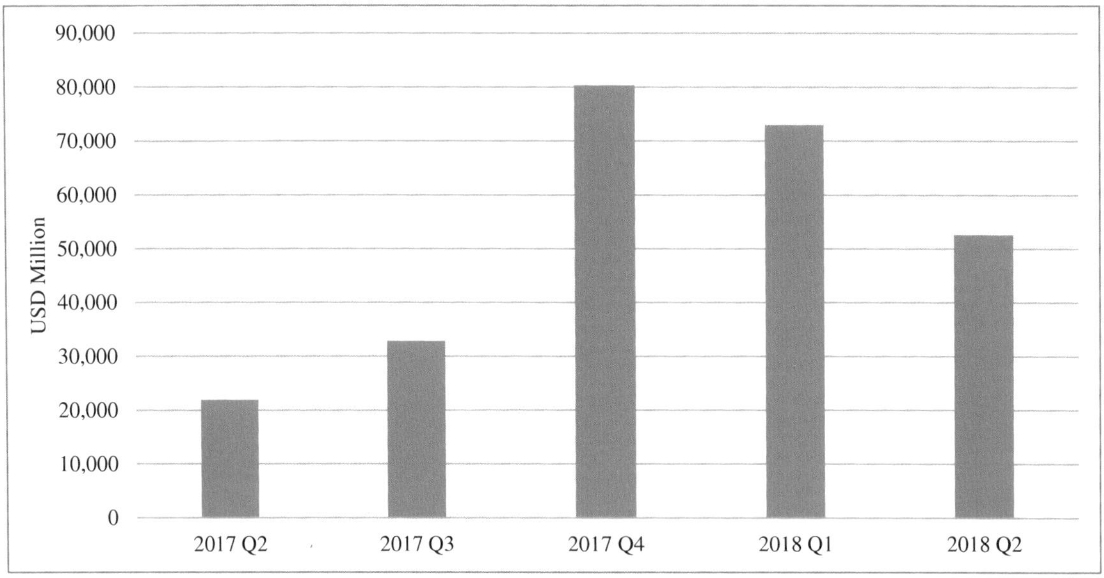

Source: Asia Competitiveness Institute based on information retrieved from OECD October 2018 FDI Report.

From China's perspective, firstly, the trade war escalates China's growth slowdown. According to the National Bureau of Statistics, China's 2018 GDP growth is 6.6 percent. Even though it is higher than the 6.5 percent objective set at the beginning of the year, the growth rate is the lowest over the past 28 years. According to IMF's projection, the growth will continue to fall to 6.2 percent in 2019 (IMF 2018).

Secondly, after two quarters of net capital inflows, rising trade tensions and uncertainty contributed to USD 19 billion of net outflows in the third quarter of 2018 (World Bank Group 2018). Foreign investors sharply reduced purchases in the bond and stock market. The FDI, thus, is lowered (Figure 1.3).

Thirdly, financial markets have declined. The Shanghai Composite Index lost 20 percent and the Renminbi depreciated by 5.5 percent against the US dollar in 2018 (World Bank Group 2018). Even though the depreciation helps to alleviate the pressure from the import tariff, it weakens the confidence of foreign investors. Policymakers should be alerted that under the depreciation pressure in 2016, the Chinese foreign reserve shrank by USD one trillion, equivalent to 25 percent of the total reserve value.

Even though China's economy is under huge pressure, President Xi still holds an optimistic view. During the annual Central Economic Work Conference, he highlighted the potential opportunity hidden behind the trade war, "the world is facing unprecedented changes in a century, bringing both challenges and opportunities (Xin Hua News Agency 2018a)."

The trade war is not beneficial to both countries. Firstly, as shown in Figure 1.4, the US trade deficits against China still increased by almost 40 percent, from USD 30.8 billion in December 2017 to USD 43.1 billion in October 2018.

Secondly, as China is the largest importer of US soybeans, accounting for 60 percent of the export, its retaliation tariff has severely struck the agriculture sector. As shown in Figure 1.5, the

Figure 1.4: US Monthly Trade Deficit with China from December 2017 to October 2018

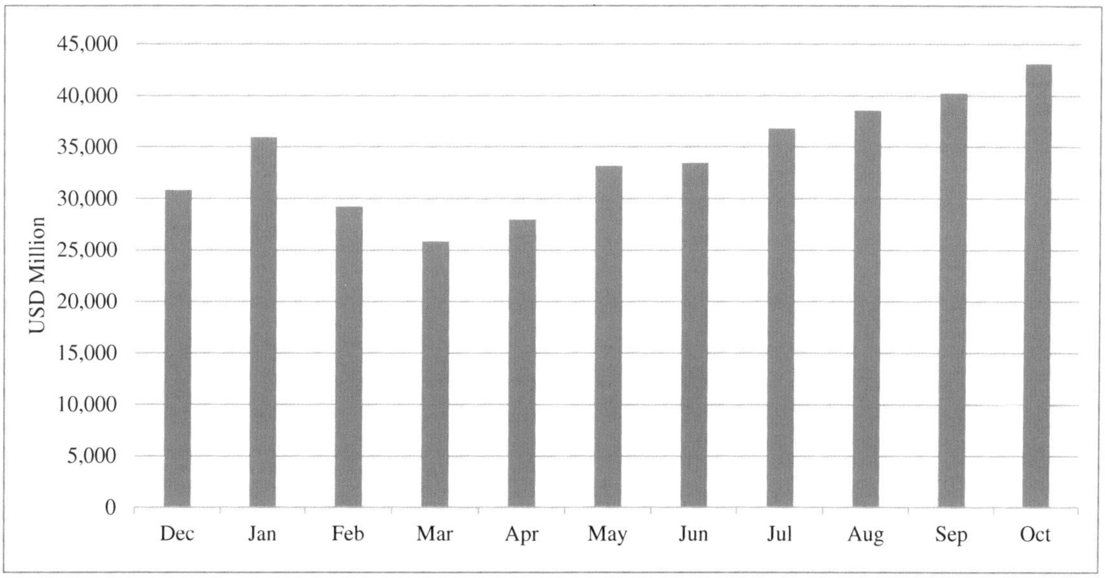

Source: Asia Competitiveness Institute based on information retrieved from the US Census Bureau.

Figure 1.5: Soybean Price in the US, from January 2018 to October 2018

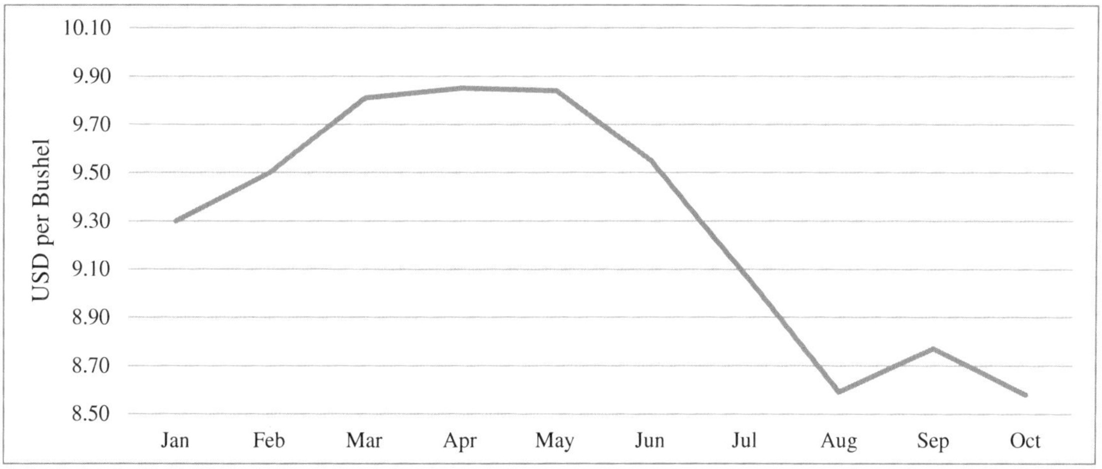

Source: Asia Competitiveness Institute based on information retrieved from USDA, NASS.

market price of soybeans has been dropping since June 2018, likely resulting in a significant loss for the farmers.

Thirdly, the US's consumers and producers face high inflationary pressure, as 97 percent of the imports from China are merchandised goods (Office of the United State Trade Representative). The price effect of rising import tariff has transferred to them. As shown in Figures 1.6 and 1.7, during the trade war period, the monthly CPI and PPI in 2018 are higher than the values in the same period of 2017.

Under the severe economic repercussions from the trade war, a peaceful resolution will be beneficial for both countries and the world. As noted by President Xi Jinping, "The Changes we

Figure 1.6: US Monthly Inflation Rate (CPI)

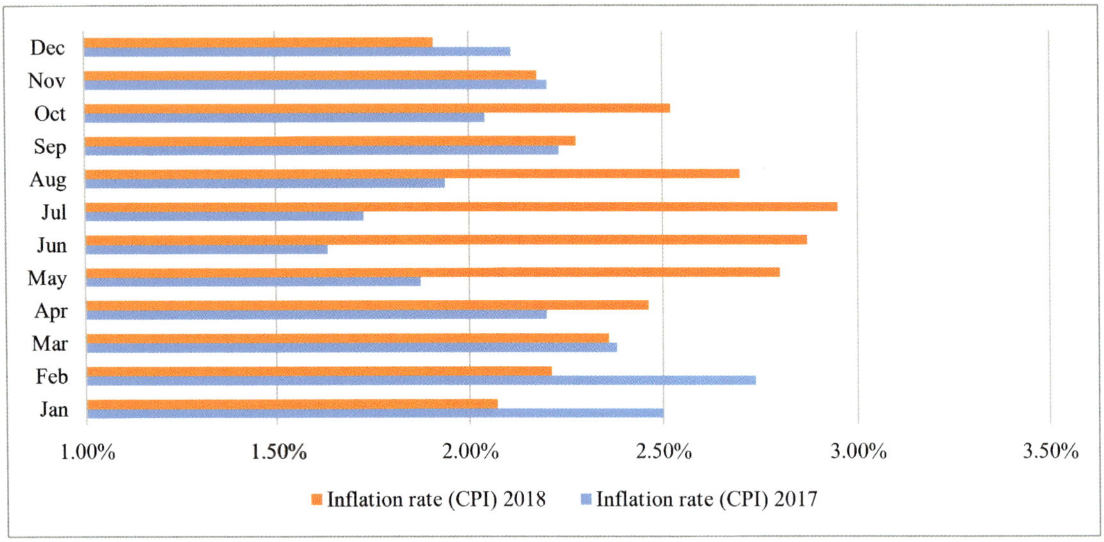

Source: Asia Competitiveness Institute based on information retrieved from the Bureau of Labour Statistic.

Figure 1.7: US Monthly Inflation Rate (PPI)

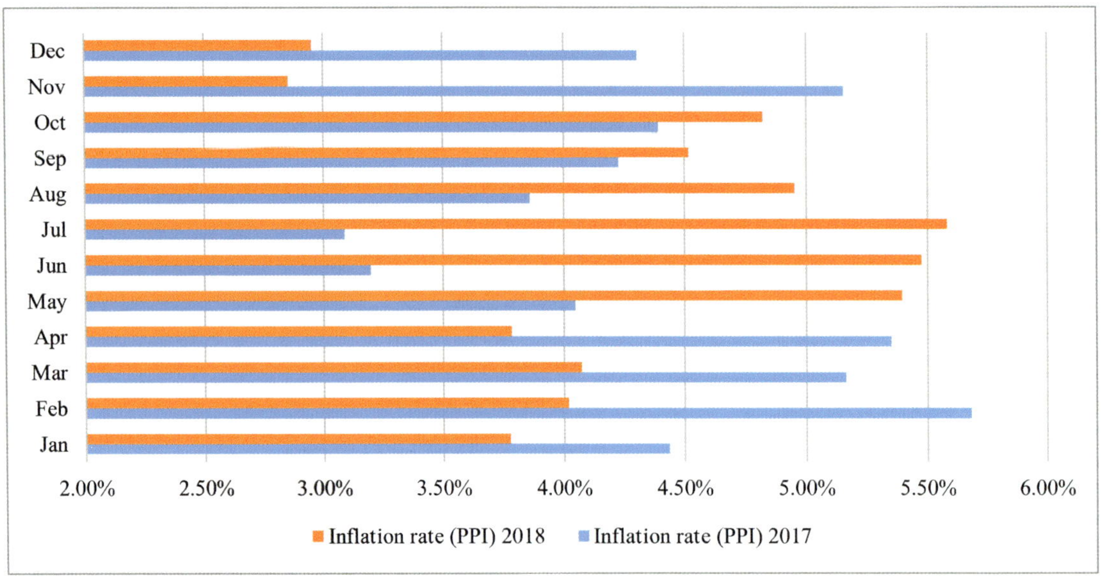

Source: Asia Competitiveness Institute based on information retrieved from the Bureau of Labour Statistic.

are encountering in the world are unseen in a century. Changes create opportunities, but more often than not, they are accompanied by risks and challenges. Mankind has once again reached a crossroad. Which direction should we choose? Cooperation or confrontation? Openness or closing one's door? Win–win progress or a zero-sum game? The interest of all countries and indeed, the future of mankind hinges on the choice we make (Xin Hua News Agency 2018b)."

China and the US, at this moment, are at a critical juncture. Their actions and attitude towards each other will have tremendous impacts on the trajectory of the world's development. Section 1.2 is a speech delivered by Professor Zheng Yongnian, Director of East Asian Institute, at National University of Singapore, on the topic of "US–China Trade War". Drawing on a vast range of historical and contemporary examples, Professor Zheng highlighted several interesting questions. Why is it "inevitable"? To whom does it benefit? What can China achieve? How may this war end? In Section 1.3, the motivation and roadmap for the rest of the book will be outlined.

1.2 The US–China Trade War[1]

I would like to thank the organiser, particularly Professor Tan, for giving me this opportunity to exchange views with you on the ongoing trade war between China and the United States (US). Now, let me share my personal views with you on three possible implications about this ongoing trade war. First, the trade war is inevitable. Second, this trade war has no winner. Third, China's takeaway from a trade war.

The first point I would like to make is that the trade war between the two countries is perhaps inevitable. This is largely due to the changes on both sides. It is easy to understand that when you are weak, people will not be afraid of you. When you are poor, people will probably be sympathetic to you. Hence, when you are strong and rich, people will have a different attitude towards you. This is human nature. In the past four decades and this year, when it celebrated the 40th anniversary of the "Reform and Opening-up" policy, China has changed drastically.

In 1981, when I went to Beijing University, China's per capita GDP was much less than US$300, but today its per capita GDP is approximate USD 9,000. There is a huge change in wealth, in which China transformed from one of the poorest countries at that time to the second largest economy now in the world. People now criticise President Xi Jinping for his foreign policies, which gives potential businesses low profiles. However, I am very sympathetic towards President Xi Jinping because it is now very difficult for China to keep its profile low. China is now too big to pretend to be small, so a trade war is somehow inevitable.

Similarly, the US has also changed drastically, and many of its domestic problems could give rise to the occurrence of a trade war. For example, one indicator is the size of the middle class. The US figure was about 70 percent at its peak but is shrinking to less than 50 percent now. During Obama's eight years of presidency, the size of the middle class was dropping by more than one percent each year. This has shown a huge impact. This is also the reason why populism comes back and why Donald Trump is able to garner sizeable support.

Beyond the shrinkage of the middle class, another problem in the US is its huge stock of trade deficits. The fiscal position of a country will be unsustainable if its trade deficits are too large. I strongly believe that we should remember the 1840s Opium War. During that period, China had

[1] This section includes the keynote address by Professor Zheng Yongnian, director of East Asian Institute of National University of Singapore, at 2018 The World Bank Group — Asia Competitiveness Institute Annual Conference on 27 November 2018, reprinted with permission.

many items exporting to the UK, but the UK had nothing of interest to China. Eventually, the UK began selling opium to China. In another way, both countries will have to find a way to deal with the huge trade deficits; otherwise, it will not be beneficial to both sides. Nevertheless, the trade deficit problem cannot be easily resolved. On the one hand, China always says that they are not actively pursuing a trade surplus. On the other hand, the US is reluctant to sell technologies that encompass the comparative advantages of the US because these technologies are sensitive, and the US is afraid that China will use them in military areas.

Furthermore, the US and China have disputes over intellectual property rights and technological transfers. In March, when Premier Li Keqiang met our group, one of the delegates from the United States asked him why China has a policy that forces the US to perform technological transfers. Premier Li Keqiang answered that he did not know why the government of China has such a policy. He said, "China has 1.3 billion populations and roughly 100 million enterprises. Therefore, definitely, there are some enterprises that constantly request the US to transfer technologies to China." As per his words, the requirement of technology transfer is not a formal policy from the government but a de facto practice in China. This angers the US.

From a political point of view, the US and China do not trust each other. In the 80s, the US optimistically believed that China would eventually democratise and become a democracy. Economic optimisation and political democratisation were the two slogans at that time. Eventually, the US found that China's economy did not embrace the free market ideology from western countries and China did not become a democracy. However, we have to keep in mind that the US is still a missionary country and it still has a strong will to change other countries' political system.

The relationship between the US and China are even worse in military areas, particularly the South China Sea issues as well as the issues regarding North Korea and Taiwan. The US military industrial complex has been strong, ever since the end of the "Cold War". In order to obtain more military budget, the US needs an enemy. Similarly, China also wants more budget so that they can maintain their influence in the South China Sea area. Such motivation of self-interest is understandable.

Given all the backgrounds, I would say that the collision between these two countries would escalate to a new state. China has also made some huge mistakes, one of which I would call the "over-propaganda of their policy". This mistake is reflected mainly in three areas.

The first area that makes the US upset is the "Made in China 2025" plan. Just like German Industry 4.0, which aims only at upgrading industries, the plan *per se* is actually not a big deal. However, China's propaganda is very awful. The advocacy of this plan, as a means to surpass the US and to defeat the US and Europe, is an over-propaganda and an over-publicity.

The second area is known as the "China Model". I believe that China has its model, which allows China to be differentiated from the US or Europe. President Xi Jinping himself made strong emphases on this model over a few occasions, particularly last year when President Xi Jinping initiated a dialogue between the Communist Party and the world. During that dialogue, more than 300 political parties and international organisations gathered in Beijing. Some of the developing countries were interested in the "China Model", but President Xi Jinping told them, "Yes! You can learn if you are interested, but we are not going to export our model." However,

China's propaganda is different from what he said. There has been strong propaganda for promoting the Chinese model everywhere and that the model is better than the US. This triggered many controversies in the West.

The third area is the "One Belt, One Road". It is officially defined as an initiative. However, the propaganda of "One Belt, One Road" is China's global strategy. This is again an over-propaganda that could give rise to many negative consequences.

Considering the mistake that China made, we could say that a war between the US and China is inevitable. However, a trade war, rather than wars in other areas, is the best outcome for China. Wars such as those arising from the conflicts in the South China Sea, in Taiwan and Korea Peninsula could be worse off. As of today, a trade war is still the best option.

My second point is that there will be no winner in this trade war. In reality, I do not believe that the US is afraid of China's political system. I strongly believe that China's political system does not have any influence over the US or Europe. Most people consider China's political regime primitive or underdeveloped. Thus, I do not think that China's political system would be attractive to so many countries. However, there are still some African and Latin America countries expressing slight interests in the system, but I do not think that it will be attractive to the US. Similarly, I do not believe that the US is afraid of China's military because the gap between the military of the US and China is too huge. However, the Pentagon wants more budget so it will still label China as a major threat. I personally feel that what the US is afraid of is China's huge market. The market is extremely important because it is the key to China's strong growth.

I have heard that the US is now ceasing the issuance of visas to Chinese students and scholars in certain areas. It seems that a "Cold War" is now taking place between the US and China. Despite so, I do not think that the US will give up on China's market.

Since the 80s, China has been the last to adopt capitalism. While India is growing rapidly, it is still in the early stage of development, and its capitalist development will be slower than China's development before. China's rapid development can be attributed to Chairman Mao because he eliminated almost all barriers to develop capitalism. However, Japan will not give up, and similarly, Europe will not give up. Even the White House has a military-industrial complex interest different from that the Wall Street does. For the moment, the US has obviously formed a unanimous policy against China. However, I think that different groups have different attitudes toward China. The Military Industrial Complex group wants a "Cold War" while Wall Street wants China to open up its door wider.

My last point is that China will develop even faster if it learns a lesson from this trade war. However, it is a big "IF". However, for the moment, everything looks fine since President Xi Jinping has emphasised many times that China will open its door wider.

For China, I do not think that it would want to be in a trade war with the US. The China-US relationship has always been important to China ever since the late Deng Xiaoping era. A working and feasible China-US relationship is the most important KPI for the leader. This also gives rise to many rumours that President Xi Jinping is facing high pressure within the party due to the tension between China and the US.

China has also emphasised multilateralism — perhaps I should say that China has overemphasised it. The "16 + 1" initiative in East European is an example. China always likes to invite many leaders to come together to discuss certain things, but yet the business has never covered more than two countries.

For the US, I believe that it is not wise to discontinue its relationship with China. For example, after the Tiananmen Square protest on 4 June 1989, the West imposed economic sanctions on China, particularly in its military domain, but China decided to develop its own system at that time. If China's military system is independent of that of the US, it will be much more difficult for the US to deal with. It is the same in other areas as well. Another example is that the supercomputer of China has developed more advanced than that of the US is. Many examples can also be found in other areas like aerospace, speed train and cashless payment. Additionally, China has the BATs — Baidu, Alibaba and Tencent. The key advantage of China is its huge market. While the US has accused China of intellectual property right violation, we have to remember that China has also been the biggest market for the US to sell technology applications.

Technology is very expensive. In Singapore, unlike China, the market is very small. Even if we have new technologies, we would have to spend a lot of money, and we do not have the market for it. For the middle class in China, although its per capita GDP is still much lower than that of the US, its sheer size is almost equal to that of the US. The middle class is shrinking in the US but is still growing in China. For instance, China has experienced five- to six-point worth of growth in a decade time. Eventually, China's middle class will be much bigger than that of the US are. A big market is in favour of technological progress. If you neglect the market in China, you are not going to benefit from this.

Nonetheless, there is a possibility that China is irrational or too nationalistic. If China retaliates to the strike from the US immediately, a "Cold War" will probably take place. A "Hot War" is almost impossible since both the US and China have nuclear capabilities but a "Cold War" or a new type of the "Cold War" could still be triggered. However, it seems that everything is well for now and that the US and China will not enter into a "Cold War". President Xi Jinping and Donald Trump will meet in a few days. Hopefully, they can strike a deal, and the US–China relationship could be adjusted.

Once again, thank you for giving me this opportunity to exchange views with you. Looking forward to any further questions during the Q&A session.

1.3 Motivation and Roadmap of the Book

This final section of the chapter will discuss the motivation of this project and provide the roadmap of the book.

Notwithstanding the increasingly significant role played by China in the global economy, the unbalanced regional development continues to impede sustainable and inclusive growth that deserves policy attention. In the tradition of the Asia Competitiveness Institute (ACI) at the Lee Kuan Yew School of Public Policy (LKYSPP), National University of Singapore (NUS), our work and publications make a distinctive contribution to the literature on economic development in the region by focusing on competitiveness analysis and rankings at the subnational level, beyond the traditional analysis at the national level.

Moreover, it is in this spirit that ACI has crafted a comprehensive methodology and framework to assess competitiveness at the subnational level, which is employed here in this book, as well as in ACI's previous publications on Greater China, Indonesia, India, and ASEAN.

Since the publication of ACI's inaugural volume on Greater China economies, the comprehensive competitiveness index developed by ACI has been used for ranking the 34 Greater China economies in various dimensions. As ACI aims to provide an annual update by extending all studies, this updated book thus includes data from 2000 to 2015, which was the latest available at the time of data collection in 2017.

ACI's evidence-based analysis, which is supported by quantitative methodology, is of great value to policymakers. Together with academics, experts, practitioners, the business community and non-government organisations are all among ACI's target audience. To ensure the quality of policy and business interactions among these parties, ACI follows the academic tradition of holding Review Seminars prior to any book publication. As noted in the Acknowledgements, for example, ACI conducted the Greater China–India Economic Forum in August 2018 to solicit feedback regarding our studies on Greater China economies.

This book consists of six chapters, with Chapter 1 as the introduction focusing on the background of the US–China Trade War. Chapter 2 will elaborate on the research methodology used for this project. The chapter will start with the literature review on competitiveness, followed by details about the research framework of ACI's competitiveness study for Greater China at the subnational level.

Subsequently, Chapters 3 and 4 will present the results related to competitiveness analysis of Greater China economies, at the economy and regional levels, respectively. Each chapter will provide the overall competitiveness rankings and scores based on 2015 data for indicators, as well as the rankings and scores within each of the four environments. Furthermore, *What-if* Competitiveness Simulation analysis will also be conducted in order to gain more insights about effective policy responses and their effects on improving competitiveness at both economy and regional levels.

The entire Chapter 5 will be dedicated to the empirical study of the relationship between REER and Exports of Mainland China provinces. The chapter will start with an overview of China's exports. The literature review will also be divided into general and China-specific studies. Subsequently, empirical models will be developed, followed by empirical results and robustness checks. The chapter will end with concluding notes and policy implications.

Finally, Chapter 6 will be the concluding chapter. The chapter will start with ESM Goh's opening address about the confrontations between US and China. After that, there will be comprehensive discussions on the US–China Trade War, including issues about China's protection on Intellectual Property Rights, its violation of World Trade Organisation rules, challenges to its economic growth, the development of its three regional megalopolises, and how to mitigate the impact and ramification of its trade war against the US. This chapter will conclude with directions for future research. Appendices will be provided at the end of the book.

References

Donald Trump. 2017. "The Inaugural Address." January 20, 2017. https://www.whitehouse.gov/briefings-statements/the-inaugural-address/.

FDI China. 2017. "Catalogue of Industries for Guiding Foreign Investment (Revision 2017)." 2017. http://www.fdi.gov.cn/1800000121_39_4851_0_7.html.

IMF. 2018. "World Economic Outlook Update, July 2018." https://www.imf.org/en/Publications/WEO/Issues/2018/07/02/world-economic-outlook-update-july-2018.

Mario, Mesquita. 2019. "How a Trade War Would Impact Global Growth." January 18, 2019. https://www.weforum.org/agenda/2019/01/how-trade-war-would-impact-global-growth-tariff/.

Ministry of Commerce People's Republic of China. 2018. "商务部新闻发言人就中方发布针对美国进口钢铁和铝产品232措施的中止减让产品清单发表谈话 A Spokesperson for the Ministry of Commerce Made a Statement on China's Announcement on a List of 232 Measures against US's Import of Steel and Aluminium Product (In Chinese)." March 23, 2018. http://www.mofcom.gov.cn/article/ae/ag/201803/20180302722664.shtml.

Office of the United States Trade Representative. 2018a. "The People's Republic of China." 2018. https://ustr.gov/countries-regions/china-mongolia-taiwan/peoples-republic-china.

———. 2018b. "Findings of The Investigation Into China's Acts, Policies, And Practices Related To Technology Transfer, Intellectual Property, and Innovation Under Section 301 Of The Trade Act Of 1974." https://ustr.gov/sites/default/files/Section%20301%20FINAL.PDF.

———. 2018c. "Under Section 301 Action, USTR Releases Proposed Tariff List on Chinese Products." April 3, 2018. https://ustr.gov/about-us/policy-offices/press-office/press-releases/2018/april/under-section-301-action-ustr.

———. 2018d. "USTR Finalizes Tariffs on $200 Billion of Chinese Imports in Response to China's Unfair Trade Practices." September 18, 2018. https://ustr.gov/about-us/policy-offices/press-office/press-releases/2018/september/ustr-finalizes-tariffs-200.

Patrick H., Hu. 1996. "Mickey Mouse in China: Legal and Cultural Implications in Protecting US Copyrights."

Peter K., Yu. 2000. "From Pirates to Partners: Protecting Intellectual Property in China in the Twenty First Century."

The Commission on the Theft of American Intellectual Property. 2017. "IP Commission Report Update."

The White House. 2018a. "Joint Statement of the United States and China Regarding Trade Consultations." May 19, 2018. https://www.whitehouse.gov/briefings-statements/joint-statement-united-states-china-regarding-trade-consultations/.

———. 2018b. "Statement by the President Regarding Trade with China." June 15, 2018. https://www.whitehouse.gov/briefings-statements/statement-president-regarding-trade-china/.

World Bank Group. 2018. "China Economic Update." http://pubdocs.worldbank.org/en/917591545202039807/CEU-Dec-2018-EN.pdf.

Xin Hua News Agency. 2018a. "China Holds Key Economic Meeting to Plan for 2019." December 2018. http://www.xinhuanet.com/english/2018-12/22/c_137690369.htm.

———. 2018b. "Full Text of Chinese President Xi's Speech at APEC CEO Summi." November 17, 2018. http://www.xinhuanet.com/english/2018-11/17/c_137613904.htm.

Chapter 2

Research Methodology

2.1 Literature Review on Competitiveness

This chapter will detail the methodology and data used to derive the competitiveness rankings as well as how Asia Competitiveness Institute (ACI) conducts policy-induced simulation analysis on the 34 Greater China economies, which can improve their competitiveness on various dimensions. This makes the contribution much more constructive than other indices that merely report their rankings.

The notion of regional or *in situ* competitiveness has been explored in various ways. Initially, in the 1980s, "competitiveness" was considered as part of the private sector domain, especially in relation to firm performance (Porter 1980). Over time, the discourse expanded into the domain of macroeconomics, as shown by the establishment of "Council on Competitiveness" or similar institution in various advanced industrialised countries. Some scholars acknowledge that it is primarily firms that compete, not nations, regions, or places (Krugman 1994). However, the performance of those firms depends on various factors that are embedded in the firm's location. These include quality of labour and infrastructure, governance, costs of doing business, as well as the performance of competing and complementary firms around the area (Bristow 2010; Camagni 2002; Kitson, Martin, and Tyler 2004).

Two of the most highly cited cross-country competitiveness studies at the moment are the World Competitiveness Yearbook (International Institute for Management Development 2018) and the Global Competitiveness Report (World Economic Forum 2018). The World Competitiveness Yearbook defines competitiveness as composed of four factors: (1) economic performance, (2) government efficiency, (3) business efficiency, and (4) infrastructure. Each factor is further made up of five criteria so that there are 20 criteria in total. The World Competitiveness Yearbook uses equal weights such that each criterion contributes 5 percent weight, and each factor contributes 25 percent weight to the Overall Competitiveness Index. Most of the data used are statistical indicators sourced from international, regional and national organizations. However, substantial perception data sourced from executive surveys supplement the statistical data.

The Global Competitiveness Report breaks down its Global Competitiveness Index into four sub-indices: (1) enabling environment, (2) human capital, (3) markets and (4) innovation ecosystem. Each of the four sub-indices has a different number of pillars. The enabling environment sub-index has four pillars: institutions, infrastructure, ICT adoption and macroeconomic environment. The human capital sub-index has two pillars: health and skills. The markets sub-index is composed of four pillars: product market, labour market, financial system and market size. Lastly, the innovative ecosystem sub-index consists of two pillars: business dynamism and innovation capability. Most of the data that make up these pillars and sub-indices come from executive opinion surveys.

2.2 Four Environments and 11 Sub-Environments

ACI's approach to competitiveness is comprehensive because it takes into account different factors that collectively shape the ability of an economy to achieve substantial and inclusive economic development over a sustainable period of time.

Guiding this overarching context, ACI has defined competitiveness according to four environments: (1) Macroeconomic Stability, (2) Government and Institutional Setting, (3) Financial, Businesses and Manpower Conditions and (4) Quality of Life and Infrastructure Development. In this section, these four environments are assumed to have the same impact on Overall Competitiveness, which is to say that each environment counts for 25 percent of the Overall Competitiveness score (see Figure 2.1).

ACI's competitiveness framework also uses a nested approach, creating two to three sub-environments under each of the four environments. There are a total of 11 sub-environments for the 34 Greater China economies. Each sub-environment under each environment has the same influence as the others under the same environment.

ACI uses a simple averaging mechanism to integrate all sub-environments (each is given the same weight) into their respective environment and then combines each environment into an Overall Competitiveness ranking.

Section 2.6 introduces the new concept of *Shapley values* to calculate the exact weight that each environment, sub-environment and individual indicator should carry.

The ACI competitiveness framework, with its four environments, is an overarching, comprehensive and systematic way of examining competitiveness. Two of these environments are directly linked to the economy. Macroeconomic Stability expresses aggregate economic activity

Figure 2.1: Asia Competitiveness Institute's Competitiveness Framework

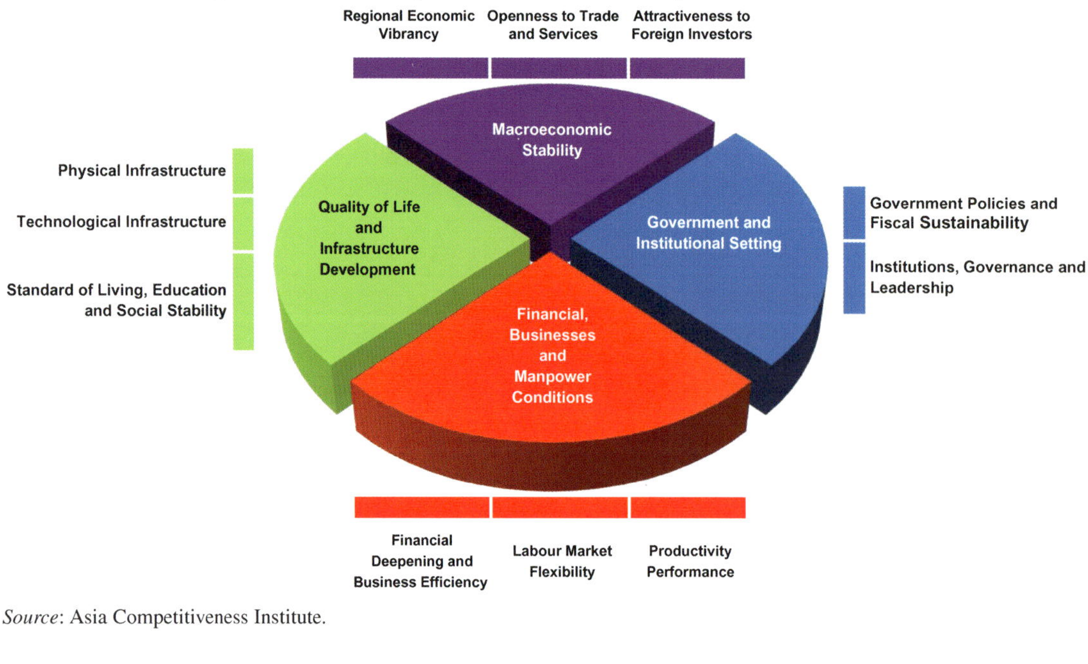

Source: Asia Competitiveness Institute.

and includes three sub-environments: (1) Regional Economic Vibrancy, (2) Openness to Trade and Services, and (3) Attractiveness to Foreign Investors. Regional Economic Vibrancy includes data on and economy's Gross Regional Domestic Product (GRDP), value-added of the three economic sectors, Consumer Price Index (CPI), tourism and investment. Openness to Trade and Services goes further to examine how international an economy is, taking into consideration the position of its merchandise on the international market, as well as the performance of trade and tourism. Attractiveness to Foreign Investors includes the state of foreign direct investment and foreign-funded companies that are active in a particular economy.

Financial, Businesses and Manpower Conditions mainly looks at the microeconomic state of the economy, examining its financial strength and understanding the factors that can affect a company's productivity, especially labour force. This environment includes three sub-environments: (1) Financial Deepening and Business Efficiency, (2) Labour Market Flexibility, and (3) Productivity Performance. Financial Deepening and Business Efficiency reflects the state of financing and investment in economic activities in an economy. Labour Market Flexibility includes data on employment and wages. Productivity Performance includes the value-added per worker for each of the three economic sectors, investment in fixed asset and overall labour productivity.

The other two environments focus on Government and Institutional Setting, and the Quality of Life and Infrastructure Development. Government and Institutional Setting includes the fiscal state of government and economic structures of a particular economy. This environment includes two sub-environments: (1) Government Policies and Fiscal Sustainability and (2) Institutions, Governance and Leadership. Government Policies and Fiscal Sustainability examines the expenses, revenue and tax collection for each economy, while Institutions, Governance and Leadership looks at the corporate structure of an economy to measure how market-oriented it is. The data used here capture the distribution of different types of enterprises by ownership.

Finally, Quality of Life and Infrastructure Development takes an overall view of basic infrastructure and public services as well as the overall quality of life. The three sub-environments under this environment include: (1) Physical Infrastructure, (2) Technological Infrastructure, and (3) Standard of Living, Education and Social Stability. Physical Infrastructure mainly refers to the level of development in the economy in terms of transportation (railways, highways, navigable inland waterways, civil aviation routes). In addition to transportation, Physical Infrastructure also includes the production levels of the natural resources (for example, coal, oil and iron) of an economy. A range of transportation and natural resource data has been collected to reflect the advantages and disadvantages of each economy as accurately as possible. Technological Infrastructure generally includes information and communications technology (ICT), such as personal computers, televisions, fixed telephones, mobile telephones, internet access and patents. Meanwhile, health care, education, population structure and the state of the environment are all included in the Standard of Living, Education and Social Stability sub-environment.

2.3 Indicators

A total of 102 indicators are used in the competitiveness ranking of the 34 Greater China economies. The availability of this data is greater for indicators in some environments and sub-environments than others. See Appendix 1 for a complete list of indicators. To a certain extent, having more indicators ensures a more robust interpretation of the aggregated sub-environment score. However, the uneven distribution of indicators across sub-environments due to data availability is not an issue. Regardless of the number of indicators in a sub-environment, they will simply average out. This provides a certain amount of flexibility in deciding whether to add or reduce the number of indicators when making changes in the future, as long as the overall framework of four environments and 11 sub-environments remains unchanged.

2.4 Data Sources and Aggregation of Indicators Data for Regions

The 102 indicators used in this research come from a number of sources. First among these are official government statistics from the National Bureau of Statistics of China, various statistical bureaus at the provincial level, the Hong Kong Census and Statistics Department, the Macau Statistics and Census Service, the National Statistics of the Republic of China (Taiwan), the World Bank and the United Nations.

The way to construct the competitiveness ranking by region follows the same methodology used for the competitiveness ranking by economy, with the appropriate dataset for indicators at the regional level. Because each region consists of a few economies, the main problem that needs to be solved in order to extend the ranking analysis from sub-regional level to regional level is data aggregation.

Many of the indicators used for the ranking at the economy level can be directly aggregated to get the indicator values for a region by summing across all the constituent economies in that region, as long as those indicators are based on absolute quantities, such as GRDP and Population. For those indicators that are defined as ratios, they can be computed according to their definition once the absolute quantities have been aggregated upon which they are defined (i.e. aggregating the denominator and numerator first).

As an illustration, following are four examples of data aggregation to derive the regional indicator values. The first example is for indicator GRDP. Since it is based on absolute quantity, the regional value can be obtained by summing across all the economies within this region. The second example is for indicator GRDP Growth. Once the GRDP has been computed for each region across the years according to the way shown in Example 1, it is straightforward to calculate GRDP Growth by region according to its definition. The third example is for Gross Capital Formation. According to its definition, it is calculated as the ratio between the Gross Capital Formation in the region and the GRDP for that region. Since both the numerator and denominator are absolute quantities, they are aggregated across all the economies within the region to get the regional values from which a ratio is computed, hence arriving at the regional value for indicator Gross Capital Formation. Lastly, the fourth example is for Inflation Rate, or equivalently CPI. Since the data are in the form of a percentage that cannot be easily disaggregated into numerator and denominator, the regional value for this indicator is obtained by taking the weighted average of economy-level data. In this case, the weighted average can be based on population size. In other instances, the weighted average can also be based on land size, depending on the nature of the indicator.

***Example 1*: Gross Regional Domestic Product (GRDP); Unit: 100 million yuan, Constant Prices at 2000**

For Region A with n economies at time t,

$$GRDP_{A,t} = \sum_{i=1}^{n} GRDP_{i,t}$$

***Example 2*: GRDP Growth; Unit: Percentage Change Per Annum**

For Region A with n economies at time t,

$$GRDP\ Growth_{A,t} = \frac{GRDP_{A,t} - GRDP_{A,t-1}}{GRDP_{A,t-1}}$$

***Example 3*: Gross Capital Formation; Unit: Percentage of GRDP**

For Region A with n economies at time t,

$$Gross\ Capital\ Formation_{A,t} = \frac{\sum_{i=1}^{n} Gross\ Capital\ Formation_{i,t}}{\sum_{i=1}^{n} GRDP_{i,t}}$$

***Example 4*: Inflation Rate (Consumer Price Index); Unit: Percentage Change per Annum**

For Region A with n economies at time t,

$$Inflation\ Rate_{A,t} = \frac{\sum_{i=1}^{n} \left(Population_{i,t} \times Inflation\ Rate_{i,t}\right)}{\sum_{i=1}^{n} Population_{i,t}}$$

For a complete list of indicators used for the regional competitiveness analysis and how to derive regional indicator data from data at the economy level, please refer to Appendix 2. Once the data aggregation is completed for all relevant indicators, the computational procedure is adopted to perform the competitiveness ranking analysis as listed in Appendix 3.

2.5 Standardised Score

The following section details the method of standardisation for further systematic analysis of indicators. The total of 102 indicators used in this research have not only different definitions but also different units of measurement. For instance, GRDP is measured in RMB100 million whereas the population size is measured in terms of the number of people. The remainder of this section will explain how to resolve issues caused by differences in definitions and units of measurement for each indicator.

ACI uses the "standardised score" or *z-score* statistical method. The standardised score measures the performance difference between a specific economy and the average level. There is no need to consider the use of different units of measurement for different indicators because the standardised score itself involves no unit of measurement as it simply measures the relative performance of various economies. In statistical terms, the standardised score measures how many standard deviations each economy is away from the average level.

The mean and standard deviation of all economies are firstly computed for each indicator, in which the standardised value is calculated as follows:

$$Standardised\ Value = \frac{Original\ Value - Mean}{Standard\ Deviation}$$

0 (zero) = same as the average of all economies
– (negative) = below the average of all economies
+ (positive) = above the average of all economies

An economy with a zero standardised score is an average performer. In the context of this competitiveness index, a negative score posits a performance worse than the average, and this argument is also inversely true. In addition to the sign of the standardised score, the magnitude of it demonstrates the difference between the performance of its corresponding economy and the average of the 34 economies. In this regard, a large absolute value of a negative score indicates very weak competitiveness performance, while that of a positive score indicates very strong competitiveness performance.

For each economy, the standardised scores across indicators are first aggregated at the sub-environment level, subsequently re-aggregated at the environment level, and finally aggregated again at the overall level. This enables us to examine the competitiveness performance of each of the 34 economies at various levels, from the overall performance to specific indicators.

As a convention of ACI's studies, all the environments are assumed to carry the same weight, i.e. 1/4. The sub-environments enclosed under each of the environments are also assigned the same weight. A similar weighting scheme is assumed at the indicator level.

While the assumption on Equal Weightage simplifies the aggregation of the index, the subjectivity of this approach raises a caveat on the robustness of the results. To address this issue, an objective weighting method named the Shapley Weightage was introduced into the study, and details of this method will be discussed in Section 2.6.

2.6 Shapley Method: A Novel Approach to Assignment of Weights

2.6.1 Shapley Value

The Shapley value is the most commonly used solution concept in cooperative game theory. Formally, a coalition game (N,v) in cooperative game theory is defined by a set of players N and a characteristic function $v(S):2^N \rightarrow R$, where it maps coalition S (or a subset of players) to a real number. The function describes the expected payoffs the S players can obtain by cooperation. The Shapley value of the coalition game is an n-vector, denoted by $\Phi(v)$, satisfying a set of axioms, i.e. Individual Rationality, Efficiency, Symmetry, Additivity and Null Player.

The i-th component of $\Phi(v)$ can be determined by

$$\Phi(v) = \sum_{S \subseteq N \setminus \{i\}} \frac{|S|!\left(N - |S| - 1\right)!}{N!}\left(v\left(S \cup i\right) - v\left(S\right)\right)$$

In the context of ACI's competitiveness index, the players will be the indicators used for the construction of the index. The coalition will be the sub-environments and environments which the indicators belong to. The desirable properties, i.e. the axioms, are meaningful for general index ranking. Individual Rationality ensures that each indicator has a positive contribution to the index score. An indicator must satisfy the Null Player axiom, so that it is economically meaningful for that indicator to be considered relevant to the index. Symmetry guarantees that if two indicators carry the same value, they are equally important in the index scoring. Efficiency and Additivity are also important mathematical properties for the construction of the index.

The application of Shapley value has been well studied in various strands of literature. The concept has been used to solve the taxation and redistribution problem, as described by Aumann and Kurz (1977). It is also used in voting for public goods problems. Aumann and Myerson (1988), for instance, have studied the link or coalition formation among players using the Shapley value. Moulin (1992) studies the application of the Shapley value in fair division of unproduced goods under monetary transfer and quasi-linear utilities. Petrosjan and Zaccour (2003) study the Shapley value cost allocation in a pollution reduction setting. More recently, Hougaard *et al.* (2017) have applied the Shapley value concept to licensing under FRAND terms.[1] However, related articles about applying the Shapley value to index ranking analysis were not found during the search of the relevant literature.

As a robustness check for the Equal Weightage approach, an objective weighting method — the "Bottom-Up" approach — is proposed based on Shapley value.

2.6.2 Shapley Weightage — The "Bottom-Up" Approach

The Shapley value of each indicator is firstly computed based on the standardised value of the indicator for every economy. In the context of this index, it defines the aggregate dispersion of the indicator, thus reflecting the inequality among the economies. More weights are assigned to those indicators with a higher Shapley value. The weights of sub-environments are computed based on both the absolute performance (standardised score) and the relative performance (weights) of indicators under that particular sub-environment. The weights of environments are computed in a similar way by considering the relevant absolute performance and the relative performance of sub-environments. The detailed description of the methodology can be found in Appendix 4.

[1] FRAND is a short notation for Fair Reasonable and Non-Discriminatory.

2.6.3 Comparison between the Shapley Method and the Entropy Method

Another objective weight assignment method, commonly applied in the area of decision science, is entropy (Zeleny 1982). The entropy for the indicator i is defined as

$$Entropy_i = -\frac{1}{\ln(E)}\sum_{e=1}^{E} p_{ei}\ln(p_{ei})$$

where E is the number of economies, $p_{ei} = \frac{v_{ei}}{\sum_{e=1}^{E} v_{ei}}$ and v_{ei} is the characteristic of the raw data x_{ei}. The weightage of indicator i is, then, defined by

$$w_i = 1 - Entropy_i$$

The interpretation of the entropy of an indicator concerns the information that the particular indicator transmits. The higher the entropy, the lesser the information carried, implying a lower weight assigned to that indicator.

While this method appears to be an improvement over a subjective weighting scheme, it is inapplicable to this competitiveness index because using the logarithm operator restricts the entropy computation in the domain of positive values. Since *z-scores* could be either positive or negative, an alternative standardisation method is required for the application of the Entropy Method. In the report "Assessing Provincial Development under the Five Development Concepts", Institute of Applied Economics Shanghai Academy of Social Sciences has applied the entropy method to assign weights to indicators. To avoid negative values, they deploy the max–min standardisation method, where

$$v_{ei} = \frac{x_{ei} - \min(x_i)}{\max(x_i) - \min(x_i)}$$

Another reason that the entropy method is less appropriate than the Shapley method is that, when applied to the field of index construction, the former method is very sensitive to indicators containing outliers. Consider the following example. As shown in Table 2.1, there are 11 economies and three indicators with different measurement units. Indicator 1 contains an outlier. All the economies perform equally in Indicator 2. There is a clear divergence of performance among all the economies in Indicator 3. The *z-score* standardisation is used for the Shapley method, while max–min standardisation for the entropy method.

Under the entropy method, the weights of indicators are

$$w_1^{Entropy} = 0.866,\ w_2^{Entropy} = 0.045,\ w_3^{Entropy} = 0.089$$

Under the Shapley method, the weights of indicators are

$$w_1^{Shapley} = 0.308,\ w_2^{Shapley} = 0.229,\ w_3^{Shapley} = 0.463$$

Table 2.1: Example to Compare the Shapley and Entropy Weight Methods

Economy	Indicator 1	Indicator 2	Indicator 3
A	10	2	1
B	1	3	2
C	1	2	3
D	1	2	4
E	1	2	5
F	1	2	6
G	1	2	7
H	1	1	8
I	1	2	9
J	1	2	10
K	1	2	11

Source: Asia Competitiveness Institute.

Due to the presence of an outlier under Indicator 1, i.e. Economy A, the entropy method predicts that Indicator 1 carries the most information, thus assigning it a much higher weight relative to the rest. Similar to the entropy method, the Shapley weights assign a relatively higher weight to Indicator 1 than Indicator 2 because of the presence of the outlier. However, the highest weight is assigned to Indicator 3 because of the dispersion observed, overcoming the bias that the entropy method generates due to its inability to handle outliers.

To summarise the preceding discussion, the derivation of the final index score must be done with the help of aggregation of all relevant information, implying that all the indicators are the determinants. Reflecting on the importance of indicators shows that the economies are unequally developed (e.g. Indicator 3). However, as noted earlier, the entropy method fails to capture this feature, due to the fact that such indicators convey less information than those with an outlier (e.g. Indicator 1). The Shapley method, on the other hand, offers a better alternative as it captures both the fact that economies are most unequally developed under Indicator 3 as well as the existence of the outlier in Indicator 1.

2.7 *What-if* Competitiveness Simulation Analysis

Pure competitiveness rankings alone are like beauty pageants because they only show a list of those that perform well and those that face challenges without providing constructive recommendations that can help improve competitiveness. ACI takes one step further by tackling the "so what" question. What impact do competitiveness rankings have on the policy of a specific economy? The data used by ACI enable the examination of the indicators, sub-environments and environments of each economy in a targeted way. By analysing these data, it is possible to not only provide a competitiveness ranking but also identify weak and strong indicators. This then allows us to provide policy suggestions that are specific to each economy.

ACI's *What-if* Competitiveness Simulation Analysis looks at how to improve the top 20 percent weakest indicators for an economy, then recalculate the standardised scores based on this improvement. First, the indicators for a specific economy are placed in order from lowest to highest based on their score. It is then possible to identify the top 20 weakest indicators for that economy (20 percent of the total 102 indicators is about 20).

Under most situations, the values of the top 20 weakest indicators are raised to the average values for all 34 Greater China economies. There are special cases for some economies in which some of the top 20 percent weakest indicators are in fact above the average values. For these specific indicators, the values remain at the original value so that the score of the economy is not discounted. After increasing the values for the top 20 percent weakest indicators, rankings are recalculated by assuming that the scores of other economies remain unchanged. Only one economy is analysed during each simulation analysis. After completing the simulation analysis of each of the 34 Greater China economies, each is given a new standardised score based on the simulated model. This can help us answer the question of how a particular economy's competitiveness ranking would change if its weakest indicators improved while other economies' scores stayed the same.

With the research methodology elaborated, Chapters 3 and 4 will detail the results of the competitiveness studies at the economy and regional levels, respectively.

References

Aumann, Robert J., and Mordecai Kurz. 1977. "Power and Taxes." *Econometrica* (JSTOR) 45: 1137. doi:10.2307/1914063.

Aumann, Robert J., and Roger B. Myerson. 1988. "Endogenous Formation of Links between Players and of Coalitions: An Application of the Shapley Value." In *The Shapley value*, edited by Alvin E. Roth, 175–192. Cambridge University Press. doi:10.1017/cbo9780511528446.013.

Bristow, Gillian. 2010. *Critical Reflections on Regional Competitiveness: Theory, Policy, Practice (Routledge Studies in Human Geography)*. Routledge.

Camagni, Roberto. 2002. "On the Concept of Territorial Competitiveness: Sound or Misleading?" *Urban Studies* (SAGE Publications) 39: 2395–2411. doi:10.1080/0042098022000027022.

Hougaard, Jens Leth, Chiu Yu Ko, and Xuyao Zhang. 2017. "A Welfare Economic Interpretation of FRAND." IFRO Working Paper, University of Copenhagen, Department of Food and Resource Economics.

Institute of Applied Economics Shanghai Academy of Social Sciences. 2016. "五大发展理念指标体系及省级区域评估报告 Assessing Provincial Development under the Five Development Concepts (in Chinese)." Shanghai Academy of Social Sciences.

International Institute for Management Development. 2018. *IMD World Competitiveness Yearbook 2018*. IMD. https://www.imd.org/research-knowledge/books/world-competitiveness-yearbook-2018/.

Kitson, Michael, Ron Martin, and Peter Tyler. 2004. "Regional Competitiveness: An Elusive yet Key Concept?" Regional Studies (Informa UK Limited) 38: 991–999. doi:10.1080/0034340042000320816.

Krugman, Paul. 1994. "Competitiveness: A Dangerous Obsession." *Foreign Affairs* (JSTOR) 73: 28. doi:10.2307/20045917.

Moulin, Herve. 1992. "An Application of the Shapley Value to Fair Division with Money." *Econometrica* (JSTOR) 60: 1331. doi:10.2307/2951524.

Petrosjan, Leon, and Georges Zaccour. 2003. "Time-consistent Shapley value allocation of pollution cost reduction." *Journal of Economic Dynamics and Control* (Elsevier BV) 27: 381–398. doi:10.1016/s0165-1889(01)00053-7.

Porter, Michael E. 1980. *Competitive Strategy: Techniques for Analyzing Industries and Competitors.* Free Press.

World Economic Forum. 2018. "The Global Competitiveness Report 2018." Geneva: World Economic Forum. http://www3.weforum.org/docs/GCR2018/05FullReport/TheGlobalCompetitivenessReport2018.pdf.

Zeleny, Milan. 1982. *Multiple Criteria Decision Making.* New York: McGraw-Hill.

Chapter 3

2018 Annual Update on Competitiveness Rankings and Simulation Studies for 34 Greater China Economies

3.1 Introduction

This chapter will present the 2018 annual update on competitiveness rankings and simulation studies for 34 Greater China economies. Disparities among Mainland China's provinces in terms of their Gross Regional Domestic Product (GRDP) growth, GRDP shares in the Chinese economy, and the provinces' overall contribution to economic growth still persist. Figure 3.1 illustrates the distribution of the provinces of Mainland China by their provincial Gross Domestic Product (GDP) growth rates, or GRDP growth rates, between the years 2016 and 2017. Figure 3.2 ranks the provinces in terms of their growth rates and is colour-coded in the same manner as Figure 3.1. On average, the 31 provinces have grown at around 9.3 percent over this period. However, there are considerable heterogeneities as 20 out of 31 provinces achieved above-average growth rates whereas 11 provinces performed below the average. In particular, as shown in Figure 3.1, Inner Mongolia showed a sharp economic contraction with a negative GRDP growth rate of –11.17 percent. Together with Tianjin, Jilin and Qinghai, which experienced GRDP growth rates of less than 4 percent, these provinces were the bottom four in terms of provincial GDP growth rates (see Figure 3.2).

On the flip side, 16 out of 31 provinces experienced GRDP growth rates of more than 10 percent, thus underlining the significant economic disparity and growth performance between the many provinces in China. Out of these 16 provinces, Guizhou, Shanxi and Tibet experienced the strongest growth rates at 14.98 percent, 14.74 percent and 13.83 percent, respectively. The other provinces with growth rates higher than 10 percent were Tibet, Xinjiang, Shaanxi, Anhui, Jiangxi, Sichuan, Hebei, Fujian, Hubei, Yunnan, Guanxi, Guangdong, Henan, and Jiangsu, in respective order of their GRDP growth rates. Provinces that had growth rates of 7–10 percent include Hainan, Chongqing, Hunan, Zhejiang, Beijing, Ningxia and Liaoning, while Shanghai, Shandong, Gansu and Heilongjiang had growth rates of 4–7 percent over 2016–2017.

The strong growth performances of many central and western provinces, such as Guizhou, Shanxi and Tibet, are indeed heartening as they bode well for the realisation of balanced development in China. However, it should be noted that these provinces started from low bases. They are still at earlier stages of development as compared with other Mainland China provinces, especially those located in the Eastern Coastal Area.[1] For instance, in terms of GRDP size,

[1] The four economic zones in Mainland China as defined by the National Bureau of Statistics of the People's Republic of China are Eastern Coastal Area in China, Central China, Western China and North-eastern China. The Eastern Coastal Area includes Beijing, Fujian, Guangdong, Hainan, Hebei, Jiangsu, Shandong, Shanghai, Tianjin and

Figure 3.1: Provincial GRDP Growth Rate in 2017

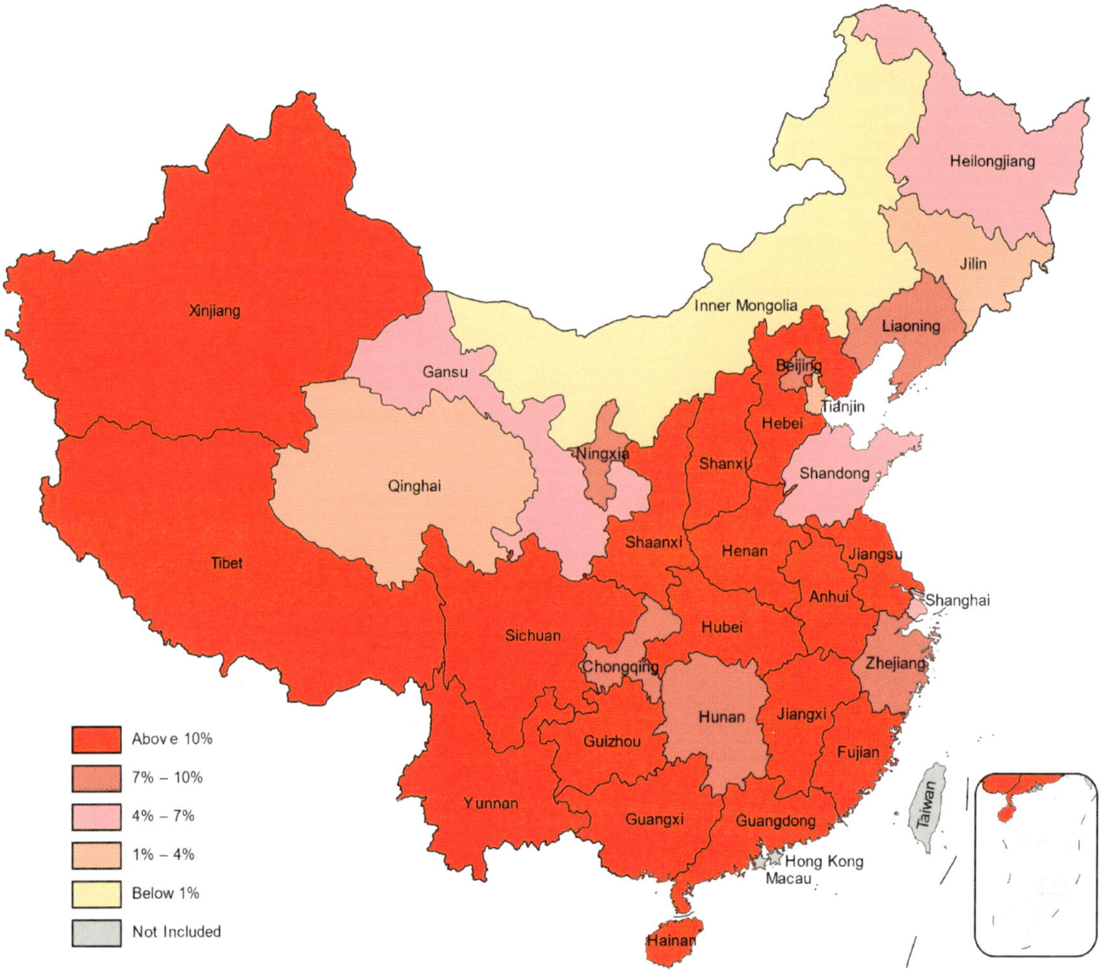

Source: Asia Competitiveness Institute based on data from the National Bureau of Statistics of China.

Guizhou, Shanxi and Tibet were still ranked among the bottom third of all 31 provinces as of 2017, together constituting a mere 3.5 percent of the Chinese economy.[2] Hence, despite their high growth rates, the actual contribution of these provinces to China's growth performance is still very modest, as seen in Figure 3.5.

For China to continue to achieve prosperity and economic development, the growth performances of the largest provinces in terms of GRDP shares, particularly Guangdong, Jiangsu, Shandong and Zhejiang, will be especially important. With a combined GRDP of more than 23

Zhejiang. Central China includes Anhui, Henan, Hubei, Hunan, Jiangxi and Shanxi. Western China includes Chongqing, Gansu, Guangxi, Guizhou, Inner Mongolia, Ningxia, Qinghai, Shaanxi, Sichuan, Tibet, Xinjiang and Yunnan, while North-eastern China includes Heilongjiang, Jilin and Liaoning. See http://www.stats.gov.cn/tjzs/cjwtjd/201308/t20130829_74318.html.

[2] There are minor discrepancies between the sum of the provinces' GRDP and the national GDP for China reported by the National Bureau for Statistics. For this book, the sum of the provinces' GRDP was used to calculate the GRDP share of each province.

Figure 3.2: Ranking of Mainland China Provinces in Terms of Provincial GRDP Growth Rates in 2017

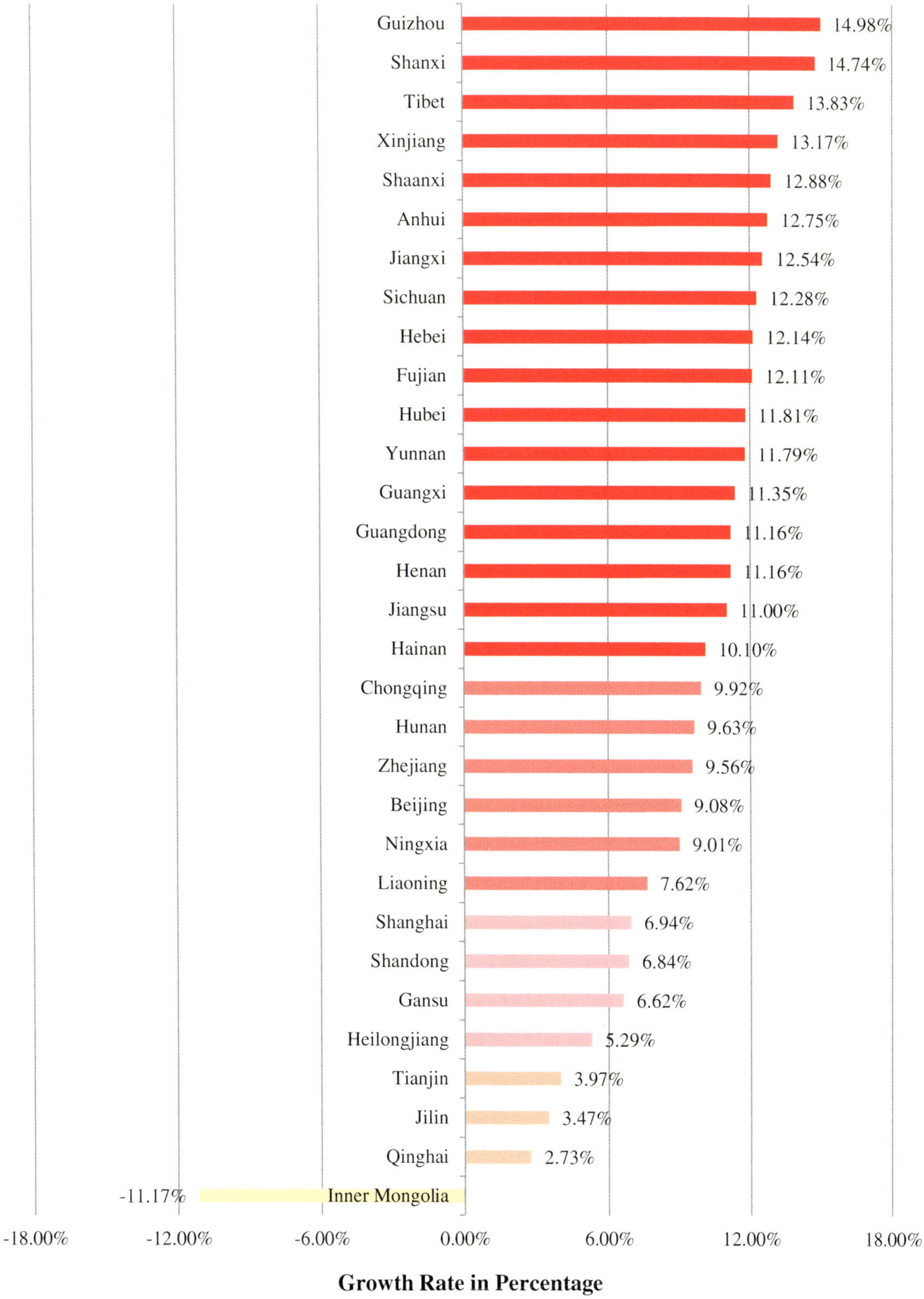

Source: Asia Competitiveness Institute based on data from the National Bureau of Statistics.

Figure 3.3: Provincial GRDP as a Share of National Nominal GDP in 2017

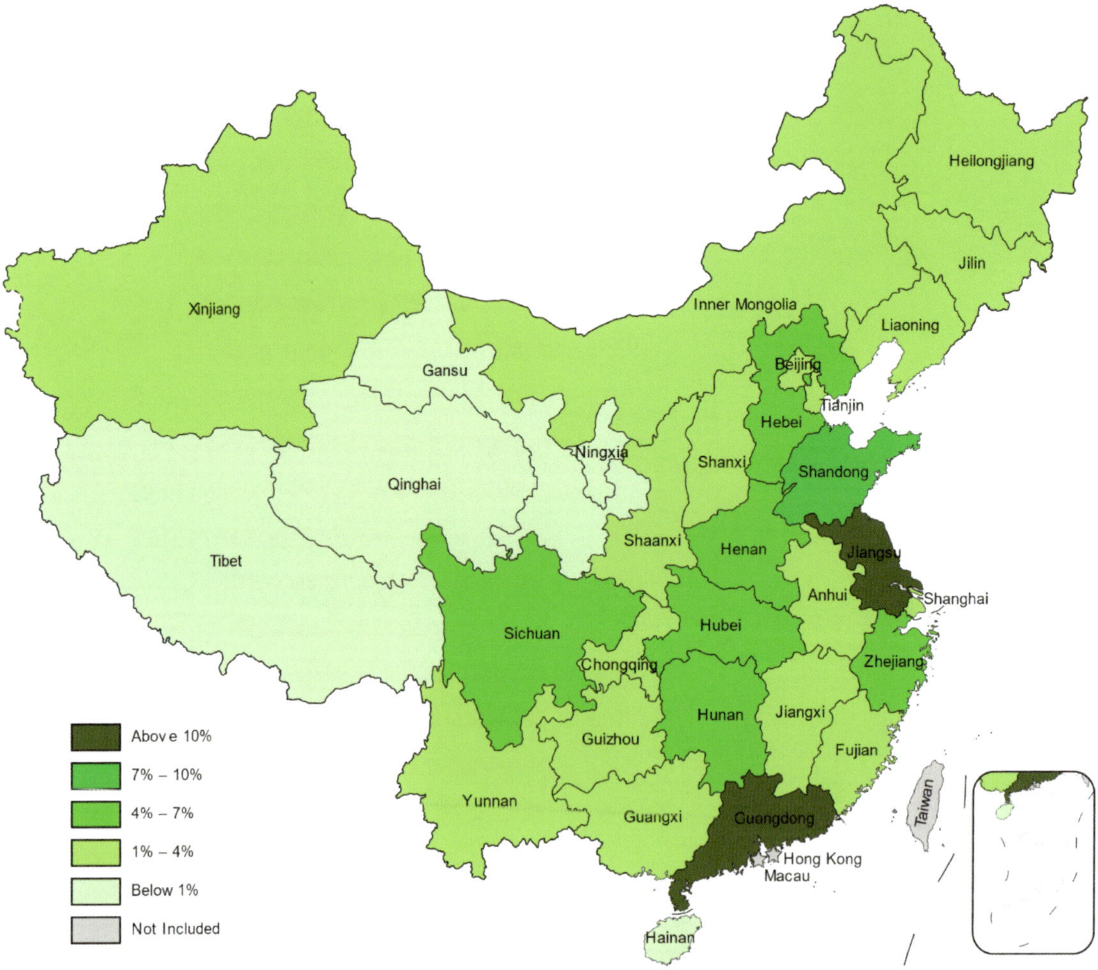

Source: Asia Competitiveness Institute based on data from the National Bureau of Statistics of China.

trillion RMB, these four provinces constituted more than 35 percent of the Chinese economy. They are therefore the most important contributors to China's economic growth, as Figure 3.3 illustrates. Between 2016 and 2017, Guangdong and Jiangsu have both grown above 11 percent while Zhejiang and Shandong experienced growth rates of 9.56 percent and 6.84 percent, respectively (see Figure 3.2). Going forward, as these provinces are at relatively mature stages of development, future growth must be driven by productivity improvement, innovation, as well as high value-added services on top of advanced manufacturing.

On the other hand, continued weak performance in the North-eastern area remains an issue of concern. While Liaoning experienced a substantial GRDP growth rate of 7.62 percent in 2017, Heilongjiang and Jilin lag behind at 5.29 percent and 3.47 percent, respectively. Once robust industrial bases of China, these provinces are now straggling behind the rest. It remains to be seen if the government's push to revitalise the North-east will bear fruit and transform the region into one of China's economic growth engines once again. More alarmingly, as mentioned above, Inner Mongolia's GRDP growth rates fell to a drastic low of –11.17 percent, with Qinghai performing second worst at 2.73 percent. Significant resources need to be directed to these areas to ensure equal development across all areas in China.

Figure 3.3 depicts the distribution of the provinces according to their GRDP as a share of national nominal GDP as of 2017. It shows the contribution of each province to the Chinese economy, which in 2017 ranged from 0.15 percent (Tibet) to 10.51 percent (Guangdong). Figure 3.4 ranks each province's contribution and is colour-coded in the same manner as Figure 3.3. The figures also indicate economic development at the provincial level.

Provinces have been categorised into five groups based on contributions to national GDP, i.e. provinces with GRDP share below 1 percent; provinces with GRDP shares between 1 percent and 4 percent; provinces with GRDP shares between 4 percent and 7 percent; provinces with GRDP shares between 7 percent and 10 percent; and provinces with GRDP shares above 10 percent. As of 2017, there were three provinces contributing more than 7 percent to China's national GDP. Besides the Eastern Coastal provinces (Guangdong, Jiangsu, Shandong, Hebei and Zhejiang), which are among the most developed provinces in China, the Central provinces of Henan and Hubei and the South-western province of Sichuan also contributed significantly to national GDP (see Figure 3.3). This indicates that economic development is more balanced in China as of 2017. Meanwhile, 17 out of 31 provinces contributed between 1 percent and 4 percent each to national GDP. Among these 17 provinces, Fujian was the one with the highest GRDP level, contributing 3.78 percent to the national GDP. Meanwhile, the shares for Shanghai and Beijing were 3.52 percent and 3.27 percent, respectively (see Figure 3.4). Among 31 provinces, Gansu, Hainan, Ningxia, Qinghai and Tibet contributed the lowest GRDP, and their positions remained the same as last year.

There are three outstanding provinces which contributed to more than 28 percent of the Chinese economy in 2017. These were Guangdong, Jiangsu and Shandong, whose contributions were 10.51 percent, 10.04 percent and 8.50 percent, respectively. Guangdong has been the top province in terms of GRDP since 1989, but Jiangsu comes close behind. The proximity of these two provinces is demonstrated not only by the numbers of nominal GRDP but by the growth of it. As shown in Figure 3.2, Jiangsu's economic growth rate is only 0.16 percent less than the 11.16 percent growth of Guangdong. Meanwhile, Shandong exceeded 7 trillion RMB in GRDP for the first time, becoming the third province to join the "7 trillion RMB club".

Due to the deepening of supply-side structural reforms in China, local governments have put more effort into reducing steel, iron and coal production. Provinces which derive most of their economic development from these sectors have thus been significantly affected. In particular, Hebei, known for its steel and iron production, experienced a severe decrease in GRDP contribution from 8.01 percent in 2016 to 4.20 percent in 2017. Likewise, Liaoning has followed in the same suit with a decrease from 5.56 percent in 2016 to 2.80 percent in 2017. Inner Mongolia, noted for its coal production, has also seen a drop in GRDP share from 2.16 percent in 2016 to 1.88 percent in 2017.

Figure 3.4: Ranking of Mainland China Provinces in Terms of Provincial GRDP as a Share of National Nominal GDP in 2017

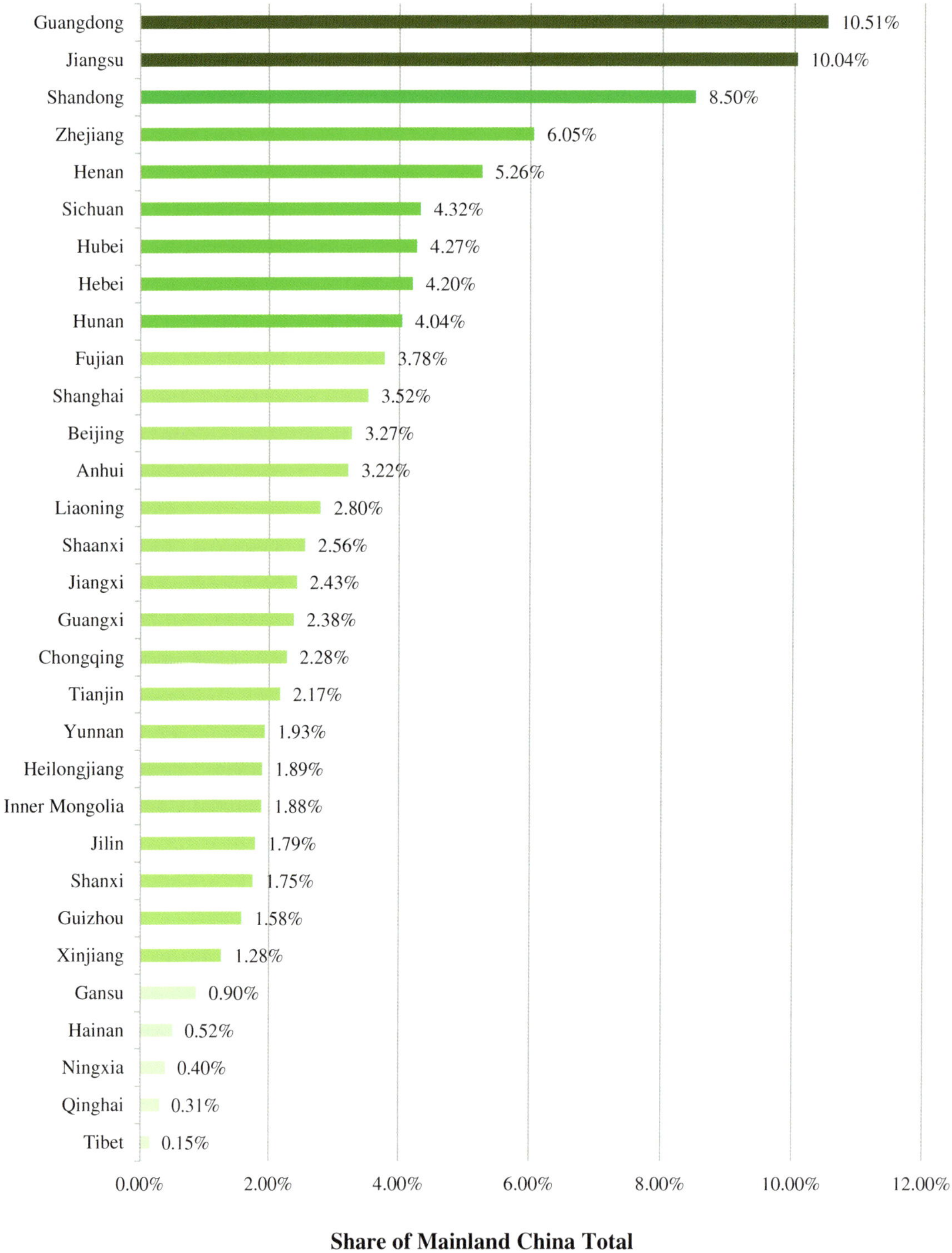

Source: Asia Competitiveness Institute based on data from the National Bureau of Statistics of China.

Figure 3.5: Provincial Share of GRDP Growth in 2017

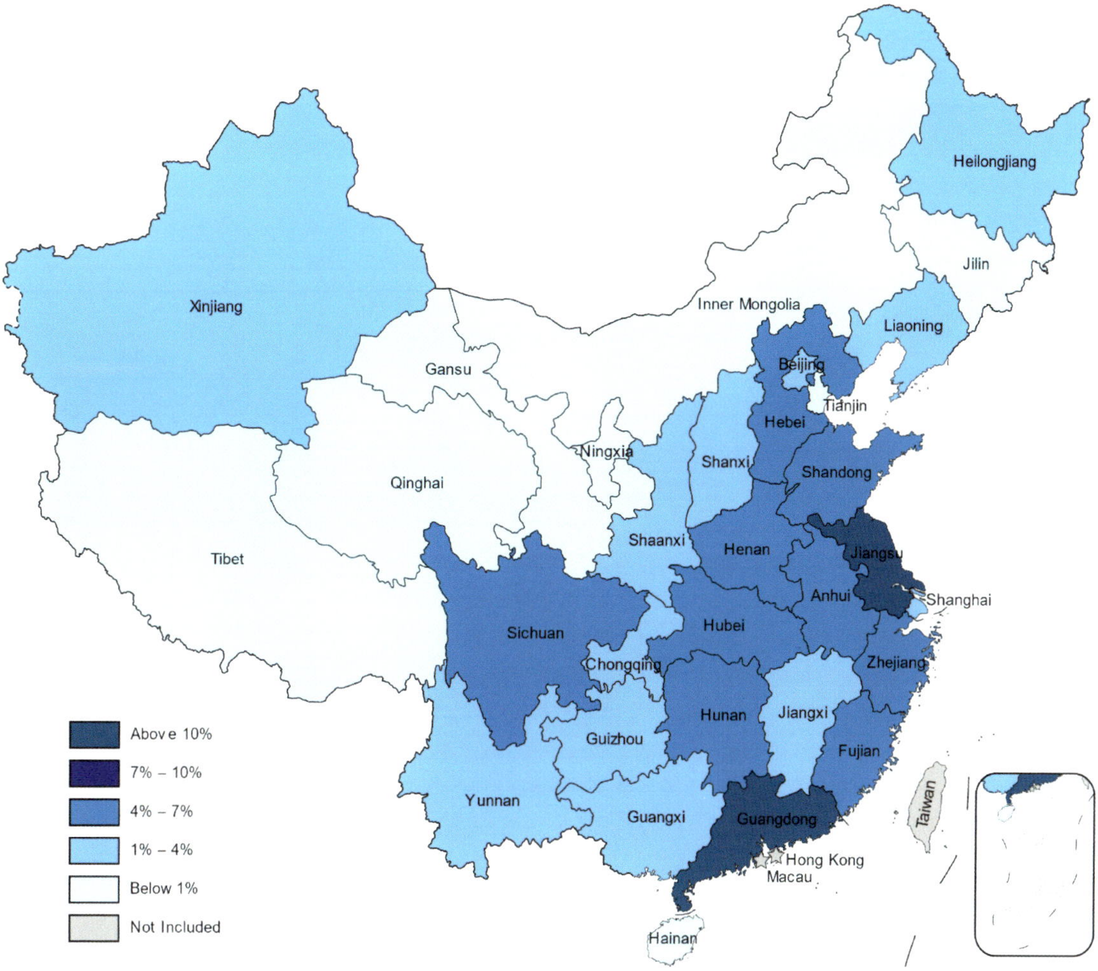

Source: Asia Competitiveness Institute based on data from the National Bureau of Statistics of China.

Figures 3.5 and 3.6 demonstrate the shares of individual provinces in the overall GDP growth of China from 2016 to 2017. Among all the 31 provinces in the framework of the regional ranking analysis, Guangdong contributed the greatest proportion of 11.97 percent to annual GDP growth in China for the year 2017. Jiangsu made nearly as high a contribution at 11.29 percent. In addition, the contributions of Shandong and Zhejiang constitute the next two provinces at 6.17 percent and 5.99 percent, respectively. It is worth noting that none of these four provinces achieved extraordinarily high GRDP growth rates in 2017; more specifically, according to Figure 3.2, while the GRDP growth rates of Guangdong and Jiangsu were a substantial 11.16 percent and 11 percent, respectively, they were still outperformed by provinces like Guizhou (14.98 percent) and Tibet (13.83 percent).

However, when considering the contributions of individual provinces to GDP growth, one must take into account not only the provincial GRDP growth rate, but also the comparative significance of different provinces in terms of their relative shares of nominal GDP. Hence, while

Figure 3.6: Ranking of Mainland China Provinces in Terms of Provincial Share of GDP Growth in 2017

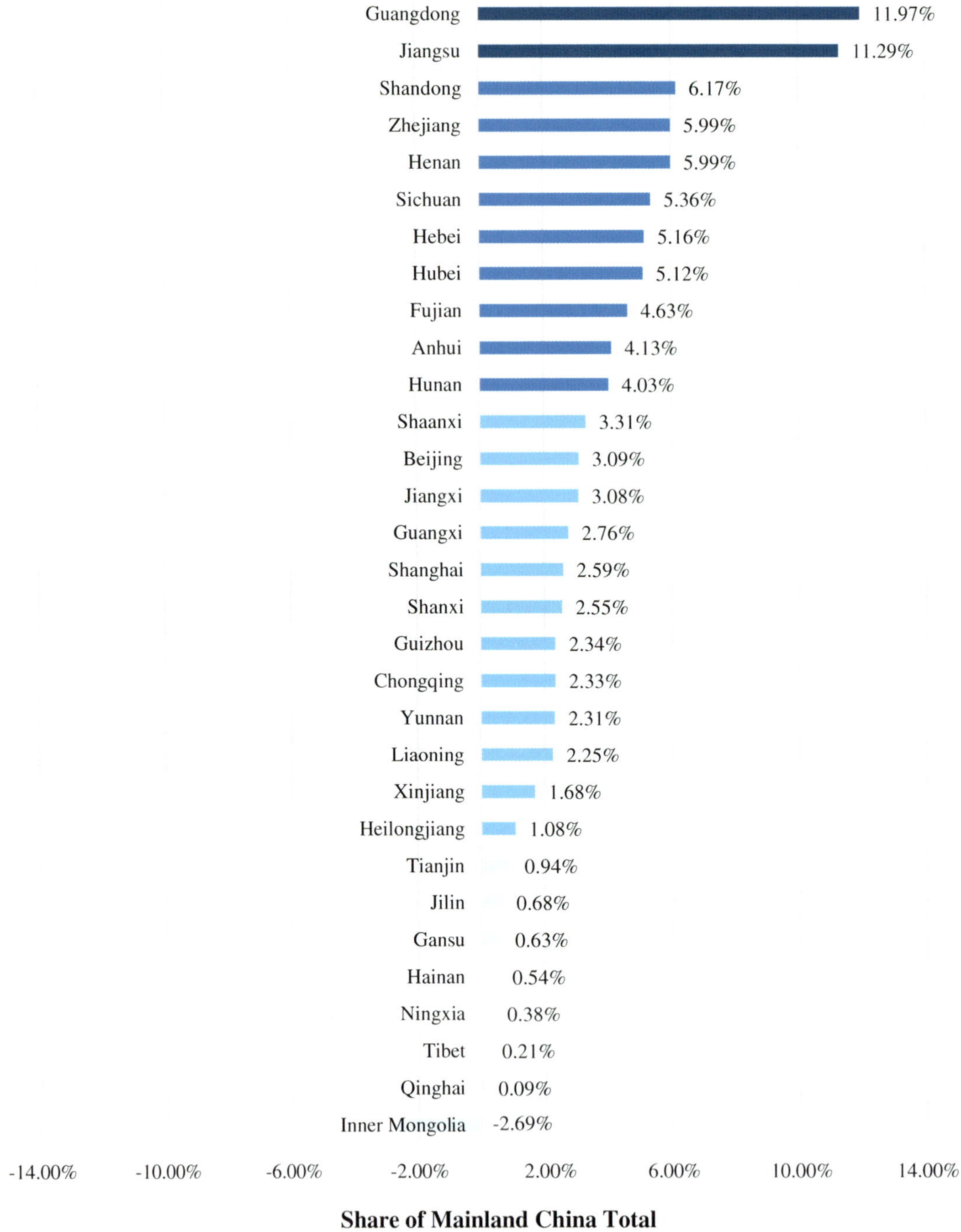

Source: Asia Competitiveness Institute based on data from the National Bureau of Statistics of China.

it can be observed that Guizhou and the Tibet Autonomous Region do indeed have outstanding GRDP growth rates, their shares of the aggregate nominal GDP of China are in fact not as significant, with the specific figure being 2.34 percent for Guizhou (18th of the 31 provinces) and as low as 0.21 percent for Tibet (29th of the 31 provinces). On the other hand, the above-mentioned four provinces of Guangdong, Jiangsu, Shandong and Zhejiang have consistently been the top contributors to national GDP over the decades with, for instance, Guangdong contributing 9.63 percent and Jiangsu contributing 9.22 percent of China's GDP in year 2016 — figures that evidently increased in 2017.

Therefore, the ranking results of the shares of individual provinces in the overall GDP growth in Figure 3.5 are not surprising. It is fairly reasonable that some provinces, such as Guizhou and Tibet, experience extremely strong economic performances with their higher GRDP growth rates. However, it does not necessarily lead to the conclusion that these provinces will also make vital contributions to the GDP growth of China. The explanation for this is rather simple and straightforward: their economic shares at the national level may not be as large as that of the provinces in the East Coast area, like Jiangsu and Guangdong. Even though the provinces in the East Coast do not achieve relatively high rankings regarding GRDP growth rates during some years, they still remain the major engines of economic development in China.

Figure 3.6 presents the ranking of the provincial share of GDP growth in detail. The top five provinces that contributed the most shares among all the provinces include Guangdong, Jiangsu, Shandong, Zhejiang and Henan. Meanwhile, the contributions of Inner Mongolia, Qinghai, Tibet, Ningxia and Hainan to China's economic growth were the smallest among all 31 provinces.

After an overview of the Greater China economies and their GRDP dynamics, the rest of this chapter will zoom into the various dimensions of the competitiveness assessment, investigating the specific factors driving the growth of these economies. The remaining sections of this chapter are organised as follows: Section 3.2 will present ACI's research findings which include overall competitiveness rankings as well as the competitiveness rankings of the four environments of Macroeconomic Stability; Government and Institutional Setting; Financial, Businesses and Manpower Conditions; and lastly, Quality of Life and Infrastructure Development. Besides providing a snapshot of the 2018 ACI rankings, this section will flesh out in further detail the robustness check conducted through the Shapley method. Moreover, a *What-if* competitiveness simulation analysis will also be carried out in order to visualise the effects of policy responses on improving competitiveness performance. Section 3.3 will then provide an overall conclusion by summarising the results and policy implications of this study.

3.2 Research Findings

Following the research methodology as elaborated in Chapter 2, the 2018 rankings for the 34 Greater China economies are obtained and discussed in this section. All rankings, the Overall Competitiveness ranking as well as the rankings under the four environments, are ordered based on the standardised scores of each economy. The results of the *What-if* Competitiveness Simulation Analysis are also included in this section.

3.2.1 ACI 2018 Overall Competitiveness Rankings and Scores

Table 3.1 shows the 2018 Overall Competitiveness ranking. In terms of spread, the maximum score for the 34 Greater China economies is 2.3977 and the minimum score is –1.5241. Guangdong is ranked top among the 34 economies with the highest score while Tibet is ranked #34.

Table 3.1: ACI 2018 Overall Competitiveness Ranking and Scores

Rank	Economy	Score
1	Guangdong	2.3977
2	Jiangsu	2.0168
3	Hong Kong	1.7073
4	Taiwan	1.6619
5	Beijing	1.6214
6	Zhejiang	1.3749
7	Shanghai	1.1922
8	Shandong	0.8301
9	Macau	0.5398
10	Fujian	0.1196
11	Hubei	0.0631
12	Hebei	0.0175
13	Liaoning	0.0000
14	Tianjin	–0.0381
15	Sichuan	–0.0754
16	Henan	–0.2087
17	Inner Mongolia	–0.2806
18	Xinjiang	–0.3733
19	Anhui	–0.3825
20	Shaanxi	–0.4058
21	Hunan	–0.4676
22	Chongqing	–0.5246
23	Jilin	–0.6048
24	Heilongjiang	–0.6212
25	Shanxi	–0.6574
26	Yunnan	–0.7322
27	Jiangxi	–0.7458
28	Hainan	–0.8435

Table 3.1: (*Continued*)

Rank	Economy	Score
29	Guizhou	–0.8803
30	Guangxi	–0.9117
31	Ningxia	–0.9723
32	Qinghai	–1.1045
33	Gansu	–1.1878
34	Tibet	–1.5241

Note: The results are based on 2015 data, collated and analysed in 2018.
Source: Asia Competitiveness Institute.

The average-performing economy (with a standardised score of 0) is the #13-ranked Liaoning (0.0000). As for the median, which is in the middle of a ranking, it is situated between the #17-ranked Inner Mongolia (–0.2806) and the #18-ranked Xinjiang (–0.3733). The median score for the 2018 Overall Competitiveness ranking is thus –0.3270. It can be seen clearly that the average score (0) is higher than the median score (–0.3270). In other words, the average value is positioned in the upper half of the ranking, above the centre of the list, which indicates that more than half of the economies score below-average performances.

In terms of the distribution of the Overall Competitiveness scores, there are several gaps in scores between economies. For example, there is a relatively large gap between the #1-ranked Guangdong (2.3977) and the #2-ranked Jiangsu (2.0168), as well as between the #2-ranked Jiangsu (2.0168) and the #3-ranked Hong Kong (1.7073). The score differences are 0.3809 and 0.3095, respectively. There is also a considerable gap of 0.3621 between the #7-ranked Shanghai (1.1922) and the #8-ranked Shandong (0.8301), and a large gap of 0.4202 between the #9-ranked Macau (0.5398) and the #10-ranked Fujian (0.1196). At the bottom of the list, the #33-ranked Gansu (–1.1878) differs from the #34-ranked Tibet (–1.5241) by a considerable gap of 0.3363. These large gaps in scores warrant attention because the economies are only one ranking apart, yet their differences in scores are sizeable.

The ranking of the 34 Greater China economies can also be analysed from a geographical and spatial perspective. In Figure 3.7, the 2018 Overall Competitiveness ranking map, each economy is colour-coded according to three categories. Green represents the top 10 economies, yellow, the middle 14 economies, and red, the 10 lowest ranking economies. As can be observed, green covers most of the Eastern Coastal Area in Mainland China, except for three economies, Hebei, Tianjin and Hainan. Hong Kong, Macau and Taiwan are in green as well. This indicates that economies in Hong Kong, Macau, Taiwan and the Eastern Coastal Area of Mainland China are more competitive than the rest of the economies in the Greater China Region.

Figure 3.7: ACI 2018 Overall Competitiveness Ranking Map

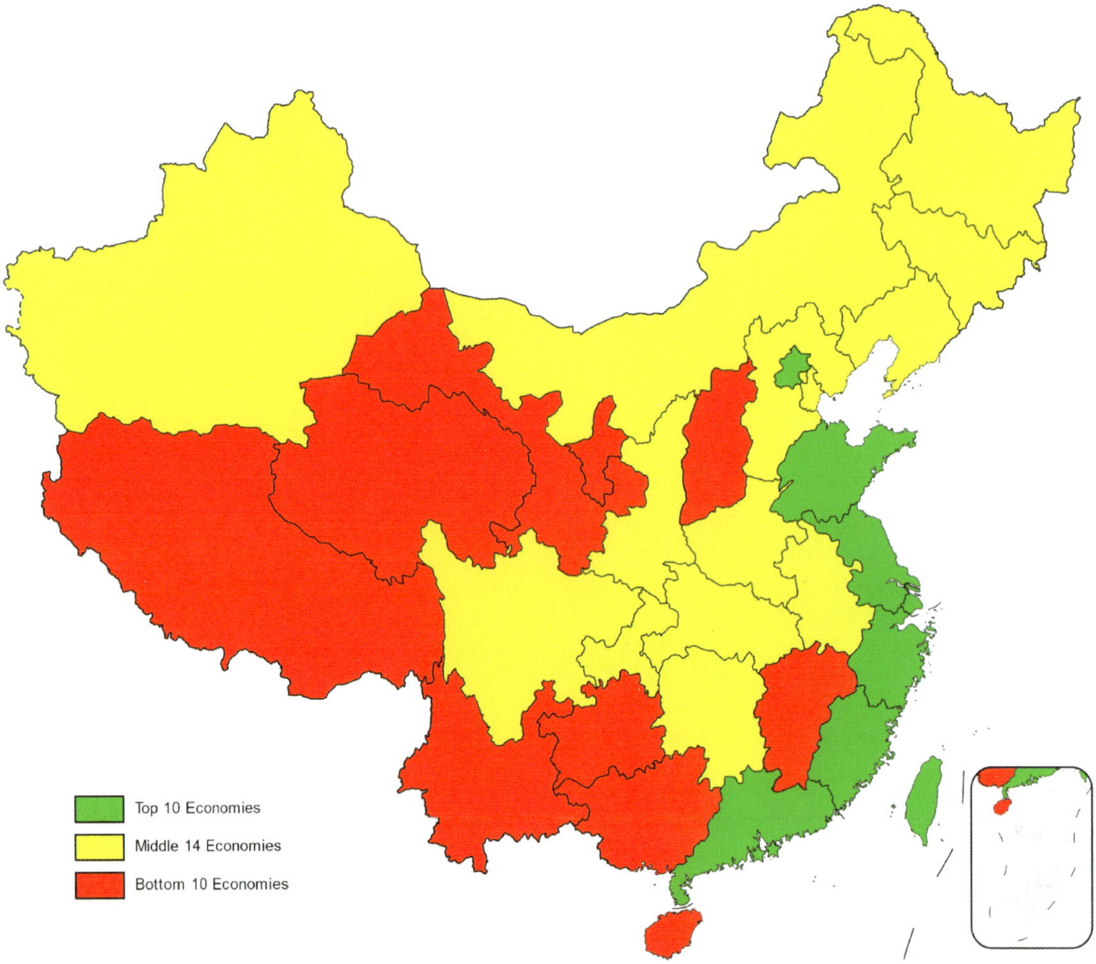

Note: The results are based on 2015 data, collated and analysed in 2018.
Source: Asia Competitiveness Institute.

On the other hand, economies located in the Central and North-eastern areas of Mainland China are largely in yellow while economies in Western China tend to be coloured in red. This seems to be in line with the stepped development theory. However, a closer look reveals that the green, yellow and red demarcations of economies do not exactly match the official regional classification announced by the National Bureau of Statistics of China. Not only does the competitiveness of each region differ from one another, but economies within the same region also have varying competitiveness. For example, while Anhui, Henan, Hubei and Hunan from Central China are in yellow, Jiangxi and Shanxi from the same region are in red. Significant parts of Western China including Chongqing, Inner Mongolia, Shaanxi, Sichuan and Xinjiang are in yellow instead of red, indicating substantial heterogeneity in the competitiveness levels among the economies in Western China.

Table 3.2 illustrates the Overall Competitiveness rankings and scores of the 34 Greater China economies from 2000 to 2015. It can be seen that the Overall Competitiveness rankings of only two economies, namely Henan (#16) and Tibet (#34), have remained unchanged from 2000 to 2015. Meanwhile, the rankings of 16 economies have improved in the same period (2000–2015). Shandong and Macau each has risen one spot; Guangdong, Zhejiang and Hainan each has risen two spots; Hebei and Inner Mongolia each has risen three spots; Jiangsu, Fujian, Sichuan and Guizhou have risen four spots; Hunan has risen five spots; Hubei has risen six spots; Shaanxi and Chongqing each has risen seven spots and Anhui has risen 12 spots. There are also 16 economies for which the rankings have fallen between 2000 and 2015. Hong Kong, Beijing and Gansu each has fallen one spot; Shanghai and Guangxi each has fallen two spots; Taiwan, Tianjin and Jiangxi have fallen three spots; Shanxi and Yunnan each has fallen four spots; Xinjiang and Jilin each has fallen five spots; Liaoning has fallen six spots; Qinghai has fallen seven spots; Ningxia has fallen eight spots and Heilongjiang has fallen 12 spots.

Table 3.2: ACI 2018 Overall Competitiveness Rankings and Scores: Evolution Over Time

Overall Competitiveness								
	1		**2**		**3**		**4**	
Rank	**Economy**	**Score**	**Economy**	**Score**	**Economy**	**Score**	**Economy**	**Score**
2000	Taiwan	3.7970	Hong Kong	2.5397	Guangdong	1.3272	Beijing	1.0538
2001	Taiwan	3.4512	Hong Kong	2.6536	Guangdong	1.5371	Beijing	1.1532
2002	Taiwan	3.4035	Hong Kong	2.2595	Guangdong	1.8006	Shanghai	1.1423
2003	Taiwan	3.1662	Hong Kong	2.3530	Guangdong	1.7957	Shanghai	1.2173
2004	Taiwan	3.0799	Hong Kong	2.3016	Guangdong	1.7440	Beijing	1.2586
2005	Taiwan	2.8703	Hong Kong	2.2335	Guangdong	1.8071	Shanghai	1.3154
2006	Taiwan	2.7058	Hong Kong	2.1533	Guangdong	1.8774	Jiangsu	1.3894
2007	Taiwan	2.4576	Hong Kong	2.1906	Guangdong	1.8511	Beijing	1.4786
2008	Taiwan	2.1993	Hong Kong	2.0059	Guangdong	1.8921	Jiangsu	1.5940
2009	Taiwan	1.9678	Guangdong	1.9594	Hong Kong	1.9014	Jiangsu	1.7800
2010	Guangdong	1.9946	Taiwan	1.8627	Jiangsu	1.8074	Hong Kong	1.7286
2011	Guangdong	1.9920	Jiangsu	1.9154	Taiwan	1.8209	Hong Kong	1.6937
2012	Guangdong	2.1103	Jiangsu	1.9878	Taiwan	1.7538	Beijing	1.5862
2013	Guangdong	2.3053	Jiangsu	2.0014	Beijing	1.6747	Taiwan	1.5873
2014	Guangdong	2.2485	Jiangsu	1.9838	Beijing	1.7279	Hong Kong	1.6406
2015	Guangdong	2.3977	Jiangsu	2.0168	Hong Kong	1.7073	Taiwan	1.6619

(*Continued*)

Table 3.2: (*Continued*)

Overall Competitiveness								
	5		6		7		8	
Rank	Economy	Score	Economy	Score	Economy	Score	Economy	Score
2000	Shanghai	0.8845	Jiangsu	0.5941	Liaoning	0.4883	Zhejiang	0.4481
2001	Shanghai	0.9869	Jiangsu	0.6790	Zhejiang	0.6319	Shandong	0.4814
2002	Beijing	1.1238	Jiangsu	0.8288	Zhejiang	0.6812	Shandong	0.5831
2003	Beijing	1.1650	Jiangsu	1.0330	Zhejiang	0.7838	Shandong	0.6869
2004	Shanghai	1.2081	Jiangsu	1.1103	Zhejiang	0.8497	Shandong	0.7533
2005	Jiangsu	1.2860	Beijing	1.2528	Zhejiang	0.9150	Shandong	0.8368
2006	Beijing	1.3285	Shanghai	1.2111	Zhejiang	1.0252	Shandong	0.9728
2007	Jiangsu	1.4622	Shanghai	1.4243	Zhejiang	1.0181	Shandong	0.8755
2008	Beijing	1.5512	Shanghai	1.5002	Zhejiang	1.0875	Shandong	0.9647
2009	Beijing	1.5270	Shanghai	1.4826	Zhejiang	1.1601	Shandong	0.9862
2010	Beijing	1.5818	Shanghai	1.5419	Zhejiang	1.1979	Shandong	0.9349
2011	Shanghai	1.5950	Beijing	1.5645	Zhejiang	1.2324	Shandong	0.8908
2012	Hong Kong	1.5251	Shanghai	1.4756	Zhejiang	1.3180	Shandong	0.9111
2013	Hong Kong	1.5199	Shanghai	1.3992	Zhejiang	1.3324	Shandong	0.8797
2014	Taiwan	1.6001	Shanghai	1.4052	Zhejiang	1.3551	Shandong	0.8245
2015	Beijing	1.6214	Zhejiang	1.3749	Shanghai	1.1922	Shandong	0.8301

Overall Competitiveness								
	9		10		11		12	
Rank	Economy	Score	Economy	Score	Economy	Score	Economy	Score
2000	Shandong	0.3822	Macau	0.1590	Tianjin	–0.0624	Heilongjiang	–0.0710
2001	Liaoning	0.4576	Macau	0.1122	Tianjin	0.0333	Fujian	–0.0504
2002	Liaoning	0.4649	Macau	0.2777	Tianjin	0.0233	Fujian	0.0205
2003	Macau	0.3915	Liaoning	0.3491	Tianjin	0.0261	Hebei	–0.0256
2004	Macau	0.6314	Liaoning	0.2611	Hebei	0.0882	Tianjin	0.0560
2005	Macau	0.4911	Liaoning	0.2838	Tianjin	0.1282	Hebei	0.1110
2006	Macau	0.4615	Liaoning	0.2754	Tianjin	0.1389	Hebei	0.0401
2007	Macau	0.5928	Liaoning	0.2678	Hebei	0.1217	Tianjin	0.0880
2008	Macau	0.5213	Liaoning	0.3362	Tianjin	0.1823	Hebei	0.1353
2009	Liaoning	0.4231	Macau	0.3875	Tianjin	0.2152	Hebei	0.1426
2010	Macau	0.5750	Liaoning	0.4146	Tianjin	0.2276	Hebei	0.1323
2011	Macau	0.5283	Liaoning	0.4154	Fujian	0.1415	Hebei	0.0909
2012	Macau	0.4966	Liaoning	0.4349	Fujian	0.1786	Hebei	0.0513
2013	Macau	0.5300	Liaoning	0.3409	Fujian	0.1663	Tianjin	–0.0095
2014	Macau	0.5843	Fujian	0.1677	Liaoning	0.1583	Hebei	0.0029
2015	Macau	0.5398	Fujian	0.1196	Hubei	0.0631	Hebei	0.0175

Table 3.2: (*Continued*)

Overall Competitiveness								
	13		14		15		16	
Rank	Economy	Score	Economy	Score	Economy	Score	Economy	Score
2000	Xinjiang	–0.0815	Fujian	–0.0886	Hebei	–0.1062	Henan	–0.1392
2001	Hebei	–0.1019	Henan	–0.1256	Heilongjiang	–0.1538	Hubei	–0.2260
2002	Hebei	–0.0532	Heilongjiang	–0.1517	Henan	–0.1677	Jilin	–0.2566
2003	Fujian	–0.0366	Heilongjiang	–0.1296	Henan	–0.1898	Xinjiang	–0.2125
2004	Fujian	–0.0618	Henan	–0.2326	Xinjiang	–0.2536	Sichuan	–0.2555
2005	Fujian	–0.0276	Henan	–0.1907	Heilongjiang	–0.1945	Xinjiang	–0.2772
2006	Fujian	–0.0361	Henan	–0.0900	Heilongjiang	–0.2374	Inner Mongolia	–0.2434
2007	Henan	–0.0869	Fujian	–0.0912	Xinjiang	–0.3012	Inner Mongolia	–0.3030
2008	Fujian	–0.0116	Henan	–0.1026	Inner Mongolia	–0.2221	Heilongjiang	–0.3023
2009	Fujian	0.0677	Henan	–0.1193	Inner Mongolia	–0.1837	Hubei	–0.2479
2010	Fujian	0.1202	Inner Mongolia	–0.1675	Henan	–0.2033	Hubei	–0.2222
2011	Tianjin	0.0843	Inner Mongolia	–0.1261	Hubei	–0.1937	Sichuan	–0.2199
2012	Tianjin	0.0107	Hubei	–0.1453	Sichuan	–0.1546	Inner Mongolia	–0.1878
2013	Hebei	–0.0379	Hubei	–0.0899	Sichuan	–0.1336	Henan	–0.1893
2014	Hubei	0.0024	Tianjin	–0.0986	Sichuan	–0.1237	Henan	–0.2272
2015	Liaoning	0.0000	Tianjin	–0.0381	Sichuan	–0.0754	Henan	–0.2087

Overall Competitiveness								
	17		18		19		20	
Rank	Economy	Score	Economy	Score	Economy	Score	Economy	Score
2000	Hubei	–0.1856	Jilin	–0.1945	Sichuan	–0.2740	Inner Mongolia	–0.2956
2001	Xinjiang	–0.2539	Jilin	–0.2555	Sichuan	–0.2689	Shanxi	–0.3062
2002	Sichuan	–0.2625	Xinjiang	–0.2769	Shanxi	–0.3589	Hubei	–0.4015
2003	Sichuan	–0.2284	Hubei	–0.3079	Jilin	–0.3535	Shanxi	–0.3923
2004	Heilongjiang	–0.2799	Hubei	–0.3387	Inner Mongolia	–0.3568	Shanxi	–0.4211
2005	Inner Mongolia	–0.3026	Hubei	–0.3564	Sichuan	–0.3960	Shanxi	–0.4323
2006	Xinjiang	–0.2988	Sichuan	–0.3360	Hubei	–0.3415	Jilin	–0.4053
2007	Heilongjiang	–0.3127	Sichuan	–0.3318	Hubei	–0.3537	Jilin	–0.4239
2008	Hubei	–0.3032	Xinjiang	–0.3344	Sichuan	–0.4111	Jilin	–0.4228
2009	Sichuan	–0.3123	Jilin	–0.3637	Heilongjiang	–0.3644	Xinjiang	–0.4139
2010	Sichuan	–0.2585	Xinjiang	–0.3011	Heilongjiang	–0.3475	Shaanxi	–0.4613
2011	Henan	–0.2489	Xinjiang	–0.3289	Heilongjiang	–0.3543	Anhui	–0.4509
2012	Henan	–0.2179	Shaanxi	–0.3379	Anhui	–0.3650	Xinjiang	–0.3869
2013	Inner Mongolia	–0.2480	Xinjiang	–0.3362	Anhui	–0.3671	Shaanxi	–0.3969
2014	Anhui	–0.2996	Inner Mongolia	–0.3073	Xinjiang	–0.3384	Shaanxi	–0.3955
2015	Inner Mongolia	–0.2806	Xinjiang	–0.3733	Anhui	–0.3825	Shaanxi	–0.4058

(*Continued*)

Table 3.2: (*Continued*)

Overall Competitiveness								
	21		22		23		24	
Rank	Economy	Score	Economy	Score	Economy	Score	Economy	Score
2000	Shanxi	–0.3179	Yunnan	–0.3201	Ningxia	–0.5509	Jiangxi	–0.5980
2001	Yunnan	–0.3423	Inner Mongolia	–0.3480	Ningxia	–0.5675	Jiangxi	–0.5977
2002	Inner Mongolia	–0.4130	Hunan	–0.4251	Yunnan	–0.4329	Ningxia	–0.5872
2003	Inner Mongolia	–0.4077	Yunnan	–0.5548	Ningxia	–0.6299	Jiangxi	–0.6700
2004	Jilin	–0.4376	Yunnan	–0.6247	Shaanxi	–0.6356	Jiangxi	–0.6603
2005	Jilin	–0.4355	Yunnan	–0.5897	Shaanxi	–0.6107	Hunan	–0.6801
2006	Shaanxi	–0.5628	Shanxi	–0.5784	Hunan	–0.6114	Yunnan	–0.6469
2007	Shanxi	–0.4778	Hunan	–0.5865	Shaanxi	–0.6042	Jiangxi	–0.6849
2008	Shanxi	–0.4631	Shaanxi	–0.5202	Hunan	–0.6146	Yunnan	–0.6572
2009	Shaanxi	–0.5188	Shanxi	–0.5364	Anhui	–0.5429	Hunan	–0.5479
2010	Anhui	–0.5051	Jilin	–0.5228	Hunan	–0.5346	Shanxi	–0.5428
2011	Shaanxi	–0.4887	Jilin	–0.5179	Shanxi	–0.5499	Hunan	–0.5661
2012	Jilin	–0.4378	Heilongjiang	–0.4459	Shanxi	–0.5764	Hunan	–0.5940
2013	Heilongjiang	–0.4062	Jilin	–0.5190	Hunan	–0.5258	Shanxi	–0.5901
2014	Heilongjiang	–0.4292	Hunan	–0.4818	Chongqing	–0.5759	Jilin	–0.6086
2015	Hunan	–0.4676	Chongqing	–0.5246	Jilin	–0.6048	Heilongjiang	–0.6212

Overall Competitiveness								
	25		26		27		28	
Rank	Economy	Score	Economy	Score	Economy	Score	Economy	Score
2000	Qinghai	–0.6446	Hunan	–0.6911	Shaanxi	–0.6974	Guangxi	–0.7383
2001	Hunan	–0.6659	Shaanxi	–0.6843	Qinghai	–0.7465	Guangxi	–0.7515
2002	Chongqing	–0.6084	Jiangxi	–0.6683	Shaanxi	–0.7222	Qinghai	–0.7410
2003	Shaanxi	–0.6955	Chongqing	–0.7191	Hunan	–0.7257	Anhui	–0.7518
2004	Ningxia	–0.6622	Hunan	–0.6945	Qinghai	–0.7511	Anhui	–0.7525
2005	Jiangxi	–0.6862	Ningxia	–0.7110	Qinghai	–0.7429	Chongqing	–0.7753
2006	Jiangxi	–0.6884	Anhui	–0.7739	Qinghai	–0.7892	Ningxia	–0.7909
2007	Yunnan	–0.6941	Anhui	–0.7281	Chongqing	–0.7867	Guangxi	–0.7928
2008	Jiangxi	–0.6595	Anhui	–0.7015	Guangxi	–0.7903	Chongqing	–0.8017
2009	Jiangxi	–0.6385	Yunnan	–0.7355	Chongqing	–0.7384	Guangxi	–0.7721
2010	Jiangxi	–0.7178	Yunnan	–0.7358	Chongqing	–0.7495	Guangxi	–0.8057
2011	Chongqing	–0.6713	Yunnan	–0.6761	Jiangxi	–0.6854	Guangxi	–0.8536
2012	Yunnan	–0.6408	Chongqing	–0.6696	Jiangxi	–0.7751	Guangxi	–0.8515
2013	Chongqing	–0.6146	Yunnan	–0.6781	Jiangxi	–0.7554	Hainan	–0.8603
2014	Shanxi	–0.6822	Jiangxi	–0.7552	Yunnan	–0.7783	Hainan	–0.8466
2015	Shanxi	–0.6574	Yunnan	–0.7322	Jiangxi	–0.7458	Hainan	–0.8435

Table 3.2: (*Continued*)

Overall Competitiveness								
	29		30		31		32	
Rank	Economy	Score	Economy	Score	Economy	Score	Economy	Score
2000	Chongqing	–0.7453	Hainan	–0.8281	Anhui	–0.8453	Gansu	–0.8708
2001	Chongqing	–0.7574	Anhui	–0.7978	Hainan	–0.8281	Gansu	–0.9113
2002	Anhui	–0.8188	Hainan	–0.8693	Guangxi	–0.8934	Gansu	–0.9853
2003	Qinghai	–0.7776	Hainan	–0.8873	Guangxi	–0.9216	Gansu	–0.9898
2004	Chongqing	–0.8298	Guangxi	–0.8663	Hainan	–0.8878	Gansu	–0.9756
2005	Anhui	–0.8162	Guangxi	–0.8615	Hainan	–0.9154	Gansu	–1.0419
2006	Guangxi	–0.7957	Chongqing	–0.8002	Hainan	–0.8899	Gansu	–1.0046
2007	Ningxia	–0.8396	Hainan	–0.8875	Qinghai	–0.9071	Gansu	–1.1022
2008	Ningxia	–0.8596	Hainan	–0.9511	Qinghai	–0.9592	Guizhou	–1.1859
2009	Hainan	–0.9198	Ningxia	–0.9347	Qinghai	–1.0615	Guizhou	–1.1897
2010	Hainan	–0.8850	Ningxia	–0.9506	Qinghai	–1.1383	Guizhou	–1.2438
2011	Hainan	–0.8589	Ningxia	–0.9364	Qinghai	–1.0974	Gansu	–1.3130
2012	Hainan	–0.8533	Ningxia	–0.9763	Qinghai	–1.1274	Guizhou	–1.1713
2013	Guangxi	–0.9237	Ningxia	–1.0237	Guizhou	–1.1155	Qinghai	–1.1300
2014	Guangxi	–0.9190	Guizhou	–0.9753	Ningxia	–0.9971	Qinghai	–1.1361
2015	Guizhou	–0.8803	Guangxi	–0.9117	Ningxia	–0.9723	Qinghai	–1.1045

Overall Competitiveness				
	33		34	
Rank	Economy	Score	Economy	Score
2000	Guizhou	–1.0797	Tibet	–1.2479
2001	Guizhou	–1.1202	Tibet	–1.3168
2002	Guizhou	–1.1347	Tibet	–1.3808
2003	Guizhou	–1.1690	Tibet	–1.1915
2004	Guizhou	–1.1713	Tibet	–1.1928
2005	Guizhou	–1.1356	Tibet	–1.3517
2006	Guizhou	–1.1469	Tibet	–1.5116
2007	Guizhou	–1.1705	Tibet	–1.3619
2008	Gansu	–1.2564	Tibet	–1.4394
2009	Gansu	–1.3237	Tibet	–1.5354
2010	Gansu	–1.3367	Tibet	–1.4897
2011	Guizhou	–1.3397	Tibet	–1.4879
2012	Gansu	–1.2692	Tibet	–1.6560
2013	Gansu	–1.2018	Tibet	–1.5844
2014	Gansu	–1.1605	Tibet	–1.5652
2015	Gansu	–1.1878	Tibet	–1.5241

Note: The results are based on 2000–2015 data, collated and analysed in 2018.
Source: Asia Competitiveness Institute.

There are six Mainland China economies that have experienced substantial changes in their Overall Competitiveness rankings over the past 15-year period from 2000 to 2015. In particular, the rankings of Heilongjiang, Ningxia and Qinghai have dropped by 12 places, eight places and seven places, respectively. One the other hand, the ranking of Anhui has improved by 12 places, and the rankings of Shaanxi and Chongqing have improved by seven places. These six economies are located in three different regions of Mainland China. Among the economies that have experienced substantial drop in ranking, Heilongjiang is from North-eastern China, and Ningxia and Qinghai are from Western China. Among those with significant improvement in ranking, Anhui is from Central China, and Shaanxi and Chongqing are from Western China. This indicates that some major changes have occurred across the competitiveness landscape of Mainland China over the past decade or so. Such changes are by no means random fluctuations but can be linked to Mainland China's regional development strategies.

The gap in competitiveness between economies in Mainland China and in Hong Kong and Taiwan had diminished from 2000 to 2009. In 2000, Taiwan and Hong Kong scored 3.7970 and 2.5397, respectively, for Overall Competitiveness, while Guangdong from Mainland China achieved a score of 1.3272. However, in 2009, the scores of Taiwan and Hong Kong decreased substantially to 1.9678 and 1.9014, respectively, while the score of Guangdong improved to 1.9594, surpassing Hong Kong and becoming the second economy in terms of Overall Competitiveness. This means that the competition to remain at the top within Greater China had intensified over the period from 2000 to 2009. Since 2010, economies from Mainland China such as Guangdong and Jiangsu have surpassed Taiwan and Hong Kong in terms of Overall Competitiveness.

3.2.2 ACI 2018 Macroeconomic Stability Rankings and Scores

Table 3.3 shows the 2018 Macroeconomic Stability ranking. Guangdong comes first in the Macroeconomic Stability ranking with a score of 3.0011. On the other hand, Macau is ranked the lowest among the 34 Greater China economies with a score of –1.1022.

Table 3.3: ACI 2018 Macroeconomic Stability Ranking and Scores

Rank	Economy	Score
1	Guangdong	3.0011
2	Hong Kong	2.2734
3	Jiangsu	2.1197
4	Shanghai	1.5753
5	Shandong	1.1571
6	Zhejiang	1.0056
7	Taiwan	0.5317
8	Beijing	0.3584

Table 3.3: *(Continued)*

Rank	Economy	Score
9	Liaoning	0.3093
10	Fujian	0.2283
11	Hubei	0.0966
12	Sichuan	0.0543
13	Henan	–0.0201
14	Tianjin	–0.1276
15	Anhui	–0.1567
16	Chongqing	–0.1709
17	Hebei	–0.1911
18	Hunan	–0.2245
19	Shaanxi	–0.3306
20	Guangxi	–0.3814
21	Yunnan	–0.4753
22	Inner Mongolia	–0.4939
23	Jiangxi	–0.4974
24	Jilin	–0.5687
25	Guizhou	–0.6718
26	Shanxi	–0.7016
27	Heilongjiang	–0.7618
28	Xinjiang	–0.7855
29	Hainan	–0.9161
30	Ningxia	–0.9477
31	Tibet	–1.0518
32	Qinghai	–1.0625
33	Gansu	–1.0716
34	Macau	–1.1022

Note: The results are based on 2015 data, collated and analysed in 2018.
Source: Asia Competitiveness Institute.

The average-performing economy (with a standardised score of 0) for Macroeconomic Stability ranking is between the #12-ranked Sichuan (0.0543) and the #13-ranked Henan (–0.0201). The median is situated between the #17-ranked Hebei (–0.1911) and the #18-ranked Hunan (–0.2245), and the median score is –0.2078. Similar to the case of Overall Competitiveness ranking, the average score (0) of Macroeconomic Stability ranking is higher than the median score (–0.2078).

It is worth noting that there is a marked drop in score from the #1-ranked Guangdong (3.0011) to the #2-ranked Hong Kong (2.2734). The gap in scores between these two economies is as huge as 0.7277. There is also a considerable gap of 0.5444 between the #3-ranked Jiangsu

(2.1197) and the #4-ranked Shanghai (1.5753), as well as a large gap of 0.4182 between the #4-ranked Shanghai (1.5753) and the #5-ranked Shandong (1.1571). Besides, the gap between the #6-ranked Zhejiang (1.0056) and the #7-ranked Taiwan (0.5317) is also as large as 0.4739. It suggests that the top six economies, namely Guangdong, Hong Kong, Jiangsu, Shanghai, Shandong and Zhejiang, significantly outperform the rest of the 34 Greater China economies in terms of Macroeconomic Stability. Besides, within the top six economics, the gaps in Macroeconomic Stability are also sizable.

Figure 3.8 provides a snapshot of the 2018 Macroeconomic Stability ranking. Similarly, green represents the top 10 economies, yellow, the middle 14 economies, and red, the 10 lowest ranking economies. It can be observed that the Eastern Coastal Area in Mainland China is largely green, except for Hainan, Hebei and Tianjin. In general, the colour of the economy changes from green to yellow, and then to red as the location shifts westwards to

Figure 3.8: ACI 2018 Macroeconomic Stability Ranking Map

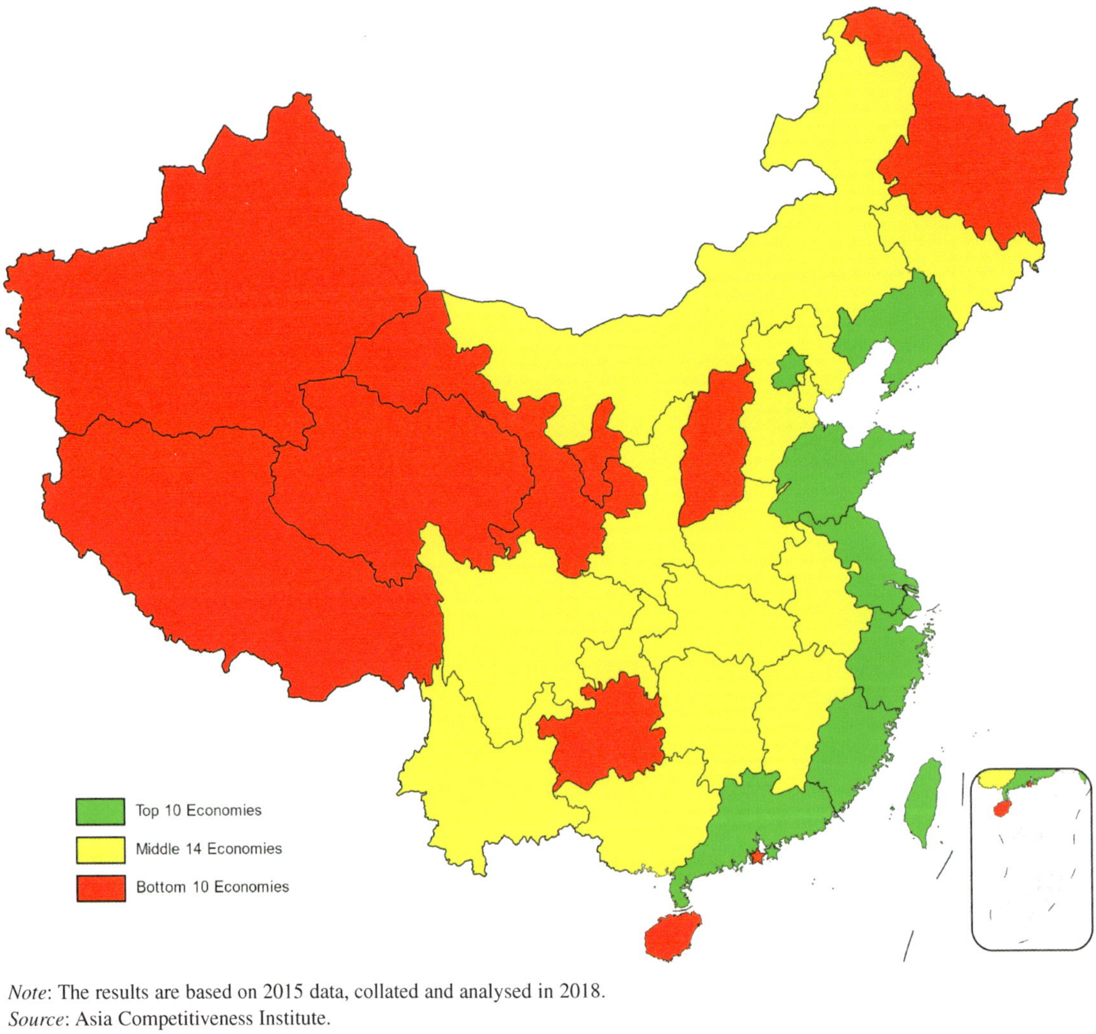

Note: The results are based on 2015 data, collated and analysed in 2018.
Source: Asia Competitiveness Institute.

the inland areas of Mainland China. Some economies that differ noticeably from this general pattern observed are Shanxi, Guizhou, Hainan, Heilongjiang and Macau. Table 3.4 shows the Macroeconomic Stability rankings and scores for the 34 Greater China economies from 2000 to 2015.

Among the 34 economies, the rankings of Liaoning (#9), Fujian (#10), Chongqing (#16), Shaanxi (#19) and Macau (#34) have not changed in 2015 as compared to 2000. Meanwhile, the rankings of 14 economies have improved over the past 15 years. Guangdong, Hubei, Henan and Guizhou have increased one place; Jiangsu, Shandong, Zhejiang, Yunnan and Tibet each has increased two places; Shanxi has increased three places; Sichuan has increased five places; Anhui and Hunan have increased seven places and Inner Mongolia has increased 10 places. The rankings of the remaining 15 economies have decreased from 2000 to 2015. Hong Kong, Shanghai and Hainan each has decreased one place; Beijing, Jiangxi, Qinghai and Gansu each has decreased two places; Taiwan, Tianjin and Ningxia have decreased three places; Hebei and Xinjiang have decreased four places; Guangxi has decreased five places; Jilin has decreased six places and Heilongjiang has decreased seven places.

Table 3.4: ACI 2018 Macroeconomic Stability Rankings and Scores: Evolution Over Time

Macroeconomic Stability								
	1		2		3		4	
Rank	**Economy**	**Score**	**Economy**	**Score**	**Economy**	**Score**	**Economy**	**Score**
2000	Hong Kong	3.5109	Guangdong	2.2679	Shanghai	1.7397	Taiwan	1.3590
2001	Hong Kong	3.1304	Guangdong	2.6864	Shanghai	1.7686	Jiangsu	1.3874
2002	Guangdong	3.0165	Hong Kong	2.1416	Shanghai	2.0341	Jiangsu	1.6650
2003	Guangdong	2.8914	Hong Kong	2.2787	Shanghai	2.0804	Jiangsu	1.9669
2004	Guangdong	2.7666	Hong Kong	2.3779	Shanghai	2.0971	Jiangsu	1.9353
2005	Guangdong	2.6591	Hong Kong	2.3215	Jiangsu	2.1394	Shanghai	2.0199
2006	Guangdong	2.6815	Jiangsu	2.1904	Hong Kong	2.0489	Shanghai	1.8908
2007	Guangdong	2.5942	Hong Kong	2.2207	Jiangsu	2.2178	Shanghai	1.8661
2008	Guangdong	2.5950	Jiangsu	2.3864	Shanghai	1.9045	Hong Kong	1.8887
2009	Guangdong	2.7025	Jiangsu	2.4802	Shanghai	1.7875	Hong Kong	1.7361
2010	Guangdong	2.6738	Jiangsu	2.4379	Shanghai	1.8183	Hong Kong	1.6835
2011	Guangdong	2.6933	Jiangsu	2.5633	Shanghai	1.7583	Hong Kong	1.6531
2012	Guangdong	2.8630	Jiangsu	2.5740	Shanghai	1.6771	Hong Kong	1.3828
2013	Guangdong	3.0394	Jiangsu	2.3054	Shanghai	1.7329	Hong Kong	1.6805
2014	Guangdong	2.9881	Jiangsu	2.2238	Hong Kong	1.9370	Shanghai	1.6597
2015	Guangdong	3.0011	Hong Kong	2.2734	Jiangsu	2.1197	Shanghai	1.5753

(Continued)

Table 3.4: (*Continued*)

Macroeconomic Stability								
	5		6		7		8	
Rank	Economy	Score	Economy	Score	Economy	Score	Economy	Score
2000	Jiangsu	1.3371	Beijing	1.0635	Shandong	0.4199	Zhejiang	0.3498
2001	Taiwan	1.1114	Beijing	0.9134	Zhejiang	0.6398	Shandong	0.5847
2002	Taiwan	1.1565	Beijing	0.9347	Zhejiang	0.8465	Shandong	0.8209
2003	Shandong	1.0096	Taiwan	0.9769	Zhejiang	0.9180	Beijing	0.6725
2004	Shandong	1.0376	Taiwan	1.0257	Zhejiang	0.8779	Beijing	0.8497
2005	Shandong	1.1305	Zhejiang	0.9732	Beijing	0.7267	Taiwan	0.6656
2006	Shandong	1.2479	Zhejiang	1.1269	Taiwan	0.8236	Beijing	0.8133
2007	Shandong	1.1345	Zhejiang	1.0659	Beijing	0.9486	Taiwan	0.7245
2008	Shandong	1.2396	Zhejiang	1.0830	Beijing	0.8331	Liaoning	0.7184
2009	Shandong	1.1920	Zhejiang	1.1182	Liaoning	0.8230	Beijing	0.5559
2010	Shandong	1.2804	Zhejiang	1.0512	Liaoning	0.9555	Beijing	0.6858
2011	Shandong	1.2477	Zhejiang	1.0535	Liaoning	0.8937	Beijing	0.6101
2012	Shandong	1.2496	Zhejiang	1.0774	Liaoning	0.9382	Beijing	0.5658
2013	Shandong	1.2103	Zhejiang	1.0081	Liaoning	0.7817	Beijing	0.5027
2014	Shandong	1.1767	Zhejiang	0.9581	Liaoning	0.6019	Beijing	0.5710
2015	Shandong	1.1571	Zhejiang	1.0056	Taiwan	0.5317	Beijing	0.3584

Macroeconomic Stability								
	9		10		11		12	
Rank	Economy	Score	Economy	Score	Economy	Score	Economy	Score
2000	Liaoning	0.2582	Fujian	0.1453	Tianjin	0.0962	Hubei	–0.1463
2001	Fujian	0.3749	Liaoning	0.2678	Tianjin	0.1466	Hubei	–0.0543
2002	Fujian	0.4631	Liaoning	0.3691	Tianjin	0.1814	Hebei	–0.1791
2003	Fujian	0.2696	Liaoning	0.2560	Tianjin	0.1676	Hebei	–0.2014
2004	Tianjin	0.2408	Liaoning	0.1639	Fujian	0.1445	Hebei	–0.1340
2005	Liaoning	0.4518	Tianjin	0.3612	Fujian	0.1236	Henan	–0.1250
2006	Liaoning	0.4542	Tianjin	0.2211	Fujian	0.2018	Henan	–0.0682
2007	Liaoning	0.5005	Tianjin	0.1793	Fujian	0.1633	Henan	–0.0564
2008	Taiwan	0.4259	Tianjin	0.2406	Fujian	0.1974	Henan	–0.0693
2009	Fujian	0.3230	Taiwan	0.2642	Tianjin	0.1440	Sichuan	–0.0394
2010	Taiwan	0.4538	Fujian	0.2345	Tianjin	0.0599	Sichuan	–0.0047
2011	Taiwan	0.3925	Fujian	0.2285	Tianjin	0.0504	Sichuan	0.0498
2012	Fujian	0.2923	Taiwan	0.2782	Sichuan	0.1382	Tianjin	0.0199
2013	Taiwan	0.3015	Fujian	0.2772	Sichuan	0.0743	Hubei	–0.0081
2014	Taiwan	0.3577	Fujian	0.2743	Sichuan	0.1332	Hubei	0.0758
2015	Liaoning	0.3093	Fujian	0.2283	Hubei	0.0966	Sichuan	0.0543

Table 3.4: (*Continued*)

Macroeconomic Stability								
	13		14		15		16	
Rank	Economy	Score	Economy	Score	Economy	Score	Economy	Score
2000	Hebei	–0.1491	Henan	–0.1653	Guangxi	–0.2028	Chongqing	–0.3171
2001	Hebei	–0.1487	Guangxi	–0.1873	Henan	–0.2320	Sichuan	–0.3969
2002	Hubei	–0.1923	Guangxi	–0.2908	Henan	–0.3045	Sichuan	–0.3220
2003	Henan	–0.2415	Sichuan	–0.2912	Hubei	–0.3302	Guangxi	–0.4090
2004	Henan	–0.2589	Sichuan	–0.2983	Hubei	–0.3874	Guangxi	–0.4258
2005	Hebei	–0.1368	Sichuan	–0.2428	Hubei	–0.4215	Shaanxi	–0.4434
2006	Hebei	–0.1736	Sichuan	–0.2046	Hubei	–0.3511	Guangxi	–0.3920
2007	Hebei	–0.1347	Sichuan	–0.1710	Hubei	–0.2660	Anhui	–0.4230
2008	Hebei	–0.1149	Sichuan	–0.1286	Hubei	–0.2725	Anhui	–0.3554
2009	Anhui	–0.0551	Hebei	–0.0669	Henan	–0.0963	Hubei	–0.1615
2010	Henan	–0.0880	Hubei	–0.0987	Hebei	–0.0992	Anhui	–0.2475
2011	Henan	–0.0762	Hubei	–0.0834	Hebei	–0.0921	Anhui	–0.2647
2012	Henan	–0.0387	Hubei	–0.0724	Hebei	–0.1421	Anhui	–0.1501
2013	Tianjin	–0.0142	Henan	–0.0714	Anhui	–0.1299	Hebei	–0.2024
2014	Tianjin	–0.0259	Henan	–0.0298	Anhui	–0.0868	Chongqing	–0.1386
2015	Henan	–0.0201	Tianjin	–0.1276	Anhui	–0.1567	Chongqing	–0.1709

Macroeconomic Stability								
	17		18		19		20	
Rank	Economy	Score	Economy	Score	Economy	Score	Economy	Score
2000	Sichuan	–0.3550	Jilin	–0.3648	Shaanxi	–0.3904	Heilongjiang	–0.4609
2001	Jiangxi	–0.4194	Anhui	–0.4278	Hunan	–0.4606	Yunnan	–0.4649
2002	Anhui	–0.4384	Shanxi	–0.4453	Shaanxi	–0.4949	Hunan	–0.5028
2003	Jiangxi	–0.4599	Chongqing	–0.5006	Anhui	–0.5134	Jilin	–0.5500
2004	Jiangxi	–0.4403	Anhui	–0.4662	Chongqing	–0.5329	Shaanxi	–0.5492
2005	Chongqing	–0.4614	Anhui	–0.4747	Guangxi	–0.4761	Jiangxi	–0.5031
2006	Anhui	–0.4308	Jiangxi	–0.4576	Inner Mongolia	–0.4608	Hunan	–0.4720
2007	Hunan	–0.4311	Inner Mongolia	–0.4499	Jilin	–0.4604	Guangxi	–0.4708
2008	Hunan	–0.3832	Jilin	–0.3977	Inner Mongolia	–0.4255	Chongqing	–0.4378
2009	Chongqing	–0.3290	Hunan	–0.3435	Guangxi	–0.3470	Jiangxi	–0.4260
2010	Hunan	–0.3183	Guangxi	–0.3703	Chongqing	–0.3714	Jiangxi	–0.4554
2011	Chongqing	–0.2985	Hunan	–0.2997	Guangxi	–0.4520	Shaanxi	–0.4758
2012	Hunan	–0.2536	Chongqing	–0.2886	Shaanxi	–0.3543	Yunnan	–0.4782
2013	Hunan	–0.2454	Chongqing	–0.2676	Shaanxi	–0.3553	Guangxi	–0.4187
2014	Hunan	–0.2253	Hebei	–0.2362	Shaanxi	–0.2613	Guangxi	–0.4643
2015	Hebei	–0.1911	Hunan	–0.2245	Shaanxi	–0.3306	Guangxi	–0.3814

(*Continued*)

Table 3.4: (*Continued*)

Macroeconomic Stability								
	21		22		23		24	
Rank	Economy	Score	Economy	Score	Economy	Score	Economy	Score
2000	Jiangxi	–0.4795	Anhui	–0.4805	Yunnan	–0.4864	Xinjiang	–0.5854
2001	Shaanxi	–0.4808	Hainan	–0.5274	Chongqing	–0.5441	Heilongjiang	–0.5984
2002	Jiangxi	–0.5145	Chongqing	–0.5400	Yunnan	–0.5513	Jilin	–0.5792
2003	Yunnan	–0.5718	Heilongjiang	–0.5746	Shanxi	–0.5747	Hunan	–0.5833
2004	Hunan	–0.5643	Inner Mongolia	–0.5650	Heilongjiang	–0.6185	Shanxi	–0.6426
2005	Inner Mongolia	–0.5318	Heilongjiang	–0.5450	Jilin	–0.5646	Hunan	–0.5791
2006	Jilin	–0.4747	Shaanxi	–0.5148	Chongqing	–0.6424	Yunnan	–0.6427
2007	Jiangxi	–0.5225	Chongqing	–0.5455	Shaanxi	–0.5561	Shanxi	–0.6244
2008	Jiangxi	–0.4716	Guangxi	–0.4907	Shaanxi	–0.5061	Heilongjiang	–0.5130
2009	Jilin	–0.4268	Inner Mongolia	–0.4607	Shaanxi	–0.5443	Yunnan	–0.5962
2010	Shaanxi	–0.5310	Inner Mongolia	–0.5464	Heilongjiang	–0.5783	Jilin	–0.5790
2011	Jiangxi	–0.4881	Yunnan	–0.5036	Inner Mongolia	–0.5386	Heilongjiang	–0.5549
2012	Jilin	–0.4947	Guangxi	–0.5075	Jiangxi	–0.5777	Heilongjiang	–0.6144
2013	Yunnan	–0.4958	Jiangxi	–0.5161	Jilin	–0.5506	Heilongjiang	–0.5914
2014	Jiangxi	–0.5352	Yunnan	–0.5895	Inner Mongolia	–0.6107	Jilin	–0.6166
2015	Yunnan	–0.4753	Inner Mongolia	–0.4939	Jiangxi	–0.4974	Jilin	–0.5687

Macroeconomic Stability								
	25		26		27		28	
Rank	Economy	Score	Economy	Score	Economy	Score	Economy	Score
2000	Hunan	–0.6471	Guizhou	–0.6562	Ningxia	–0.6979	Hainan	–0.6993
2001	Jilin	–0.6012	Shanxi	–0.6570	Guizhou	–0.7037	Ningxia	–0.7895
2002	Heilongjiang	–0.6232	Hainan	–0.6275	Guizhou	–0.7670	Ningxia	–0.8193
2003	Shaanxi	–0.6043	Xinjiang	–0.6686	Inner Mongolia	–0.6813	Guizhou	–0.7392
2004	Jilin	–0.6536	Yunnan	–0.6650	Macau	–0.6797	Xinjiang	–0.7218
2005	Yunnan	–0.6181	Xinjiang	–0.6498	Shanxi	–0.7063	Guizhou	–0.7417
2006	Heilongjiang	–0.6475	Shanxi	–0.7401	Xinjiang	–0.7511	Hainan	–0.7979
2007	Heilongjiang	–0.6533	Yunnan	–0.6582	Tibet	–0.7773	Xinjiang	–0.8257
2008	Yunnan	–0.6027	Shanxi	–0.6959	Tibet	–0.8300	Xinjiang	–0.8308
2009	Heilongjiang	–0.6196	Shanxi	–0.7455	Guizhou	–0.7525	Hainan	–0.8249
2010	Shanxi	–0.6111	Yunnan	–0.6575	Guizhou	–0.8520	Xinjiang	–0.8657
2011	Jilin	–0.5774	Shanxi	–0.6513	Guizhou	–0.8166	Xinjiang	–0.8733
2012	Inner Mongolia	–0.6481	Guizhou	–0.7021	Shanxi	–0.7230	Tibet	–0.8404
2013	Guizhou	–0.6627	Inner Mongolia	–0.6862	Shanxi	–0.7952	Xinjiang	–0.8490
2014	Heilongjiang	–0.6743	Guizhou	–0.6793	Shanxi	–0.7853	Xinjiang	–0.8264
2015	Guizhou	–0.6718	Shanxi	–0.7016	Heilongjiang	–0.7618	Xinjiang	–0.7855

Table 3.4: (*Continued*)

Macroeconomic Stability								
	29		30		31		32	
Rank	**Economy**	**Score**	**Economy**	**Score**	**Economy**	**Score**	**Economy**	**Score**
2000	Shanxi	–0.8016	Qinghai	–0.8198	Gansu	–0.8521	Inner Mongolia	–0.8766
2001	Qinghai	–0.8210	Tibet	–0.8333	Macau	–0.8424	Inner Mongolia	–0.8455
2002	Inner Mongolia	–0.8422	Xinjiang	–0.8452	Macau	–0.9015	Tibet	–0.9073
2003	Hainan	–0.7393	Ningxia	–0.7557	Gansu	–0.8601	Macau	–0.8665
2004	Tibet	–0.7509	Gansu	–0.7986	Ningxia	–0.8143	Guizhou	–0.8183
2005	Qinghai	–0.8207	Ningxia	–0.8226	Tibet	–0.8270	Hainan	–0.8280
2006	Guizhou	–0.8107	Ningxia	–0.8370	Tibet	–0.8497	Qinghai	–0.8860
2007	Hainan	–0.8416	Ningxia	–0.8612	Guizhou	–0.8661	Gansu	–0.9708
2008	Guizhou	–0.8530	Hainan	–0.8541	Ningxia	–0.9510	Gansu	–1.0754
2009	Tibet	–0.9178	Xinjiang	–0.9330	Ningxia	–0.9566	Gansu	–1.1086
2010	Tibet	–0.8725	Hainan	–0.9649	Macau	–0.9669	Ningxia	–1.0082
2011	Tibet	–0.8949	Hainan	–0.9902	Ningxia	–1.0573	Qinghai	–1.0638
2012	Xinjiang	–0.8874	Hainan	–0.9471	Ningxia	–1.0042	Qinghai	–1.0164
2013	Tibet	–0.8615	Hainan	–0.8894	Gansu	–1.0100	Qinghai	–1.0539
2014	Hainan	–0.8974	Ningxia	–0.9867	Tibet	–1.0277	Gansu	–1.0544
2015	Hainan	–0.9161	Ningxia	–0.9477	Tibet	–1.0518	Qinghai	–1.0625

Macroeconomic Stability				
	33		34	
Rank	**Economy**	**Score**	**Economy**	**Score**
2000	Tibet	–0.9539	Macau	–0.9596
2001	Gansu	–0.9829	Xinjiang	–0.9922
2002	Gansu	–0.9624	Qinghai	–0.9788
2003	Tibet	–0.8671	Qinghai	–0.9038
2004	Qinghai	–0.8452	Hainan	–0.8861
2005	Gansu	–0.8909	Macau	–1.1620
2006	Gansu	–0.8915	Macau	–1.2037
2007	Macau	–1.0151	Qinghai	–1.0342
2008	Macau	–1.1239	Qinghai	–1.1295
2009	Qinghai	–1.1812	Macau	–1.1943
2010	Gansu	–1.0922	Qinghai	–1.1553
2011	Gansu	–1.0649	Macau	–1.0771
2012	Gansu	–1.0264	Macau	–1.2891
2013	Ningxia	–1.0634	Macau	–1.1756
2014	Qinghai	–1.0810	Macau	–1.1245
2015	Gansu	–1.0716	Macau	–1.1022

Note: The results are based on 2000–2015 data, collated and analysed in 2018.
Source: Asia Competitiveness Institute.

Hong Kong only retained its top position in the Macroeconomic Stability ranking in 2000 and 2001. Since 2002, it has started to fall behind some Mainland China economies such as Guangdong, Jiangsu and Shanghai. In general, the standardised score of Hong Kong decreased over the past decade or so, from 3.5109 in 2000 to 1.3828 in 2012, and the ranking of Hong Kong fell from #1 in 2000 to #4 in 2012. It started to catch up from year 2013, with its ranking improving steadily to #2 and score increasing to 2.2734 in 2015. However, Hong Kong has not regained the top position since 2002, and the gap between Hong Kong and the #1-ranked Guangdong (3.0011) is still as large as 0.7277 in 2015.

3.2.3 ACI 2018 Government and Institutional Setting Rankings and Scores

The Government and Institutional Setting ranking is displayed in Table 3.5. The maximum and minimum scores of the 34 Greater China economies are 1.9868 and –2.0771, respectively. Taiwan occupies the highest position under this environment while Tibet is ranked at the bottom.

Table 3.5: ACI 2018 Government and Institutional Setting Ranking and Scores

Rank	Economy	Score
1	Taiwan	1.9868
2	Jiangsu	1.9224
3	Guangdong	1.8503
4	Hong Kong	1.7956
5	Beijing	1.7281
6	Zhejiang	1.3554
7	Shanghai	1.3090
8	Macau	0.9313
9	Shandong	0.8084
10	Fujian	0.0124
11	Hubei	–0.1146
12	Hebei	–0.1269
13	Henan	–0.1864
14	Anhui	–0.1897
15	Sichuan	–0.2195
16	Chongqing	–0.2616
17	Liaoning	–0.3181
18	Hainan	–0.3387
19	Jiangxi	–0.3966
20	Tianjin	–0.4731
21	Guizhou	–0.5009

Table 3.5: (*Continued*)

Rank	Economy	Score
22	Inner Mongolia	–0.5244
23	Yunnan	–0.5379
24	Ningxia	–0.5907
25	Guangxi	–0.6104
26	Heilongjiang	–0.6153
27	Xinjiang	–0.6283
28	Hunan	–0.6409
29	Shaanxi	–0.7905
30	Jilin	–0.8113
31	Shanxi	–0.8676
32	Gansu	–0.9353
33	Qinghai	–0.9443
34	Tibet	–2.0771

Note: The results are based on 2015 data, collated and analysed in 2018.
Source: Asia Competitiveness Institute.

The average-performing economy (with a score of 0) is situated between the #10-ranked Fujian (0.0124) and the #11-ranked Hubei (–0.1146) while the median score lies between the #17-ranked Liaoning (–0.3181) and the #18-ranked Hainan (–0.3387). For the Government and Institutional Setting, the median score is –0.3284, noticeably lower than the average score (0). This suggests that only less than half of the economies perform better than the average-performing economy in terms of Government and Institutional Setting.

The distribution of scores for Government and Institutional Setting is quite skewed, with only 10 out of the 34 Greater China economies scoring above the average (i.e. above 0). The difference in scores between the bottom-ranked Tibet (–2.0771) and the #33-ranked Qinghai (–0.9443) is 1.1328. Given this tremendous gap, Tibet can be viewed as an outlier under the Government and Institutional Setting environment. Moreover, the gap in scores between the #9-ranked Shandong (0.8084) and the #10-ranked Fujian (0.0124) is 0.7960, indicating that the top nine economies have much stronger Government and Institutional Setting competitiveness relative to the rest of Greater China economies.

Figure 3.9 shows the 2018 Government and Institutional Setting ranking from a spatial perspective. The top 10 economies are colour-coded in green, the middle 14 economies in yellow, and the bottom 10 in red. It can be observed that the Eastern Coastal Area of Mainland China is largely green, except for Hainan, Hebei and Tianjin. The distribution of the economies in yellow and red lacks clearly defined patterns, as these middle- or bottom-ranked economies under this environment span across all regions of Mainland China. Nevertheless, the bottom 10 economies do tend to concentrate in three clusters. The largest cluster consists of Xinjiang, Tibet, Qinghai, Gansu, Shaanxi and Shanxi in the west. The other two smaller clusters consist of Hunan and Guizhou in the south, and Heilongjiang and Liaoning in the north west, respectively.

Figure 3.9: ACI 2018 Government and Institutional Setting Ranking Map

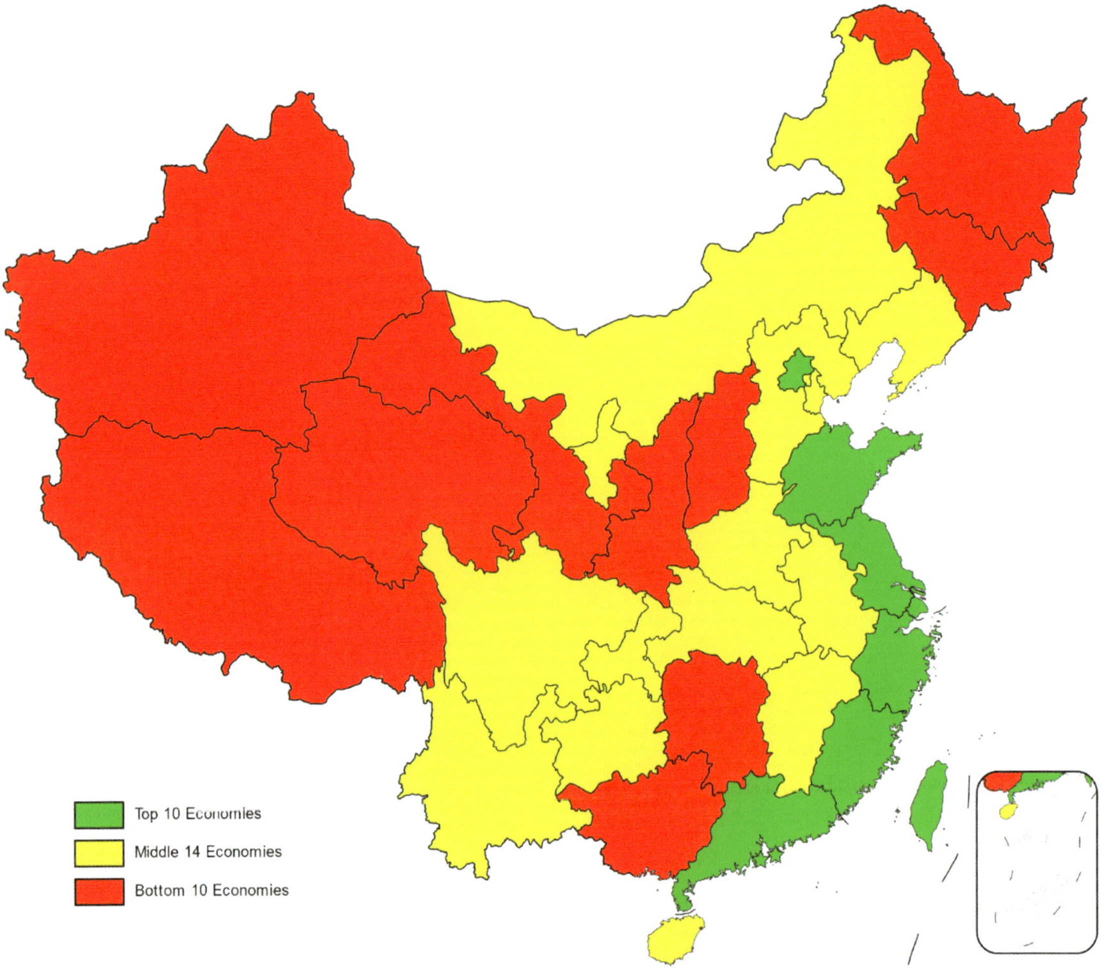

Note: The results are based on 2015 data, collated and analysed in 2018.
Source: Asia Competitiveness Institute.

Table 3.6 shows the Government and Institutional Setting rankings and scores for the 34 Greater China economies from 2000 to 2015. There are three economies for which the rankings in 2015 have remained the same as in 2000, namely Taiwan (#1), Tianjin (#20) and Tibet (#34). The rankings of 17 economies have improved over the past 15 years from 2000 to 2015. Guangdong and Henan have risen one spot; Beijing and Sichuan have risen two spots; Guizhou and Shaanxi have risen three spots; Jiangsu and Macau have risen four spots; Fujian and Hunan each has risen five spots; Guangxi has risen six spots; Hainan has risen eight spots; Jiangxi has risen 10 spots; Hubei and Chongqing each has risen 12 spots; Hebei has risen 13 spots and Anhui has risen 16 spots. On the other hand, the rankings of 14 economies have fallen over the years. Shandong has fallen one spot; Hong Kong and Shanghai have fallen two spots; Zhejiang has fallen three spots; Heilongjiang and Gansu have fallen five spots; Inner Mongolia has fallen six spots; Liaoning has fallen eight spots; Ningxia and Qinghai have fallen 11 spots; Yunnan, Jilin and Shanxi each has fallen 12 spots and Xinjiang has fallen 17 spots.

Table 3.6: ACI 2018 Government and Institutional Setting Rankings and Scores: Evolution Over Time

Government and Institutional Setting								
	1		2		3		4	
Rank	**Economy**	**Score**	**Economy**	**Score**	**Economy**	**Score**	**Economy**	**Score**
2000	Taiwan	4.4052	Hong Kong	1.4025	Zhejiang	0.9168	Guangdong	0.7153
2001	Taiwan	3.8734	Hong Kong	1.8727	Zhejiang	1.1468	Guangdong	1.0560
2002	Taiwan	3.8055	Hong Kong	1.6800	Zhejiang	1.1374	Guangdong	1.1209
2003	Taiwan	3.7444	Hong Kong	1.9001	Shanghai	1.2394	Guangdong	1.2017
2004	Taiwan	3.6446	Hong Kong	1.9426	Beijing	1.3271	Shanghai	1.2480
2005	Taiwan	3.4488	Hong Kong	2.0878	Beijing	1.3585	Shanghai	1.3094
2006	Taiwan	3.2867	Hong Kong	2.0326	Beijing	1.3848	Shanghai	1.1842
2007	Taiwan	3.0569	Hong Kong	2.1005	Beijing	1.4367	Shanghai	1.3444
2008	Taiwan	2.8513	Hong Kong	1.8870	Beijing	1.6192	Guangdong	1.4378
2009	Taiwan	2.5625	Hong Kong	1.8206	Beijing	1.6522	Jiangsu	1.6187
2010	Taiwan	2.3719	Hong Kong	1.7556	Beijing	1.7026	Jiangsu	1.6628
2011	Taiwan	2.3616	Beijing	1.7629	Jiangsu	1.7457	Hong Kong	1.7311
2012	Taiwan	2.3142	Jiangsu	1.8193	Beijing	1.6916	Guangdong	1.6846
2013	Taiwan	2.0458	Beijing	1.8682	Guangdong	1.8577	Jiangsu	1.8510
2014	Taiwan	1.9448	Beijing	1.8730	Jiangsu	1.8167	Guangdong	1.7885
2015	Taiwan	1.9868	Jiangsu	1.9224	Guangdong	1.8503	Hong Kong	1.7956

Government and Institutional Setting								
	5		6		7		8	
Rank	**Economy**	**Score**	**Economy**	**Score**	**Economy**	**Score**	**Economy**	**Score**
2000	Shanghai	0.6504	Jiangsu	0.5720	Beijing	0.5409	Shandong	0.5040
2001	Beijing	0.9936	Shanghai	0.8212	Jiangsu	0.7886	Shandong	0.6082
2002	Beijing	1.0583	Shanghai	0.9726	Jiangsu	0.8226	Shandong	0.5536
2003	Zhejiang	1.1577	Beijing	1.0991	Jiangsu	1.0266	Shandong	0.6232
2004	Guangdong	1.1047	Zhejiang	1.0714	Jiangsu	1.0291	Macau	0.6718
2005	Guangdong	1.1362	Jiangsu	1.0773	Zhejiang	1.0752	Shandong	0.5832
2006	Jiangsu	1.1675	Guangdong	1.1543	Zhejiang	1.0341	Shandong	0.5977
2007	Jiangsu	1.3372	Guangdong	1.3295	Zhejiang	1.1281	Shandong	0.6741
2008	Jiangsu	1.4293	Shanghai	1.3669	Zhejiang	1.1607	Macau	0.7302
2009	Guangdong	1.5646	Shanghai	1.4345	Zhejiang	1.2641	Shandong	0.7848
2010	Guangdong	1.5725	Shanghai	1.3752	Zhejiang	1.3103	Macau	1.0747
2011	Guangdong	1.6442	Shanghai	1.3951	Zhejiang	1.3151	Macau	0.9839
2012	Hong Kong	1.6605	Shanghai	1.4080	Zhejiang	1.3808	Macau	0.9186
2013	Hong Kong	1.5185	Zhejiang	1.4241	Shanghai	1.3785	Macau	0.9130
2014	Hong Kong	1.7665	Zhejiang	1.4242	Shanghai	1.2944	Macau	0.9841
2015	Beijing	1.7281	Zhejiang	1.3554	Shanghai	1.3090	Macau	0.9313

(*Continued*)

Table 3.6: (*Continued*)

Government and Institutional Setting								
	9		10		11		12	
Rank	Economy	Score	Economy	Score	Economy	Score	Economy	Score
2000	Liaoning	0.4772	Xinjiang	0.3913	Yunnan	0.2329	Macau	0.1923
2001	Liaoning	0.3563	Henan	0.1652	Yunnan	0.1583	Xinjiang	0.1043
2002	Liaoning	0.2858	Henan	0.1445	Macau	0.1308	Yunnan	0.1128
2003	Macau	0.3317	Liaoning	0.1625	Henan	0.0307	Fujian	0.0070
2004	Shandong	0.6010	Liaoning	0.0420	Fujian	0.0222	Henan	–0.1239
2005	Macau	0.5498	Fujian	0.0728	Liaoning	–0.0325	Xinjiang	–0.1814
2006	Macau	0.3966	Fujian	0.0556	Henan	–0.0727	Liaoning	–0.0959
2007	Macau	0.6389	Fujian	0.0777	Henan	–0.1205	Hebei	–0.1250
2008	Shandong	0.7094	Fujian	0.0601	Hebei	–0.1254	Henan	–0.1442
2009	Macau	0.6476	Fujian	0.0614	Hebei	–0.1346	Liaoning	–0.1477
2010	Shandong	0.7107	Fujian	–0.0262	Xinjiang	–0.1201	Hebei	–0.1259
2011	Shandong	0.7093	Fujian	–0.0094	Liaoning	–0.1348	Xinjiang	–0.1369
2012	Shandong	0.7639	Fujian	–0.0422	Liaoning	–0.0714	Sichuan	–0.1416
2013	Shandong	0.8163	Fujian	0.0085	Sichuan	–0.1368	Liaoning	–0.1559
2014	Shandong	0.7635	Fujian	0.0088	Hubei	–0.1167	Sichuan	–0.1296
2015	Shandong	0.8084	Fujian	0.0124	Hubei	–0.1146	Hebei	–0.1269

Government and Institutional Setting								
	13		14		15		16	
Rank	Economy	Score	Economy	Score	Economy	Score	Economy	Score
2000	Ningxia	0.0287	Henan	0.0190	Fujian	–0.0485	Inner Mongolia	–0.0795
2001	Ningxia	0.0844	Fujian	–0.0083	Macau	–0.0940	Jilin	–0.1372
2002	Fujian	0.0383	Ningxia	0.0379	Xinjiang	–0.0323	Jilin	–0.1408
2003	Xinjiang	–0.1171	Yunnan	–0.2525	Jilin	–0.2811	Sichuan	–0.2817
2004	Xinjiang	–0.1645	Sichuan	–0.2123	Yunnan	–0.2650	Ningxia	–0.2911
2005	Henan	–0.1936	Hebei	–0.2056	Inner Mongolia	–0.2189	Yunnan	–0.2321
2006	Xinjiang	–0.1141	Inner Mongolia	–0.1377	Qinghai	–0.1488	Sichuan	–0.1659
2007	Liaoning	–0.1309	Sichuan	–0.2162	Xinjiang	–0.2736	Yunnan	–0.3201
2008	Liaoning	–0.1681	Xinjiang	–0.2206	Hubei	–0.2368	Tianjin	–0.2761
2009	Henan	–0.1795	Hubei	–0.2164	Sichuan	–0.2622	Inner Mongolia	–0.2723
2010	Liaoning	–0.1677	Hubei	–0.2442	Inner Mongolia	–0.2593	Sichuan	–0.2779
2011	Inner Mongolia	–0.1851	Hebei	–0.1983	Sichuan	–0.2080	Henan	–0.3046
2012	Hebei	–0.1839	Inner Mongolia	–0.2316	Xinjiang	–0.2321	Hubei	–0.2509
2013	Hebei	–0.1747	Hubei	–0.1916	Henan	–0.2629	Anhui	–0.2702
2014	Hebei	–0.1296	Anhui	–0.1927	Henan	–0.2630	Liaoning	–0.3155
2015	Henan	–0.1864	Anhui	–0.1897	Sichuan	–0.2195	Chongqing	–0.2616

Table 3.6: (*Continued*)

Government and Institutional Setting								
	17		18		19		20	
Rank	**Economy**	**Score**	**Economy**	**Score**	**Economy**	**Score**	**Economy**	**Score**
2000	Sichuan	–0.0891	Jilin	–0.1064	Shanxi	–0.2326	Tianjin	–0.2923
2001	Inner Mongolia	–0.1789	Sichuan	–0.2017	Heilongjiang	–0.3254	Shanxi	–0.3643
2002	Chongqing	–0.2189	Inner Mongolia	–0.2223	Sichuan	–0.2449	Heilongjiang	–0.2886
2003	Ningxia	–0.2997	Inner Mongolia	–0.3198	Hubei	–0.3204	Heilongjiang	–0.3343
2004	Qinghai	–0.2939	Hebei	–0.2946	Hubei	–0.2978	Inner Mongolia	–0.3100
2005	Sichuan	–0.2512	Qinghai	–0.2594	Hubei	–0.3107	Ningxia	–0.3109
2006	Hebei	–0.1680	Yunnan	–0.2271	Hubei	–0.2777	Heilongjiang	–0.2787
2007	Inner Mongolia	–0.3218	Hubei	–0.3299	Heilongjiang	–0.3893	Tianjin	–0.3900
2008	Inner Mongolia	–0.2819	Yunnan	–0.3366	Ningxia	–0.3677	Sichuan	–0.3730
2009	Tianjin	–0.2771	Xinjiang	–0.2951	Yunnan	–0.3320	Heilongjiang	–0.4266
2010	Henan	–0.2803	Yunnan	–0.3322	Tianjin	–0.3408	Hainan	–0.3773
2011	Anhui	–0.3251	Hubei	–0.3339	Yunnan	–0.3436	Tianjin	–0.3653
2012	Yunnan	–0.3196	Anhui	–0.3263	Henan	–0.3365	Hainan	–0.3875
2013	Inner Mongolia	–0.3057	Xinjiang	–0.3570	Yunnan	–0.3575	Hainan	–0.3619
2014	Chongqing	–0.3419	Yunnan	–0.3747	Hainan	–0.4072	Jiangxi	–0.4287
2015	Liaoning	–0.3181	Hainan	–0.3387	Jiangxi	–0.3966	Tianjin	–0.4731
Government and Institutional Setting								
	21		22		23		24	
Rank	**Economy**	**Score**	**Economy**	**Score**	**Economy**	**Score**	**Economy**	**Score**
2000	Heilongjiang	–0.3066	Qinghai	–0.3601	Hubei	–0.4486	Guizhou	–0.4684
2001	Tianjin	–0.3873	Hubei	–0.4796	Qinghai	–0.5011	Hebei	–0.5035
2002	Qinghai	–0.2948	Tianjin	–0.3609	Hebei	–0.4251	Hubei	–0.4609
2003	Tianjin	–0.3913	Hebei	–0.4144	Qinghai	–0.4734	Chongqing	–0.5140
2004	Tianjin	–0.4242	Jilin	–0.4362	Chongqing	–0.5297	Hainan	–0.5379
2005	Heilongjiang	–0.3468	Tianjin	–0.4113	Hainan	–0.4848	Guizhou	–0.5585
2006	Tianjin	–0.3121	Ningxia	–0.3228	Hainan	–0.4164	Gansu	–0.5282
2007	Hainan	–0.4459	Ningxia	–0.4794	Qinghai	–0.4943	Jilin	–0.5255
2008	Heilongjiang	–0.4117	Hainan	–0.4702	Jilin	–0.5231	Qinghai	–0.5453
2009	Hainan	–0.4675	Jiangxi	–0.5128	Jilin	–0.5290	Anhui	–0.5441
2010	Heilongjiang	–0.4023	Anhui	–0.4189	Ningxia	–0.5112	Shaanxi	–0.5335
2011	Heilongjiang	–0.3832	Hainan	–0.4040	Jiangxi	–0.5181	Ningxia	–0.5271
2012	Heilongjiang	–0.4813	Shaanxi	–0.4846	Jiangxi	–0.4906	Tianjin	–0.5192
2013	Chongqing	–0.4379	Jiangxi	–0.4688	Tianjin	–0.5255	Shaanxi	–0.5468
2014	Tianjin	–0.4809	Xinjiang	–0.4880	Heilongjiang	–0.4915	Inner Mongolia	–0.4929
2015	Guizhou	–0.5009	Inner Mongolia	–0.5244	Yunnan	–0.5379	Ningxia	–0.5907

(*Continued*)

Table 3.6: (*Continued*)

Government and Institutional Setting								
	25		26		27		28	
Rank	Economy	Score	Economy	Score	Economy	Score	Economy	Score
2000	Hebei	–0.4970	Hainan	–0.4971	Gansu	–0.5728	Chongqing	–0.5835
2001	Gansu	–0.5667	Guizhou	–0.5698	Jiangxi	–0.5921	Chongqing	–0.5979
2002	Guizhou	–0.5169	Shanxi	–0.5442	Gansu	–0.5538	Hainan	–0.7000
2003	Gansu	–0.6222	Shanxi	–0.6227	Hainan	–0.6324	Guizhou	–0.7213
2004	Gansu	–0.5828	Guizhou	–0.6352	Shanxi	–0.6494	Heilongjiang	–0.7304
2005	Jilin	–0.5850	Chongqing	–0.6199	Shanxi	–0.6291	Gansu	–0.6655
2006	Jilin	–0.5432	Chongqing	–0.5612	Guizhou	–0.5848	Jiangxi	–0.6977
2007	Jiangxi	–0.5589	Chongqing	–0.6292	Guizhou	–0.6684	Anhui	–0.6735
2008	Jiangxi	–0.5645	Shanxi	–0.5907	Shaanxi	–0.6080	Anhui	–0.6223
2009	Ningxia	–0.5859	Shaanxi	–0.6020	Chongqing	–0.6358	Shanxi	–0.6749
2010	Jiangxi	–0.5748	Chongqing	–0.5775	Jilin	–0.6391	Hunan	–0.6888
2011	Chongqing	–0.6079	Jilin	–0.6134	Shaanxi	–0.6586	Hunan	–0.8355
2012	Ningxia	–0.5416	Jilin	–0.6373	Chongqing	–0.6439	Hunan	–0.7623
2013	Heilongjiang	–0.5637	Ningxia	–0.5672	Jilin	–0.6542	Hunan	–0.7217
2014	Guizhou	–0.5402	Shaanxi	–0.6304	Guangxi	–0.6545	Hunan	–0.6635
2015	Guangxi	–0.6104	Heilongjiang	–0.6153	Xinjiang	–0.6283	Hunan	–0.6409

Government and Institutional Setting								
	29		30		31		32	
Rank	Economy	Score	Economy	Score	Economy	Score	Economy	Score
2000	Jiangxi	–0.5920	Anhui	–0.9185	Guangxi	–1.0576	Shaanxi	–1.1060
2001	Hainan	–0.7104	Anhui	–0.8664	Shaanxi	–1.0220	Guangxi	–1.0258
2002	Jiangxi	–0.7155	Anhui	–0.9079	Shaanxi	–0.9200	Hunan	–1.2169
2003	Jiangxi	–0.7312	Anhui	–0.7546	Shaanxi	–0.8719	Tibet	–1.1698
2004	Jiangxi	–0.7330	Anhui	–0.7945	Shaanxi	–0.8261	Hunan	–1.0671
2005	Anhui	–0.7588	Jiangxi	–0.7846	Shaanxi	–0.8448	Hunan	–1.0419
2006	Anhui	–0.7274	Shaanxi	–0.7880	Hunan	–0.9145	Shanxi	–0.9539
2007	Gansu	–0.6985	Shanxi	–0.7071	Shaanxi	–0.7323	Hunan	–0.9010
2008	Chongqing	–0.6797	Guizhou	–0.7268	Hunan	–0.8571	Gansu	–0.9958
2009	Qinghai	–0.6798	Hunan	–0.7323	Guizhou	–0.7538	Guangxi	–0.9239
2010	Guizhou	–0.7779	Qinghai	–0.8279	Guangxi	–0.8878	Shanxi	–0.9018
2011	Guangxi	–0.8646	Shanxi	–0.8646	Qinghai	–0.9216	Guizhou	–0.9703
2012	Guangxi	–0.8022	Shanxi	–0.8535	Guizhou	–0.9099	Qinghai	–0.9863
2013	Guizhou	–0.7480	Guangxi	–0.7593	Shanxi	–0.9195	Gansu	–1.0298
2014	Ningxia	–0.6638	Jilin	–0.7135	Gansu	–0.9087	Shanxi	–0.9999
2015	Shaanxi	–0.7905	Jilin	–0.8113	Shanxi	–0.8676	Gansu	–0.9353

Table 3.6: (*Continued*)

Government and Institutional Setting				
	33		34	
Rank	Economy	Score	Economy	Score
2000	Hunan	–1.1761	Tibet	–1.6159
2001	Hunan	–1.2442	Tibet	–1.6527
2002	Guangxi	–1.2956	Tibet	–1.8403
2003	Hunan	–1.1734	Guangxi	–1.2252
2004	Guangxi	–1.1610	Tibet	–1.3439
2005	Guangxi	–1.1044	Tibet	–1.6674
2006	Guangxi	–0.9803	Tibet	–2.2767
2007	Guangxi	–0.9885	Tibet	–2.0041
2008	Guangxi	–1.0064	Tibet	–2.1198
2009	Gansu	–1.0374	Tibet	–2.1883
2010	Gansu	–1.0749	Tibet	–2.1679
2011	Gansu	–1.0330	Tibet	–1.9021
2012	Gansu	–1.0038	Tibet	–2.0016
2013	Qinghai	–1.1619	Tibet	–2.0035
2014	Qinghai	–1.1453	Tibet	–2.0917
2015	Qinghai	–0.9443	Tibet	–2.0771

Note: The results are based on 2000–2015 data, collated and analysed in 2018.
Source: Asia Competitiveness Institute.

Taiwan has outperformed the rest of the 33 economies in Greater China in terms of Government and Institutional Setting for the past 15 years from 2000 to 2015. However, the score of Taiwan has decreased from 4.4052 in 2000 to 1.9868 in 2015. There is also a considerable decrease in the score gap between Taiwan and the #2-ranked economy. In 2015, the difference in scores between Taiwan and the #2-ranked Jiangsu (1.9224) is 0.0644, whereas in 2000, the gap in scores between Taiwan and the #2-ranked Hong Kong (1.4025) is 3.0027. As for Hong Kong, it had remained as the #2-ranked economy from 2000 to 2010. However, Beijing and Jiangsu from Mainland China surpassed Hong Kong in 2011, occupying the second and third positions, respectively, in the ranking. In 2012, Hong Kong was overtaken by another Mainland economy Guangdong, thereby dropping to the #5-ranked economy during the period from 2012 to 2014, only to improve slightly to the #4-ranked in 2015. The evolution over time suggests that more Mainland China economies are strengthening their Government and Institutional Setting competitiveness and, as a result, their performance has become comparable to that of Taiwan and Hong Kong. It's very likely that Mainland China economies will surpass Taiwan and come to the top in terms of Government and Institutional Setting in the future.

3.2.4 ACI 2018 Financial, Businesses and Manpower Conditions Rankings and Scores

Table 3.7 shows the Financial, Businesses and Manpower Conditions ranking. The top performer under this environment is Hong Kong, with a score of 2.5143. Tibet is ranked last at #34 with a score of –1.2299.

Table 3.7: ACI 2018 Financial, Businesses and Manpower Conditions Ranking and Scores

Rank	Economy	Score
1	Hong Kong	2.5143
2	Taiwan	2.4538
3	Guangdong	1.7150
4	Macau	1.7032
5	Jiangsu	1.4785
6	Beijing	1.1646
7	Zhejiang	0.9953
8	Shandong	0.6459
9	Shanghai	0.5327
10	Hubei	0.0630
11	Liaoning	0.0482
12	Tianjin	0.0222
13	Fujian	–0.0165
14	Hebei	–0.1381
15	Henan	–0.1826
16	Chongqing	–0.2466
17	Sichuan	–0.2725
18	Inner Mongolia	–0.2860
19	Anhui	–0.4052
20	Jilin	–0.4067
21	Shaanxi	–0.4177
22	Hunan	–0.4757
23	Xinjiang	–0.5844
24	Jiangxi	–0.5877
25	Hainan	–0.7487

Table 3.7: (*Continued*)

Rank	Economy	Score
26	Shanxi	–0.8080
27	Guangxi	–0.8147
28	Guizhou	–0.8801
29	Yunnan	–0.8863
30	Ningxia	–0.8895
31	Heilongjiang	–0.8918
32	Qinghai	–1.0645
33	Gansu	–1.1036
34	Tibet	–1.2299

Note: The results are based on 2015 data, collated and analysed in 2018.
Source: Asia Competitiveness Institute.

The average-performing economy (with a standardised score of 0) is situated between the #12-ranked Tianjin (0.0222) and the #13-ranked Fujian (–0.0165), while the median score is between the #17-ranked Sichuan (–0.2725) and the #18-ranked Inner Mongolia (–0.2860). The median score for Financial, Businesses and Manpower Conditions ranking is hence –0.2793, which is lower than the average score (0).

The largest drop is between the #2-ranked Taiwan (2.4538) and the #3-ranked Guangdong (1.7150), and their difference in scores is 0.7388. The gaps between most of other consecutively ranked economies appear quite moderate in size, with a value of less than 0.1 or 0.2. A few relatively larger gaps in scores include those between the #5-ranked Jiangsu (1.4785) and the #6-ranked Beijing (1.1646), the #7-ranked Zhejiang (0.9953) and the #8-ranked Shandong (0.6459) as well as between the #9-ranked Shanghai (0.5327) and the #10-ranked Hubei (0.0630). Their gaps in scores are 0.3139, 0.3494 and 0.4697, respectively.

Figure 3.10 shows the Financial, Businesses and Manpower Conditions ranking map. The colours represent each economy's competitiveness under the Financial, Businesses and Manpower Conditions Environment. The top 10 economies are all located in the Eastern Coastal Area or Hong Kong, Macau and Taiwan, except for the #10-ranked Hubei. However, among the economies in the Eastern Coastal Area, there is substantial heterogeneity in competitiveness levels as Hainan is in the bottom 10, Fujian, Hebei and Tianjin are in the middle 14 while the remaining six economies are in top 10. As for the economies in Central China, Western China and North-eastern China, most of them are either in the middle 14 or the bottom 10, which suggests that the competitiveness of these three regions is generally weaker. In addition, the bottom 10 economies are mainly located in Western China, which serves as a reminder for Western China to improve its competitiveness in terms of Financial, Businesses and Manpower Conditions.

Figure 3.10: ACI 2018 Financial, Businesses and Manpower Conditions Ranking Map

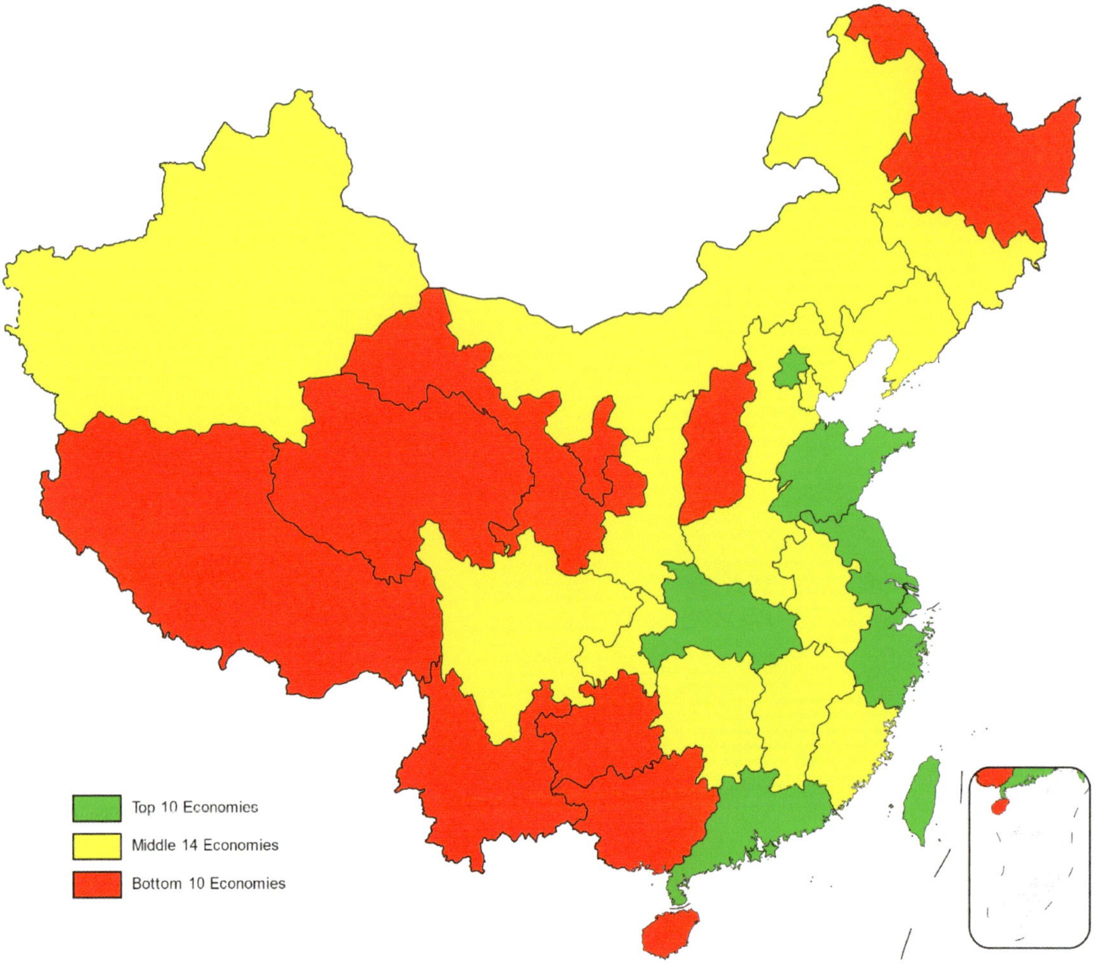

Note: The results are based on 2015 data, collated and analysed in 2018.
Source: Asia Competitiveness Institute.

The rankings and scores of the 34 Greater China economies in Financial, Businesses and Manpower Conditions from 2000 to 2015 are shown in Table 3.8. There are four economies for which the 2015 rankings have stayed the same as in 2000, including Henan (#15), Sichuan (#17), Jilin (#20) and Jiangxi (#24). There are 13 economies that have improved their standing in Financial, Businesses and Manpower Conditions over the past 15 years. Hong Kong, Guangdong, Tianjin and Inner Mongolia each has improved one spot; Zhejiang has improved two spots; Jiangsu, Hunan and Hainan each has improved three spots; Anhui, Guizhou and Ningxia each has improved four spots; Hubei has improved six spots and Chongqing has improved 14 spots. The other 17 economies have seen a decline in their rankings over the years. Taiwan, Macau, Beijing, Shandong, Liaoning, Fujian, Xinjiang, Guangxi and Tibet each has fallen one spot; Yunnan and Gansu each has fallen two spots; Shanghai, Hebei, Shaanxi and Qinghai have fallen three spots; Shanxi has fallen five spots and Heilongjiang has fallen 17 spots.

Table 3.8: ACI 2018 Financial, Businesses and Manpower Conditions Rankings and Scores: Evolution Over Time

Financial, Businesses and Manpower Conditions								
	1		2		3		4	
Rank	Economy	Score	Economy	Score	Economy	Score	Economy	Score
2000	Taiwan	3.9877	Hong Kong	3.3184	Macau	1.3617	Guangdong	0.6137
2001	Taiwan	3.7396	Hong Kong	3.4870	Macau	1.3892	Guangdong	0.7348
2002	Taiwan	3.6944	Hong Kong	3.2902	Macau	1.5584	Guangdong	0.8242
2003	Taiwan	3.5080	Hong Kong	3.3427	Macau	1.7053	Guangdong	0.9772
2004	Taiwan	3.6358	Hong Kong	3.1362	Macau	1.7320	Guangdong	0.9623
2005	Taiwan	3.6459	Hong Kong	2.9827	Macau	1.6729	Guangdong	1.0508
2006	Taiwan	3.4349	Hong Kong	3.0294	Macau	1.7558	Guangdong	1.0998
2007	Taiwan	3.2217	Hong Kong	3.1035	Macau	1.8302	Guangdong	1.1371
2008	Hong Kong	3.0655	Taiwan	3.0499	Macau	1.7261	Guangdong	1.2416
2009	Hong Kong	2.9141	Taiwan	2.8812	Macau	1.6504	Guangdong	1.3403
2010	Taiwan	2.9675	Hong Kong	2.7237	Macau	1.6264	Guangdong	1.3895
2011	Taiwan	2.8304	Hong Kong	2.6854	Macau	1.6420	Guangdong	1.3887
2012	Taiwan	2.8096	Hong Kong	2.6335	Macau	1.7425	Guangdong	1.4063
2013	Hong Kong	2.5927	Taiwan	2.5748	Macau	1.7494	Guangdong	1.6146
2014	Hong Kong	2.5370	Taiwan	2.4146	Macau	1.8337	Guangdong	1.7005
2015	Hong Kong	2.5134	Taiwan	2.4538	Guangdong	1.7150	Macau	1.7032
Financial, Businesses and Manpower Conditions								
	5		6		7		8	
Rank	Economy	Score	Economy	Score	Economy	Score	Economy	Score
2000	Beijing	0.3038	Shanghai	0.2230	Shandong	0.0415	Jiangsu	0.0386
2001	Beijing	0.3889	Shanghai	0.2540	Zhejiang	0.1305	Jiangsu	0.0991
2002	Hunan	0.5351	Beijing	0.3702	Shanghai	0.2829	Zhejiang	0.1811
2003	Beijing	0.5285	Jiangsu	0.3718	Shanghai	0.3599	Zhejiang	0.3362
2004	Beijing	0.6248	Jiangsu	0.4593	Shanghai	0.3800	Zhejiang	0.3361
2005	Beijing	0.6789	Jiangsu	0.5832	Shanghai	0.4274	Shandong	0.4261
2006	Beijing	0.7602	Jiangsu	0.6729	Zhejiang	0.5318	Shandong	0.4594
2007	Beijing	0.7731	Jiangsu	0.7300	Zhejiang	0.6012	Shanghai	0.5034
2008	Beijing	0.8750	Jiangsu	0.8373	Shanghai	0.6519	Zhejiang	0.6426
2009	Beijing	1.0110	Jiangsu	0.9771	Zhejiang	0.7608	Shanghai	0.6777
2010	Jiangsu	1.0344	Beijing	0.9980	Zhejiang	0.8031	Shanghai	0.6996
2011	Beijing	1.1068	Jiangsu	1.0557	Zhejiang	0.8846	Shanghai	0.8646
2012	Beijing	1.1229	Jiangsu	1.1021	Zhejiang	0.9404	Shanghai	0.6245
2013	Jiangsu	1.3575	Beijing	1.1394	Zhejiang	0.9091	Shandong	0.5677
2014	Jiangsu	1.4210	Beijing	1.1146	Zhejiang	0.9578	Shandong	0.5889
2015	Jiangsu	1.4785	Beijing	1.1646	Zhejiang	0.9953	Shandong	0.6459

(Continued)

Table 3.8: (*Continued*)

Financial, Businesses and Manpower Conditions								
	9		10		11		12	
Rank	Economy	Score	Economy	Score	Economy	Score	Economy	Score
2000	Zhejiang	0.0079	Liaoning	–0.0670	Hebei	–0.0974	Fujian	–0.1461
2001	Shandong	0.0961	Liaoning	0.0495	Tianjin	–0.1458	Hebei	–0.1476
2002	Jiangsu	0.1487	Shandong	0.1239	Liaoning	–0.1292	Tianjin	–0.1461
2003	Shandong	0.2356	Liaoning	–0.1195	Tianjin	–0.1284	Hebei	–0.2386
2004	Shandong	0.2664	Tianjin	–0.1188	Liaoning	–0.1625	Fujian	–0.2273
2005	Zhejiang	0.4182	Tianjin	–0.0711	Liaoning	–0.1178	Fujian	–0.2213
2006	Shanghai	0.4498	Liaoning	–0.0698	Tianjin	–0.0873	Fujian	–0.2112
2007	Shandong	0.4347	Liaoning	0.0586	Tianjin	–0.0628	Fujian	–0.2035
2008	Shandong	0.4302	Liaoning	0.1809	Tianjin	0.0785	Fujian	–0.2049
2009	Shandong	0.5063	Liaoning	0.2937	Tianjin	0.2285	Henan	–0.1753
2010	Shandong	0.4736	Liaoning	0.3065	Tianjin	0.2627	Fujian	–0.1633
2011	Shandong	0.4733	Liaoning	0.2864	Tianjin	–0.0194	Inner Mongolia	–0.0799
2012	Shandong	0.4860	Liaoning	0.3164	Tianjin	0.0050	Fujian	–0.0564
2013	Shanghai	0.4434	Liaoning	0.2465	Tianjin	0.0199	Fujian	–0.0772
2014	Shanghai	0.5134	Liaoning	0.1531	Tianjin	0.0185	Hubei	0.0042
2015	Shanghai	0.5327	Hubei	0.0630	Liaoning	0.0482	Tianjin	0.0222

Financial, Businesses and Manpower Conditions								
	13		14		15		16	
Rank	Economy	Score	Economy	Score	Economy	Score	Economy	Score
2000	Tianjin	–0.1626	Heilongjiang	–0.2204	Henan	–0.2229	Hubei	–0.2764
2001	Fujian	–0.2266	Henan	–0.2674	Hubei	–0.3013	Heilongjiang	–0.3017
2002	Hebei	–0.2036	Fujian	–0.2809	Henan	–0.2980	Hubei	–0.3149
2003	Fujian	–0.2559	Heilongjiang	–0.2771	Henan	–0.2891	Hubei	–0.3143
2004	Hebei	–0.2512	Henan	–0.2860	Hubei	–0.3115	Xinjiang	–0.3226
2005	Hebei	–0.2499	Henan	–0.2960	Heilongjiang	–0.3469	Xinjiang	–0.3651
2006	Hebei	–0.2393	Henan	–0.2887	Xinjiang	–0.3722	Inner Mongolia	–0.3729
2007	Hebei	–0.2562	Henan	–0.2938	Inner Mongolia	–0.3401	Jilin	–0.3825
2008	Inner Mongolia	–0.2440	Hebei	–0.2470	Henan	–0.2477	Jilin	–0.3527
2009	Fujian	–0.1811	Inner Mongolia	–0.1867	Hebei	–0.2163	Jilin	–0.3325
2010	Inner Mongolia	–0.1854	Hebei	–0.2051	Henan	–0.2165	Hubei	–0.3040
2011	Fujian	–0.0883	Hebei	–0.1610	Hubei	–0.2374	Henan	–0.2635
2012	Inner Mongolia	–0.1096	Hebei	–0.1428	Hubei	–0.2139	Henan	–0.2307
2013	Hubei	–0.0812	Inner Mongolia	–0.1016	Hebei	–0.1025	Henan	–0.2221
2014	Fujian	–0.0339	Inner Mongolia	–0.1352	Hebei	–0.1405	Henan	–0.1880
2015	Fujian	–0.0165	Hebei	–0.1381	Henan	–0.1826	Chongqing	–0.2466

Table 3.8: (*Continued*)

Financial, Businesses and Manpower Conditions								
	17		18		19		20	
Rank	**Economy**	**Score**	**Economy**	**Score**	**Economy**	**Score**	**Economy**	**Score**
2000	Sichuan	–0.3236	Shaanxi	–0.3504	Inner Mongolia	–0.3527	Jilin	–0.3662
2001	Sichuan	–0.3222	Xinjiang	–0.3268	Jilin	–0.3347	Inner Mongolia	–0.3654
2002	Heilongjiang	–0.3281	Sichuan	–0.3335	Xinjiang	–0.3681	Inner Mongolia	–0.4128
2003	Sichuan	–0.3270	Xinjiang	–0.3291	Inner Mongolia	–0.4539	Anhui	–0.4574
2004	Heilongjiang	–0.3431	Sichuan	–0.3501	Jilin	–0.4588	Shaanxi	–0.4652
2005	Hubei	–0.3971	Inner Mongolia	–0.4023	Sichuan	–0.4110	Jilin	–0.4405
2006	Heilongjiang	–0.3842	Hubei	–0.3926	Sichuan	–0.4195	Jilin	–0.4530
2007	Hubei	–0.4169	Xinjiang	–0.4209	Sichuan	–0.4223	Heilongjiang	–0.4256
2008	Xinjiang	–0.3739	Hubei	–0.3927	Heilongjiang	–0.4578	Sichuan	–0.4830
2009	Hubei	–0.3327	Sichuan	–0.3962	Anhui	–0.4390	Xinjiang	–0.4694
2010	Jilin	–0.3381	Xinjiang	–0.3710	Anhui	–0.3818	Sichuan	–0.3962
2011	Chongqing	–0.3103	Jilin	–0.3392	Sichuan	–0.4216	Xinjiang	–0.4326
2012	Chongqing	–0.2692	Jilin	–0.3081	Sichuan	–0.3914	Anhui	–0.4345
2013	Chongqing	–0.2903	Sichuan	–0.3559	Anhui	–0.3569	Jilin	–0.3589
2014	Chongqing	–0.2780	Anhui	–0.3154	Sichuan	–0.3654	Jilin	–0.3762
2015	Sichuan	–0.2725	Inner Mongolia	–0.2860	Anhui	–0.4052	Jilin	–0.4067

Financial, Businesses and Manpower Conditions								
	21		22		23		24	
Rank	**Economy**	**Score**	**Economy**	**Score**	**Economy**	**Score**	**Economy**	**Score**
2000	Shanxi	–0.3999	Xinjiang	–0.4093	Anhui	–0.4288	Jiangxi	–0.4353
2001	Shaanxi	–0.4053	Hunan	–0.4295	Shanxi	–0.4535	Anhui	–0.4579
2002	Jilin	–0.4217	Shaanxi	–0.4473	Anhui	–0.4687	Jiangxi	–0.4982
2003	Shaanxi	–0.4648	Hunan	–0.4837	Jiangxi	–0.4962	Shanxi	–0.4982
2004	Anhui	–0.4672	Jiangxi	–0.4726	Inner Mongolia	–0.4801	Shanxi	–0.4966
2005	Jiangxi	–0.4679	Shanxi	–0.4746	Hunan	–0.4873	Anhui	–0.5133
2006	Jiangxi	–0.4870	Anhui	–0.5113	Shanxi	–0.5181	Hunan	–0.5242
2007	Anhui	–0.4892	Chongqing	–0.4967	Shanxi	–0.5177	Jiangxi	–0.5235
2008	Anhui	–0.4961	Chongqing	–0.5108	Shaanxi	–0.5306	Jiangxi	–0.5509
2009	Chongqing	–0.4893	Hunan	–0.5674	Heilongjiang	–0.5780	Jiangxi	–0.5822
2010	Chongqing	–0.5080	Heilongjiang	–0.5408	Jiangxi	–0.5417	Shanxi	–0.5657
2011	Anhui	–0.4569	Hunan	–0.5019	Heilongjiang	–0.5510	Jiangxi	–0.5753
2012	Shaanxi	–0.4977	Xinjiang	–0.5240	Hunan	–0.5294	Heilongjiang	–0.5445
2013	Shaanxi	–0.4461	Hunan	–0.5342	Heilongjiang	–0.5428	Jiangxi	–0.5738
2014	Shaanxi	–0.4522	Hunan	–0.4957	Jiangxi	–0.5760	Xinjiang	–0.5777
2015	Shaanxi	–0.4177	Hunan	–0.4757	Xinjiang	–0.5844	Jiangxi	–0.5877

(*Continued*)

Table 3.8: (*Continued*)

Financial, Businesses and Manpower Conditions								
	25		26		27		28	
Rank	Economy	Score	Economy	Score	Economy	Score	Economy	Score
2000	Hunan	−0.4408	Guangxi	−0.4416	Yunnan	−0.4473	Hainan	−0.4921
2001	Yunnan	−0.4736	Jiangxi	−0.4751	Guangxi	−0.4787	Hainan	−0.5225
2002	Guangxi	−0.5244	Shanxi	−0.5527	Yunnan	−0.5549	Hainan	−0.5567
2003	Chongqing	−0.5049	Jilin	−0.5175	Guangxi	−0.5404	Yunnan	−0.5458
2004	Hunan	−0.5047	Chongqing	−0.5188	Yunnan	−0.5516	Guangxi	−0.5891
2005	Chongqing	−0.5247	Shaanxi	−0.5397	Yunnan	−0.5790	Guangxi	−0.6186
2006	Shaanxi	−0.5283	Chongqing	−0.5346	Guangxi	−0.6416	Yunnan	−0.6447
2007	Shaanxi	−0.5560	Hunan	−0.5630	Guangxi	−0.6488	Yunnan	−0.6531
2008	Shanxi	−0.5591	Hunan	−0.5941	Guangxi	−0.6978	Yunnan	−0.7077
2009	Shaanxi	−0.5829	Shanxi	−0.6136	Yunnan	−0.7679	Guangxi	−0.7796
2010	Hunan	−0.5748	Shaanxi	−0.6057	Hainan	−0.7716	Guangxi	−0.7884
2011	Shaanxi	−0.5874	Shanxi	−0.6033	Hainan	−0.6595	Guangxi	−0.8115
2012	Jiangxi	−0.6208	Shanxi	−0.6303	Hainan	−0.7624	Guangxi	−0.8249
2013	Xinjiang	−0.5988	Shanxi	−0.6574	Hainan	−0.7681	Guangxi	−0.8748
2014	Heilongjiang	−0.5822	Hainan	−0.7522	Shanxi	−0.7772	Guangxi	−0.8858
2015	Hainan	−0.7487	Shanxi	−0.8080	Guangxi	−0.8147	Guizhou	−0.8801

Financial, Businesses and Manpower Conditions								
	29		30		31		32	
Rank	Economy	Score	Economy	Score	Economy	Score	Economy	Score
2000	Qinghai	−0.5389	Chongqing	−0.5508	Gansu	−0.6426	Guizhou	−0.6573
2001	Chongqing	−0.5325	Gansu	−0.6141	Qinghai	−0.6166	Guizhou	−0.6934
2002	Chongqing	−0.5571	Qinghai	−0.6558	Gansu	−0.7029	Ningxia	−0.7326
2003	Hainan	−0.6293	Ningxia	−0.6585	Qinghai	−0.6784	Tibet	−0.6948
2004	Hainan	−0.6201	Ningxia	−0.6459	Qinghai	−0.6969	Tibet	−0.7002
2005	Hainan	−0.6594	Ningxia	−0.6954	Qinghai	−0.6958	Tibet	−0.7429
2006	Ningxia	−0.6690	Hainan	−0.6909	Qinghai	−0.7632	Gansu	−0.7823
2007	Hainan	−0.7131	Ningxia	−0.7140	Tibet	−0.7843	Qinghai	−0.8058
2008	Hainan	−0.7563	Ningxia	−0.7733	Qinghai	−0.8641	Gansu	−0.8652
2009	Ningxia	−0.7875	Hainan	−0.8077	Tibet	−0.9440	Qinghai	−0.9695
2010	Ningxia	−0.8056	Yunnan	−0.8237	Qinghai	−1.0135	Gansu	−1.0338
2011	Ningxia	−0.8199	Yunnan	−0.8746	Tibet	−1.0567	Qinghai	−1.0662
2012	Ningxia	−0.8298	Yunnan	−0.8908	Qinghai	−1.0273	Guizhou	−1.0730
2013	Qinghai	−0.9236	Yunnan	−0.9287	Ningxia	−0.9916	Guizhou	−1.0687
2014	Qinghai	−0.9619	Ningxia	−0.9665	Yunnan	−0.9762	Guizhou	−1.0556
2015	Yunnan	−0.8863	Ningxia	−0.8895	Heilongjiang	−0.8918	Qinghai	−1.0645

Table 3.8: (*Continued*)

Financial, Businesses and Manpower Conditions				
	33		34	
Rank	Economy	Score	Economy	Score
2000	Tibet	–0.6957	Ningxia	–0.7300
2001	Ningxia	–0.7383	Tibet	–0.7384
2002	Guizhou	–0.7371	Tibet	–0.7839
2003	Gansu	–0.7272	Guizhou	–0.7348
2004	Guizhou	–0.7434	Gansu	–0.7486
2005	Guizhou	–0.7807	Gansu	–0.7879
2006	Tibet	–0.7843	Guizhou	–0.8237
2007	Gansu	–0.8134	Guizhou	–0.8903
2008	Tibet	–0.8767	Guizhou	–0.9932
2009	Gansu	–0.9845	Guizhou	–1.0580
2010	Tibet	–1.0530	Guizhou	–1.0974
2011	Gansu	–1.1458	Guizhou	–1.1547
2012	Tibet	–1.1277	Gansu	–1.1501
2013	Gansu	–1.1354	Tibet	–1.2246
2014	Gansu	–1.1295	Tibet	–1.2359
2015	Gansu	–1.1036	Tibet	–1.2299

Note: The results are based on 2000–2015 data, collated and analysed in 2018.
Source: Asia Competitiveness Institute.

From 2000 to 2014, Taiwan, Hong Kong and Macau have always occupied the top three positions in the Financial, Businesses and Manpower Conditions ranking. However, the gap between the #3-ranked Macau and the #4-ranked Guangdong has diminished over the years, from 0.7480 in 2000 to merely 0.1332 in 2014, showing a rising trend of Mainland China economies in terms of Financial, Businesses and Manpower Conditions. In 2015, Guangdong has surpassed Macau and edged itself into the top three positions for the first time since 2000, indicating a small success in the effort of Mainland China economies to catch up with Taiwan, Hong Kong and Macau. Nevertheless, the gap between the #3-ranked Guangdong (1.7150) and the #4-ranked Macau (1.7032) is as small as 0.0118 while the gap between Guangdong and the #2-ranked Taiwan (2.4538) is as large as 0.7388. Besides, the gap between the #5-ranked Jiangsu (1.4785) and Macau is also relatively large with a value of 0.3139. This suggests that it is still not an easy path for economies in Mainland China to take over Taiwan, Hong Kong and Macau and to secure their positions in the top three in terms of Financial, Businesses and Manpower Conditions.

3.2.5 ACI 2018 Quality of Life and Infrastructure Development Rankings and Scores

Table 3.9 shows the ranking of Quality of Life and Infrastructure Development. Beijing is ranked first with the highest score (2.6077) among the 34 Greater China economies, while Guangxi is ranked last with a score of –1.4880.

Table 3.9: ACI 2018 Quality of Life and Infrastructure Development Ranking and Scores

Rank	Economy	Score
1	Beijing	2.6077
2	Guangdong	2.0978
3	Jiangsu	1.7672
4	Zhejiang	1.6118
5	Taiwan	1.0331
6	Shanghai	0.8911
7	Xinjiang	0.6492
8	Hebei	0.5192
9	Tianjin	0.4410
10	Macau	0.4180
11	Shandong	0.3884
12	Inner Mongolia	0.2903
13	Fujian	0.2080
14	Hubei	0.1830
15	Sichuan	0.1652
16	Shaanxi	0.0723
17	Heilongjiang	0.0243
18	Shanxi	0.0016
19	Liaoning	–0.0393
20	Hunan	–0.3487

Table 3.9: *(Continued)*

Rank	Economy	Score
21	Henan	–0.3649
22	Jilin	–0.3989
23	Hong Kong	–0.4139
24	Anhui	–0.6306
25	Yunnan	–0.7463
26	Qinghai	–0.9199
27	Hainan	–1.0447
28	Ningxia	–1.0855
29	Guizhou	–1.1281
30	Tibet	–1.1487
31	Gansu	–1.1817
32	Jiangxi	–1.2133
33	Chongqing	–1.2165
34	Guangxi	–1.4880

Note: The results are based on 2015 data, collated and analysed in 2018.
Source: Asia Competitiveness Institute.

The average-performing economy (with a standardised score of 0) is between the #18-ranked Shanxi (0.0016) and the #19-ranked Liaoning (–0.0393). The median score falls between the #17-ranked Heilongjiang (0.0243) and the #18-ranked Shanxi (0.0016). The median score 0.0130 is only slightly above the average score (0), indicating that the numbers of economies performing better and worse than average in terms of Quality of Life and Infrastructure Development are quite evenly distributed.

Some of the larger gaps in scores include those between the #1-ranked Beijing (2.6077) and the #2-ranked Guangdong (2.0978), as well as between the #4-ranked Zhejiang (1.6118) and the #5-ranked Taiwan (1.0331). Their differences in scores are 0.5099 and 0.5787, respectively.

Figure 3.11 provides a snapshot of the Quality of Life and Infrastructure Development ranking. Green represents the economies that are in the top 10, yellow in the middle 14, and red in the bottom 10. The overall pattern of competitiveness increasing from west to east in Greater China still largely persists, as shown in this map, except for Xinjiang and Jiangxi.

Figure 3.11: ACI 2018 Quality of Life and Infrastructure Development Ranking Map

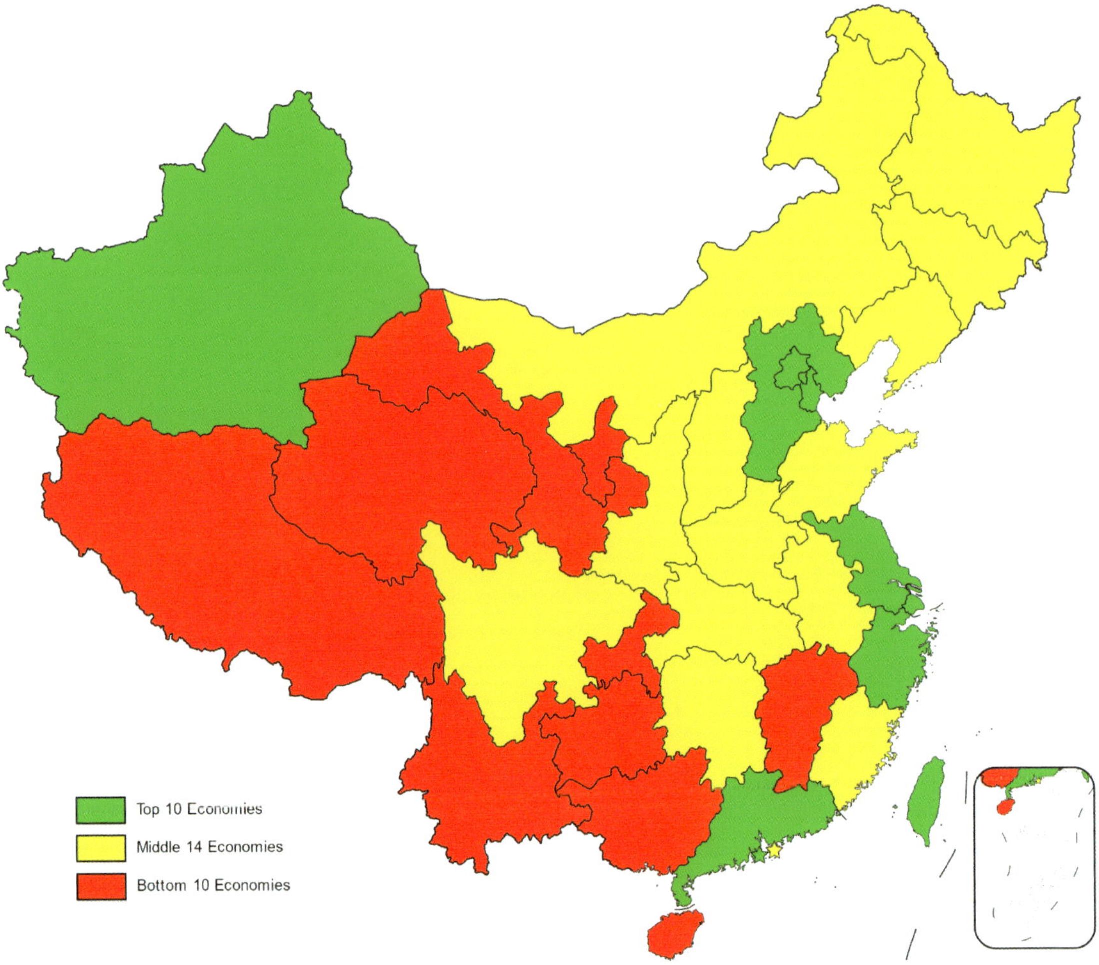

Note: The results are based on 2015 data, collated and analysed in 2018.
Source: Asia Competitiveness Institute.

Table 3.10 displays the Quality of Life and Infrastructure Development rankings and scores for the 34 Greater China economies from 2000 to 2015. There are three economies that have retained the same ranking in 2015 as compared to 2000, which are Hubei (#14), Hunan (#20) and Tibet (#30). Meanwhile, 16 economies have moved up the Quality of Life and Infrastructure Development ranking over the past 15 years. Beijing, Guangdong, Shanghai, Hebei and Inner Mongolia have risen one spot; Xinjiang has risen three spots; Guizhou has risen five spots; Sichuan and Hainan have risen six spots; Anhui has risen seven spots; Zhejiang, Tianjin and Macau each has risen eight spots; Fujian has risen nine spots; Shaanxi has risen 11 spots and Jiangsu has risen 13 spots. From 2000 to 2015, the rankings of 15 economies have dropped. Qinghai and Chongqing have fallen one spot; Henan, Yunnan and Gansu each has fallen two spots; Shandong has fallen three spots; Taiwan and Ningxia have fallen four spots; Jiangxi and Guangxi have fallen six spots; Shanxi and Jilin each has fallen seven spots; Heilongjiang has fallen 12 spots; Liaoning has fallen 15 spots and Hong Kong has fallen 17 spots.

Table 3.10: ACI 2018 Quality of Life and Infrastructure Development Rankings and Scores: Evolution Over Time

Quality of Life and Infrastructure Development								
	1		2		3		4	
Rank	Economy	Score	Economy	Score	Economy	Score	Economy	Score
2000	Taiwan	3.6387	Beijing	1.8082	Guangdong	1.0836	Liaoning	1.0538
2001	Taiwan	3.5247	Beijing	1.7969	Guangdong	0.9784	Liaoning	0.9507
2002	Taiwan	3.3566	Beijing	1.6035	Guangdong	1.3936	Liaoning	1.1154
2003	Taiwan	3.0869	Beijing	1.8635	Guangdong	1.3476	Liaoning	0.9488
2004	Taiwan	2.7524	Beijing	1.7173	Guangdong	1.4281	Hebei	0.9966
2005	Taiwan	2.4967	Beijing	1.7128	Guangdong	1.6116	Hebei	0.9889
2006	Taiwan	2.1504	Beijing	1.8020	Guangdong	1.7914	Shandong	1.1806
2007	Beijing	2.1847	Taiwan	1.8774	Guangdong	1.6283	Shanghai	1.4327
2008	Beijing	2.2706	Taiwan	1.6096	Guangdong	1.5536	Shanghai	1.4906
2009	Beijing	2.2955	Guangdong	1.4688	Shanghai	1.4547	Taiwan	1.3990
2010	Beijing	2.3260	Shanghai	1.6755	Guangdong	1.5675	Jiangsu	1.3921
2011	Beijing	2.2081	Shanghai	1.7810	Jiangsu	1.5991	Guangdong	1.5160
2012	Beijing	2.3241	Jiangsu	1.6530	Guangdong	1.6353	Shanghai	1.5971
2013	Beijing	2.5183	Guangdong	1.7868	Jiangsu	1.6907	Shanghai	1.4821
2014	Beijing	2.6826	Jiangsu	1.7043	Guangdong	1.6448	Shanghai	1.6082
2015	Beijing	2.6077	Guangdong	2.0978	Jiangsu	1.7672	Zhejiang	1.6118

Quality of Life and Infrastructure Development								
	5		6		7		8	
Rank	Economy	Score	Economy	Score	Economy	Score	Economy	Score
2000	Heilongjiang	0.7375	Hong Kong	0.7248	Shanghai	0.5062	Shandong	0.3827
2001	Hong Kong	0.9281	Heilongjiang	0.6795	Shanghai	0.6590	Tianjin	0.5045
2002	Hong Kong	0.8635	Shanghai	0.7421	Heilongjiang	0.7044	Hebei	0.6201
2003	Hong Kong	0.8882	Hebei	0.7629	Heilongjiang	0.7230	Shanghai	0.6709
2004	Liaoning	0.8940	Hong Kong	0.8070	Shandong	0.7998	Zhejiang	0.7653
2005	Shanghai	0.9439	Shandong	0.8502	Zhejiang	0.8032	Jiangsu	0.7957
2006	Zhejiang	0.9808	Jiangsu	0.9477	Shanghai	0.8147	Hebei	0.7246
2007	Jiangsu	0.9989	Hebei	0.9558	Shandong	0.9205	Zhejiang	0.8839
2008	Shandong	1.1023	Jiangsu	1.0994	Zhejiang	1.0383	Hebei	0.9755
2009	Jiangsu	1.3524	Shandong	1.0786	Zhejiang	1.0464	Hebei	0.9326
2010	Zhejiang	1.1615	Taiwan	0.9338	Shandong	0.9114	Hebei	0.9082
2011	Zhejiang	1.2273	Taiwan	1.0355	Shandong	0.8083	Hebei	0.7816
2012	Zhejiang	1.3410	Taiwan	0.9049	Shandong	0.7769	Hebei	0.6533
2013	Zhejiang	1.4551	Taiwan	0.7919	Xinjiang	0.5946	Shandong	0.5725
2014	Zhejiang	1.5547	Taiwan	1.0625	Xinjiang	0.6697	Hebei	0.5168
2015	Taiwan	1.0331	Shanghai	0.8911	Xinjiang	0.6492	Hebei	0.5192

(Continued)

Table 3.10: (*Continued*)

Quality of Life and Infrastructure Development								
	9		10		11		12	
Rank	Economy	Score	Economy	Score	Economy	Score	Economy	Score
2000	Hebei	0.3689	Xinjiang	0.3159	Shanxi	0.3131	Zhejiang	0.3059
2001	Hebei	0.4380	Shandong	0.4197	Shanxi	0.3879	Zhejiang	0.3258
2002	Shandong	0.5598	Tianjin	0.4079	Jiangsu	0.2890	Shanxi	0.2753
2003	Shandong	0.5864	Tianjin	0.4455	Zhejiang	0.3895	Xinjiang	0.3551
2004	Heilongjiang	0.6872	Shanghai	0.6123	Jiangsu	0.5627	Macau	0.5431
2005	Liaoning	0.7128	Macau	0.6941	Hong Kong	0.5895	Tianjin	0.5794
2006	Macau	0.7050	Liaoning	0.6985	Tianjin	0.6760	Hong Kong	0.6049
2007	Macau	0.6881	Tianjin	0.5914	Liaoning	0.5394	Hong Kong	0.4911
2008	Tianjin	0.6148	Macau	0.5488	Liaoning	0.4822	Hong Kong	0.3976
2009	Tianjin	0.6817	Liaoning	0.5592	Hong Kong	0.3963	Heilongjiang	0.3083
2010	Tianjin	0.8403	Liaoning	0.4029	Fujian	0.3892	Inner Mongolia	0.3862
2011	Tianjin	0.6406	Liaoning	0.4650	Fujian	0.3835	Macau	0.3719
2012	Tianjin	0.5327	Fujian	0.4487	Macau	0.4140	Liaoning	0.3807
2013	Tianjin	0.4854	Macau	0.4211	Fujian	0.3902	Liaoning	0.3549
2014	Shandong	0.4491	Macau	0.4171	Fujian	0.3565	Heilongjiang	0.1975
2015	Tianjin	0.4410	Macau	0.4180	Shandong	0.3884	Inner Mongolia	0.2903
Quality of Life and Infrastructure Development								
	13		14		15		16	
Rank	Economy	Score	Economy	Score	Economy	Score	Economy	Score
2000	Inner Mongolia	0.2662	Hubei	0.2166	Jilin	0.1516	Jiangsu	0.1475
2001	Xinjiang	0.3135	Jilin	0.1664	Inner Mongolia	0.1546	Jiangsu	0.1347
2002	Xinjiang	0.2683	Zhejiang	0.2394	Jilin	0.2361	Macau	0.1925
2003	Jiangsu	0.3265	Shanxi	0.2936	Macau	0.2287	Jilin	0.0854
2004	Tianjin	0.5033	Xinjiang	0.2985	Shanxi	0.2764	Inner Mongolia	0.0742
2005	Heilongjiang	0.5437	Shanxi	0.2652	Xinjiang	0.2056	Inner Mongolia	0.0715
2006	Heilongjiang	0.4599	Xinjiang	0.1667	Shanxi	0.1398	Henan	0.1072
2007	Xinjiang	0.4319	Heilongjiang	0.3381	Henan	0.1568	Shanxi	0.1228
2008	Heilongjiang	0.2916	Xinjiang	0.2186	Shanxi	0.1744	Inner Mongolia	0.1498
2009	Macau	0.2958	Inner Mongolia	0.2562	Xinjiang	0.2026	Shanxi	0.0969
2010	Macau	0.3425	Xinjiang	0.2695	Heilongjiang	0.2665	Shanxi	0.1184
2011	Inner Mongolia	0.3449	Xinjiang	0.2471	Heilongjiang	0.2011	Shanxi	0.1200
2012	Inner Mongolia	0.3138	Xinjiang	0.2524	Shanxi	0.1338	Shaanxi	0.1213
2013	Hebei	0.3430	Shanxi	0.2479	Heilongjiang	0.2358	Inner Mongolia	0.2007
2014	Tianjin	0.1324	Liaoning	0.1321	Inner Mongolia	0.1288	Shanxi	0.0984
2015	Fujian	0.2080	Hubei	0.1830	Sichuan	0.1652	Shaanxi	0.0723

Table 3.10: (*Continued*)

Quality of Life and Infrastructure Development								
	17		18		19		20	
Rank	**Economy**	**Score**	**Economy**	**Score**	**Economy**	**Score**	**Economy**	**Score**
2000	Tianjin	0.1388	Macau	–0.0338	Henan	–0.1218	Hunan	–0.1732
2001	Hubei	0.0331	Sichuan	–0.0338	Macau	–0.0545	Henan	–0.1116
2002	Inner Mongolia	0.0196	Sichuan	–0.0261	Henan	–0.1339	Fujian	–0.1479
2003	Sichuan	0.0835	Inner Mongolia	–0.0019	Hubei	–0.1355	Fujian	–0.1514
2004	Jilin	–0.0227	Sichuan	–0.0566	Fujian	–0.1614	Henan	–0.1663
2005	Jilin	0.0337	Henan	–0.0667	Fujian	–0.0736	Hubei	–0.1442
2006	Inner Mongolia	0.0991	Jilin	0.0187	Fujian	–0.1754	Shaanxi	–0.1856
2007	Inner Mongolia	0.0170	Jilin	–0.1634	Hunan	–0.2243	Hubei	–0.2654
2008	Henan	0.0908	Fujian	–0.0943	Hubei	–0.1921	Shaanxi	–0.2325
2009	Fujian	0.0411	Henan	0.0201	Jilin	–0.0253	Shaanxi	–0.1444
2010	Hong Kong	0.0799	Shaanxi	0.0044	Henan	–0.1493	Hubei	–0.1557
2011	Hong Kong	0.0879	Hubei	–0.0496	Shaanxi	–0.0551	Sichuan	–0.2197
2012	Heilongjiang	0.0365	Hubei	0.0146	Jilin	–0.1343	Sichuan	–0.1613
2013	Hubei	–0.0426	Sichuan	–0.0624	Shaanxi	–0.0807	Henan	–0.1251
2014	Hubei	0.0455	Shaanxi	–0.0848	Sichuan	–0.0852	Hong Kong	–0.3146
2015	Heilongjiang	0.0243	Shanxi	0.0016	Liaoning	–0.0393	Hunan	–0.3487

Quality of Life and Infrastructure Development								
	21		22		23		24	
Rank	**Economy**	**Score**	**Economy**	**Score**	**Economy**	**Score**	**Economy**	**Score**
2000	Sichuan	–0.1985	Fujian	–0.2632	Yunnan	–0.4281	Ningxia	–0.5439
2001	Hunan	–0.2291	Fujian	–0.3190	Yunnan	–0.4345	Shaanxi	–0.5206
2002	Hunan	–0.3159	Hubei	–0.4490	Yunnan	–0.5345	Ningxia	–0.5586
2003	Henan	–0.1787	Hunan	–0.3533	Ningxia	–0.5374	Shaanxi	–0.5446
2004	Hubei	–0.2192	Hunan	–0.3575	Shaanxi	–0.4416	Ningxia	–0.6265
2005	Hunan	–0.3221	Shaanxi	–0.3546	Sichuan	–0.5102	Yunnan	–0.6782
2006	Hubei	–0.2021	Hunan	–0.2802	Sichuan	–0.4141	Yunnan	–0.8033
2007	Shaanxi	–0.3388	Fujian	–0.3672	Sichuan	–0.3894	Guangxi	–0.7567
2008	Jilin	–0.2523	Hunan	–0.3836	Sichuan	–0.4990	Guangxi	–0.6573
2009	Hubei	–0.1848	Hunan	–0.3356	Sichuan	–0.4300	Guangxi	–0.7381
2010	Sichuan	–0.2548	Jilin	–0.3319	Hunan	–0.3487	Anhui	–0.7758
2011	Henan	–0.2606	Jilin	–0.3530	Hunan	–0.4209	Anhui	–0.5925
2012	Henan	–0.1778	Hong Kong	–0.1920	Anhui	–0.4018	Hunan	–0.5909
2013	Jilin	–0.3046	Hong Kong	–0.3204	Hunan	–0.3914	Anhui	–0.5647
2014	Henan	–0.3398	Hunan	–0.3558	Anhui	–0.4873	Jilin	–0.4920
2015	Henan	–0.3649	Jilin	–0.3989	Hong Kong	–0.4139	Anhui	–0.6306

(*Continued*)

Table 3.10: (*Continued*)

Quality of Life and Infrastructure Development								
	25		26		27		28	
Rank	Economy	Score	Economy	Score	Economy	Score	Economy	Score
2000	Qinghai	–0.5543	Jiangxi	–0.6021	Shaanxi	–0.6127	Guangxi	–0.9017
2001	Ningxia	–0.5706	Jiangxi	–0.6349	Qinghai	–0.7108	Guangxi	–0.9755
2002	Jiangxi	–0.6306	Qinghai	–0.6860	Shaanxi	–0.6868	Chongqing	–0.8313
2003	Yunnan	–0.6129	Jiangxi	–0.7072	Qinghai	–0.7237	Anhui	–0.9616
2004	Jiangxi	–0.7250	Yunnan	–0.7615	Qinghai	–0.8608	Guangxi	–0.9344
2005	Jiangxi	–0.6964	Ningxia	–0.7117	Qinghai	–0.8787	Guangxi	–0.8796
2006	Jiangxi	–0.8245	Guangxi	–0.8372	Ningxia	–1.0052	Qinghai	–1.0300
2007	Jiangxi	–0.8702	Yunnan	–0.8769	Qinghai	–0.9434	Ningxia	–0.9793
2008	Yunnan	–0.7248	Jiangxi	–0.7929	Qinghai	–0.9228	Ningxia	–1.0101
2009	Jiangxi	–0.7851	Anhui	–0.9224	Yunnan	–0.9602	Qinghai	–1.0030
2010	Yunnan	–0.8440	Guangxi	–0.8633	Jiangxi	–1.0201	Hainan	–1.0823
2011	Yunnan	–0.7363	Jiangxi	–0.9104	Qinghai	–0.9380	Guangxi	–0.9753
2012	Yunnan	–0.6157	Guangxi	–0.9274	Hainan	–0.9715	Qinghai	–1.0245
2013	Yunnan	–0.6589	Qinghai	–0.9286	Ningxia	–1.0631	Hainan	–1.0777
2014	Yunnan	–0.8710	Qinghai	–0.9155	Ningxia	–0.9846	Hainan	–1.0011
2015	Yunnan	–0.7463	Qinghai	–0.9199	Hainan	–1.0447	Ningxia	–1.0855

Quality of Life and Infrastructure Development								
	29		30		31		32	
Rank	Economy	Score	Economy	Score	Economy	Score	Economy	Score
2000	Gansu	–1.0033	Tibet	–1.1355	Anhui	–1.1531	Chongqing	–1.1769
2001	Chongqing	–1.0136	Gansu	–1.0706	Anhui	–1.0795	Hainan	–1.1789
2002	Guangxi	–1.0426	Anhui	–1.0751	Hainan	–1.1841	Gansu	–1.2585
2003	Chongqing	–1.0506	Guangxi	–1.1194	Hainan	–1.1702	Gansu	–1.3281
2004	Anhui	–0.9741	Hainan	–1.1434	Gansu	–1.3729	Chongqing	–1.3978
2005	Chongqing	–1.1644	Anhui	–1.1700	Hainan	–1.2989	Gansu	–1.3789
2006	Anhui	–1.1037	Chongqing	–1.1292	Hainan	–1.2836	Gansu	–1.3978
2007	Anhui	–1.0454	Chongqing	–1.1714	Hainan	–1.2063	Tibet	–1.3556
2008	Anhui	–1.0577	Chongqing	–1.2648	Hainan	–1.3518	Tibet	–1.3682
2009	Ningxia	–1.0456	Chongqing	–1.2125	Hainan	–1.2219	Tibet	–1.4949
2010	Ningxia	–1.1082	Qinghai	–1.1141	Chongqing	–1.2498	Tibet	–1.2865
2011	Ningxia	–1.0000	Hainan	–1.0690	Chongqing	–1.2240	Gansu	–1.5300
2012	Jiangxi	–1.0981	Ningxia	–1.1354	Chongqing	–1.2064	Gansu	–1.3840
2013	Gansu	–1.1513	Jiangxi	–1.1605	Chongqing	–1.2167	Guangxi	–1.2724
2014	Gansu	–1.0992	Jiangxi	–1.1878	Guizhou	–1.2476	Tibet	–1.2984
2015	Guizhou	–1.1281	Tibet	–1.1487	Gansu	–1.1817	Jiangxi	–1.2133

Table 3.10: (*Continued*)

Quality of Life and Infrastructure Development				
	33		34	
Rank	**Economy**	**Score**	**Economy**	**Score**
2000	Hainan	−1.2319	Guizhou	−2.0259
2001	Tibet	−1.4492	Guizhou	−2.0089
2002	Tibet	−1.3422	Guizhou	−1.9841
2003	Tibet	−1.5268	Guizhou	−1.9826
2004	Tibet	−1.4878	Guizhou	−2.0086
2005	Tibet	−1.5931	Guizhou	−1.9770
2006	Tibet	−1.5059	Guizhou	−1.8902
2007	Gansu	−1.5003	Guizhou	−1.8047
2008	Gansu	−1.5975	Guizhou	−1.7067
2009	Gansu	−1.6502	Guizhou	−1.7322
2010	Gansu	−1.6266	Guizhou	−1.7645
2011	Tibet	−1.5557	Guizhou	−1.9290
2012	Guizhou	−1.5273	Tibet	−1.9854
2013	Guizhou	−1.5361	Tibet	−1.6138
2014	Guangxi	−1.3148	Chongqing	−1.3218
2015	Chongqing	−1.2165	Guangxi	−1.4880

Note: The results are based on 2000–2015 data, collated and analysed in 2018.
Source: Asia Competitiveness Institute.

Hong Kong, Macau and Taiwan do not occupy the top three positions on the ranking of Quality of Life and Infrastructure Development, unlike other environments. Hong Kong's best performance occurred between 2000 and 2004 when it was ranked #5 or #6. Since then, its ranking has decreased drastically over the years to #23 in 2015. Macau's ranking was #18 in 2000, and it improved to between #9 and #13 during the period from 2004 to 2015. While Taiwan was in the top two positions from 2000 to 2008, it has dropped out from the top three since 2009. Instead, Beijing, Guangdong and Jiangsu have been performing well under this particular environment.

3.2.6 ACI 2018 Robustness Check Using Shapley Method

In this section, the Shapley method as delineated in Chapter 2 is implemented to compute a set of more objective weights for competitiveness rankings as a robustness check for the Equal Weightage Method. Figure 3.12 shows the weight of each environment under the two different weightage assignment methods. Differed from the Equal Weightage where each of the four environments is assigned with 25 percent weightage, the Shapley Weightage shows a diverse distribution of weights among the environments, ranging from 23.9 percent for Macroeconomic Stability to 26.0 percent for Government and Institutional Setting.

It was introduced in Chapter 2 that the Shapley Weightage of an environment measures the unequal competitiveness performance among all the 34 Greater China economies under that environment. Consequently, the more divergent the cross-economy performance is within a given environment, the higher its associated Shapley Weightage will be. An economy will thus receive a higher score if it performs well in an environment in which there is higher inequality across all assessed economies. Therefore, the weightage of an environment represents the relative importance of that environment in contributing to the overall competitiveness performance. In this way, the Shapley Weightage method marks a significant change from the Equal Weightage method by accounting for and capturing the unequal performances across different economies.

The comparatively high weightage of Government and Institutional Setting, which is weighted at 26.0 percent reflects the unequal performances among the 34 Greater China economies with regard to this environment. Correspondingly, Financial, Businesses and Manpower Conditions contains the second highest degree of unequal performances, as indicated by its weight of 25.1 percent. The environment with the least divergent performance is Macroeconomic Stability, which is denoted by its relatively low weight of 23.9 percent.

Figure 3.12: Comparison of Equal Weight and Shapley Weight Methods

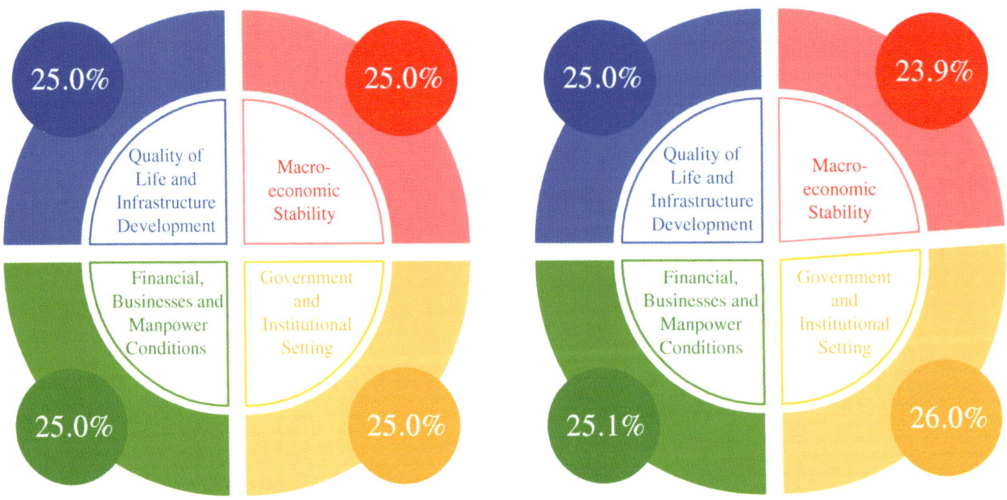

Source: Asia Competitiveness Institute.

Although the weightages are different, the Shapley Weightage of each environment does not significantly deviate from the 25 percent that is assumed in the Equal Weightage approach. Mathematically, there are two reasons that could account for this phenomenon. The first is that every economy has become more equally developed in all aspects, and across all indicators, sub-environments and hence environments. This is clearly not the case for Greater China, where regional inequality still exists. Thus, the second explanation is more applicable, which is that the aggregate level of inequality, i.e. the Shapley value, among the 34 Greater China economies is relatively uniform across all indicators, sub-environments, and hence environments. The stronger economies outperform the weaker ones by a similar extent in one environment as in the other environments. Using the range between the top- and bottom-ranked economies as a simplified illustration, the values for all environments are relatively similar, with 4.1033 for Macroeconomic Stability, 4.0639 for Government and Institutional Setting, 3.7441 for Financial, Businesses and Manpower Conditions, and 4.0957 for Quality of Life and Infrastructure Development.

Table 3.11 shows the Overall Competitiveness Performance of the 34 Greater China economies under both the Equal Weightage method and the Shapley Weightage method. The difference in rankings between the two methods is not significant as it only involves the swapping of positions for four pairs of economies, i.e. Taiwan–Beijing, Hebei–Liaoning, Tianjin–Sichuan and Xinjiang–Anhui. This demonstrates the robustness of the Equal Weightage approach. Even though the use of Equal Weightage is a subjective assumption in weight assigning, the ranking is consistent with the objective Shapley approach.

Using the pair of Taiwan and Beijing as an illustration, there are two possible explanations to account for the ranking differences between the two methods. Beijing is ranked #4 under the Shapley Weightage method while it is #5 under the Equal Weightage method. The first plausible reason is that the indicators under which Beijing performs well are associated with higher weights when the Shapley method is used, meaning all economies perform diversely and Beijing has a larger comparative advantage in those indicators. Second, indicators under which Beijing performed not so well might be associated with lower weights, meaning that performances across all economies are not as diverse and Beijing's weakness in these areas is thus not as significant as the Equal Weightage method has assumed.

Since the two methods give relatively consistent rankings, the following discussions will focus on the Equal Weightage results.

3.2.7 ACI 2018 *What-if* Competitiveness Simulation Analysis for Overall Competitiveness

All figures and tables shown in earlier sections reflect results before the *What-if* simulation analysis. In this section, the results of the *What-if* Competitiveness Simulation Analysis for the 34 Greater China economies are analysed. The simulation analysis indicates the potential of each economy to improve its standings. It is based on improving the top 20 percent weakest indicators of an economy to the average, while assuming that the performance of all other economies remains constant.

Table 3.11: Comparison of Results based on Equal Weight and Shapley Weight Methods

Economy	Rank		Score	
	Equal Weight	Shapley Weight	Equal Weight	Shapley Weight
Guangdong	1	1	2.3977	2.4534
Jiangsu	2	2	2.0168	2.0597
Hong Kong	3	3	1.7073	1.6414
Taiwan	4	5	1.6619	1.5730
Beijing	5	4	1.6214	1.6298
Zhejiang	6	6	1.3749	1.4105
Shanghai	7	7	1.1922	1.2134
Shandong	8	8	0.8301	0.8573
Macau	9	9	0.5398	0.4736
Fujian	10	10	0.1196	0.1406
Hubei	11	11	0.0631	0.0852
Hebei	12	13	0.0175	–0.0170
Liaoning	13	12	0.0000	0.0074
Tianjin	14	15	–0.0381	–0.0719
Sichuan	15	14	–0.0754	–0.0619
Henan	16	16	–0.2087	–0.1855
Inner Mongolia	17	17	–0.2806	–0.2764
Xinjiang	18	19	–0.3733	–0.3852
Anhui	19	18	–0.3825	–0.3618
Shaanxi	20	20	–0.4058	–0.4023
Hunan	21	21	–0.4676	–0.4735
Chongqing	22	22	–0.5246	–0.5433
Jilin	23	23	–0.6048	–0.5905
Heilongjiang	24	24	–0.6212	–0.6105
Shanxi	25	25	–0.6574	–0.6934
Yunnan	26	26	–0.7322	–0.7397
Jiangxi	27	27	–0.7458	–0.7452
Hainan	28	28	–0.8435	–0.8364
Guizhou	29	29	–0.8803	–0.8751
Guangxi	30	30	–0.9117	–0.9262
Ningxia	31	31	–0.9723	–1.0123
Qinghai	32	32	–1.1045	–1.0931
Gansu	33	33	–1.1878	–1.1789
Tibet	34	34	–1.5241	–1.4655

Source: Asia Competitiveness Institute.

Table 3.12 summarises the Overall Competitiveness results before and after the *What-if* simulation for each economy. Comparing the results, 19 out of the 34 economies have their rankings improved by more than five spots. Among them, nine economies demonstrate major potential for improvement, namely Tibet (up 16 spots from #34), Guangxi (up 13 spots from #30), Guizhou (up 11 spots from #29), Jiangxi (up 11 spots from #27), Qinghai (up 10 spots from #32), Ningxia (up 10 spots from #31), Hainan (up 10 spots from #28), Yunnan (up 10 spots from #26) and Hunan (up 10 spots from #21). These economies are ranked among the bottom 15 before the simulation analysis. Economies for which the ranking remains the same after the simulation are Guangdong (#1), Jiangsu (#2) and Fujian (#10). For Jiangsu, although its score improves after the simulation, it is insufficient to overcome the large gap of 0.3809 between the original score of Jiangsu and that of its immediately better-ranked counterpart Guangdong. The same explanation can also be applied to Fujian for which the gap between its original score and that of Macau is as large as 0.4202.

Table 3.12: ACI 2018 *What-if* Competitiveness Simulation Analysis on Overall Competitiveness Ranking and Scores

	Rank			Score	
Economy	**Before**	**After**	**Improvement**	**Before**	**After**
Anhui	19	11	8	–0.3825	0.0486
Beijing	5	3	2	1.6214	1.9636
Chongqing	22	15	7	–0.5246	–0.0742
Fujian	10	10	0	0.1196	0.3940
Gansu	33	26	7	–1.1878	–0.7029
Guangdong	1	1	0	2.3977	2.6430
Guangxi	30	17	13	–0.9117	–0.2876
Guizhou	29	18	11	–0.8803	–0.3383
Hainan	28	18	10	–0.8435	–0.3567
Hebei	12	10	2	0.0175	0.3420
Heilongjiang	24	16	8	–0.6212	–0.1516
Henan	16	10	6	–0.2087	0.3823
Hong Kong	3	2	1	1.7073	2.2949
Hubei	11	10	1	0.0631	0.3558
Hunan	21	11	10	–0.4676	0.0475
Inner Mongolia	17	11	6	–0.2806	0.1084
Jiangsu	2	2	0	2.0168	2.2909
Jiangxi	27	16	11	–0.7458	–0.2117
Jilin	23	17	6	–0.6048	–0.2444
Liaoning	13	10	3	0.0000	0.4595

(Continued)

Table 3.12: (*Continued*)

	Rank			Score	
Economy	**Before**	**After**	**Improvement**	**Before**	**After**
Macau	9	7	2	0.5398	1.2409
Ningxia	31	21	10	−0.9723	−0.4513
Qinghai	32	22	10	−1.1045	−0.4896
Shaanxi	20	13	7	−0.4058	−0.0124
Shandong	8	7	1	0.8301	1.2254
Shanghai	7	3	4	1.1922	1.7331
Shanxi	25	16	9	−0.6574	−0.1988
Sichuan	15	10	5	−0.0754	0.3369
Taiwan	4	2	2	1.6619	2.1985
Tianjin	14	10	4	−0.0381	0.3916
Tibet	34	18	16	−1.5241	−0.3804
Xinjiang	18	12	6	−0.3733	0.0243
Yunnan	26	16	10	−0.7322	−0.1966
Zhejiang	6	4	2	1.3749	1.6423

Note: The results are based on 2015 data, collated and analysed in 2018.
Source: Asia Competitiveness Institute.

It is worth noting that Hong Kong, Taiwan and Beijing, which are ranked from #2 to #5 before the simulation, all rise to be within top three after the simulation analysis. This shows that Hong Kong, Taiwan and Beijing are not far from the #2-ranked Jiangsu or from each other in terms of Overall Competitiveness. By improving on the top 20 percent weakest indicators, Hong Kong, Taiwan and Beijing have the potential to outperform Jiangsu and join the top two in the league. Meanwhile, given the relatively large gap between Jiangsu and the #1-ranked Guangdong, it is important for Jiangsu to further improve its competitiveness to retain its top two position in the ranking.

3.2.8 ACI 2018 *What-if* Competitiveness Simulation Analysis for Four Environments

Table 3.13 illustrates the 2018 *What-if* Competitiveness Simulation Analysis for Macroeconomic Stability. There are only five economies that can improve their rankings by more than five spots, which is much lower than the other environments. Among them, Macau has a large potential to improve its ranking by 17 spots from the original #34. The other four economies include Gansu (up seven spots from #33), Qinghai (up seven spots from #32), Ningxia (up six spots from #30) and Xinjiang (up seven spots from #28).

Table 3.13: ACI 2018 *What-if* Competitiveness Simulation Analysis on Macroeconomic Stability Ranking and Scores

Economy	Rank			Score	
	Before	After	Improvement	Before	After
Anhui	15	15	0	–0.1567	–0.1319
Beijing	8	7	1	0.3584	0.8014
Chongqing	16	14	2	–0.1709	–0.1047
Fujian	10	10	0	0.2283	0.2549
Gansu	33	26	7	–1.0716	–0.7190
Guangdong	1	1	0	3.0011	3.1064
Guangxi	20	20	0	–0.3814	–0.3814
Guizhou	25	24	1	–0.6718	–0.5330
Hainan	29	25	4	–0.9161	–0.5851
Hebei	17	14	3	–0.1911	–0.0285
Heilongjiang	27	25	2	–0.7618	–0.6395
Henan	13	11	2	–0.0201	0.1493
Hong Kong	2	2	0	2.2734	2.7020
Hubei	11	10	1	0.0966	0.2287
Hunan	18	18	0	–0.2245	–0.2245
Inner Mongolia	22	21	1	–0.4939	–0.4585
Jiangsu	3	3	0	2.1197	2.1902
Jiangxi	23	21	2	–0.4974	–0.4078
Jilin	24	21	3	–0.5687	–0.4310
Liaoning	9	8	1	0.3093	0.4062
Macau	34	17	17	–1.1022	–0.1942
Ningxia	30	24	6	–0.9477	–0.5284
Qinghai	32	25	7	–1.0625	–0.6256
Shaanxi	19	16	3	–0.3306	–0.1693
Shandong	5	5	0	1.1571	1.1706
Shanghai	4	4	0	1.5753	1.8136
Shanxi	26	21	5	–0.7016	–0.4259
Sichuan	12	11	1	0.0543	0.1051
Taiwan	7	7	0	0.5317	0.9161
Tianjin	14	13	1	–0.1276	0.0161
Tibet	31	27	4	–1.0518	–0.7214
Xinjiang	28	21	7	–0.7855	–0.4714
Yunnan	21	20	1	–0.4753	–0.3731
Zhejiang	6	6	0	1.0056	1.1279

Note: The results are based on 2015 data, collated and analysed in 2018.
Source: Asia Competitiveness Institute.

Besides the above-mentioned ones, the other five economies originally among the bottom 10 also show moderate improvement in rankings, namely Tibet (up four spot from #31), Hainan (up four spots from #29), Heilongjiang (up two spots from #27), Shanxi (up five spots from #26) and Guizhou (up one spots from #25). Nevertheless, the rankings of 11 economies remain the same even after the simulation. They are Guangdong (#1), Hong Kong (#2), Jiangsu (#3), Shanghai (#4), Shandong (#5), Zhejiang (#6), Taiwan (#7), Fujian (#10), Anhui (#15), Hunan (#18) and Guangxi (#20).

Unlike the case of Overall Competitiveness, whereby the competition for top-notch is highly intense, the ranking of the top five economies in terms of Macroeconomic Stability does not change after the simulation. One possible explanation is that the competitiveness gaps among the top five economies in terms of Macroeconomic Stability are relatively large. In the original analysis before the simulation, the #1-ranked Guangdong surpasses the #2-ranked Hong Kong by 0.7277; the #3-ranked Jiangsu outperforms the #4-ranked Shanghai by 0.5444 and Shanghai's score is higher than the #5-ranked Shandong by 0.5444. As a result, even with some increases in scores, these economies are still unable to improve their rankings. The second possible explanation is that most indicators under Macroeconomic Stability are not among the top 20 percent weakest areas for some of these economies. This applies to Jiangsu and Shandong for which the improvement in score after the simulation is only 0.0705 and 0.0135, respectively. For other economies that cannot improve their rankings after the simulation, these two explanations are also applicable.

Among the 11 economies for which the rankings remain unchanged after the simulation, the scores of Hunan and Guangxi remain the same after the simulation. Hunan retains its #18 position in the Macroeconomic Stability ranking with a score of –0.2245. Guangxi retains its #20 position with a score of –0.3814. This is due to the fact that the top 20 percent weakest indicators of Hunan and Guangxi are not from Macroeconomic Stability.

Table 3.14 shows the Government and Institutional Setting simulation results for the 34 Greater China economies. From the results, a relatively large number of 15 economies demonstrate the potential to improve their rankings by more than five spots and the magnitude of improvement in terms of increase in ranking is also very significant. Five economies show massive improvements after the simulation, with Qinghai rising by 22 spots from #33, Tibet by 19 spots from #34, Shaanxi by 19 spots from #29, Hunan by 17 spots from #28 and Heilongjiang by 16 spots from #26. There are also five other economies that can increase their rankings by more than 10 spots, namely Shanxi (up 13 spots from #31), Jilin (up 13 spots from #30), Gansu (up 12 spots from #32), Xinjiang (up 12 spots from #27) and Inner Mongolia (up 11 spots from #22). It is worth noting that these 10 economies are all among the bottom 15 in the original ranking. The result that bottom-ranked economies can enjoy such a huge improvement after the simulation sheds light on three points. First, the competitiveness differences among the bottom 15 economies are very small as their original score differences are all below 0.03 with the only exception of 1.1329 between #33-ranked Qinghai and #34-ranked Tibet. Second, it is possible that a large portion of these economies' top 20 percent weakest indicators fall under Government and Institutional Setting. Third, these economies are likely to be far below the average in terms of these indicators, resulting in large potential for improvement.

Table 3.14: ACI 2018 *What-if* Competitiveness Simulation Analysis on Government and Institutional Setting Ranking and Scores

Economy	Rank			Score	
	Before	After	Improvement	Before	After
Anhui	14	11	3	–0.1897	–0.0891
Beijing	5	5	0	1.7281	1.7281
Chongqing	16	10	6	–0.2616	0.1257
Fujian	10	10	0	0.0124	0.2119
Gansu	32	20	12	–0.9353	–0.4721
Guangdong	3	1	2	1.8503	1.9726
Guangxi	25	20	5	–0.6104	–0.4123
Guizhou	21	21	0	–0.5009	–0.5009
Hainan	18	10	8	–0.3387	0.1693
Hebei	12	12	0	–0.1269	–0.1269
Heilongjiang	26	10	16	–0.6153	0.0041
Henan	13	10	3	–0.1864	0.0477
Hong Kong	4	4	0	1.7956	1.7956
Hubei	11	10	1	–0.1146	0.2209
Hunan	28	11	17	–0.6409	–0.1158
Inner Mongolia	22	11	11	–0.5244	–0.1153
Jiangsu	2	1	1	1.9224	2.1789
Jiangxi	19	15	4	–0.3966	–0.2192
Jilin	30	17	13	–0.8113	–0.2870
Liaoning	17	10	7	–0.3181	0.0492
Macau	8	8	0	0.9313	0.9313
Ningxia	24	16	8	–0.5907	–0.2663
Qinghai	33	11	22	–0.9443	–0.1135
Shaanxi	29	10	19	–0.7905	0.0063
Shandong	9	8	1	0.8084	1.1404
Shanghai	7	6	1	1.3090	1.4678
Shanxi	31	18	13	–0.8676	–0.3393
Sichuan	15	11	4	–0.2195	–0.0982
Taiwan	1	1	0	1.9868	1.9868
Tianjin	20	11	9	–0.4731	–0.0568
Tibet	34	15	19	–2.0771	–0.2018
Xinjiang	27	15	12	–0.6283	–0.2179
Yunnan	23	19	4	–0.5379	–0.3890
Zhejiang	6	6	0	1.3554	1.6154

Note: The results are based on 2015 data, collated and analysed in 2018.
Source: Asia Competitiveness Institute.

On the other hand, the rankings for eight economies remain constant after the simulation. They are Taiwan (#1), Hong Kong (#4), Beijing (#5), Zhejiang (#6), Macau (#8), Fujian (#10), Hebei (#12) and Guizhou (#21). Among them, Zhejiang and Fujian have their scores improved to a certain extent. The reason for these two economies' inability to improve their respective rankings after the simulation lies in the large gaps in scores between these economies and the economies that are ranked immediately ahead of them. For example, while the Government and Institutional Setting score of Fujian improves from 0.0124 to 0.2119 after the simulation, it is still insufficient to raise Fujian's ranking as the original score difference between Fujian (#10) and the #9-ranked Shandong is as large as 0.7960. As for Taiwan, Hong Kong, Beijing, Macau, Hubei and Guizhou, both their scores and rankings are unaffected by the simulation. This is because none of their top 20 percent weakest indicators fall under Government and Institutional Setting.

The *What-if* Competitiveness Simulation Analysis on Financial, Businesses and Manpower Conditions is shown in Table 3.15. Notably, 12 out of 34 economies have bettered their performances by more than five spots in the ranking after the simulation, but no economy experiences an improvement of more than 10 spots. Gansu and Tibet demonstrate the largest potential as their rankings have risen by 10 spots from #33 and by nine spots from #34, respectively. Heilongjiang (originally #31), Ningxia (originally #30), Yunnan (originally #29) and Guangxi (originally #27) have their rankings improved by eight spots. Qinghai (originally #32), Xinjiang (originally #23) and Sichuan (originally #17) have risen by seven spots. There are also three economies that have improved by six spots, namely Hainan (originally #25), Hunan (originally #22) and Jilin (originally #20).

Table 3.15: ACI 2018 *What-if* Competitiveness Simulation Analysis on Financial, Businesses and Manpower Conditions Ranking and Scores

	Rank			Score	
Economy	**Before**	**After**	**Improvement**	**Before**	**After**
Anhui	19	14	5	–0.4052	–0.0299
Beijing	6	6	0	1.1646	1.2930
Chongqing	16	16	0	–0.2466	–0.2101
Fujian	13	10	3	–0.0165	0.1191
Gansu	33	23	10	–1.1036	–0.5338
Guangdong	3	3	0	1.7150	1.7623
Guangxi	27	19	8	–0.8147	–0.4146
Guizhou	28	23	5	–0.8801	–0.5418
Hainan	25	19	6	–0.7487	–0.3504
Hebei	14	10	4	–0.1381	0.0879
Heilongjiang	31	23	8	–0.8918	–0.5592
Henan	15	10	5	–0.1826	0.2833

Table 3.12: (*Continued*)

	Rank			Score	
Economy	**Before**	**After**	**Improvement**	**Before**	**After**
Macau	9	7	2	0.5398	1.2409
Ningxia	31	21	10	–0.9723	–0.4513
Qinghai	32	22	10	–1.1045	–0.4896
Shaanxi	20	13	7	–0.4058	–0.0124
Shandong	8	7	1	0.8301	1.2254
Shanghai	7	3	4	1.1922	1.7331
Shanxi	25	16	9	–0.6574	–0.1988
Sichuan	15	10	5	–0.0754	0.3369
Taiwan	4	2	2	1.6619	2.1985
Tianjin	14	10	4	–0.0381	0.3916
Tibet	34	18	16	–1.5241	–0.3804
Xinjiang	18	12	6	–0.3733	0.0243
Yunnan	26	16	10	–0.7322	–0.1966
Zhejiang	6	4	2	1.3749	1.6423

Note: The results are based on 2015 data, collated and analysed in 2018.
Source: Asia Competitiveness Institute.

It is worth noting that Hong Kong, Taiwan and Beijing, which are ranked from #2 to #5 before the simulation, all rise to be within top three after the simulation analysis. This shows that Hong Kong, Taiwan and Beijing are not far from the #2-ranked Jiangsu or from each other in terms of Overall Competitiveness. By improving on the top 20 percent weakest indicators, Hong Kong, Taiwan and Beijing have the potential to outperform Jiangsu and join the top two in the league. Meanwhile, given the relatively large gap between Jiangsu and the #1-ranked Guangdong, it is important for Jiangsu to further improve its competitiveness to retain its top two position in the ranking.

3.2.8 ACI 2018 *What-if* Competitiveness Simulation Analysis for Four Environments

Table 3.13 illustrates the 2018 *What-if* Competitiveness Simulation Analysis for Macroeconomic Stability. There are only five economies that can improve their rankings by more than five spots, which is much lower than the other environments. Among them, Macau has a large potential to improve its ranking by 17 spots from the original #34. The other four economies include Gansu (up seven spots from #33), Qinghai (up seven spots from #32), Ningxia (up six spots from #30) and Xinjiang (up seven spots from #28).

Table 3.16 illustrates the 2018 *What-if* Competitiveness Simulation Analysis on Quality of Life and Infrastructure Development. This environment shows the greatest potential for improvement among all four environments as each of the 34 Greater China economies demonstrates a rise in ranking except the top-ranked Beijing. Moreover, the extent of improvement is also considerable as 11 economies have their rankings raised by more than 10 places. Guangxi has improved by 21 places from #34, Jiangxi by 19 places from #32, Tibet, Guizhou and Hong Kong by 18 places from #30, #29 and #23, respectively, Yunnan by 17 places from #25, Anhui and Henan by 15 places from #24 and #21, respectively, Chongqing and Liaoning by 14 places from #33 and #19, respectively, and Hunan by 13 places from #20. Besides, there are also nine other economies the rankings of which have risen by more than five spots. Shanxi, Heilongjiang and Sichuan have improved their rankings by 10 spots from #18, #17 and #15, respectively; the rankings of Ningxia, Hubei and Macau have risen by seven spots from #28, #14 and #10, respectively; and the rankings of Fujian, Inner Mongolia and Shandong have improved by six spots from #13, #12 and #11, respectively. Although Beijing is already at the top of the Quality of Life and Infrastructure Development ranking, the simulation analysis suggests the possibility of Beijing to further enhance its competitiveness. According to the analysis, Beijing's score in this environment can increase from 2.6077 to 3.2784 if the top 20 percent weakest indicators were to be improved to the average level.

Table 3.16: ACI 2018 *What-if* Competitiveness Simulation Analysis on Quality of Life and Infrastructure Development Ranking and Scores

	Rank			Score	
Economy	**Before**	**After**	**Improvement**	**Before**	**After**
Anhui	24	9	15	–0.6306	0.4262
Beijing	1	1	0	2.6077	3.2784
Chongqing	33	19	14	–1.2165	–0.0791
Fujian	13	7	6	0.2080	0.8373
Gansu	31	26	5	–1.1817	–0.8073
Guangdong	2	1	1	2.0978	2.7547
Guangxi	34	13	21	–1.4880	0.1715
Guizhou	29	11	18	–1.1281	0.3567
Hainan	27	24	3	–1.0447	–0.5202
Hebei	8	5	3	0.5192	1.3004
Heilongjiang	17	7	10	0.0243	0.6481
Henan	21	6	15	–0.3649	0.9008
Hong Kong	23	5	18	–0.4139	1.3828
Hubei	14	7	7	0.1830	0.6640
Hunan	20	7	13	–0.3487	0.7124
Inner Mongolia	12	6	6	0.2903	0.9852

Table 3.16: *(Continued)*

Economy	Rank			Score	
	Before	After	Improvement	Before	After
Jiangsu	3	1	2	1.7672	2.4580
Jiangxi	32	13	19	−1.2133	0.2466
Jilin	22	20	2	−0.3989	−0.0613
Liaoning	19	5	14	−0.0393	1.0256
Macau	10	3	7	0.4180	1.8925
Ningxia	28	21	7	−1.0855	−0.3698
Qinghai	26	22	4	−0.9199	−0.3880
Shaanxi	16	12	4	0.0723	0.3196
Shandong	11	5	6	0.3884	1.2960
Shanghai	6	2	4	0.8911	2.1666
Shanxi	18	8	10	0.0016	0.5028
Sichuan	15	5	10	0.1652	1.1041
Taiwan	5	1	4	1.0331	2.6464
Tianjin	9	5	4	0.4410	1.2664
Tibet	30	12	18	−1.1487	0.2212
Xinjiang	7	6	1	0.6492	0.9958
Yunnan	25	8	17	−0.7463	0.4854
Zhejiang	4	2	2	1.6118	2.1226

Note: The results are based on 2015 data, collated and analysed in 2018.
Source: Asia Competitiveness Institute.

It is worth noting that rankings for Guangdong, Jiangsu and Taiwan are #2, #3 and #5, respectively, before the simulation, but all of the three economies have the potential to rise to #1, as suggested by the simulation analysis. This shows that Guangdong, Jiangsu and Taiwan are not far from the #1-ranked Beijing in terms of Quality of Life and Infrastructure Development. The competition to obtain the top position is very intense and the key to ranking higher in the competitiveness race lies upon whether the economy could improve its top 20 percent weakest indicators faster.

3.3 Concluding Notes and Policy Implications

In summary, the top three performers for ACI 2018 Overall Competitiveness ranking are Guangdong, Jiangsu and Hong Kong. The gaps in scores among the top three ranked economies had been steadily diminishing from 2000 to 2010, indicating an intensification of the competition to remain at the top within Greater China during this period. Since 2010, economies from Mainland China, such as Guangdong and Jiangsu, have surpassed Taiwan and Hong Kong to secure their top two positions in the Overall Competitiveness ranking. Thereafter, there has been a rising trend in the score gaps among the top three economies, which suggests that the competitiveness of Guangdong and Jiangsu as compared to the other top-performing economies in Greater China has been increasing. On the other hand, the competition among the #3-, #4- and #5-ranked economies has become more intense, as can be reflected from the narrowing gaps in the scores of these economies over the past few years.

The relative strengths of the top three economies are shown in Figure 3.13, whereby the sub-environment scores of Guangdong, Jiangsu and Hong Kong are compared to the maximum score of the 34 Greater China economies. For the #1-ranked Guangdong, it achieves the maximum score in four sub-environments, namely Openness to Trade and Services, Government Policies and Fiscal Sustainability, Financial Deepening and Business Efficiency, and Physical Infrastructure. As for the #2-ranked Jiangsu, it achieves the maximum score of the 34 Greater China economies in the sub-environment of Regional Economic Vibrancy. Jiangsu's performance is also close to the maximum score in the sub-environments of Government Policies and Fiscal Sustainability as well as Physical Infrastructure. Meanwhile, the #3-ranked Hong Kong performs remarkably in three sub-environments, Institutions, Governance and Leadership; Openness to Trade and Services; and Financial Deepening and Business Efficiency. However, the strength of Hong Kong is rather unevenly distributed among all the sub-environments. For example, it performs rather poorly compared to the maximum score in the sub-environments of Regional Economic Vibrancy, Physical Infrastructure, and Standard of Living, Education and Social Stability.

Figure 3.13: ACI 2018 Maximum Competitiveness Web — Guangdong, Jiangsu and Hong Kong

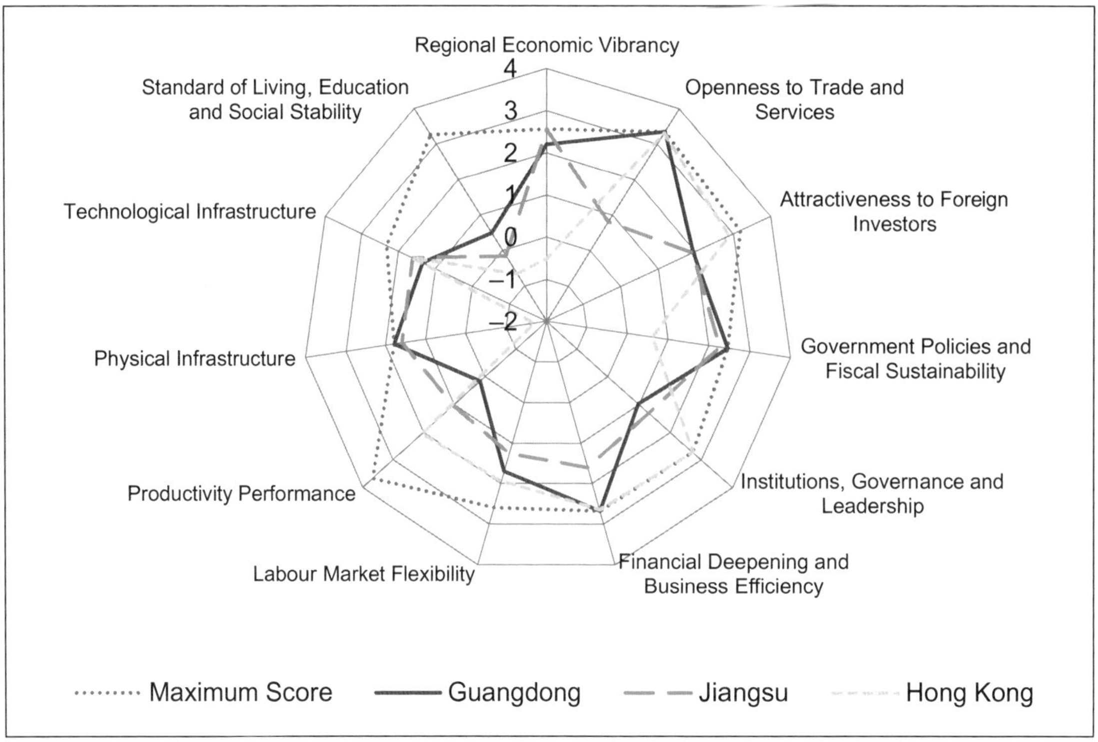

Note: The results are based on 2015 data, collated and analysed in 2018.
Source: Asia Competitiveness Institute.

The potential of Jiangsu, Hong Kong, Taiwan and Beijing, which are currently ranked among the top five in the 2018 Overall Competitiveness ranking, to become the most competitive economies in Greater China is demonstrated in the *What-if* Competitiveness Simulation Analysis. Based on the results, Jiangsu retains its current position of #2, while both Hong Kong (currently #3) and Taiwan (currently #4) rise to join Jiangsu as the #2 after the simulation analysis. Beijing's ranking is also improved by two spots to become #3. This shows that Hong Kong, Taiwan and Beijing are not far from the #2-ranked Jiangsu or from each other in terms of Overall Competitiveness. These top-performing economies should not be complacent about their Overall Competitiveness standings. When each economy improves on its relative weaknesses while capitalising on its strengths, the competitiveness landscape at the top of the ranking will change. Meanwhile, the observation that no economy rises to #1 after the simulation also demonstrates the considerable strengths of Guangdong in terms of Overall Competitiveness as compared to the other top-performing economies in Greater China. Therefore, for Jiangsu, Hong Kong, Taiwan and Beijing to compete with Guangdong, the governments should not only focus on improving the economies' weaknesses but also strive to develop new sources of economic growth.

The bottom three performers of ACI 2018 Overall Competitiveness shown in Figure 3.14 are Qinghai, Gansu and Tibet. The ranking of Gansu has dropped from #32 to #33 in the past 15 years (2000–2015), while Tibet has always occupied the bottom position. At the same time, Qinghai's ranking has declined steadily from #25 in 2000 to #32 in 2015. Figure 3.14 is thus

Figure 3.14: ACI 2018 Median Competitiveness Web — Qinghai, Gansu and Tibet

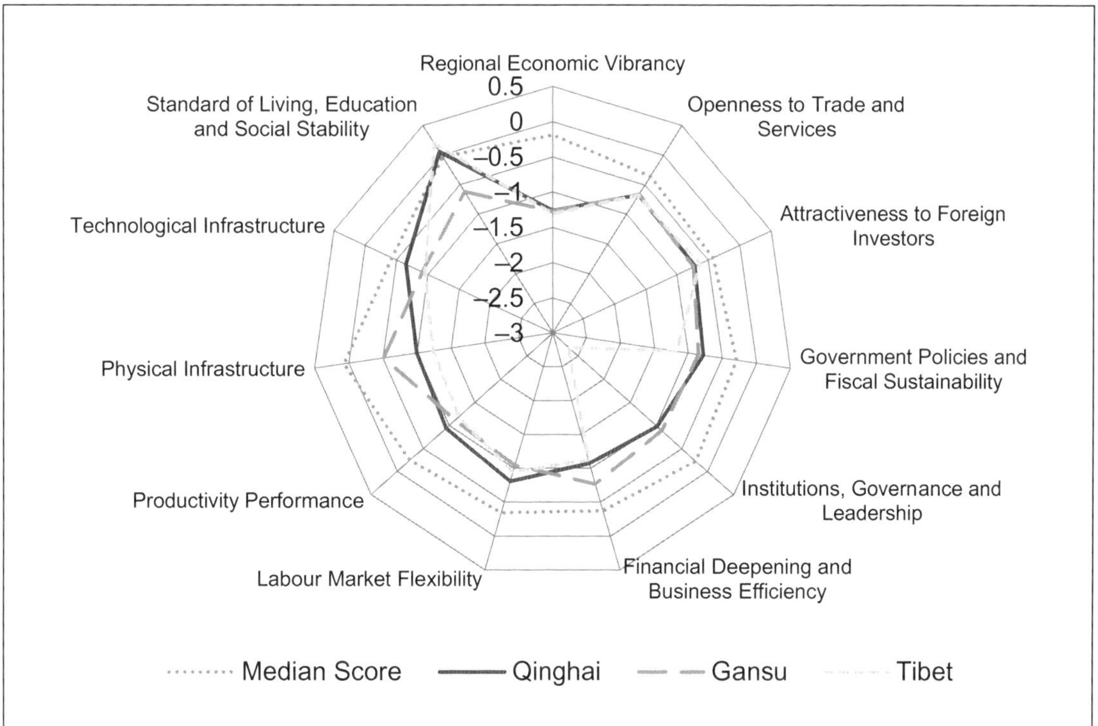

Note: The results are based on 2015 data, collated and analysed in 2018.
Source: Asia Competitiveness Institute.

devised to further illustrate the relative strengths and weaknesses of these economies, whereby the scores of Qinghai, Gansu and Tibet in each sub-environment are compared to the median scores of the 34 Greater China economies.

The three bottom-ranked economies score below the median in all sub-environments, with the only exceptions being Qinghai and Tibet which score slightly above median in the sub-environment of Standard of Living, Education and Social Stability. While the economies have poor performances in all sub-environments, their weaknesses are most significant in four sub-environments, namely Regional Economic Vibrancy; Institutions, Governance and Leadership; Productivity Performance; and Physical Infrastructure. Meanwhile, there are also two sub-environments under which the scores of these economies are relatively closer to the median; they are Openness to Trade and Services, and Attractiveness to Foreign Investors.

Another observation is that the scores of these three economies are comparable to each other in a number of sub-environments such as Regional Economic Vibrancy, Openness to Trade and Services, Attractiveness to Foreign Investors, Labour Market Flexibility, Productivity Performance, and Technological Infrastructure. This implies a certain level of competition among the economies which is healthy for their development. Nevertheless, the results also suggest that Tibet falls behind significantly in a few sub-environments, especially Government Policies and Fiscal Sustainability, and Institutions, Governance and Leadership, which warrants policy responses from the government.

The analysis results paint a relatively bleak picture of the competitiveness of Qinghai, Gansu and Tibet as compared to the rest of the Greater China economies. However, based on the *What-if* Competitiveness Simulation Analysis on Overall Competitiveness, Qinghai, Gansu and Tibet have the potential to attain #22, #26 and #18 positions, respectively, should they choose to improve upon their top 20 percent weakest indicators to the average level. This result is indeed encouraging. While the thrust of this ACI study has been focused on discovering the relative competitiveness of the 34 Greater China economies, the policy-induced *What-if* simulations offer useful insights for each economy to enhance its competitiveness, enabling the proposal of appropriate development strategies or policies.

Discussant Notes 3.1

Comments on "2018 Annual Update on Competitiveness Rankings and Simulation Studies for 34 Greater China Economies"

Dr Fan Yubo

Associate Professor, Policy Research Office, Shandong Academy of Social Sciences

The Economist once drew an interesting analogy between Chinese provinces and other countries, comparing their GDP, population and export volumes. This analogy was made with the aim of identifying the countries that a Chinese province may be potentially comparable to in these aspects. China is now the world's second largest economy, where some of its provinces by themselves would rank fairly high in the global economic league. For example, at a time, Guangdong's GDP (at market exchange rates) was almost as big as Indonesia's while the outputs of both Jiangsu and Shandong exceeded Switzerland's. Now, Guangdong's GDP (at market exchange rates) is almost as large as Spain's, and the output of both Jiangsu and Shandong exceed Indonesia's. Therefore, it is of great significance to study Chinese provinces and to identify the pathways that economic development takes in a large country like China. In recent years, the Asia Competitiveness Institute (ACI) of the Lee Kuan Yew School of Public Policy, National University of Singapore has been paying close attention to the development of China. The Annual Update of Competitiveness Analysis for 34 Greater China Economies provides us with an important reference for China's future development

1 This Project Has Strengthened My Understanding of the Following Three Points

1.1 Competition Amongst Local Governments Has Promoted China's Economic Development

Competition amongst local governments has been considered a major driver for economic growth after the implementation of China's reform and opening-up policy. Following the market-based reform, economic decentralization was implemented and the subsequent hierarchies in political institutions caused local governments to compete against each other for economic resources. Local decentralization and a performance-oriented assessment model gave local governments the power to pursue economic development within their jurisdictions, leading to competition amongst local governments. The competition was spurred on by the drive to expand capital investment and the motivation of pursuing a larger scale of local economies. Owing to the restrictions of administration and the liquidity of resources, however, competition does not necessarily lead to economic increases. If local governments chose to adopt a protectionist strategy or the plunder strategy, transaction costs would increase while economic growth would decrease. China's provinces are not homogeneous and resources endowments vary greatly among them. The setting of the index system of the project has also reflected the huge differences in resource distribution among the various provinces in China.

1.2 Regional Competitiveness Ranking Provides a Reference Frame for Development

The ACI Competitiveness Yearbook is an important annual report on the competitiveness of the provinces in China. It benchmarks the performance of the 34 economies of China based on more than 102 criteria measuring different facets of competitiveness. The four dimensions of competitiveness evaluation are: Macroeconomic Stability; Government and Institutional Setting; Financial, Businesses and Manpower Conditions; and Quality of Life and Infrastructure Development. The research model designed by ACI team follows the basic concepts of competition and cooperation, and their division of the concept of competitiveness into these four dimensions corresponds to the four variables of regional development. In ACI, this ranking of regional competitiveness has been a long-standing research project, which not only contributes to the academic research of regional economies, but is also a useful development reference system for each region. Through this reference system, we can realise our own advantages and disadvantages, gain an understanding of our competitors, discover potential areas of collaboration, help to remove both tangible and intangible obstacles that hinder cooperation and so on. Leveraging on respective strengths of regions and converging interests, provinces can put in place a development cooperation framework that covers wide-ranging areas on multiple levels.

1.3 The Risk of Europeanisation of China's Economy

As far as Chinese research is concerned, China is a big developing country with a highly decentralised economy and highly centralised politics. The relationship between central and local governments is an important link in understanding the negative problems caused by China's "growth miracle", the inadequate provision of public goods and serious environmental pollution. Under the current relationship between central and local governments in China, the most important and direct way for local government officials to develop the economy is through infrastructure construction and the development of other government investment projects to promote short-term economic growth. The subsequent increase in local government debt then triggered concerns over how local government debt incurred and the best way to address it. Many economists have analysed the conflict between insufficient labor mobility and common currency area, which led to China's local government debt. The former generates huge geographical disparities in labor productivity, while the latter reduces the possibility of increasing exports through depreciation in the less developed areas in China. As a result, borrowing becomes the channel for local governments' financing. What's worse, the expectation of bailout from central government provides even more incentive for local governments to borrow.

2 Two Suggestions

2.1 Incorporate Indicators Measuring the Comparative Advantages Among the Main Functional Zones

For mainland China, the characteristics of homogeneity in development between provinces in the past few years are obvious. This reflects the provinces' intensive pursuit of comparative advantage as well as large and comprehensive industrial development, leading to serious ecological damage, degradation of ecosystem functions, intense resource exploitation, serious environmental problems, unreasonable spatial structure and low utilization efficiency. In 2010, China began to implement the National Main Functional Zoning Plan, which aimed to plan a reasonable distribution of population and industries, map out sustainable land use and urbanization patterns, determine the main functions of different regions, and define the direction of development according to the capacity of resources and the prevailing environment. These development policies control the intensity of development, standardise the order of development, and gradually form a pattern of land and space development in which population, economy, resources and environment are coordinated. It is suggested that more indicators should be incorporated to highlight the differences between the main functional zones, such that the ranking of competitiveness may be more conducive to guiding the region to embark on the route of differentiation and synergy.

2.2 Enhance the Analysis of the Change in Annual Rankings

The rankings of some provinces may change in the annual ranking, and even change across regions if a long-term comparison is made. This reflects changes in the overall competitiveness of each regional economy, as well as the process of China's supply-side reform and industrial restructuring. On the basis of carrying out annual competitiveness rankings, it is advisable to also carry out temporal competitiveness ranking analysis and prediction. If a comprehensive ranking analysis of 3–5 years can be carried out, it may have more guiding value for the medium-term and long-term development of the region. The team should consider carrying out the prediction of the temporal competitiveness based on 3–5 years competitiveness ranking.

Discussant Notes 3.2

Comments on "2018 Annual Update on Competitiveness Rankings and Simulation Studies for 34 Greater China Economies"

Dr He Dongni

Deputy Director, China Institute for Reform and Development

1 General Comments

The study Annual Update of Competitiveness Analysis for 34 Greater China Economies conducted by ACI has three characteristics:

Firstly, the topic of this study is "competitiveness", one of the main concerns of the Chinese government today. This topic is highly integrated into China's long-term economic development. In fact, it is a key issue that needs to be solved in order for China to transform from an economy with high-speed growth to an economy with high-quality development.

Secondly, this study is based on a scientific methodology. It builds a competitiveness assessment framework including hundreds of indicators.

Thirdly, this study provided clear and pertinent policy recommendations. It emphasised that ranking is less important than scores and used simulation to uncover the best way to improve competitiveness scores. This is a very valuable contribution.

2 Questions for Further Discussion Regarding Economic Competitiveness

Let's first come back to the essential question: what does competitiveness mean? ACI proposes four environments to capture competitiveness: Macroeconomic Stability; Government and Institutional Setting; Financial, Business and Manpower Conditions; and Quality of Life and Infrastructure Development. There are two judging criteria for an economy to be competitive. The first criterion is how much money an economy attracts or how much investments and consumptions that economy attracts. The second one is how many people or talents an economy attracts. More importantly, the attractiveness should not be a short-term phenomenon simply achieved by short-term and preferential policies.

As you may know, in 2016, China experienced a sharp drop in private investment. The government responded through various measures, especially by relaxing market access and "streamlining the administration" to reduce institutional costs. However, the probability of private investment growth going down still remains relatively high today. A drop in investment is more likely to happen in the northeast and the west than in other regions of China.

Consumption expenditure, as a percentage of GDP, grew from 50.0 percent in 2013 to 58.8 percent in 2017. In the first half of 2018, consumption expenditure even contributed nearly 80 percent of the GDP. The rapid increase in demand for services such as education, medical care and health services reflects the trend of "consumption upgrade" in China. However, the inequality between a strong demand for service consumption and an insufficient supply for it is significant, hence leading to consumption outflows. On the one hand there is an outflow of investments; on the other hand there is an outflow of consumption. This phenomenon also reflects the contradictory situation, in which the growing demand cannot be met due to the lack of supply. An important reason for this is that the market, in particular the services market, is not open enough. Nevertheless, the openness of the market cannot be measured simply by looking at the numbers or the proportion of companies with different ownerships.

The second question to ask is: what is the key to attract investment, consumption and talent? We have talked quite a lot about improving business environments today. Actually, the business environment has become the most important factor for a region to attract investments and people. What constitutes a good business environment? At minimum, it includes strict property rights protection, an open and convenient market access, fair competition policies, an appropriate corporate tax rate, and good legal protection.

For example, the registration process and registration cost of starting a business in different regions are different. In China, it takes an average of 22.9 days and requires 7 steps, or procedures, to start a new business. In OECD countries, it takes an average of 4.9 procedures and 8.5 days to start a new business, and in South Korea, it takes only 4 days and requires 2 procedures to start a new business. These facts show that institutional costs are very different for enterprises in different countries. I can even use my visa application to Singapore as a personal example. My visa was approved in less than 2 hours upon submitting the application — this is high efficiency and competitiveness.

The third question to ask is: what is the most fundamental condition for being competitive? While the openness of the market and the comprehensiveness of the business environment indeed play a part, the fundamental condition is still attributed to the relationship between the government and the market. Essentially, whether the market plays a decisive role in resource allocation is the fundamental condition.

Chapter 4

2018 Annual Update on Regional Competitiveness Rankings and Simulation Studies for Greater China

4.1 Introduction

This chapter will present the 2018 annual update on regional competitiveness rankings and simulation studies for Greater China. As demonstrated by the rankings and analysis in Chapter 3, the distribution of economic competitiveness among sub-national economies exhibits a rather unbalanced pattern. Led by economies along the eastern coastlines while dragged by economies in the west, China's economic development varies across the five regions shown in Figure 4.1.

Figure 4.1: Map of Greater China by Region

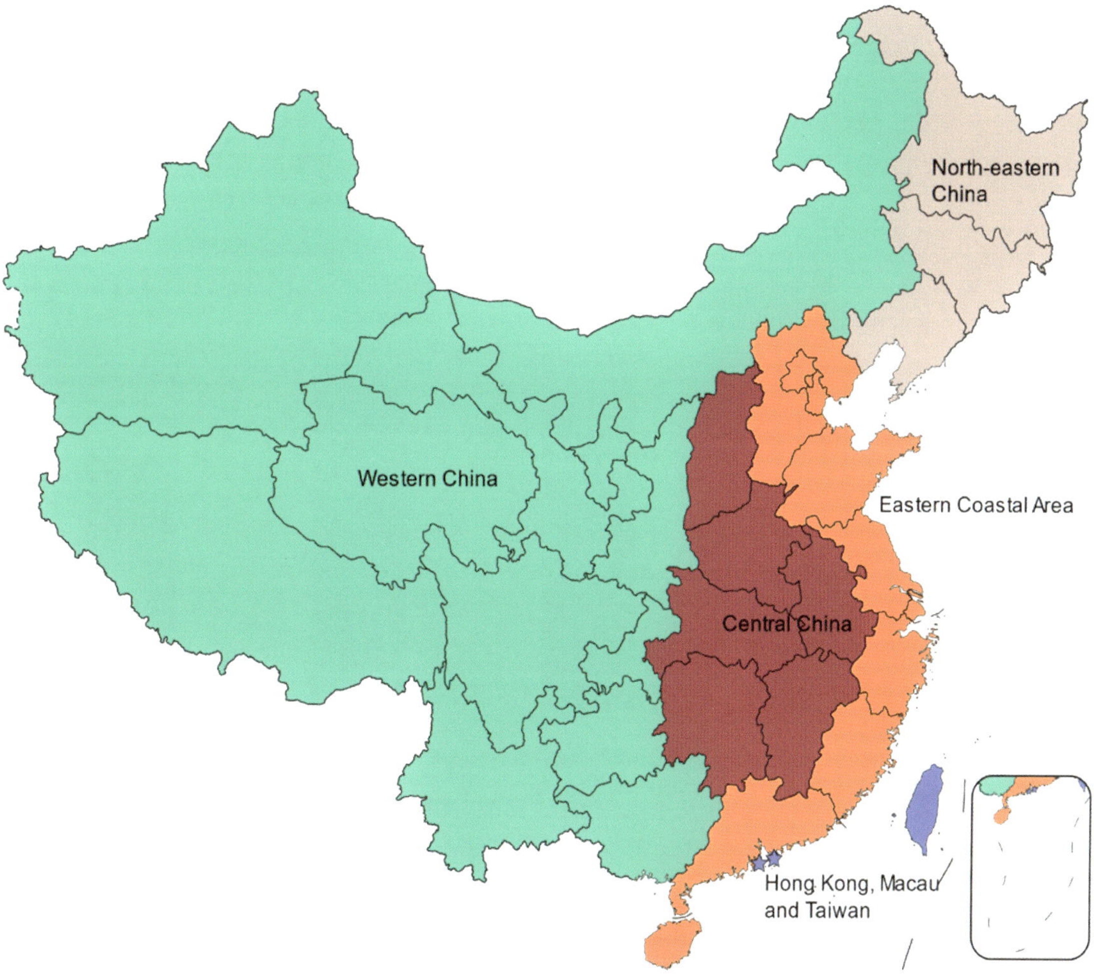

Source: Asia Competitiveness Institute.

4.1.1 Overview of Regional Disparities

While there has been a general consensus that regional disparity arises from the unbalanced geographical spreading of resources and preferential policies implemented in history, this socio-economic issue remains as a hot topic among scholars and policymakers. One reason for this popularity lies upon the fact that regional disparity is a multi-dimensional problem. Various manifestations of regional disparities exist, as suggested by different economic indicators. For instance, as shown in Figure 4.2, regional disparities in terms of Gross Regional Domestic Product (GRDP), Imports, Exports and Foreign Direct Investment (FDI) are clearly demonstrated by their unevenly distributed spectrums. Eastern Coastal Area exhibits disproportionately high share of GRDP, exports, imports and FDI. Together with Hong Kong, Macau and Taiwan, these two regions contribute a sizable amount of economic values, dominating all other regions of the Greater China.

The multi-dimensionality poses a strong hindrance to proposing a quick and simple solution for all regional imbalances. Nevertheless, this complexity also underpins the necessity of an in-depth analysis of each aspect of regional disparities. In the context of this book, the relationship between trade and regional disparities is of pivotal concern. Notably, the unbalanced import and export patterns have already illustrated that trade *per se* contributes differently to the regional economies in Greater China. However, the interaction between trade and other types of regional disparities is not yet unveiled. One sentiment emphasises that the co-existence of trade

Figure 4.2: Share of Gross Regional Domestic Products; International Imports and Exports; and Foreign Direct Investment by Region, 2015

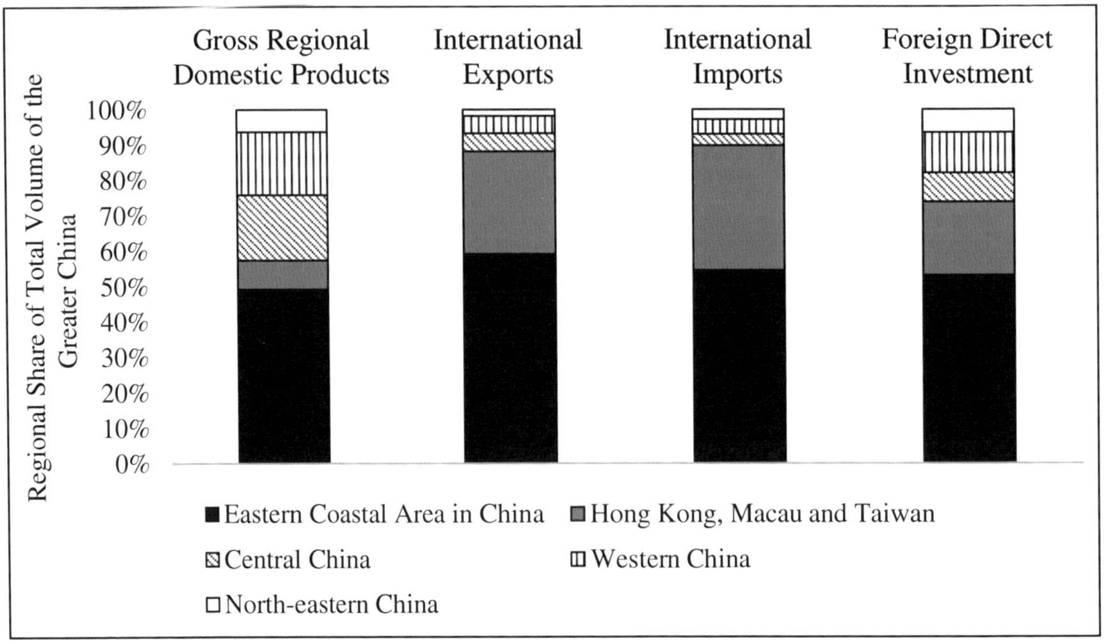

Note: Calculations are based on constant prices at 2000.
Source: Asia Competitiveness Institute based on data retrieved from National Bureau of Statistics of China, Hong Kong Statistical Yearbook, Macau Statistical Yearbook, and Taiwan Statistical Yearbook.

flourishment and economic vibrancy in the Eastern Coastal Area is not a mere coincidence. Import and export growth have benefitted this region but also accelerated the formation of economic disparities. Thus, the development of the Eastern Coastal Area is at the cost of forgoing other regions in Mainland China, with trade catalysing the entire process. In fact, some studies in the literature argue that trade growth facilitates regional disparities (Jian, Sachs, and Warner 1996; Yang 2002; Zhang and Zhang 2003; Kanbur and Zhang 2005). This argument motivates a thorough evaluation, as presented in Section 4.1.2.

4.1.2 The Nexus among Regional Disparities, Trade and Policies

The growth of the Eastern Coastal Area started in the early 1980s, riding on the trend of rising globalisation. Trade, indeed, played an important role in facilitating growth due to the formation of the global value chain. To take advantage of the low labour cost, manufacturing companies outsourced the production of labour-intensive goods to China (Ozawa 2006). Inevitably, import and export activities have to be involved, which created economic values in two aspects. On the one hand, to build up the capacity for producing intermediate goods, a large amount of Foreign Direct Investment (FDI) was injected into the Eastern Coastal Area. For example, in the 1980s, Guangdong and Fujian together amounted up to 56.2 percent of the total FDI pledged to Mainland China (Chen, Chang, and Zhang 1995). Newly established companies created employment opportunities for the local market as well as an increase in tax revenues for the local governments. On the other hand, exporting those goods would still create a positive trade balance, which is directly accounted in the GRDP of the Eastern Coastal Area, even though there is only limited value addition from raw materials to intermediate goods.

Other than opportunities from trade and globalisation, benefits from preferential policies should also be considered. Embracing the trend of "Reform and Opening-up" in the 1980s, five designated Special Economic Zones (SEZs) were created in the Eastern Coastal Area to attract foreign investors with preferential corporate tax rate, derestriction and more liberal laws (Nashitateno 1983; Crane *et al.* 2018). This prioritisation, according to the plan of the government, should be beneficial to the rest of Greater China. A key argument supporting this belief is the "spillover effect", which suggests that the strong growth from the Eastern Coastal Area would trickle down to the Central and Western Regions of Greater China (Crane *et al.* 2018). Essentially, this effect predicts that the unbalanced development will eventually even out.

Unexpectedly, after the four decades of development, the "spillover effect" has not fully materialised, but rather the regional disparites widened. There are many plausible reasons why the "spillover" is difficult to achieve. Firstly, the prioritised development gave Eastern Coastal Area distinct advantages on technology, infrastructure and human capital. Compared with inland regions, Eastern Coastal Area was, therefore, more attractive to foreign capitals. The comparative advantages of Eastern Coastal Area reinforced its position against other regions. Foreign capitals were thus less likely to migrate to other places (Crane *et al.* 2018). Secondly, the dominant positions of large State-Owned Enterprises in inland regions gave less room to the development of foreign private ownership (Crane *et al.* 2018). Last but not least, the local government implemented policies only favouring local enterprises. Such regional protectionism created strong interregional trade barriers, blocking away the opportunity for "spillover effect" to take place (Li, Qiu, and Sun 2003).

Since the development of the Eastern Coastal Area was contemporarily affected by preferential policies and trade globalisation, two conditions should be taken into account when evaluating regional disparities in Greater China. The first one is the domestic background set by policies; the second one is trade flourishment. In this regard, only evaluating the effect of the trade on regional disparities could be difficult because the relationship between trade and regional disparities may vary across different countries due to policy influences. This argument is supported by conclusions from empirical studies in the literature. The influence of trade on regional inequalities could be neutral if not accounted for country-specific factors. Changes in trade shape the local economies in a more polarised way when the cost of internal transactions and the chance that only developed regions have access to foreign markets are jointly high (Rodríguez-Pose and Gill 2006; Rodríguez-Pose 2012).

That being said, effects from both policies and trade need to be considered when addressing regional disparities. To mitigate regional disparities, policymakers could focus on enabling isolated economies to be fully integrated into the global value chain. The Belt and Road Initiative of China is a *de facto* practice of this strategy. The initiative features infrastructure investment in Western and Central regions as well as surrounding countries. The investment, if succeeded, could help improve inland connectivity across countries, thus offering Central and Western regions access to foreign markets. However, caveats should be raised concerning the relocation cost of manufacturing companies. Companies may hesitate to relocate to the Central and Western Regions due to high opportunity cost on divesting established factories and facilities in the Eastern Coastal Regions. Without relocation, trade flourishment in the Central and Western Regions of Greater China may be difficult to realise.

Given the importance of both trade and regional disparities, a dedicated analysis will be conducted on each topic. The discussion about import and export will be carried out in Chapter 5, along with an investigation on instrumental factors affecting export effectiveness. Asia Competitiveness Institute (ACI) is continuously spending efforts to track and analyse the evolving competitiveness landscape at the regional level for Greater China so that each region could use the results as benchmarks to evaluate its strengths and weaknesses (Tan *et al.* 2016). This chapter focuses on the regional competitiveness analysis of Greater China, diving into different aspects of regional disparities. The remaining sections are organised as follows. Section 4.2 presents the research findings including the Overall Competitiveness ranking of five regions as well as the competitiveness rankings of four environments. Besides providing a snapshot of the 2018 ACI rankings, this section will also track the changes of each region in terms of competitiveness over time. Details of the sub-environments under each environment will also be discussed. Section 4.3 concludes by summarising salient results of the study.

4.2 Research Findings

This section presents and discusses the performance of the five regions of Greater China in the 2018 Overall Competitiveness rankings and the four identified environments. Following the research methodology outlined in Chapter 2 and the competitiveness study on the 34 Greater China economies in Chapter 3, the scores and rankings in this section are generated by standardising the scores across regions and ordering the regions based on these standardised scores. As a result of this procedure, it is imperative to note that the scores reported in this section do not constitute a metric of regional competitiveness, but rather, reflect the relative competitive strength of each region against the other regions.

4.2.1 ACI 2018 Overall Competitiveness Rankings and Scores

Table 4.1 shows the 2018 Overall Competitiveness rankings and scores of the five regions in Greater China. The Eastern Coastal Area in China ranks first with a score of 1.7823, followed by Hong Kong, Macau and Taiwan, Western China, Central China and North-eastern China which rank second, third, fourth and fifth, respectively.

From the Overall Competitiveness scores, it can be inferred that the Eastern Coastal Area in China and Hong Kong, Macau and Taiwan are more competitive than the regional average. This is evident from the positive Overall Competitiveness scores the two regions attain. Western China, Central China and North-eastern China, on the other hand, attain negative Overall Competitiveness scores, indicative of their below-average performance.

Studying the distribution of the Overall Competitiveness scores, a negative skew is observed with the mean score exceeding the median score, where the mean is taken as a conceived region with a score of 0 and the median as the region ranked third (Western China with a score of –0.4841). This suggests a disparity in the competitiveness between the top-performing regions and the bottom-performing regions. This disparity is further emphasised by the large gap in scores between the Eastern Coastal Area (1.7823), ranked first, Hong Kong, Macau and Taiwan (0.3870), ranked second, and all the other regions which have their scores closely clustered together. The Eastern Coastal Area, Hong Kong, Macau and Taiwan and Western China have the respective score differences of 1.3953 and 0.8711. These are sizeable when contrasted against the score differences among the bottom-performing regions of Central China and North-eastern China, 0.2609 and 0.1953. These observations reflect the Eastern Coastal Area's significant lead

Table 4.1: ACI 2018 Overall Competitiveness Rankings and Scores

Rank	Region	Score
1	Eastern Coastal Area in China	1.7823
2	Hong Kong, Macau and Taiwan	0.3870
3	Western China	–0.4841
4	Central China	–0.7450
5	North-eastern China	–0.9403

Note: The results are based on 2015 data, collated and analysed in 2018.
Source: Asia Competitiveness Institute.

Figure 4.3: ACI 2018 Overall Competitiveness Ranking Map

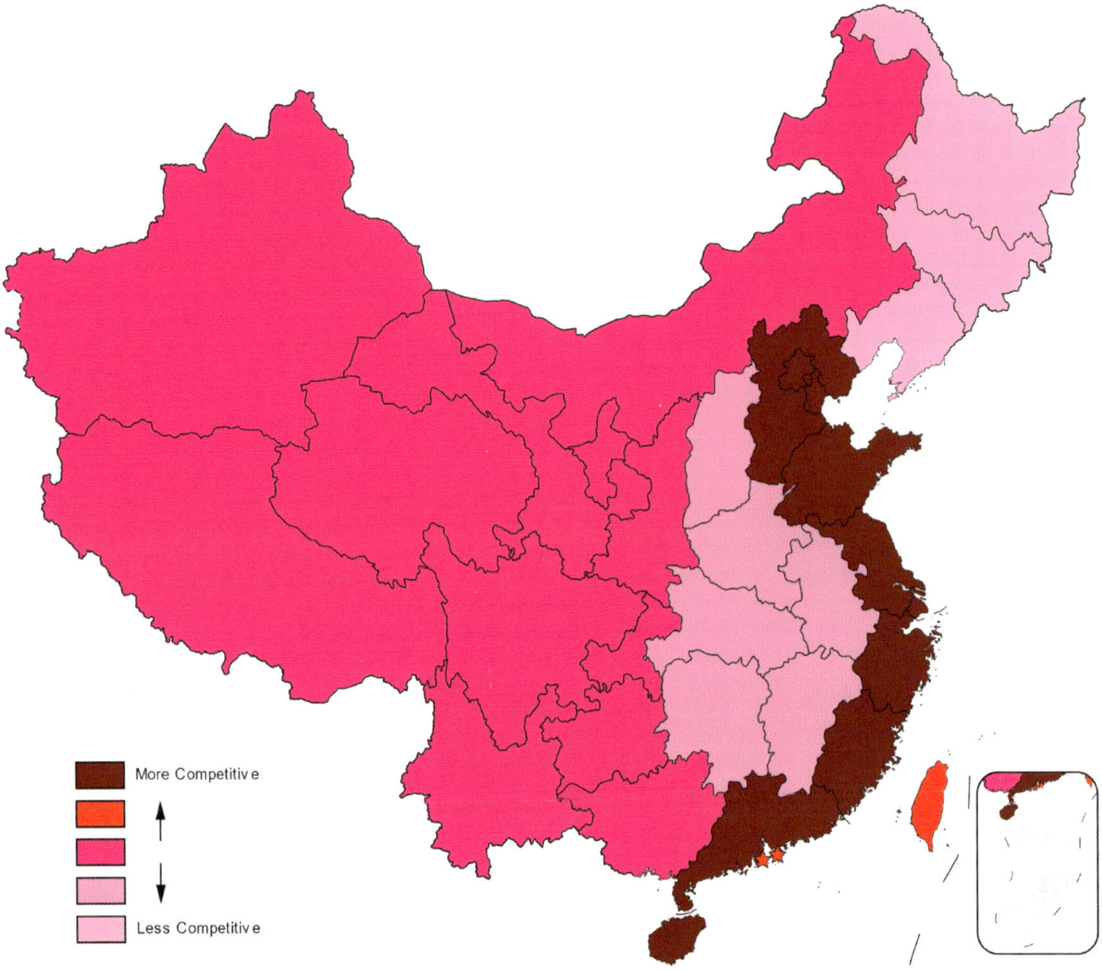

Note: The results are based on 2015 data, collated and analysed in 2018.
Source: Asia Competitiveness Institute.

in competitive strength over all the other regions and Hong Kong, Macau and Taiwan's edge over the remaining mainland regions.

The Overall Competitiveness scores and rankings of the five regions can also be visualised geographically. Figure 4.3 colour-codes the regions by their level of competitiveness, with more competitive regions in a darker shade and less competitive regions in a lighter shade.

Table 4.2 presents the Overall Competitiveness rankings and scores of the five regions from 2000 to 2015. Discerning the patterns and changes in rankings over the decade and half, it can be observed that the Eastern Coastal Area has surpassed Hong Kong, Macau and Taiwan to rank first since 2002, with its score climbing steadily from 1.0526 in 2000 to 1.8132 in 2013, only experiencing a slight drop in 2014 and 2015. In contrast, in the same period, Hong Kong, Macau and Taiwan, having fallen to place second in the rankings, has seen its score decline from 1.3524 in 2000 to 0.3554 in 2013, experiencing only subtle improvements in 2014 and 2015. As a result of these trends, the gap in scores between the top two ranked regions has widened considerably

Table 4.2: ACI 2018 Overall Competitiveness Rankings and Scores: Evolution Over Time

	Overall Competitiveness					
	1		2		3	
Rank	**Region**	**Score**	**Region**	**Score**	**Region**	**Score**
2000	Hong Kong, Macau and Taiwan	1.3524	Eastern Coastal Area in China	1.0526	North-eastern China	–0.5851
2001	Hong Kong, Macau and Taiwan	1.3023	Eastern Coastal Area in China	1.1343	North-eastern China	–0.7041
2002	Eastern Coastal Area in China	1.2795	Hong Kong, Macau and Taiwan	1.1557	North-eastern China	–0.6563
2003	Eastern Coastal Area in China	1.2837	Hong Kong, Macau and Taiwan	1.1438	North-eastern China	–0.6755
2004	Eastern Coastal Area in China	1.3098	Hong Kong, Macau and Taiwan	1.1184	Western China	–0.6850
2005	Eastern Coastal Area in China	1.4627	Hong Kong, Macau and Taiwan	0.9288	North-eastern China	–0.6569
2006	Eastern Coastal Area in China	1.5048	Hong Kong, Macau and Taiwan	0.8902	North-eastern China	–0.7047
2007	Eastern Coastal Area in China	1.5157	Hong Kong, Macau and Taiwan	0.8776	Western China	–0.7236
2008	Eastern Coastal Area in China	1.6167	Hong Kong, Macau and Taiwan	0.7272	North-eastern China	–0.6746
2009	Eastern Coastal Area in China	1.7212	Hong Kong, Macau and Taiwan	0.5486	North-eastern China	–0.6558
2010	Eastern Coastal Area in China	1.7614	Hong Kong, Macau and Taiwan	0.4719	Western China	–0.6826
2011	Eastern Coastal Area in China	1.7871	Hong Kong, Macau and Taiwan	0.4145	Western China	–0.6472
2012	Eastern Coastal Area in China	1.8149	Hong Kong, Macau and Taiwan	0.3454	Western China	–0.5842
2013	Eastern Coastal Area in China	1.8132	Hong Kong, Macau and Taiwan	0.3554	Western China	–0.6385
2014	Eastern Coastal Area in China	1.7843	Hong Kong, Macau and Taiwan	0.4119	Western China	–0.5767
2015	Eastern Coastal Area in China	1.7823	Hong Kong, Macau and Taiwan	0.3870	Western China	–0.4841

	Overall Competitiveness			
	4		5	
Rank	**Region**	**Score**	**Region**	**Score**
2000	Western China	–0.7301	Central China	–1.0898
2001	Western China	–0.7645	Central China	–0.9680
2002	Western China	–0.8054	Central China	–0.9735
2003	Western China	–0.7132	Central China	–1.0387
2004	North-eastern China	–0.7222	Central China	–1.0210
2005	Western China	–0.6914	Central China	–1.0431
2006	Western China	–0.7503	Central China	–0.9400
2007	North-eastern China	–0.7489	Central China	–0.9208
2008	Western China	–0.7666	Central China	–0.9026
2009	Western China	–0.7638	Central China	–0.8502
2010	North-eastern China	–0.7188	Central China	–0.8319
2011	North-eastern China	–0.7161	Central China	–0.8383
2012	North-eastern China	–0.7461	Central China	–0.8300
2013	North-eastern China	–0.7028	Central China	–0.8273
2014	Central China	–0.7728	North-eastern China	–0.8466
2015	Central China	–0.7450	North-eastern China	–0.9403

Note: The results are based on 2000–2015 data, collated and analysed in 2018.
Source: Asia Competitiveness Institute.

since the Eastern Coastal Area claimed the top position in 2002. With the score difference of 0.1238 in 2002 growing to 1.4695 in 2012 before a slight decline to 1.3953 in 2015, the Eastern Coastal Area has gained significant competitive strength over Hong Kong, Macau and Taiwan over the years, with the disparity only ameliorating slightly in recent years.

The scores of Central, Western and North-eastern China, on the other hand, have remained negative over the past decade and half, indicating the regions' below-average performance. North-eastern China and Western China occupied the third and fourth ranks from 2000 to 2013, interchanging positions over the years until 2014 when Western China ranked third and North-eastern China, outperformed by Central China, fell to rank fifth among the five regions.

Another pattern can be discerned from the range of the Overall Competitiveness scores from 2000 to 2015. The difference in scores between the top-ranked and bottom-ranked regions has displayed a general increasing trend over the 15-year observation period, fluctuating without a distinct pattern from 2000 to 2006 before increasing with a clear trend from 2007 to 2015. While the increment has been relatively small, growing from 2.4422 in 2000 to 2.7226 in 2015, it signals a growing disparity in the competitiveness of the five regions of Greater China.

To extend the competitiveness analysis of the five regions over time, a break in the Overall Competitiveness scores is introduced at 2007, during the occurrence of the Global Financial Crisis. The 15-year period is partitioned into two segments, 2000–2006 (Period A) and 2007–2015 (Period B) and the Overall Competitiveness scores of each region over each period are averaged and plotted as points on the graph in Figure 4.4. The graph can be interpreted in the following manner. Regions locatcd above the 45-degree line perform better in the period of 2007–2015 than 2000–2006, whereas regions located below the line perform better in the period of 2000–2006 than 2007–2015.

From the graph, it is observed that the points representing the Eastern Coastal Area, Western China and Central China fall above the 45-degree line. This indicates that the three regions exhibit an improvement in their Overall Competitiveness standings from 2000–2006 to 2007–2015. Of the three regions, the Eastern Coastal Area makes the most significant improvement, evidenced by the large vertical distance between the point representing the region and the line. In contrast, Western and Central China, represented by points situated closer to the 45-degree line, make only marginal progress over the same duration.

The remaining points representing Hong Kong, Macau and Taiwan and North-eastern China are located below the 45-degree line. This indicates a decline in the Overall Competitiveness standings of the two regions. The decline is especially sharp for Hong Kong, Macau and Taiwan given the large vertical distance between the point representing the region and the line. North-eastern China, on the other hand, located closer to the 45-degree line, experiences only a subtle drop over the same duration.

To examine the factors contributing to the observed patterns in the Overall Competitiveness rankings, the five regions and their performance in the four environments of Macroeconomic Stability; Government and Institutional Setting; Financial, Businesses and Manpower Conditions; and Quality of Life and Infrastructure Development are studied in closer detail.

Figure 4.4: ACI 2018 Competitiveness Over Time for Overall Competitiveness

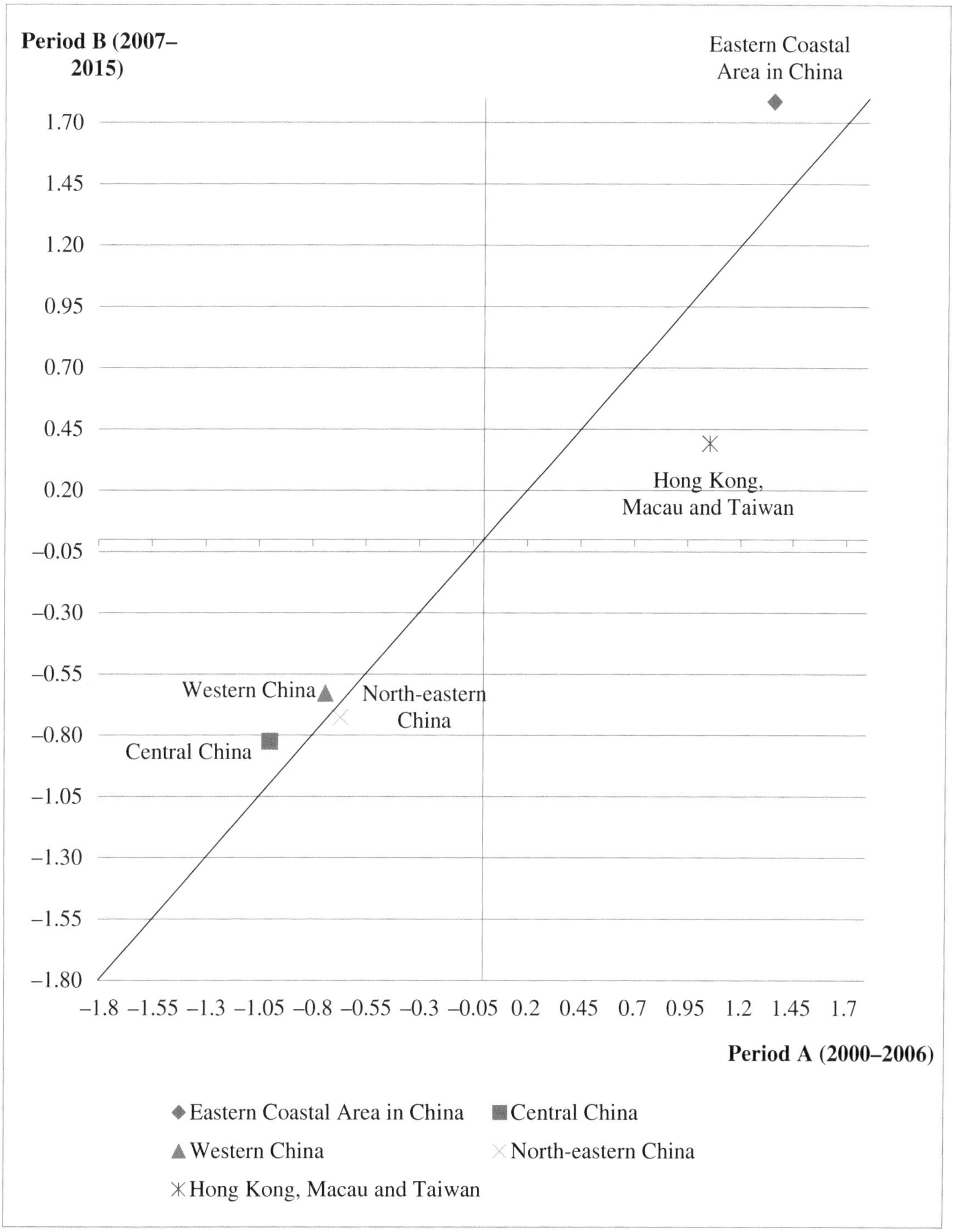

Note: The results are based on 2000–2015 data, collated and analysed in 2018.
Source: Asia Competitiveness Institute.

4.2.2 ACI 2018 Macroeconomic Stability Rankings and Scores

Table 4.3 shows the 2018 rankings and scores of the five regions in the first environment of Macroeconomic Stability. Similar to the Overall Competitiveness scores and rankings, the Eastern Coastal Area in China ranks first with a score of 1.8701. The region is followed by Hong Kong, Macau and Taiwan, Western China, Central China and North-eastern China, which rank second, third, fourth and fifth, respectively.

From the Macroeconomic Stability scores, it can be inferred that the Eastern Coastal Area in China and Hong Kong, Macau and Taiwan perform above the regional average in this environment. This is evident from the positive Macroeconomic Stability scores the two regions attain. Conversely, Western China, Central China and North-eastern China, which record negative scores, perform below average in Macroeconomic Stability.

In terms of the distribution of the Macroeconomic Stability scores, a negative skew is observed, with the mean score exceeding the median score; where the mean is taken as a conceived region with a score of 0 and the median as the region ranked third (Western China with a score of –0.4439). The score differences between the ranked regions are also notable; a large gap in scores can be observed between the Eastern Coastal Area (1.8701), ranked first, and all the other regions which have their scores clustered together. The Eastern Coastal Area and Hong Kong, Macau and Taiwan are separated by a score difference of 1.7603. This difference is substantial when contrasted against the score differences of 0.5537, 0.0855 and 0.4772 among the other regions. These aspects of the Macroeconomic Stability score distribution are congruent with that of the Overall Competitiveness scores, suggesting regional characteristics in Macroeconomic Stability influence the Eastern Coastal Area's lead in Overall Competitiveness.

The Macroeconomic Stability scores and rankings of the five regions can also be represented geographically. Figure 4.5 colour-codes the regions by their performance in the Macroeconomic Stability environment, with better-performing regions in a darker shade and poorer-performing regions in a lighter shade.

Table 4.3: ACI 2018 Macroeconomic Stability Rankings and Scores

Rank	Region	Score
1	Eastern Coastal Area in China	1.8701
2	Hong Kong, Macau and Taiwan	0.1098
3	Western China	–0.4439
4	Central China	–0.5294
5	North-eastern China	–1.0066

Note: The results are based on 2015 data, collated and analysed in 2018.
Source: Asia Competitiveness Institute.

Figure 4.5: ACI 2018 Macroeconomic Stability Ranking Map

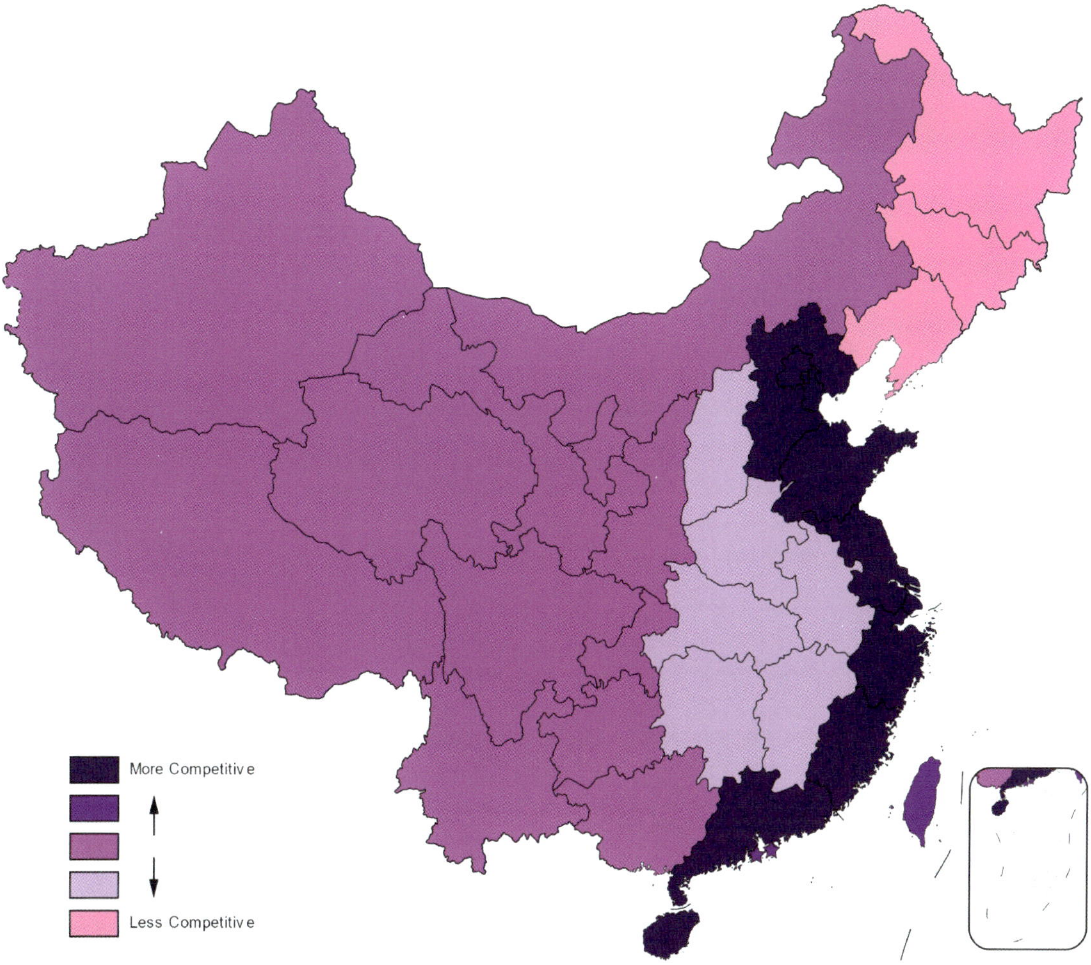

Note: The results are based on 2015 data, collated and analysed in 2018.
Source: Asia Competitiveness Institute.

Table 4.4 presents the Macroeconomic Stability rankings and scores of the five regions from 2000 to 2015. Discerning the patterns and changes in the rankings over the decade and a half, it can be observed that the Eastern Coastal Area and Hong Kong, Macau and Taiwan have consistently ranked first and second, respectively, with the exception of 2011 and 2012 when Western China outperformed Hong Kong, Macau and Taiwan to take the second place. The Eastern Coastal Area's undefeated lead in this environment has been a result of a growing divergence of the region's Macroeconomic Stability score from the average score of 0; the region's score has seen an improvement from 1.6917 in 2000 to 1.8701 in 2015, representative of the Eastern Coastal Area's growing edge over the other regions. In contrast, although Hong Kong, Macau and Taiwan has retained its position in second place, it has seen a steep decline in its score over the same period, from 0.5804 in 2000 to 0.1098 in 2015. These trends have contributed to a widening disparity in Macroeconomic Stability scores between the top two ranked regions over the past decade and half.

Over the same period, the Macroeconomic Stability scores of Western, Central and Northeastern China have remained negative, indicating the regions' below-average performance.

Table 4.4: ACI 2018 Macroeconomic Stability Rankings and Scores: Evolution Over Time

Macroeconomic Stability						
	1		2		3	
Rank	**Region**	**Score**	**Region**	**Score**	**Region**	**Score**
2000	Eastern Coastal Area in China	1.6917	Hong Kong, Macau and Taiwan	0.5804	Western China	–0.6259
2001	Eastern Coastal Area in China	1.7035	Hong Kong, Macau and Taiwan	0.5719	Central China	–0.5934
2002	Eastern Coastal Area in China	1.8629	Hong Kong, Macau and Taiwan	0.2254	North-eastern China	–0.5861
2003	Eastern Coastal Area in China	1.8210	Hong Kong, Macau and Taiwan	0.3287	Western China	–0.6001
2004	Eastern Coastal Area in China	1.8228	Hong Kong, Macau and Taiwan	0.3303	Western China	–0.5962
2005	Eastern Coastal Area in China	1.9328	Hong Kong, Macau and Taiwan	–0.0837	North-eastern China	–0.4595
2006	Eastern Coastal Area in China	1.9439	Hong Kong, Macau and Taiwan	–0.0318	Central China	–0.6140
2007	Eastern Coastal Area in China	1.9317	Hong Kong, Macau and Taiwan	0.0188	North-eastern China	–0.6408
2008	Eastern Coastal Area in China	1.9432	Hong Kong, Macau and Taiwan	–0.0727	North-eastern China	–0.4407
2009	Eastern Coastal Area in China	1.9860	Hong Kong, Macau and Taiwan	–0.2788	Central China	–0.5146
2010	Eastern Coastal Area in China	1.9826	Hong Kong, Macau and Taiwan	–0.2585	Western China	–0.5205
2011	Eastern Coastal Area in China	1.9941	Western China	–0.3924	Hong Kong, Macau and Taiwan	–0.4594
2012	Eastern Coastal Area in China	1.9858	Western China	–0.3499	Central China	–0.4072
2013	Eastern Coastal Area in China	1.9761	Hong Kong, Macau and Taiwan	–0.2148	Western China	–0.5095
2014	Eastern Coastal Area in China	1.9590	Hong Kong, Macau and Taiwan	–0.2834	Western China	–0.3299
2015	Eastern Coastal Area in China	1.8701	Hong Kong, Macau and Taiwan	0.1098	Western China	–0.4439

Macroeconomic Stability				
	4		5	
Rank	**Region**	**Score**	**Region**	**Score**
2000	North-eastern China	–0.6578	Central China	–0.9884
2001	Western China	–0.7934	North-eastern China	–0.8885
2002	Western China	–0.6923	Central China	–0.8099
2003	North-eastern China	–0.6872	Central China	–0.8624
2004	North-eastern China	–0.7587	Central China	–0.7982
2005	Western China	–0.4942	Central China	–0.8954
2006	North-eastern China	–0.6333	Western China	–0.6649
2007	Central China	–0.6485	Western China	–0.6611
2008	Western China	–0.6798	Central China	–0.7499
2009	Western China	–0.5654	North-eastern China	–0.6273
2010	Central China	–0.5421	North-eastern China	–0.6615
2011	Central China	–0.5165	North-eastern China	–0.6258
2012	Hong Kong, Macau and Taiwan	–0.5330	North-eastern China	–0.6958
2013	Central China	–0.5721	North-eastern China	–0.6798
2014	Central China	–0.4887	North-eastern China	–0.8569
2015	Central China	–0.5294	North-eastern China	–1.0066

Note: The results are based on 2000–2015 data, collated and analysed in 2018.
Source: Asia Competitiveness Institute.

These three regions have occupied the third, fourth and fifth positions for the past decade and half (with the exception of 2011 and 2012), and interchange positions without a discernible pattern. The ranking of the three regions, however, has stabilised since 2013, with Western, Central and North-eastern China occupying the third, fourth and fifth positions in that order.

Another observation can be discerned from the range of the Macroeconomic Stability scores from 2000 to 2015. The difference in scores between the top-ranked and bottom-ranked regions has shown a general increasing trend over the 15-year period, increasing from 2.6801 in 2000 to 2.8767 in 2015. Though relatively small, this increment is indicative of a growing disparity among the five regions of Greater China in the Macroeconomic Stability environment. This observation is aligned with that gleaned from the Overall Competitiveness scores.

The Macroeconomic Stability environment can be further deconstructed into the sub-environments of Regional Economic Vibrancy, Openness to Trade and Services and Attractiveness to Foreign Investors. To examine the patterns in the Macroeconomic Stability scores more closely, the five regions' performance in each of the three sub-environments is studied. This information is summarised in Figure 4.6.

From the sub-environment scores, it is evident that the Eastern Coastal Area performs exceedingly well, attaining the highest score among the five regions in every sub-environment. This is consistent with the region's significant lead over the other regions in its Macroeconomic Stability score. On the contrary, despite ranking second and attaining a positive Macroeconomic Stability score, Hong Kong, Macau and Taiwan's performance in the sub-environment of Regional Economic Vibrancy leaves much to be desired. While the region does reasonably well in the

Figure 4.6: ACI 2018 Sub-Environment Scores of Macroeconomic Stability

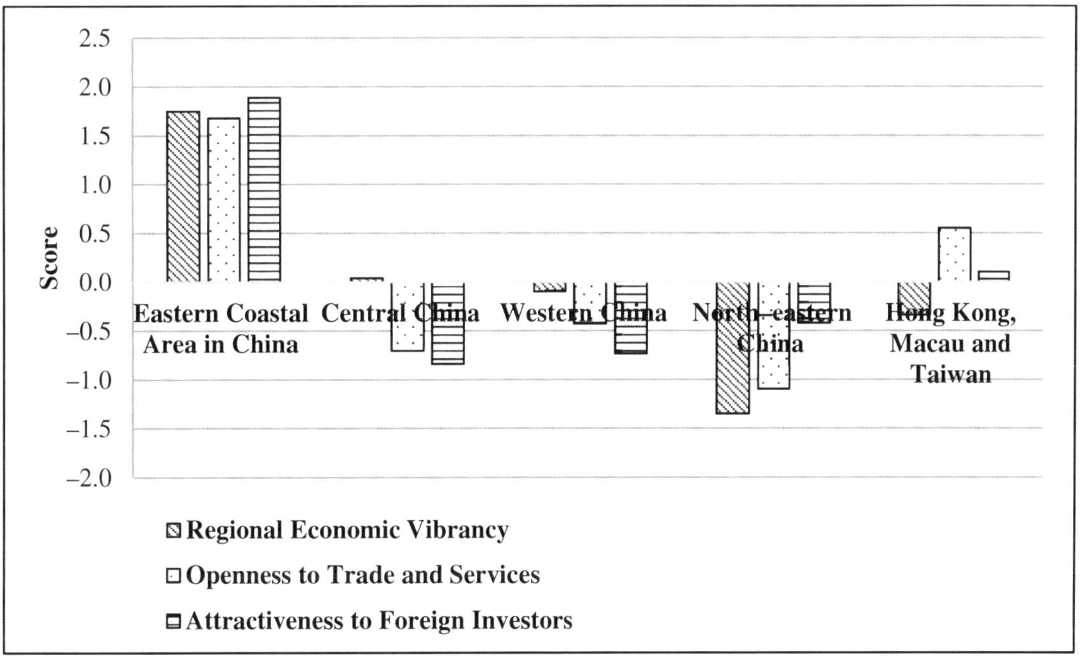

Note: The results are based on 2015 data, collated and analysed in 2018.
Source: Asia Competitiveness Institute.

sub-environments of Openness to Trade and Services and Attractiveness to Foreign Investors, coming in second to the Eastern Coastal Area in these sub-environments, it attains a negative score in Regional Economic Vibrancy. Evident from Figure 4.6, this score is lower than that attained by the lower ranked Central and Western China. The remaining regions of Western, Central and North-eastern China attain negative scores and perform below the average in all three sub-environments. This observation is unsurprising given the three regions' negative Macroeconomic Stability scores.

Further, while the regions vary in their performance in the Macroeconomic Stability environment, it is worth noting that each region exhibits relative strengths and weaknesses in their sub-environment scores. This information provides a useful indication of the areas each region can focus its efforts on to improve their standings in the Macroeconomic Stability environment. In this respect, Central and Western China should concentrate efforts on improving the sub-environment of Attractiveness to Foreign Investors while North-eastern China and Hong Kong, Macau and Taiwan should do the same in the sub-environment of Regional Economic Vibrancy.

To study the intertemporal shifts in the regions' performance in the Macroeconomic Stability sub-environments, a break in the sub-environment scores is introduced at 2007. For each sub-environment, the 15-year observation period is partitioned into two segments, 2000–2006 (Period A) and 2007–2015 (Period B) and the scores of each region over each period are averaged and plotted in a graph. The graph can be interpreted in the following manner. Regions above the 45-degree line perform better in the sub-environment in the period are of 2007–2015 than 2000–2006, whereas regions below the line perform better in the sub-environment in the period of 2000–2006 than 2007–2015.

Figure 4.7 summarises the intertemporal shifts in each region's performance in the sub-environment of Regional Economic Vibrancy. In the graph, the points representing the Eastern Coastal Area of China, Western China and North-eastern China fall close to the 45-degree line. From this, it can be inferred that the Regional Economic Vibrancy scores of these three regions remained nearly constant over the two time periods, suggesting only marginal changes, if any, in the regions' relative standings in the sub-environment. A key distinction between the three regions, however, is their location on the 45-degree line. The Eastern Coastal Area, situated close to the top, is steeply more competitive than the other regions in the sub-environment of Regional Economic Vibrancy. Western China, situated close to the graph's origin, comes close to the average performance of the five regions in both time periods. Finally, North-eastern China, situated close to the bottom, falls behind the other regions in its performance in this sub-environment by a large gap.

The points representing Central China and Hong Kong, Macau and Taiwan, on the other hand, do not coincide with the 45-degree line. Central China, located above the 45-degree line, displays an improvement in its standing in the Regional Economic Vibrancy sub-environment over the two periods. Hong Kong, Macau and Taiwan, in contrast, is situated below the line, reflecting a decline in its competitive strength in this sub-environment.

Figure 4.7: ACI 2018 Competitiveness Over Time for Regional Economic Vibrancy

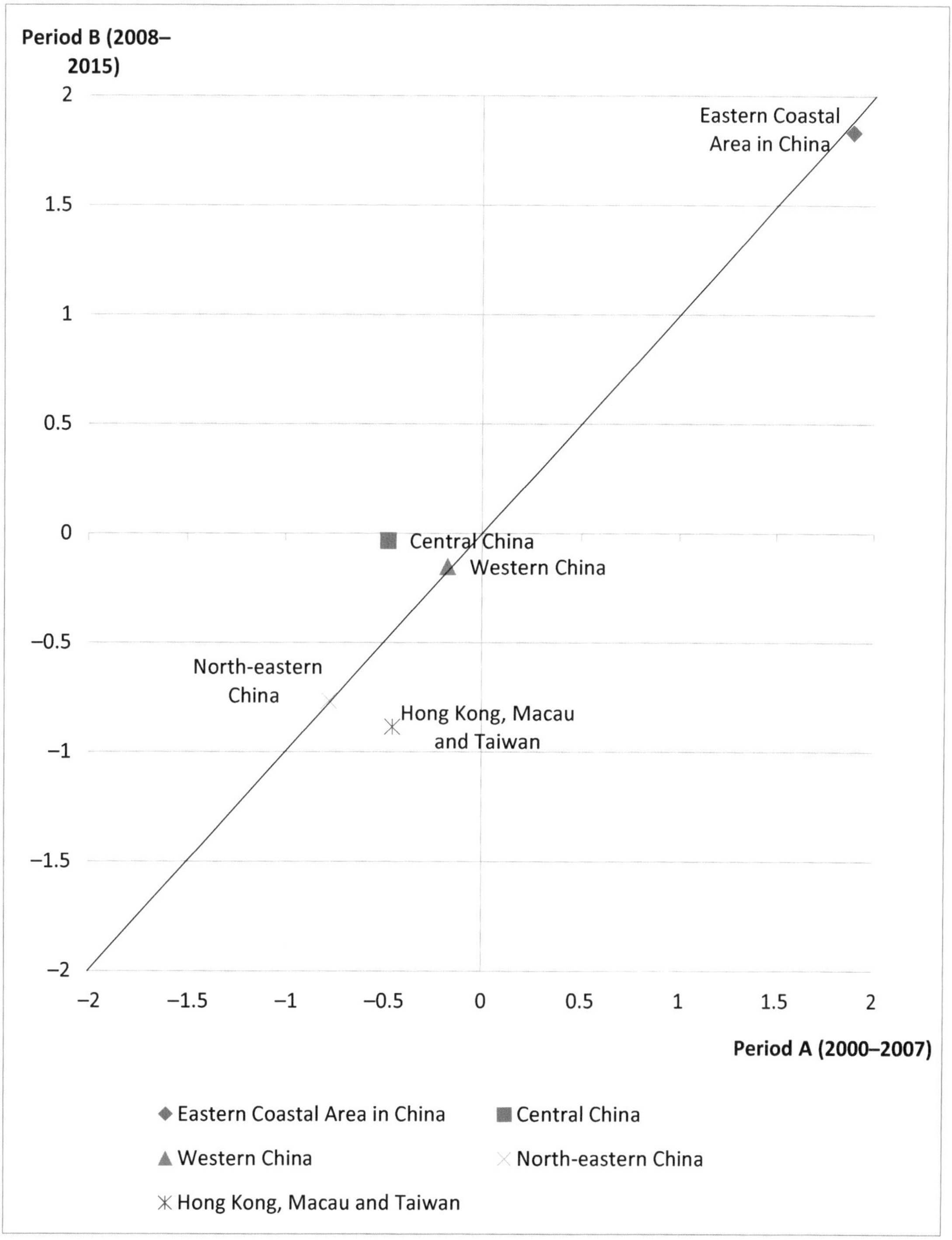

Note: The results are based on 2000–2015 data, collated and analysed in 2018.
Source: Asia Competitiveness Institute.

Figure 4.8: ACI 2018 Competitiveness Over Time for Openness to Trade and Services

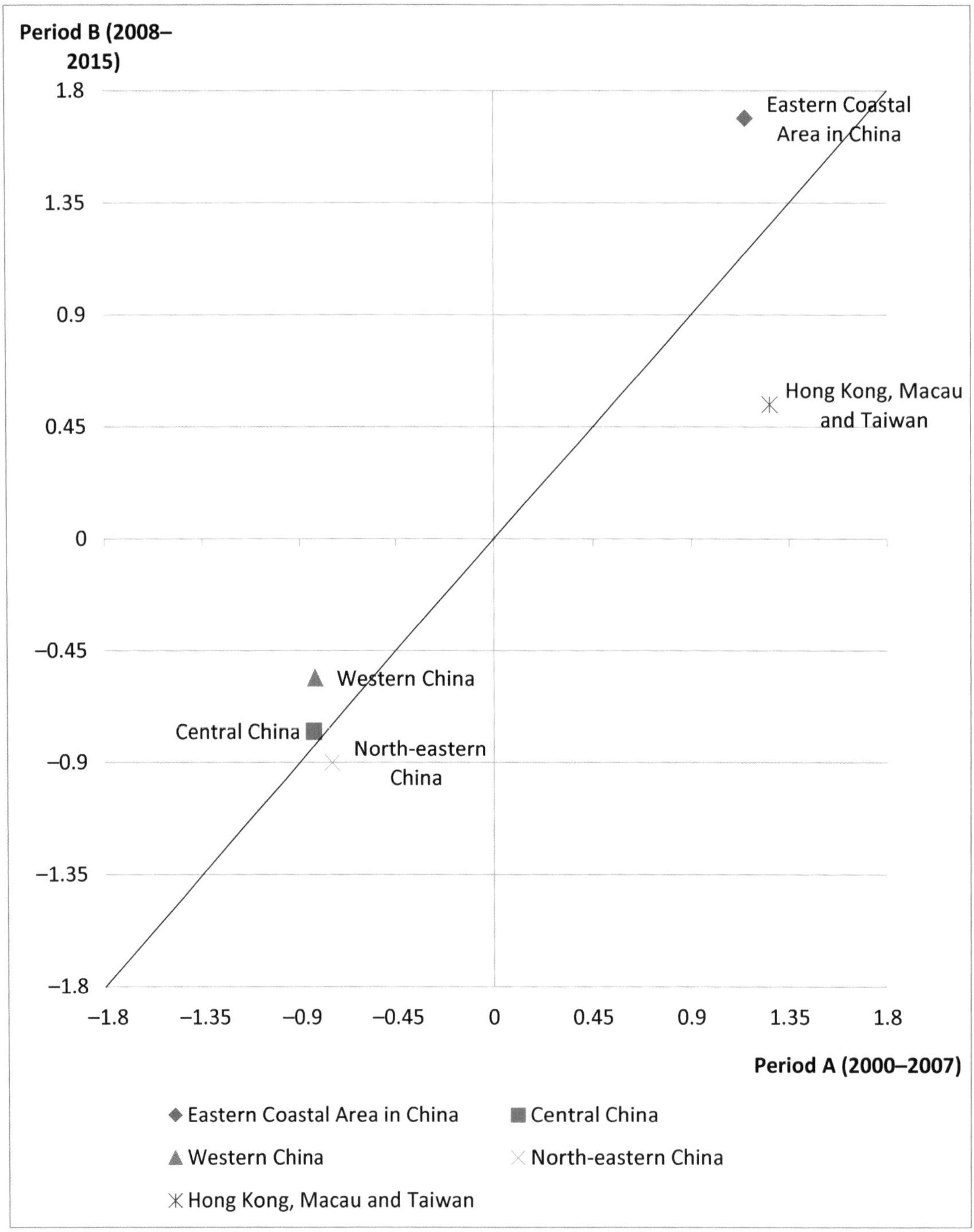

Note: The results are based on 2000–2015 data, collated and analysed in 2018.
Source: Asia Competitiveness Institute.

Figure 4.8 captures the intertemporal shifts in each region's performance in the sub-environment of Openness to Trade and Services. In the graph, the points representing the Eastern Coastal Area, Western China and Central China are above the 45-degree line. This indicates an improvement in the regions' standings in the Openness to Trade and Services sub-environment. Of the three regions, the Eastern Coastal Area makes the largest progress. This can be seen from the large vertical distance between the point representing the region and the 45-degree line. Western China and Central China, by contrast, are situated close to the 45-degree line, implying the two regions make only subtle improvements.

The other points representing Hong Kong, Macau and Taiwan and North-eastern China are located below the 45-degree line, indicating a drop in the regions' standings in the Openness to Trade and Services sub-environment. The decline is especially sharp for Hong Kong, Macau and Taiwan, as seen from the significant vertical distance separating the point representing the region and the line. North-eastern China, in contrast, is located closer to the 45-degree line, suggesting that the region experiences only a marginal decline in its performance in the sub-environment.

Figure 4.9 reflects the intertemporal shifts in the regions' performance in the sub-environment of Attractiveness to Foreign Investors. In the graph, the point representing North-eastern China falls close to the 45-degree line. It can hence be gathered that the region's Attractiveness to Foreign Investors score has remained nearly constant over the two time periods, suggesting only subtle changes, if any, in its relative standing in this sub-environment.

The points representing the Eastern Coastal Area, Western China and Central China are above the 45-degree line, indicating that these regions show an improvement in their Attractiveness to Foreign Investors score over the identified break. The point representing Hong Kong, Macau and Taiwan, on the other hand, is below the 45-degree line, indicating a decline in the region's standing in the sub-environment. These points, however, are all close to the 45-degree line, suggesting that any shifts in the performance of the five regions in this sub-environment over the identified break are marginal.

The patterns identified under the Macroeconomic Stability environment and its sub-environments are generally consistent with the broad trends and movements in the Overall Competitiveness scores, reasserting the environment as an informative indicator of Overall Competitiveness.

4.2.3 ACI 2018 Government and Institutional Setting Rankings and Scores

Table 4.5 shows the 2018 rankings and scores of the five regions in the second environment of Government and Institutional Setting. Similar to the Overall Competitiveness scores and rankings, the Eastern Coastal Area in China ranks first with a score of 1.8970. The region is followed by Hong Kong, Macau and Taiwan, Western China, Central China and North-eastern China, which rank second, third, fourth and fifth, respectively.

From the Government and Institutional Setting scores, it can be inferred that the Eastern Coastal Area in China performs above the average of the five regions in the environment. This is evident from the positive Government and Institutional Setting score the region attains. On the other hand, Hong Kong, Macau and Taiwan, Western China, Central China, and North-eastern China, which record negative scores, perform below average in the Government and Institutional Setting environment.

Figure 4.9: ACI 2018 Competitiveness Over Time for Attractiveness to Foreign Investors

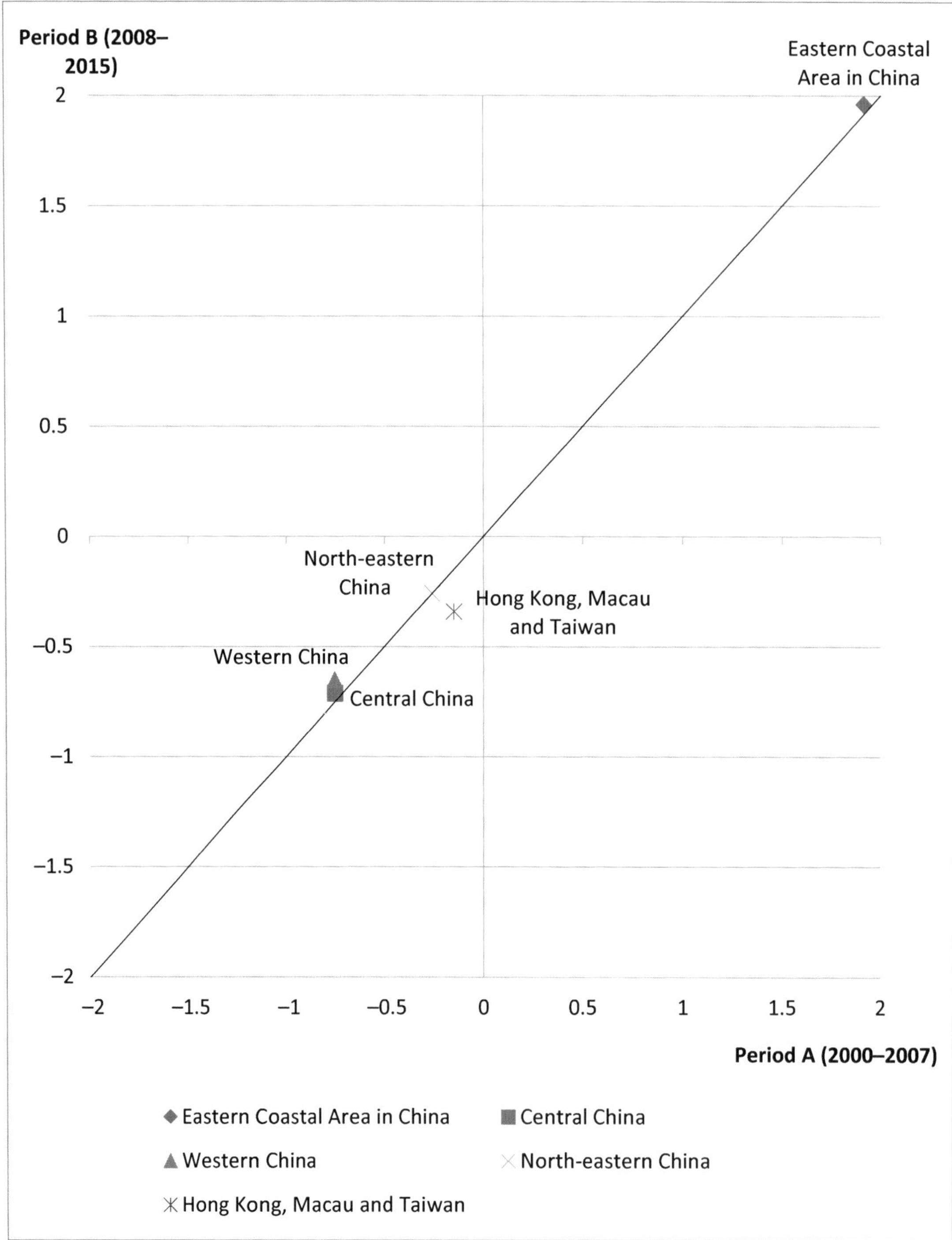

Note: The results are based on 2015 data, collated and analysed in 2018.
Source: Asia Competitiveness Institute.

Table 4.5: ACI 2018 Government and Institutional Setting Rankings and Scores

Rank	Region	Score
1	Eastern Coastal Area in China	1.8970
2	Hong Kong, Macau and Taiwan	–0.0379
3	Western China	–0.3888
4	Central China	–0.4453
5	North-eastern China	–1.0250

Note: The results are based on 2015 data, collated and analysed in 2018.
Source: Asia Competitiveness Institute.

In terms of the distribution of the Government and Institutional Setting scores, a negative skew is observed, with a mean score exceeding the median score, where the mean is taken as a conceived region with a score of 0 and the median as the region ranked third (Western China with a score of –0.3888). The score differences between the regions are also notable; there is a large gap in the scores of the Eastern Coastal Area (1.8970), ranked first, and all the other regions which have their scores clustered together. The Eastern Coastal Area and Hong Kong, Macau and Taiwan are separated by a score difference of 1.9349. This difference is substantial when contrasted against the score differences of 0.3509, 0.0565 and 0.5797 between the other regions. These aspects of the Government and Institutional Setting score distribution are consistent with that observed in the Overall Competitiveness scores, suggesting that the regional characteristics in this environment contribute to the Eastern Coastal Area's lead in Overall Competitiveness.

The Government and Institutional Setting scores and rankings of the five regions can also be visualised geographically. Figure 4.10 colour-codes the regions by their performance in the Government and Institutional Setting environment, with better performing regions in a darker shade and poorer performing regions in a lighter shade.

Table 4.6 presents the Government and Institutional Setting scores and rankings of the five regions from 2000 to 2015. Distilling the patterns and changes in the rankings over the decade and half, it can be observed that the Eastern Coastal Area has outperformed Hong Kong, Macau and Taiwan to rank first since 2001, with its score increasing markedly from 1.0356 in 2000 to 1.8970 in 2015, only experiencing slight dips in 2004 and 2014. In contrast, over the same period, Hong Kong, Macau and Taiwan, having fallen to rank second, has seen its score decline from 1.3224 in 2000 to –0.0379 in 2015, with only minor improvements in 2004 and 2014. As a result of these trends, the gap in scores between the top two ranked regions has widened considerably since the Eastern Coastal Area claimed the top position in 2001. With a growing difference of 0.2868 in 2000 to 1.9349 in 2015, the Eastern Coastal Area has gained significant strength in its performance in the Government and Institutional Setting environment over Hong Kong, Macau and Taiwan over the years.

The Government and Institutional Setting scores of Central, Western and North-eastern China, on the other hand, have remained negative over the same period, indicative of their below-average

Figure 4.10: ACI 2018 Government and Institutional Setting Ranking Map

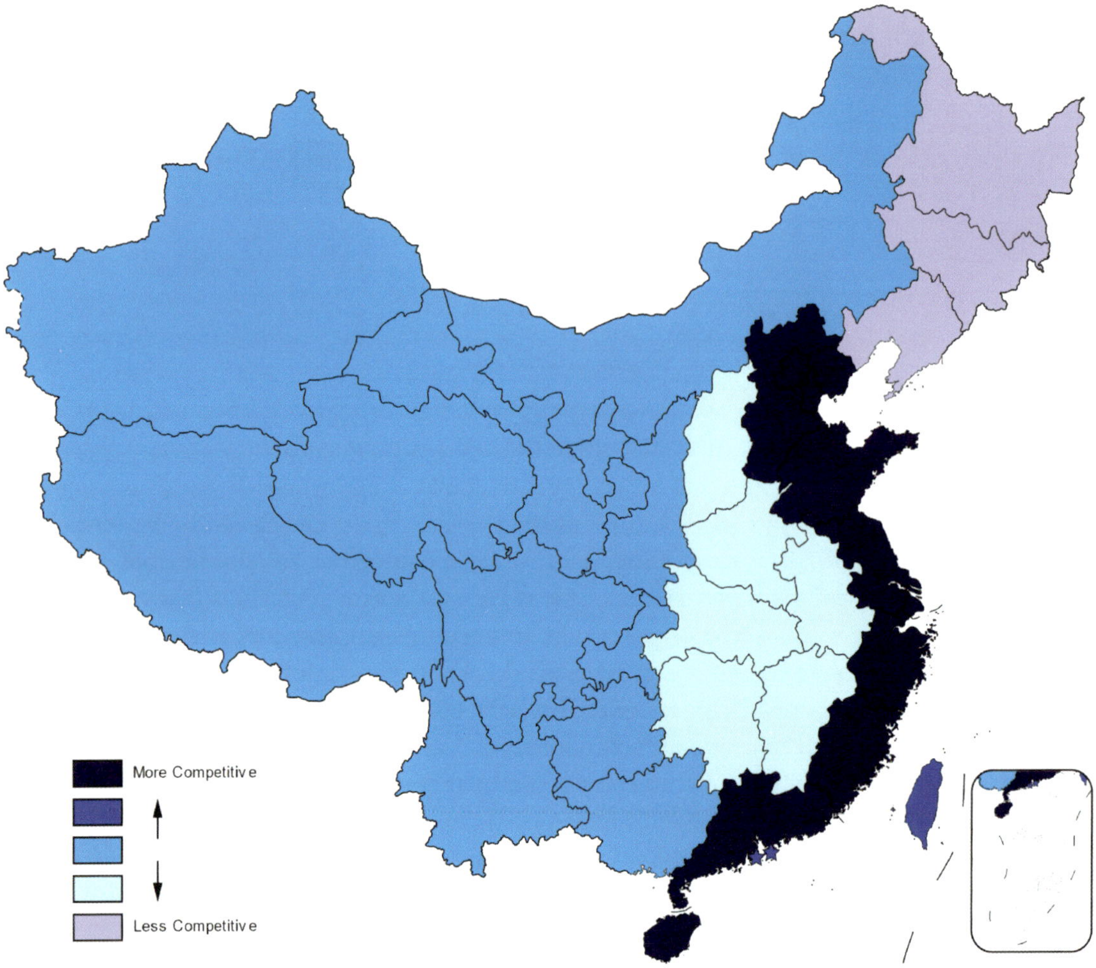

Note: The results are based on 2015 data, collated and analysed in 2018.
Source: Asia Competitiveness Institute.

performance in the environment. North-eastern, China has experienced a significant decline in its performance over the decade and half, falling from the third position in 2000 and 2002 to the fourth position in 2001 and 2003–2006 and eventually remaining at the last position from 2007. Western China, on the other hand, has shown its strength in the environment, surpassing North-eastern China and maintaining its third position since 2003. Meanwhile, Central China has seen an improvement in recent years, taking over North-eastern China's fourth position since 2007.

A distinct increasing trend in the range of the Government and Institutional Setting scores from 2000 to 2015 is also observed. The difference in scores between the top-ranked and bottom-ranked regions has grown from 2.5673 in 2000 to 2.9220 in 2015, signifying a growing disparity in Government and Institutional Setting scores among the five regions of Greater China. This observation is congruent with that gleaned from the Overall Competitiveness scores.

The Government and Institutional Setting environment can be further broken down into the two sub-environments of Government Policies and Fiscal Sustainability and Institutions, Governance and Leadership. To examine the patterns in the Government and Institutional Setting

Table 4.6: ACI 2018 Government and Institutional Setting Rankings and Scores: Evolution Over Time

Government and Institutional Setting						
	1		2		3	
Rank	Region	Score	Region	Score	Region	Score
2000	Hong Kong, Macau and Taiwan	1.3224	Eastern Coastal Area in China	1.0356	North-eastern China	–0.4882
2001	Eastern Coastal Area in China	1.3332	Hong Kong, Macau and Taiwan	1.0517	Western China	–0.5982
2002	Eastern Coastal Area in China	1.3861	Hong Kong, Macau and Taiwan	1.0048	North-eastern China	–0.5596
2003	Eastern Coastal Area in China	1.4155	Hong Kong, Macau and Taiwan	0.9873	Western China	–0.6624
2004	Eastern Coastal Area in China	1.3561	Hong Kong, Macau and Taiwan	1.0577	Western China	–0.5734
2005	Eastern Coastal Area in China	1.3976	Hong Kong, Macau and Taiwan	1.0177	Western China	–0.5983
2006	Eastern Coastal Area in China	1.4403	Hong Kong, Macau and Taiwan	0.9632	Western China	–0.5827
2007	Eastern Coastal Area in China	1.5093	Hong Kong, Macau and Taiwan	0.8765	Western China	–0.6036
2008	Eastern Coastal Area in China	1.5853	Hong Kong, Macau and Taiwan	0.7738	Western China	–0.6622
2009	Eastern Coastal Area in China	1.6837	Hong Kong, Macau and Taiwan	0.6044	Western China	–0.6088
2010	Eastern Coastal Area in China	1.6995	Hong Kong, Macau and Taiwan	0.5579	Western China	–0.5641
2011	Eastern Coastal Area in China	1.7251	Hong Kong, Macau and Taiwan	0.5124	Western China	–0.5486
2012	Eastern Coastal Area in China	1.7498	Hong Kong, Macau and Taiwan	0.4451	Western China	–0.4964
2013	Eastern Coastal Area in China	1.8017	Hong Kong, Macau and Taiwan	0.3058	Western China	–0.4656
2014	Eastern Coastal Area in China	1.7057	Hong Kong, Macau and Taiwan	0.4865	Western China	–0.4445
2015	Eastern Coastal Area in China	1.8970	Hong Kong, Macau and Taiwan	–0.0379	Western China	–0.3888

Government and Institutional Setting				
	4		5	
Rank	Region	Score	Region	Score
2000	Western China	–0.6249	Central China	–1.2449
2001	North-eastern China	–0.6085	Central China	–1.1783
2002	Western China	–0.7170	Central China	–1.1143
2003	North-eastern China	–0.6857	Central China	–1.0548
2004	North-eastern China	–0.8209	Central China	–1.0196
2005	North-eastern China	–0.8738	Central China	–0.9432
2006	North-eastern China	–0.8925	Central China	–0.9283
2007	Central China	–0.8652	North-eastern China	–0.9171
2008	Central China	–0.7787	North-eastern China	–0.9183
2009	Central China	–0.7416	North-eastern China	–0.9377
2010	Central China	–0.6908	North-eastern China	–1.0026
2011	Central China	–0.7131	North-eastern China	–0.9757
2012	Central China	–0.6892	North-eastern China	–1.0093
2013	Central China	–0.6023	North-eastern China	–1.0396
2014	Central China	–0.6196	North-eastern China	–1.1281
2015	Central China	–0.4453	North-eastern China	–1.0250

Note: The results are based on 2000–2015 data, collated and analysed in 2018.
Source: Asia Competitiveness Institute.

Figure 4.11: ACI 2018 Sub-Environment Scores of Government and Institutional Setting

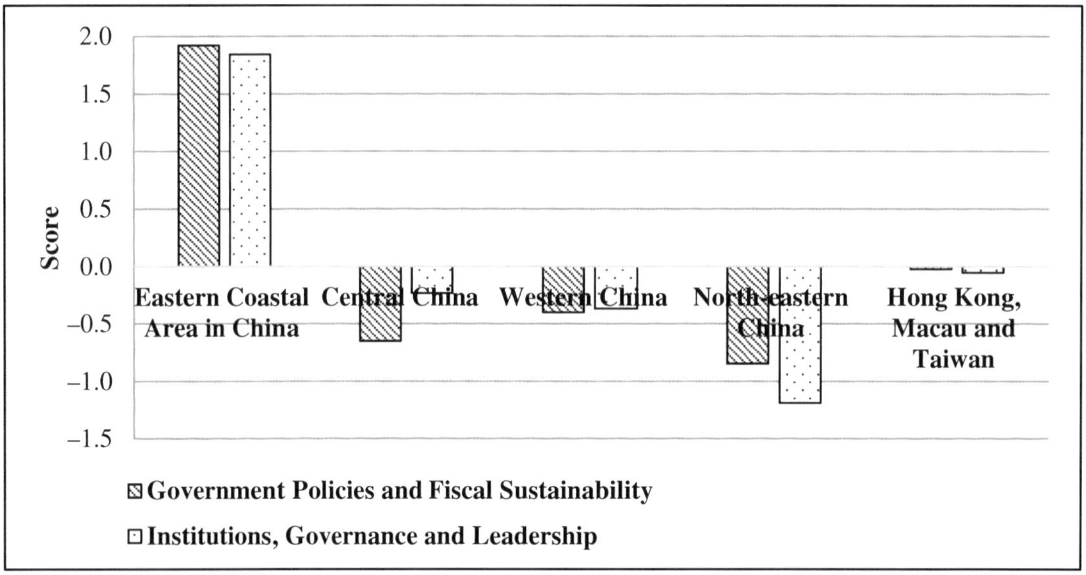

Note: The results are based on 2015 data, collated and analysed in 2018.
Source: Asia Competitiveness Institute.

scores in greater detail, the five regions' performance in each of the two sub-environments is analysed. This information is represented in Figure 4.11.

From the sub-environment scores, it is evident that the Eastern Coastal Area performs exceptionally well, holding the highest score among the five regions in both sub-environments. This is consistent with the region's lead in its Government and Institutional Setting score. The Eastern Coastal Area is also the only region which attains a positive score in the sub-environments. The remaining regions possess negative scores in the sub-environments to varying extents in a manner consistent with the overall Government and Institutional Setting rankings.

Further, while the regions attain different Government and Institutional Setting scores, each region exhibits relative strengths and weaknesses in their sub-environment scores. This provides a useful directive of the areas each region can focus on to improve their standings in the environment. In this light, Central and Western China should concentrate efforts on improving the sub-environment of Government Policies and Fiscal Sustainability while North-eastern China and Hong Kong, Macau and Taiwan should do the same in the sub-environment of Institutions, Governance and Leadership.

To study the intertemporal shifts in the regions' performance in the Government and Institutional Setting sub-environments, a break in the sub-environment scores is introduced at 2007. The procedure follows that applied to the sub-environments under Macroeconomic Stability and can be interpreted in a similar manner.

Figure 4.12 captures the temporal dynamics in each region's performance in the sub-environment of Government Policies and Fiscal Sustainability. In the graph, the points representing the Eastern Coastal Area, Western China, North-eastern China and Central China are above the

Figure 4.12: ACI 2018 Competitiveness Over Time for Government Policies and Fiscal Sustainability

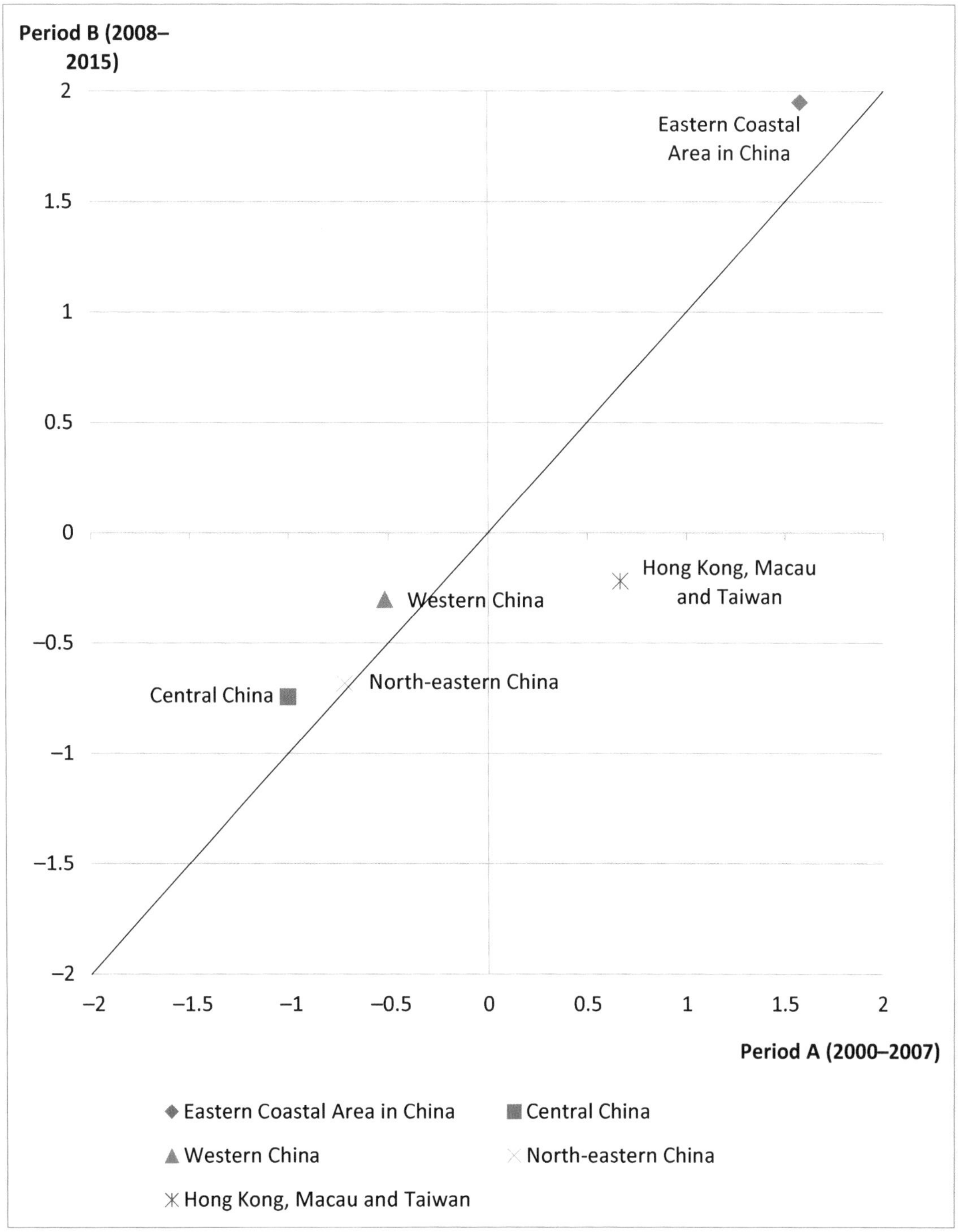

Note: The results are based on 2000–2015 data, collated and analysed in 2018.
Source: Asia Competitiveness Institute.

45-degree line. From this, it can be inferred that the Government Policies and Fiscal Sustainability scores of these four regions have shown an improvement over the break. Of the four regions, the Eastern Coastal Area and Central China show the largest progress, with a relatively large vertical distance separating the points representing these regions and the 45-degree line.

In contrast, the point corresponding to Hong Kong, Macau and Taiwan falls below the 45-degree line. The large distance of the region from the line reflects a sharp decline in Hong Kong, Macau and Taiwan's competitiveness in the sub-environment of Government Policies and Fiscal Sustainability over the two time periods.

Figure 4.13 shows the changes in the scores of the five regions in the sub-environment of Institutions, Governance and Leadership over the two time periods. The Eastern Coastal Area in China, Western China and Central China show improvements in their scores in the sub-environment, with the points corresponding to these regions located above the 45-degree line. From the distance between the points and the line, it can be drawn that Central China displayed the largest progress, followed by the Eastern Coastal Area and Western China.

The points corresponding to Hong Kong, Macau and Taiwan and North-eastern China, on the other hand, are situated below the 45-degree line, indicating a decline in the regions' relative performance in the sub-environment of Institutions, Governance and Leadership. Further, both points are located far from the line, suggesting that the decline in the two regions' performance in the sub-environment has been drastic.

The patterns identified under the environment of Government and Institutional Setting and its sub-environments are congruent with the broad trends and movements in the Overall Competitiveness scores, reasserting the environment as a useful indicator of Overall Competitiveness.

4.2.4 ACI 2018 Financial, Businesses and Manpower Conditions Rankings and Scores

Table 4.7 presents the 2018 rankings and scores of the five regions in the third environment of Financial, Businesses and Manpower Conditions. Hong Kong, Macau and Taiwan ranks first in this environment with a score of 1.2702. The region is followed by the Eastern Coastal Area in China, Western China, Central China and North-eastern China, which rank second, third, fourth and fifth, respectively.

From the Financial, Businesses and Manpower Conditions scores, it can be inferred that Hong Kong, Macau and Taiwan and the Eastern Coastal Area in China perform above the average of the five regions in the environment. This is evident from the positive Financial, Businesses and Manpower Conditions scores the two regions attain. In contrast, Western China, Central China and North-eastern China, which record negative scores in the environment, perform below average.

In terms of the distribution of the Financial, Businesses and Manpower Conditions scores, a negative skew is observed, with the mean score exceeding the median score, where the mean is taken as a conceived region with a score of 0 and the median as the region ranked third (Western China with a score of –0.6491). The score differences between the ranked regions are also notable. A large gap in scores can be observed between the Eastern Coastal Area (1.1477), ranked second, and Western China (–0.6491), ranked third. The two regions are separated by a score

Figure 4.13: ACI 2018 Competitiveness Over Time for Institutions, Governance and Leadership

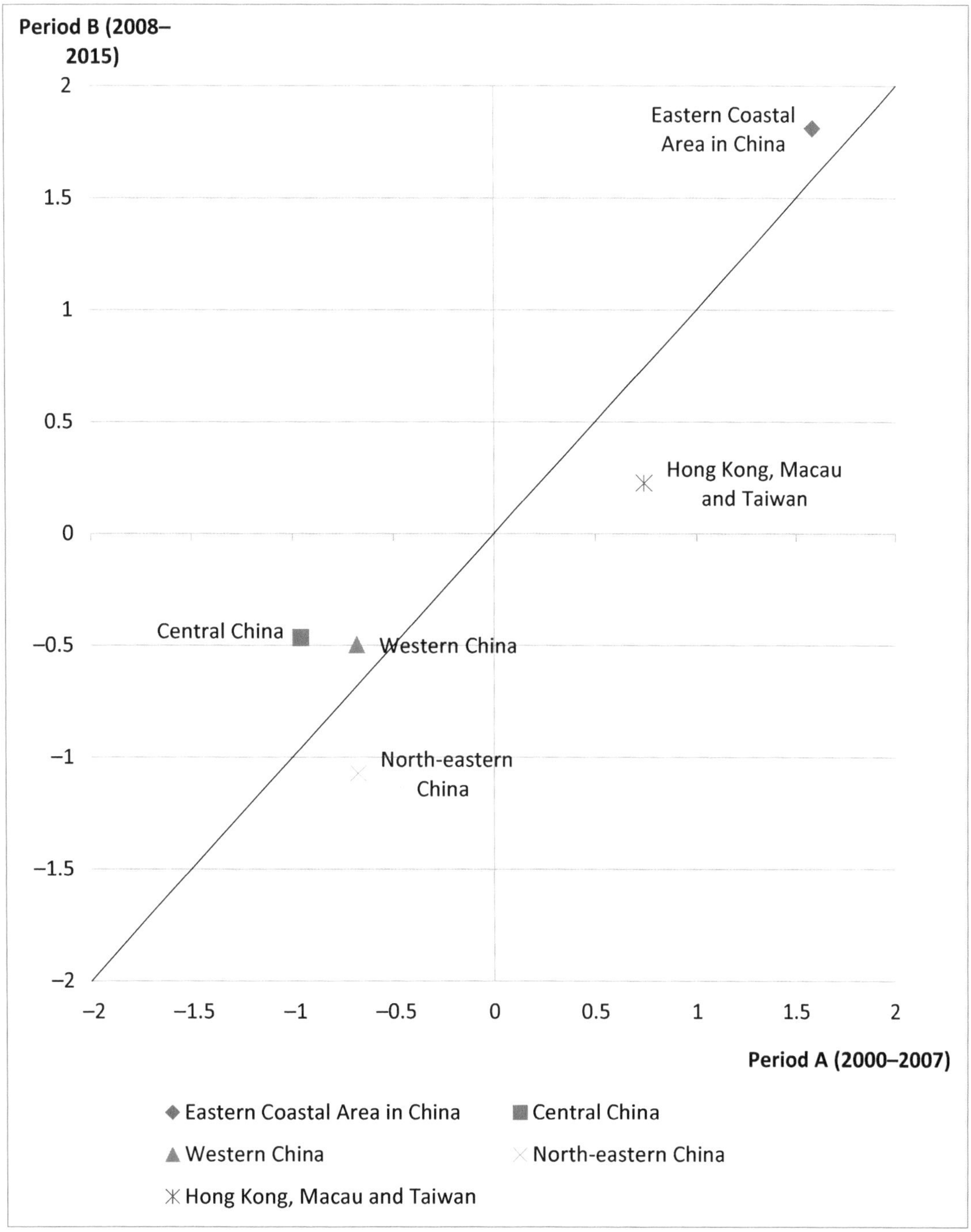

Note: The results are based on 2000–2015 data, collated and analysed in 2018.
Source: Asia Competitiveness Institute.

Table 4.7: ACI 2018 Financial, Businesses and Manpower Conditions Rankings and Scores

Rank	Region	Score
1	Hong Kong, Macau and Taiwan	1.2702
2	Eastern Coastal Area in China	1.1477
3	Western China	–0.6491
4	Central China	–0.6801
5	North-eastern China	–1.0888

Note: The results are based on 2015 data, collated and analysed in 2018.
Source: Asia Competitiveness Institute.

difference of 1.7968; this is substantial when contrasted against the score differences between Hong Kong, Macau and Taiwan and the Eastern Coastal Area (0.1225), Western China and Central China (0.031), and Central China and North-eastern China (0.4087). This indicates that the two regions of Hong Kong, Macau and Taiwan and the Eastern Coastal Area outperform the three regions of Western China, Central China and North-eastern China in the environment of Financial, Businesses and Manpower Conditions by a large extent.

The Financial, Businesses and Manpower Conditions scores and rankings of the five regions can also be represented geographically. Figure 4.14 colour-codes the regions by their performance in the Financial, Businesses and Manpower Conditions environment, with better performing regions in a darker shade and poorer performing regions in a lighter shade.

Table 4.8 presents the Financial, Businesses and Manpower Conditions rankings and scores of the five regions from 2000 to 2015. Discerning the patterns and changes in the rankings over the decade and half, it can be observed that Hong Kong, Macau and Taiwan and the Eastern Coastal Area have consistently ranked first and second, respectively, with the exception of 2014 when the Eastern Coastal Area outperformed Hong Kong, Macau and Taiwan to take the first place. Hong Kong, Macau and Taiwan's score in the Financial, Businesses and Manpower Conditions environment has experienced a decline over the decade and half, falling from 1.8409 in 2000 to 1.2702 in 2015. On the other hand, the Eastern Coastal Area has experienced a drastic improvement, with its score in the environment increasing from 0.2902 in 2000 to 1.1477 in 2015. As a result of these trends, the score gap between the top two ranked regions has narrowed significantly over the decade and half, with the difference in scores shrinking from 1.5507 in 2000 to 0.1225 in 2015. This implies that the disparity in the performance in the environment of Financial, Businesses and Manpower Conditions between Hong Kong, Macau and Taiwan and the Eastern Coastal Area has reduced over the years.

Over the same period, the Financial, Businesses and Manpower Conditions scores of Western, Central and North-eastern China have remained negative, indicating the regions' below-average performance in the environment. Western and Central China have occupied the third and fourth positions for the past decade and half, interchanging positions without a discernible pattern. North-eastern China, on the other hand, has occupied the fifth position, with little progress in its Financial, Businesses and Manpower Conditions scores over the same period.

Another observation can be discerned from the range of the Financial, Businesses and Manpower Conditions scores from 2000 to 2015. The difference in scores between the top-ranked and bottom-ranked regions has shown a general decreasing trend over the 15-year period,

Figure 4.14: ACI 2018 Financial, Businesses and Manpower Conditions Ranking Map

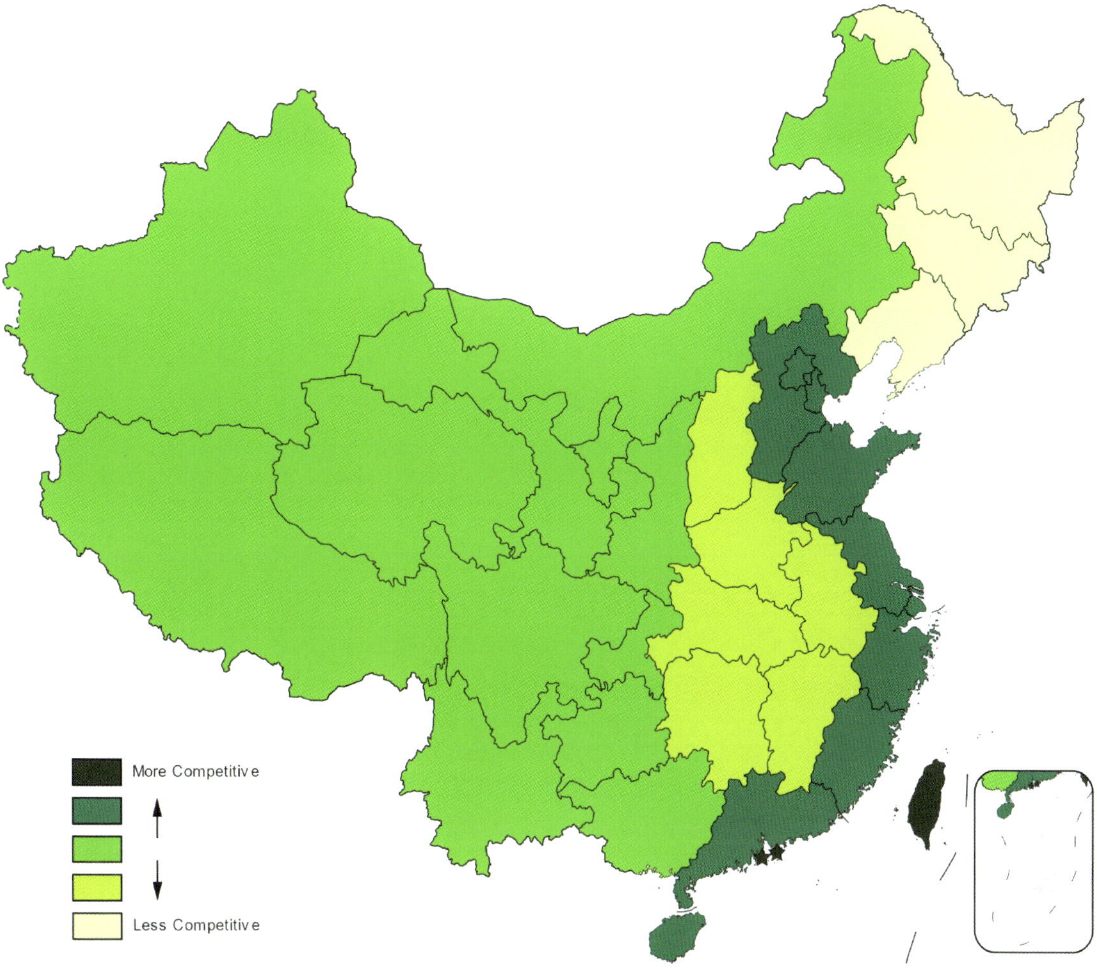

Note: The results are based on 2015 data, collated and analysed in 2018.
Source: Asia Competitiveness Institute.

decreasing from 2.6421 in 2000 to 2.3590 in 2015. Though small, the decrease is indicative of a narrowing disparity among the five regions of Greater China in the Financial, Businesses and Manpower Conditions environment.

The Financial, Businesses and Manpower Conditions environment can be further deconstructed into the three sub-environments of Financial Deepening and Business Efficiency, Labour Market Flexibility and Productivity Performance. To study the patterns in the Financial, Businesses and Manpower Conditions scores more closely, the five regions' performance in each of the three sub-environments is studied. This information is presented in Figure 4.15.

From the sub-environment scores, it is evident that the regions of the Eastern Coastal Area and Hong Kong, Macau and Taiwan perform exceedingly well, with the two regions attaining the top two highest scores among the five regions in every sub-environment. This is consistent with the regions' close scores and their significant lead over the other regions in the Financial, Businesses and Manpower Conditions environment. Specifically, Hong Kong, Macau and Taiwan, ranked first in the environment, attains the highest score in the sub-environments of Labour Market

Table 4.8: ACI 2018 Financial, Businesses and Manpower Conditions Rankings and Scores: Evolution Over Time

Financial, Businesses and Manpower Conditions						
	1		2		3	
Rank	Region	Score	Region	Score	Region	Score
2000	Hong Kong, Macau and Taiwan	1.8409	Eastern Coastal Area in China	0.2902	Central China	–0.6477
2001	Hong Kong, Macau and Taiwan	1.8127	Eastern Coastal Area in China	0.3629	Western China	–0.6821
2002	Hong Kong, Macau and Taiwan	1.7493	Eastern Coastal Area in China	0.4052	Central China	–0.3475
2003	Hong Kong, Macau and Taiwan	1.7082	Eastern Coastal Area in China	0.5723	Western China	–0.6754
2004	Hong Kong, Macau and Taiwan	1.6899	Eastern Coastal Area in China	0.6036	Western China	–0.6811
2005	Hong Kong, Macau and Taiwan	1.6445	Eastern Coastal Area in China	0.6847	Western China	–0.7074
2006	Hong Kong, Macau and Taiwan	1.6047	Eastern Coastal Area in China	0.7494	Western China	–0.7162
2007	Hong Kong, Macau and Taiwan	1.5700	Eastern Coastal Area in China	0.8046	Western China	–0.7344
2008	Hong Kong, Macau and Taiwan	1.4824	Eastern Coastal Area in China	0.9286	Western China	–0.7776
2009	Hong Kong, Macau and Taiwan	1.4202	Eastern Coastal Area in China	1.0077	Western China	–0.7788
2010	Hong Kong, Macau and Taiwan	1.3844	Eastern Coastal Area in China	1.0508	Central China	–0.7908
2011	Hong Kong, Macau and Taiwan	1.3325	Eastern Coastal Area in China	1.1098	Western China	–0.7747
2012	Hong Kong, Macau and Taiwan	1.3055	Eastern Coastal Area in China	1.1383	Western China	–0.7471
2013	Hong Kong, Macau and Taiwan	1.2315	Eastern Coastal Area in China	1.2152	Central China	–0.7604
2014	Eastern Coastal Area in China	1.2537	Hong Kong, Macau and Taiwan	1.1919	Central China	–0.7330
2015	Hong Kong, Macau and Taiwan	1.2702	Eastern Coastal Area in China	1.1477	Western China	–0.6491

Financial, Businesses and Manpower Conditions				
	4		5	
Rank	Region	Score	Region	Score
2000	Western China	–0.6822	North-eastern China	–0.8012
2001	Central China	–0.7169	North-eastern China	–0.7766
2002	Western China	–0.7983	North-eastern China	–1.0088
2003	Central China	–0.7308	North-eastern China	–0.8742
2004	Central China	–0.7162	North-eastern China	–0.8962
2005	Central China	–0.7357	North-eastern China	–0.8861
2006	Central China	–0.7516	North-eastern China	–0.8863
2007	Central China	–0.7784	North-eastern China	–0.8618
2008	Central China	–0.7890	North-eastern China	–0.8444
2009	Central China	–0.8021	North-eastern China	–0.8471
2010	Western China	–0.7928	North-eastern China	–0.8516
2011	Central China	–0.8018	North-eastern China	–0.8659
2012	Central China	–0.8114	North-eastern China	–0.8853
2013	Western China	–0.7852	North-eastern China	–0.9011
2014	Western China	–0.8128	North-eastern China	–0.8998
2015	Central China	–0.6801	North-eastern China	–1.0888

Note: The results are based on 2000–2015 data, collated and analysed in 2018.
Source: Asia Competitiveness Institute.

Figure 4.15: ACI 2018 Sub-Environment Scores of Financial, Businesses and Manpower Conditions

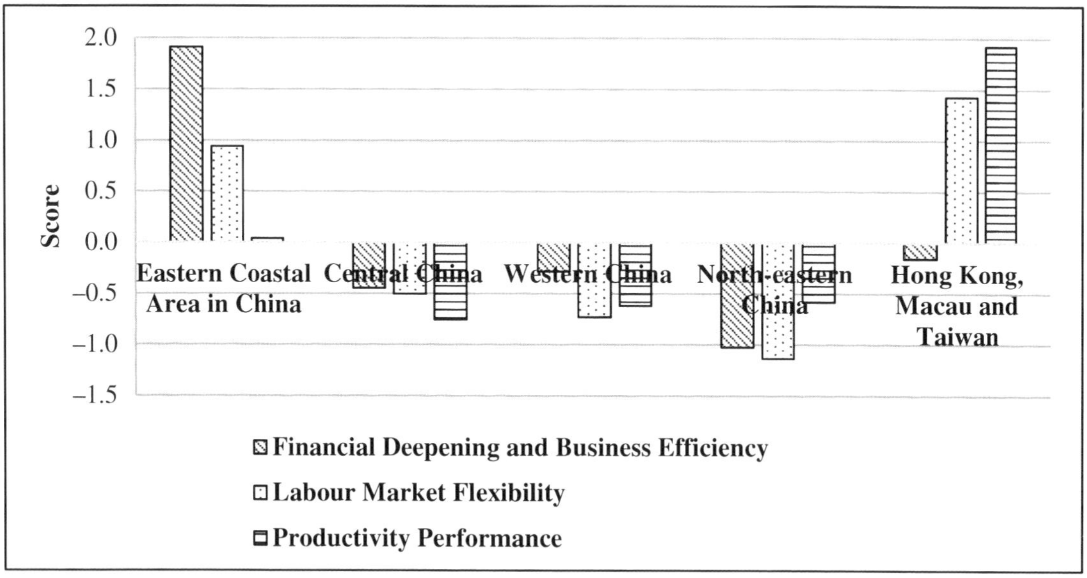

Note: The results are based on 2015 data, collated and analysed in 2018.
Source: Asia Competitiveness Institute

Flexibility and Productivity Performance and the second highest score in the sub-environment of Financial Deepening and Business Efficiency. The Eastern Coastal Area, ranked second in the environment, attains the highest score in the sub-environment of Financial Deepening and Business Efficiency and the second highest score in the sub-environments of Labour Market Flexibility and Productivity Performance. The remaining regions of Central China, Western China and North-eastern China, on the other hand, attain negative scores and perform below average in all three sub-environments. This observation is unsurprising given the three regions' negative scores in the Financial, Businesses and Manpower Conditions environment.

Further, while the regions vary in their performance in the Financial, Businesses and Manpower Conditions environment, it is worth noting that each region exhibits relative strengths and weaknesses in their sub-environment scores. This provides a useful directive of the areas each region can focus on to improve their standings in the Financial, Businesses and Manpower Conditions environment. In this respect, the Eastern Coastal Area and Central China should concentrate efforts on improving the sub-environment of Productivity Performance while Western China and North-eastern China should prioritise Labour Market Flexibility and Hong Kong, Macau and Taiwan should do the same for Financial Deepening and Business Efficiency.

To study the dynamics in the regions' performance in the Financial, Businesses and Manpower Conditions sub-environments, a break in the sub-environment scores is implemented at 2007. The procedure follows that applied to the sub-environments under the environments previously studied and can be interpreted in a similar manner.

Figure 4.16 captures the intertemporal shifts in the regions' performance in the sub-environment of Financial Deepening and Business Efficiency. In the graph, the points representing the Eastern Coastal Area, Western China, Central China and North-eastern China are above the 45-degree

Figure 4.16: ACI 2018 Competitiveness Over Time for Financial Deepening and Business Efficiency

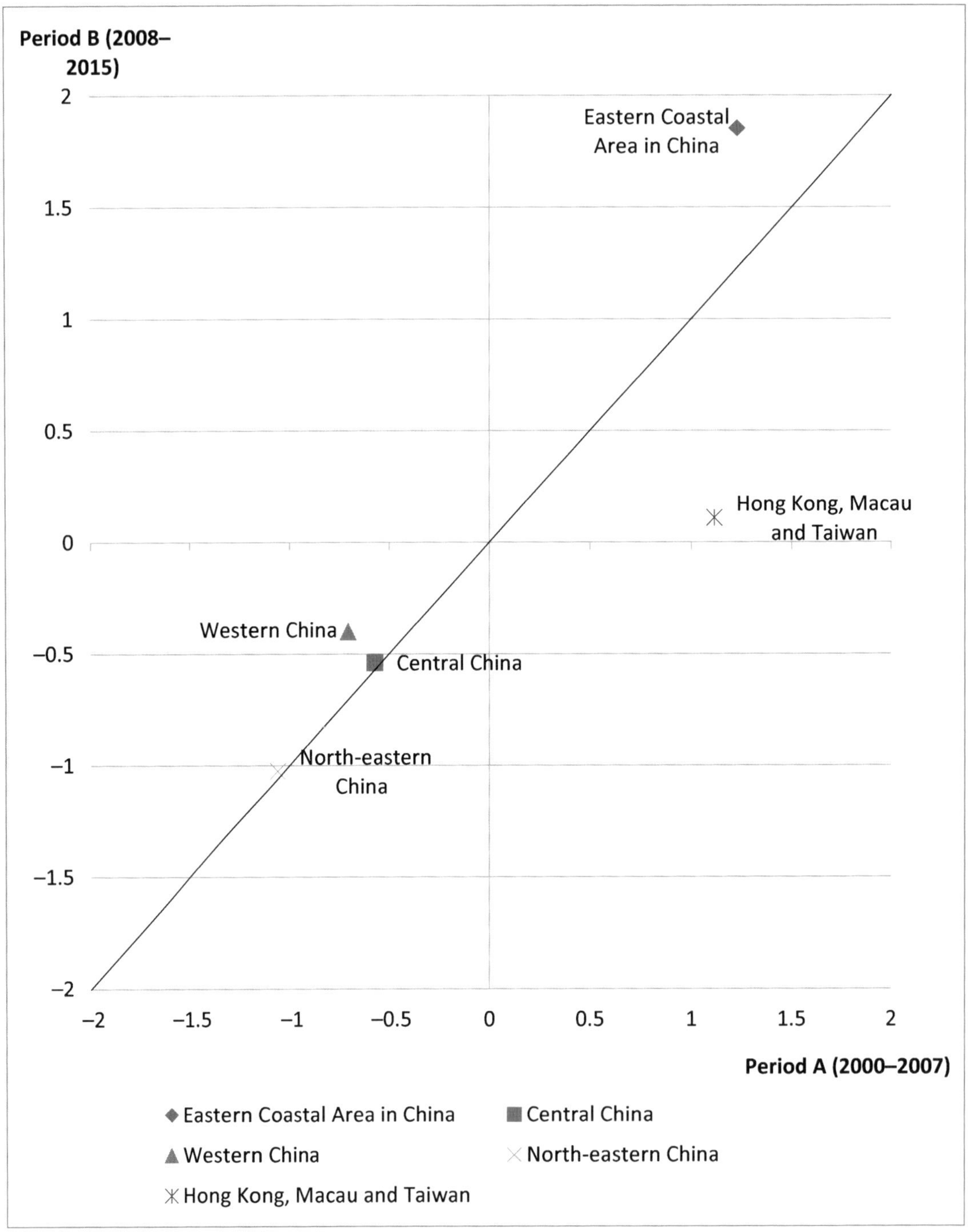

Note: The results are based on 2000–2015 data, collated and analysed in 2018.
Source: Asia Competitiveness Institute.

line. From this observation, it can be inferred that the Financial Deepening and Business Efficiency scores of these four regions have shown an improvement over the identified break. Of the four regions, the Eastern Coastal Area shows the largest progress, with a large vertical distance separating the point representing the region and the 45-degree line.

In contrast, the point corresponding to Hong Kong, Macau and Taiwan falls below the 45-degree line. The significant distance of the region from the line reflects a sharp decline in Hong Kong, Macau and Taiwan's competitiveness in the sub-environment of Financial Deepening and Business Efficiency over the two time periods.

Figure 4.17 summarises the intertemporal shifts in each region's performance in the sub-environment of Labour Market Flexibility. In the graph, the point representing the Eastern Coastal Area of China is above the 45-degree line, indicating that the region's score in the Labour Market Flexibility sub-environment has increased over the two time periods. On the other hand, the points representing Hong Kong, Macau and Taiwan, Western China and North-eastern China fall below the 45-degree line, indicating that these regions exhibit a decline in their Labour Market Flexibility scores over the identified break. The remaining point representing Central China, in contrast, is positioned near the 45-degree line, suggesting that the region's score in the sub-environment has remained nearly constant over the two time periods, with only subtle changes, if any, in its relative standing in Labour Market Flexibility.

Collectively, these observations point to a narrowing disparity between Hong Kong, Macau and Taiwan and the Eastern Coastal Area. It can also be observed from the graph that the points representing Central, Western and North-eastern China are situated closely to one another. This suggests that the three regions score similarly in the sub-environment of Labour Market Flexibility in both time periods.

Figure 4.18 reflects the intertemporal shifts in the regions' performance in the sub-environment of Productivity Performance. In the graph, all the points representing the five regions are positioned close to the 45-degree line. From this, it can be inferred that the Productivity Performance scores of the five regions remained nearly constant over the two time periods, implying marginal changes, if any, in the regions' relative standings in the sub-environment. A key distinction between the five regions, however, is their location on the 45-degree line. Hong Kong, Macau and Taiwan, situated close to the top, is steeply more competitive than the other regions in the sub-environment of Productivity Performance. The Eastern Coastal Area, positioned close to the graph's origin, comes close to the average performance of the five regions in both time periods. Finally, the three regions of North-eastern China, Western China and Central China, located close to the bottom, fall behind the other regions in their performance in this sub-environment by a large gap.

With the exception of Hong Kong, Macau and Taiwan's lead over the Eastern Coastal Area, the patterns identified under the Financial, Businesses and Manpower Conditions environment and its sub-environments are largely consistent with the general trends observed in the Overall Competitiveness scores. This reasserts the environment as a useful indicator of Overall Competitiveness.

Figure 4.17: ACI 2018 Competitiveness Over Time for Labour Market Flexibility

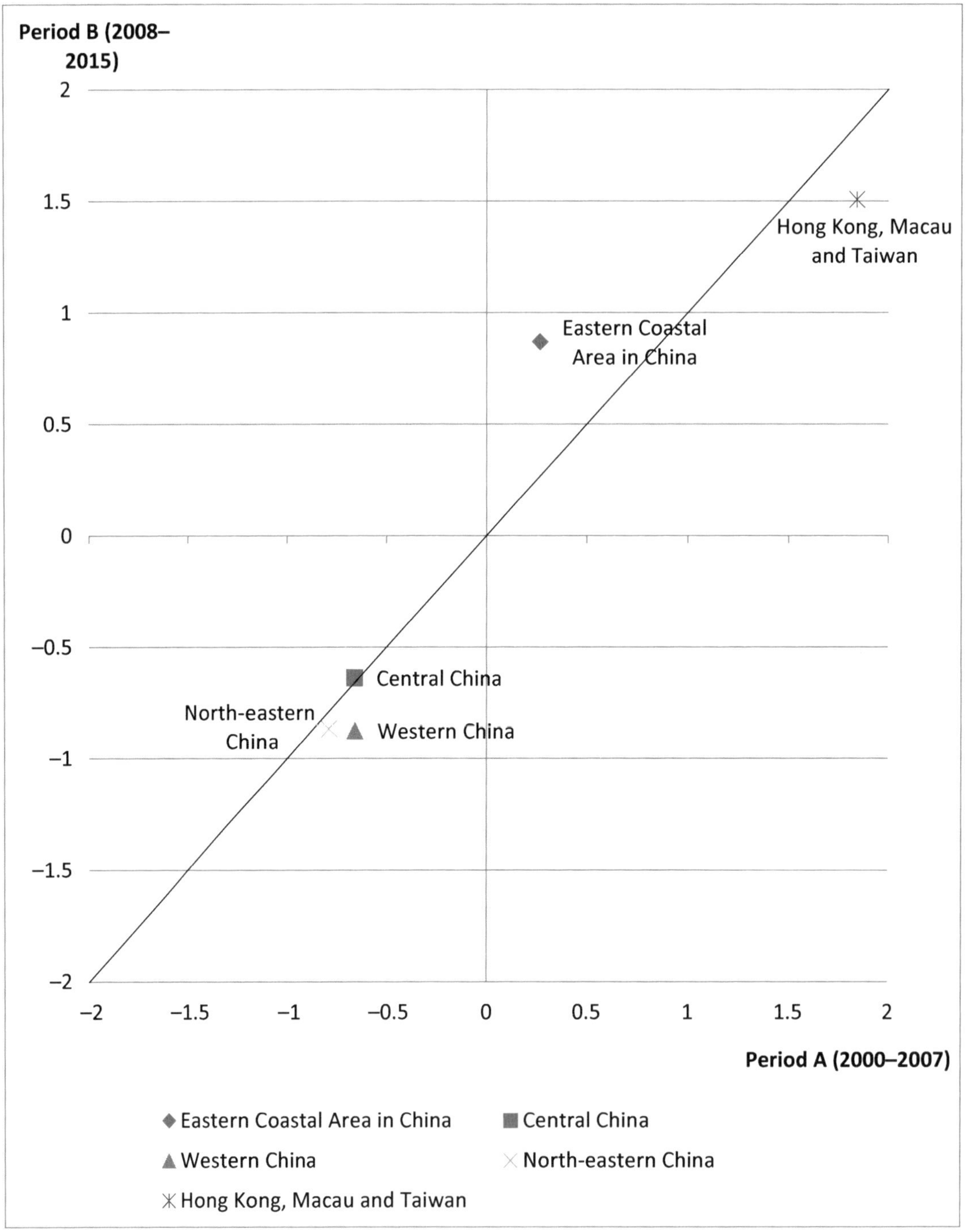

Note: The results are based on 2000–2015 data, collated and analysed in 2018.
Source: Asia Competitiveness Institute.

Figure 4.18: ACI 2018 Competitiveness Over Time for Productivity Performance

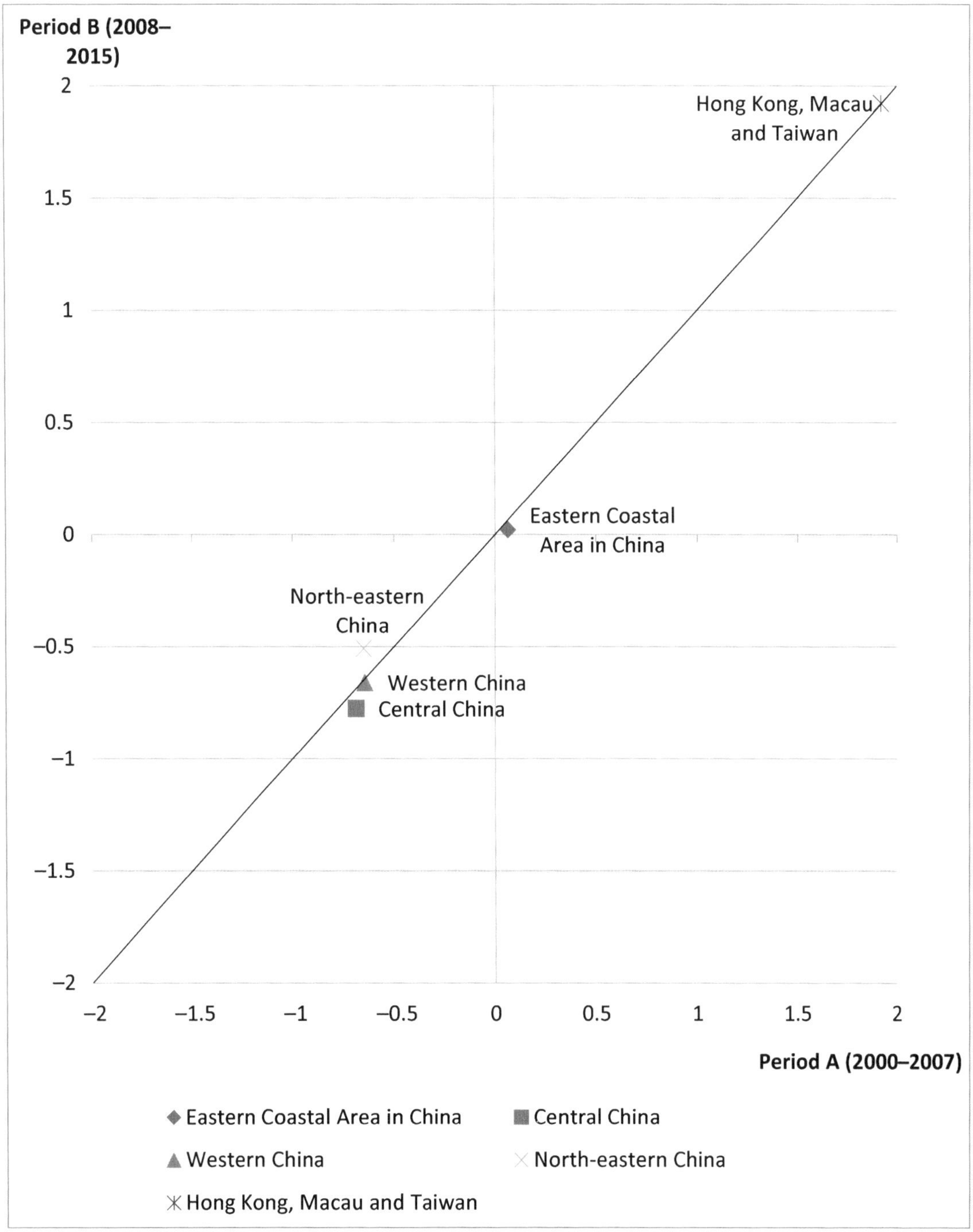

Note: The results are based on 2000–2015 data, collated and analysed in 2018.
Source: Asia Competitiveness Institute.

4.2.5 ACI 2018 Quality of Life and Infrastructure Development Rankings and Scores

Table 4.9 shows the 2018 rankings and scores of the five regions in the fourth environment of Quality of Life and Infrastructure Development. Similar to the Overall Competitiveness scores and rankings, the Eastern Coastal Area in China ranks first with a score of 1.8235. The region is followed by Hong Kong, Macau and Taiwan, Western China, North-eastern China and Central China which rank second, third, fourth and fifth, respectively.

From the Quality of Life and Infrastructure Development scores, it can be inferred that the Eastern Coastal Area in China and Hong Kong, Macau and Taiwan perform above the average of the five regions in the environment. This is evident from the positive Quality of Life and Infrastructure Development scores the regions attain. On the other hand, Western China, North-eastern China and Central China, which record negative scores, perform below average in the Quality of Life and Infrastructure Development environment.

In terms of the distribution of Quality of Life and Infrastructure Development scores, a negative skew is observed, with a mean score exceeding the median score, where the mean is taken as a conceived region with a score of 0 and the median as the region ranked third (Western China with a score of –0.3484). The score differences between the regions are also notable; there is a large gap in the scores of the Eastern Coastal Area (1.8235), ranked first, and all the other regions which have their scores clustered together. The Eastern Coastal Area and Hong Kong, Macau and Taiwan are separated by a score difference of 1.7024. This difference is substantial when compared with the score differences of 0.4695, 0.0860 and 0.7275 between the other regions. These aspects of the Quality of Life and Infrastructure Development score distribution are consistent with that observed in the Overall Competitiveness scores, suggesting that the regional characteristics in this environment to the Eastern Coastal Area's lead in Overall Competitiveness.

The Quality of Life and Infrastructure Development scores and rankings of the five regions can also be visualised geographically. Figure 4.19 colour-codes the regions by their performance in the Quality of Life and Infrastructure Development environment, with better performing regions in a darker shade and poorer performing regions in a lighter shade.

Table 4.9: ACI 2018 Quality of Life and Infrastructure Development Ranking and Scores

Rank	Region	Score
1	Eastern Coastal Area in China	1.8235
2	Hong Kong, Macau and Taiwan	0.1211
3	Western China	–0.3484
4	North-eastern China	–0.4344
5	Central China	–1.1619

Note: The results are based on 2015 data, collated and analysed in 2018.
Source: Asia Competitiveness Institute.

Figure 4.19: ACI 2018 Quality of Life and Infrastructure Development Ranking Map

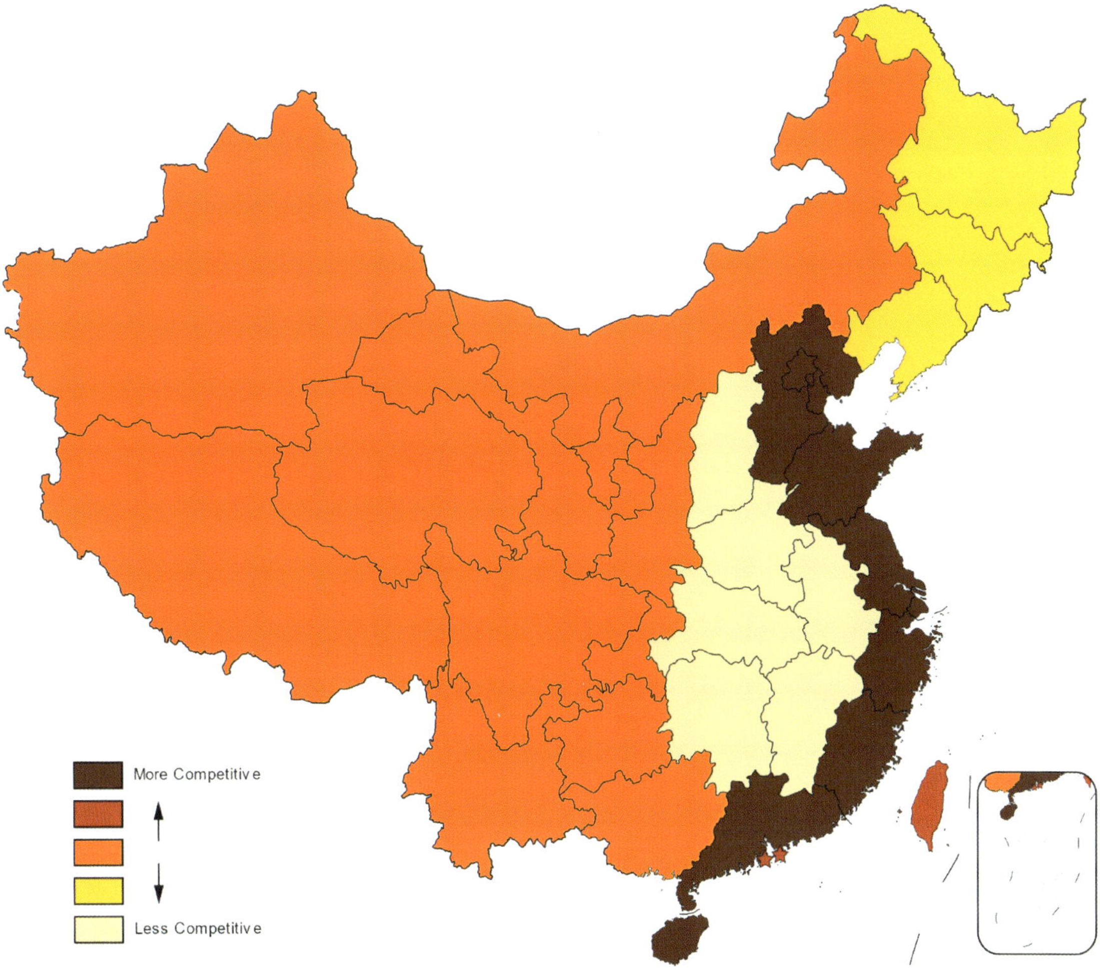

Note: The results are based on 2015 data, collated and analysed in 2018.
Source: Asia Competitiveness Institute.

Table 4.10 presents the Quality of Life and Infrastructure Development rankings and scores of the five regions from 2000 to 2015. Distilling the patterns and changes in the rankings over the decade and half, it can be observed that the Eastern Coastal Area has outperformed Hong Kong, Macau and Taiwan to rank first since 2004, with its score increasing remarkably from 0.9525 in 2000 to 1.8235 in 2015. In contrast, over the same period, Hong Kong, Macau and Taiwan, having fallen to rank second, saw its score decline drastically from 1.3569 in 2000 to 0.1211 in 2015. The drop represents the region's decline from the top-performing region to the average-performing region in the environment. As a consequence, the gap in scores between the top two regions has widened considerably since the Eastern Coastal Area ranked first in 2004; the score difference has risen from 0.4044 in 2000 to 1.7024 in 2015. This is indicative of the significant edge the Eastern Coastal Area has gained in the Quality of Life and Infrastructure Development environment over Hong Kong, Macau and Taiwan over the years.

Table 4.10: ACI 2018 Quality of Life and Infrastructure Development Rankings and Scores: Evolution Over Time

Quality of Life and Infrastructure Development						
	1		2		3	
Rank	Region	Score	Region	Score	Region	Score
2000	Hong Kong, Macau and Taiwan	1.3569	Eastern Coastal Area in China	0.9525	North-eastern China	–0.2597
2001	Hong Kong, Macau and Taiwan	1.4620	Eastern Coastal Area in China	0.8668	North-eastern China	–0.3746
2002	Hong Kong, Macau and Taiwan	1.2625	Eastern Coastal Area in China	1.0424	North-eastern China	–0.2545
2003	Hong Kong, Macau and Taiwan	1.2900	Eastern Coastal Area in China	1.0329	North-eastern China	–0.3006
2004	Eastern Coastal Area in China	1.1612	Hong Kong, Macau and Taiwan	1.1434	North-eastern China	–0.2500
2005	Eastern Coastal Area in China	1.4031	Hong Kong, Macau and Taiwan	0.8618	North-eastern China	–0.2140
2006	Eastern Coastal Area in China	1.4767	Hong Kong, Macau and Taiwan	0.7828	North-eastern China	–0.2154
2007	Eastern Coastal Area in China	1.4758	Hong Kong, Macau and Taiwan	0.8477	North-eastern China	–0.4074
2008	Eastern Coastal Area in China	1.6574	Hong Kong, Macau and Taiwan	0.5670	North-eastern China	–0.3482
2009	Eastern Coastal Area in China	1.7121	Hong Kong, Macau and Taiwan	0.2907	North-eastern China	–0.0226
2010	Eastern Coastal Area in China	1.8333	Hong Kong, Macau and Taiwan	0.0754	North-eastern China	–0.1640
2011	Eastern Coastal Area in China	1.8130	Hong Kong, Macau and Taiwan	0.1551	North-eastern China	–0.1943
2012	Eastern Coastal Area in China	1.8224	Hong Kong, Macau and Taiwan	0.0569	North-eastern China	–0.1624
2013	Eastern Coastal Area in China	1.8008	Hong Kong, Macau and Taiwan	0.0092	North-eastern China	–0.0128
2014	Eastern Coastal Area in China	1.8303	Hong Kong, Macau and Taiwan	0.1627	North-eastern China	–0.3172
2015	Eastern Coastal Area in China	1.8235	Hong Kong, Macau and Taiwan	0.1211	Western China	–0.3484

Quality of Life and Infrastructure Development				
	4		5	
Rank	Region	Score	Region	Score
2000	Western China	–0.8206	Central China	–1.2291
2001	Western China	–0.8017	Central China	–1.1525
2002	Western China	–0.7487	Central China	–1.3017
2003	Western China	–0.7523	Central China	–1.2699
2004	Western China	–0.7349	Central China	–1.3197
2005	Western China	–0.7612	Central China	–1.2897
2006	Western China	–0.8334	Central China	–1.2107
2007	Western China	–0.7325	Central China	–1.1836
2008	Western China	–0.7799	Central China	–1.0964
2009	Western China	–0.8825	Central China	–1.0977
2010	Western China	–0.6673	Central China	–1.0775
2011	Western China	–0.6896	Central China	–1.0842
2012	Western China	–0.5623	Central China	–1.1546
2013	Western China	–0.6320	Central China	–1.1651
2014	Western China	–0.5942	Central China	–1.0816
2015	North-eastern China	–0.4344	Central China	–1.1619

Note: The results are based on 2000–2015 data, collated and analysed in 2018.
Source: Asia Competitiveness Institute.

The Quality of Life and Infrastructure Development scores of the remaining three environments on the contrary have remained negative over the same duration, indicating their below-average performance in the environment. North-eastern China, Western China and Central China have occupied the third, fourth and fifth positions, respectively, over the decade and half until 2015 when Western China outperformed North-eastern China to take the third place.

An increasing trend in the range of the Quality of Life and Infrastructure Development scores from 2000 to 2015 is also observed. The difference in scores between the top-ranked and bottom-ranked regions has grown from 2.5860 in 2000 to 2.9854 in 2015, signalling a widening disparity in Quality of Life and Infrastructure Development performances among the five regions of Greater China. This observation is congruent with that gleaned from the Overall Competitiveness scores and the other environments previously analysed.

The environment of Quality of Life and Infrastructure Development can be further analysed in terms of the three sub-environments of Physical Infrastructure, Technological Infrastructure and Standard of Living, Education and Social Stability. To examine the patterns in the Quality of Life and Infrastructure Development scores in greater detail, the five regions' performance in each sub-environment is studied. This information is summarised in Figure 4.20.

From the sub-environment scores, it is evident that the Eastern Coastal Area outperforms all the other regions, attaining the highest score in all three environments among the five regions. This is consistent with the region's significant lead over the other regions in the Quality of Life and Infrastructure Development score. The Eastern Coastal Area is also the only region which attains a positive score in all three sub-environments. Meanwhile, Hong Kong, Macau and Taiwan which ranked second in the Quality of Life and Infrastructure Development attains the second highest score in the sub-environments of Technological Infrastructure and Standard of Living, Education

Figure 4.20: ACI 2018 Sub-Environment Scores of Quality of Life and Infrastructure Development

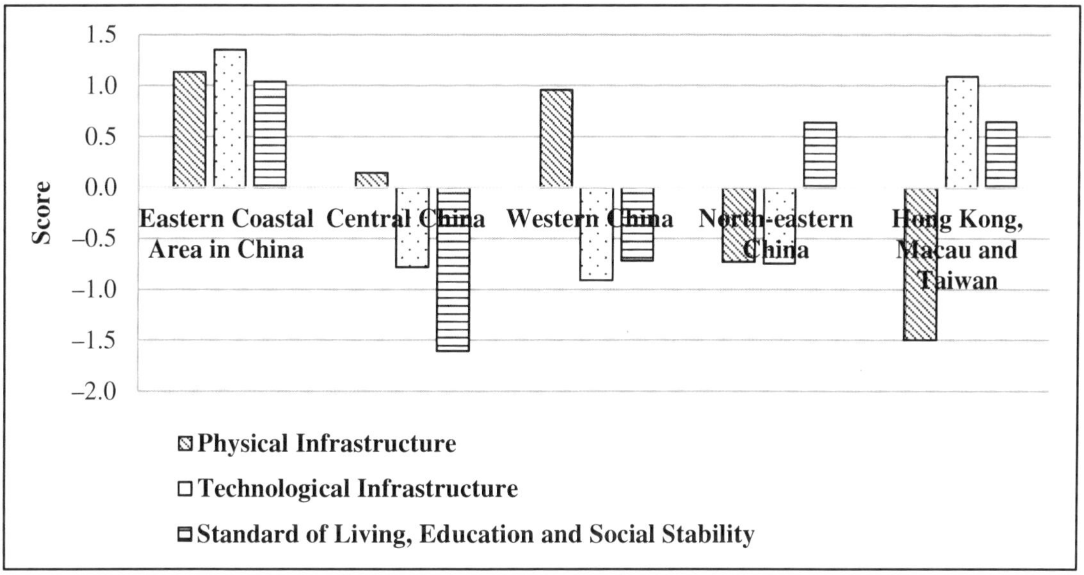

Note: The results are based on 2015 data, collated and analysed in 2018.
Source: Asia Competitiveness Institute.

and Social Stability. The region, however, performs the worst out of the five regions in the sub-environment of Physical Infrastructure. On the other hand, the remaining regions perform comparatively poorly, each with negative scores in two of the three sub-environments.

Further, while the regions attain different scores in the Quality of Life and Infrastructure Development environment, each region exhibits relative strengths and weaknesses in their sub-environment scores. This information provides a useful directive of the areas each region can focus its efforts on to improve their standings in the Quality of Life and Infrastructure Development environment. In this respect, Hong Kong, Macau and Taiwan should focus efforts on improving the sub-environment of Physical Infrastructure while Western China and North-eastern China should prioritise on the Technological Infrastructure and Central China should do the same for the Standard of Living, Education and Social Stability.

To study the intertemporal shifts in the regions' performance in the Quality of Life and Infrastructure Development sub-environments, a break in the sub-environment scores is implemented at 2007. The procedure follows that applied to the sub-environments under the environments previously studied and can be interpreted in a similar manner.

Figure 4.21 captures the dynamics in the five regions' performance in the sub-environment of Physical Infrastructure. In the graph, all the points representing the five regions are positioned close to the 45-degree line. From this, it can be inferred that the Physical Infrastructure scores of the five regions remained nearly constant over the two time periods, implying only marginal changes, if any, in the regions' relative standings in the sub-environment. A key distinction, however, is the location of the points representing each region on the 45-degree line. The Eastern Coastal Area, positioned close to the top, outperforms the other regions in the sub-environment of Physical Infrastructure. This is consistent with the region's ranking in the broader environment of Quality of Life and Infrastructure Development. The Eastern Coastal Area's performance in the sub-environment is followed by Western China, Central China, North-eastern China and Hong Kong, Macau and Taiwan in that order. This observation is surprising considering Hong Kong, Macau and Taiwan's score in the Quality of Life and Infrastructure Development environment, where it ranks second, ahead of the other regions except the Eastern Coastal Area. Hence, it appears to be especially crucial for Hong Kong, Macau and Taiwan to address this sub-environment if it wishes to improve its score in the Quality of Life and Infrastructure Development environment.

Figure 4.22 reflects the intertemporal shifts in the regions' performance in the sub-environment of Technological Infrastructure. In the graph, the points representing the Eastern Coastal Area and Central China fall above the 45-degree line, indicating that the regions' scores in the Technological Infrastructure sub-environment have increased over the two time periods. Of the two regions, the Eastern Coastal Area exhibits larger improvement, with a sizeably larger vertical distance separating its point and the line. On the other hand, the points representing Hong Kong, Macau and Taiwan and North-eastern China are below the 45-degree line. This observation indicates that the two regions' performance in the sub-environment of Technological Infrastructure has deteriorated over the identified break. This decline is especially significant for Hong Kong, Macau and Taiwan as evidenced by the distance of the region's point from the line. On the other hand, the point representing Western China falls squarely on the 45-degree line, suggesting that

Figure 4.21: ACI 2018 Competitiveness Over Time for Physical Infrastructure

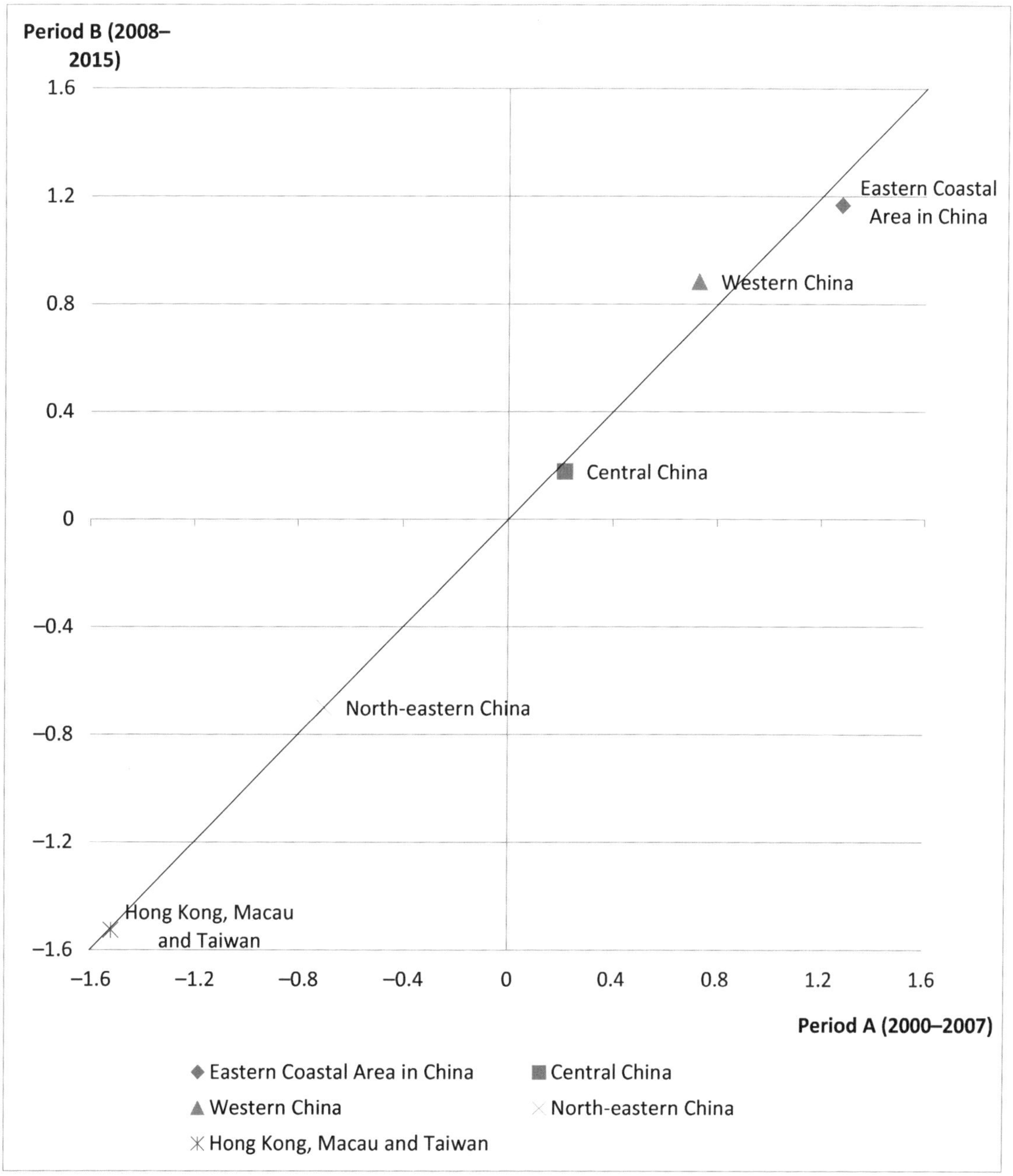

Note: The results are based on 2000–2015 data, collated and analysed in 2018.
Source: Asia Competitiveness Institute.

the region's score in the sub-environment has remained constant for the two time periods. The five regions' performance in this sub-environment is also largely consistent with that in the broader environment of Quality of Life and Infrastructure Development, with the exception of Western China which is outperformed by North-eastern and Central China.

Figure 4.22: ACI 2018 Competitiveness Over Time for Technological Infrastructure

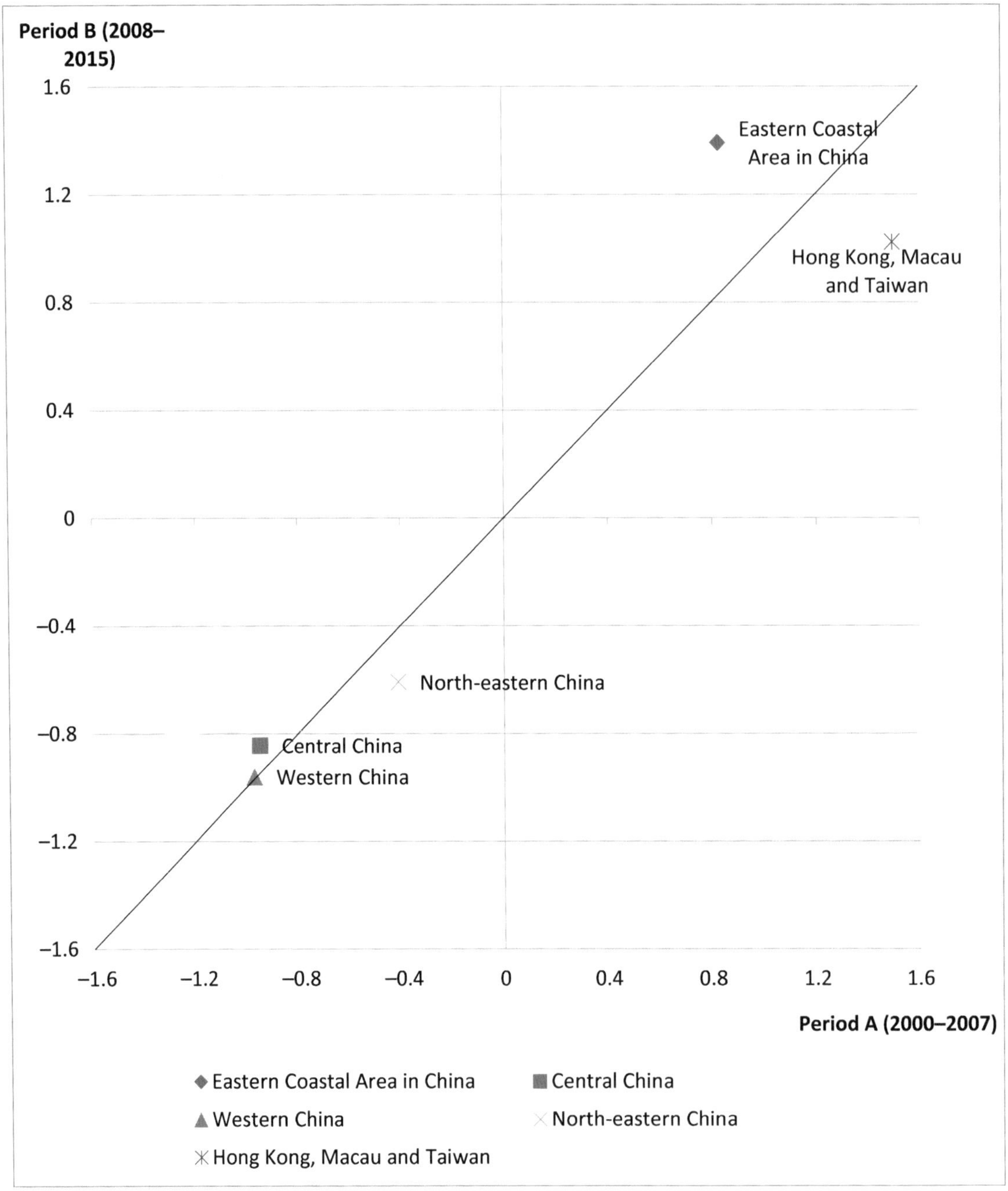

Note: The results are based on 2000–2015 data, collated and analysed in 2018.
Source: Asia Competitiveness Institute.

Figure 4.23: ACI 2018 Competitiveness Over Time for Standard of Living, Education and Social Stability

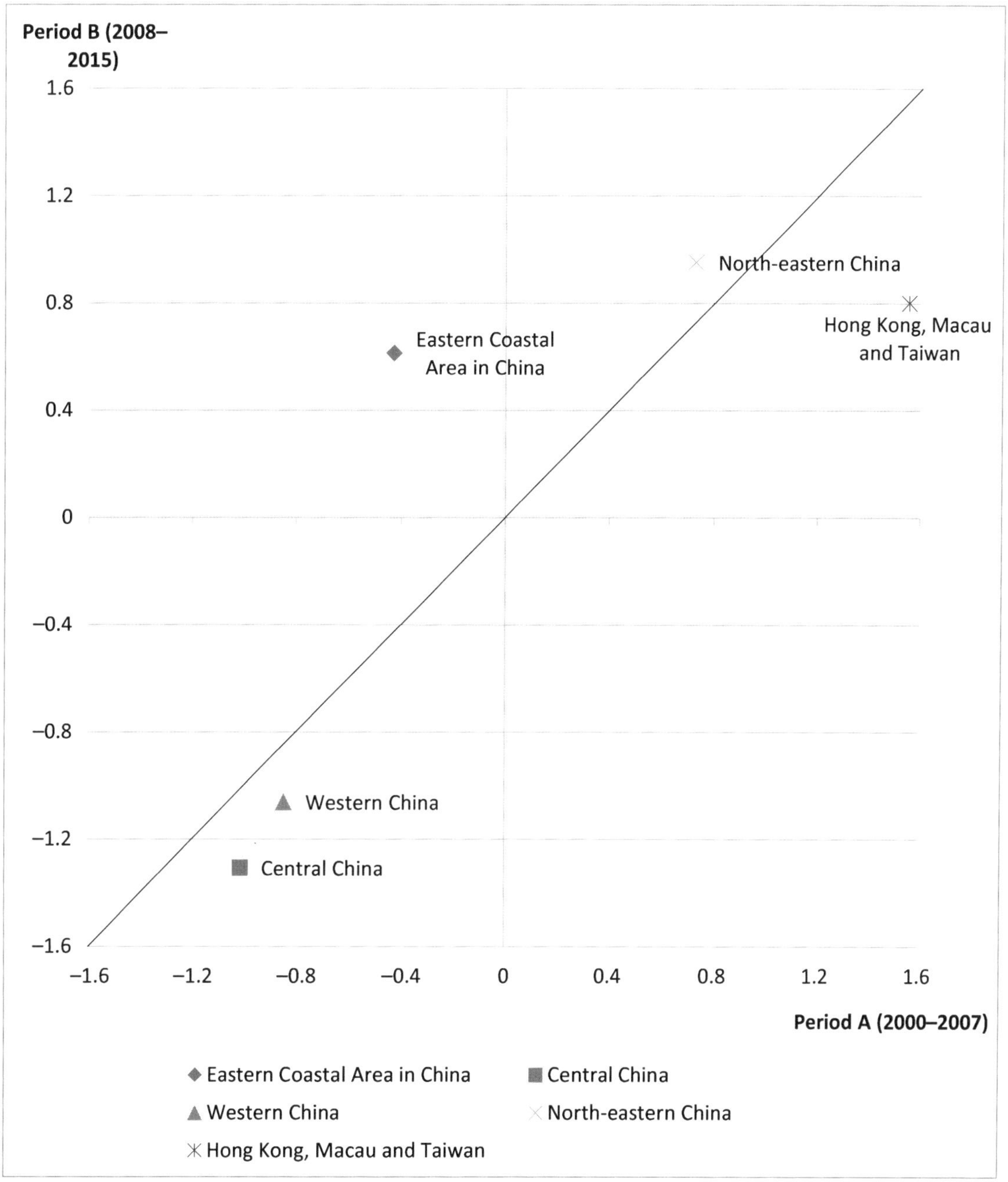

Note: The results are based on 2000–2015 data, collated and analysed in 2018.
Source: Asia Competitiveness Institute.

Figure 4.23 summarises the intertemporal shifts in each region's performance in the sub-environment of Standard of Living, Education and Social Stability. In the graph, the points representing North-eastern China and the Eastern Coastal Area in China are positioned above the 45-degree line. This is indicative of the two regions' improvements in the sub-environment. Of the two, the Eastern Coastal Area attains larger progress as seen from the sizeable distance which separates the point representing the region and the line. The remaining points representing Hong Kong, Macau and Taiwan, Western China and Central China are located below the 45-degree line, suggesting that these regions experience a decline in their scores and drop in their relative standings in the sub-environment. Of the three, Hong Kong, Macau and Taiwan shows the steepest decline, being separated from the 45-degree line by a large vertical distance.

Overall, it can be seen that North-eastern China's improvement and the Eastern Coastal Area's progress, coupled with Hong Kong, Macau and Taiwan's decline in the sub-environment over the two periods have brought the three regions' performance in the Standard of Living, Education and Social Stability sub-environment closer. This result deviates from the general trend previously observed in the environment of Quality of Life and Infrastructure Development. In contrast, the regions of Western China and Central China have remained significantly behind the three regions in their performance in this sub-environment.

The patterns identified under the environment of Quality of Life and Infrastructure Development and its sub-environments are congruent with the broad trends and movements in the Overall Competitiveness scores, reasserting the environment as a useful indicator of Overall Competitiveness.

4.3 Concluding Notes and Policy Implications

In summary, the overall development across the five regions of Greater China remains imbalanced. This study represents an attempt to identify the strengths and weaknesses in various dimensions and gauge the potential for each region such that informed policy recommendations grounded in research findings can be proposed.

From the Overall Competitiveness study, three key observations can be identified. Firstly, the Eastern Coastal Area has surpassed Hong Kong, Macau and Taiwan to rank first since 2002, with the score difference in Overall Competitiveness continually widening over the years (with the exception of 2013 and 2014). Secondly, Western China has displayed significant progress in its Overall Competitiveness, replacing North-eastern China to rank third in 2004, 2007 and since 2010. Thirdly, Central China, which previously failed to move up the ranks, has shown an improvement in its Overall Competitiveness scores and has displaced North-eastern China to rank fourth since 2014.

To understand the common and distinct strengths and weaknesses of the regions, the five regions of Greater China can be categorised into three groups based on the 2018 Overall Competitiveness rankings; the top-performing group comprising the Eastern Coastal Area in China and Hong Kong, Macau and Taiwan, the middle-performing group comprising Western China and Central China, and the bottom-performing group comprising North-eastern China.

Both top-performing regions fare comparably well in the sub-environments of Openness to Trade and Services; Institutions, Governance and Leadership; Labour Market Flexibility; and Technological Infrastructure. The key differences in two regions' performance. However, result from Hong Kong, Macau and Taiwan's poor scores in the sub-environments of Regional Economic Vibrancy; Government Policies and Fiscal Sustainability; Institutions, Governance and Leadership; Financial Deepening and Business Efficiency; and Physical Infrastructure relative to the Eastern Coastal Area.

The medium-performing regions fare well in some areas; Western China performs above the regional average for the sub-environment of Physical Infrastructure whereas Central China performs above the regional average for the sub-environments of Regional Economic Vibrancy and Physical Infrastructure. Both regions, however, score below average in the remaining sub-environments, faring especially poorly in the sub-environments of Technological Infrastructure and Standard of Living, Education and Social Stability.

The bottom-performing region, North-eastern China scores below the regional average in all sub-environments except Standard of Living, Education and Social Stability. This is in contrast to the other regions with more than one positive sub-environment score.

References

Chen, Chung, Lawrence Chang, and Yimin Zhang. 1995. "The role of foreign direct investment in Chinas post-1978 economic development." *World Development* (Elsevier BV) 23: 691–703. doi:10.1016/0305-750x(94)00143-m.

Crane, Bret, Chad Albrecht, Kristopher McKay Duffin, and Conan Albrecht. 2018. "China's special economic zones: an analysis of policy to reduce regional disparities." *Regional Studies, Regional Science* (Informa UK Limited) 5: 98–107. doi:10.1080/21681376.2018.1430612.

Jian, Tianlun, Jeffrey D. Sachs, and Andrew M. Warner. 1996. "Trends in regional inequality in China." *China Economic Review* (Elsevier BV) 7: 1–21. doi:10.1016/s1043-951x(96)90017-6.

Kanbur, Ravi, and Xiaobo Zhang. 2005. "Fifty Years of Regional Inequality in China: a Journey Through Central Planning, Reform, and Openness." *Review of Development Economics* (Wiley) 9: 87–106. doi:10.1111/j.1467-9361.2005.00265.x.

Li, Jie, Larry D. Qiu, and Qunyan Sun. 2003. "Interregional protection: Implications of fiscal decentralization and trade liberalization." *China Economic Review* (Elsevier BV) 14: 227–245. doi:10.1016/s1043-951x(03)00024-5.

Nishitateno, Sonoko. 1983. "China's Special Economic Zones: Experimental Units for Economic Reform." *The International and Comparative Law Quarterly* (Cambridge University Press) 32: 175–185. http://www.jstor.org/stable/759472.

Ozawa, Terutomo. 2006. "Asias Labour-Driven Economic Development, Flying-Geese Style." (UNU-WIDER) 2006. http://www.wider.unu.edu/publications/working-papers/research-papers/2006/en_GB/rp2006-59/_files/78091780661970692/default/rp2006-59.pdf.

Rodríguez-Pose, Andrés. 2012. "Trade and Regional Inequality." *Economic Geography* (Wiley) 88: 109-136. doi:10.1111/j.1944–8287.2012.01147.x.

Rodríguez-Pose, Andrés, and Nicholas Gill. 2006. "How does trade affect regional disparities?" *World Development* (Elsevier BV) 34: 1201–1222. doi:10.1016/j.worlddev.2005.12.003.

Tan, Khee Giap, Peng Wang, and Teleixi Xie. 2017. *2016 Growth Slowdown Analysis by Income Thresholds and Annual Update of Competitiveness Analysis for 34 Greater China Economies.* World Scientific. doi:10.1142/10618.

Yang, Dennis Tao. 2002. "What has caused regional inequality in China?" *China Economic Review* (Elsevier BV) 13: 331–334. doi:10.1016/s1043-951x(02)00088-3.

Zhang, Xiaobo, and Kevin H. Zhang. 2003. "How Does Globalisation Affect Regional Inequality within A Developing Country? Evidence from China." *Journal of Development Studies* (Informa UK Limited) 39: 47–67. doi:10.1080/713869425.

Discussant Notes

Comments on "2018 Annual Update on Regional Competitiveness Rankings and Simulation Studies for Greater China"

Dr Dániel Palotai

Chief Economist and Executive Director, The Central Bank of Hungary

Several factors determine China's competitiveness, some had been more important a long time ago, while others are becoming more relevant recently. The Belt and Road Initiative is definitely a highly important in this regard. The initiative, which was proposed in 2013 by Xi Jinping, includes the Silk Road Economic Belt and the 21st-Century Maritime Silk Road initiatives. It aims not only to create a trade and infrastructure network connecting Asia with Europe and Africa along ancient trade routes, but also to foster transformation within China. The Belt and Road initiative can also contribute to reducing regional disparities while promoting economic growth in all regions.

Xi Jinping in his speech given on the 19th party congress in 2017 also highlighted the importance of the coordinated regional development strategy, covering the coordinated development and functional transformation of regions, small towns, cities and even Beijing. The key areas of coordination include government policies, industrial economy, transportation, while the common feature is the competitiveness.

Studies of Asia Competitiveness Institute (ACI) on Greater China Competitiveness assess and compare Greater China economies annually. The studies' main goal is to understand and comprehensively and quantitatively map the competitiveness landscape of Greater China. ACI Competitiveness Ranking aims at identifying the strengths and weaknesses along various dimensions collectively defining competitiveness of China's regions. The latest study also tries to measure the potential for improvement of those regions within Greater China that have so far not achieved a higher level of competitiveness.

The ACI competitiveness framework has several advantages. Using the ACI ranking one can assess competitiveness not just at the sub-national level, but also at the regional or city level (Figure 1.). The framework is able to show the regional disparities within the same country and can provide valuable information to policymakers with regards to economic development. ACI publishes its competitiveness study annually to easily follow-up developments in regions and over time periods. The annual reviews also give the opportunity for policymakers to fine-tune their economic policy if needed.

Measuring competitiveness has become more important after the global financial crisis. Competitiveness can provide a new perspective for policy makers since fiscal and monetary policy have reached their limits all around the world. China's role in the world economy has

Figure 1: Regions of China Analysed Separately by ACI Greater China Competitiveness

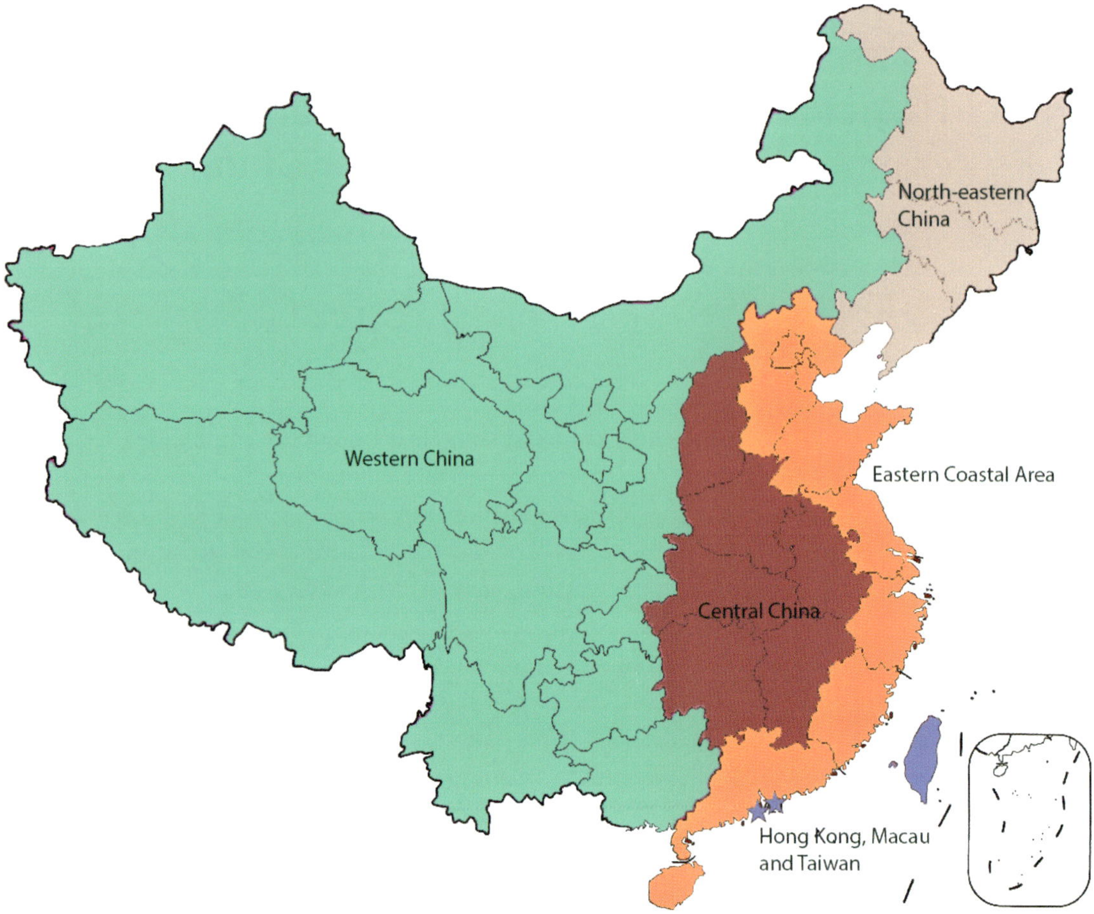

Source: Asia Competitiveness Institute.

changed significantly over the past three decades and now it has become one of the leaders of the world economy. China has managed to increase its importance in the ASEAN region more than any other major competitors (Figure 2).

In terms of nominal GDP China is already holds the second position after the Unites States but taking the GDP per capita figures into consideration China is still ranked relatively low. These macroeconomic indicators serve as a good basis for revealing the economic power of a country but cannot show whether a country utilises its resources optimally to attain the highest possible and sustainable level of welfare.

The competitive functioning of an economy requires solid fundamentals, such as stable macro-economy and financing, strong and reliable institutions, efficient regulation as well as high-quality education and health care. China performs well in the major global competitiveness reports. It ranked 27th of 137 countries in Global Competitiveness Report prepared by World Economic Forum (WEF) and has also a good position in IMD — World Competitiveness Ranking (18th of 63 countries) and in the World Bank's Doing Business (78th of 190 countries).

Figure 2: Nominal GDP in 2010 Prices (1992–2016)

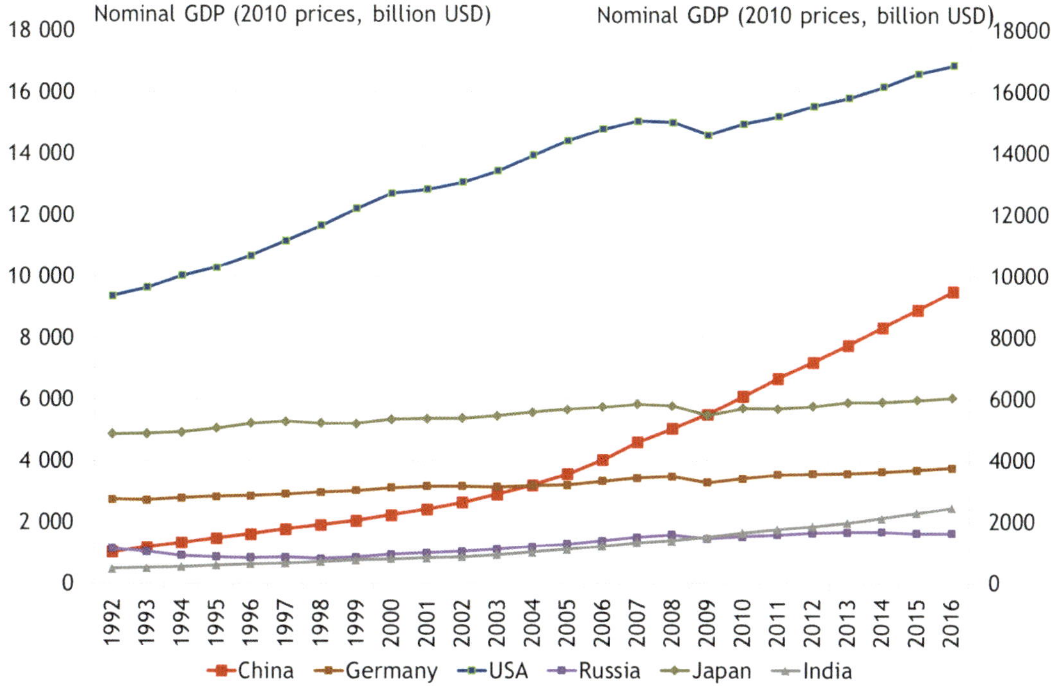

Source: The World Bank.

Table 1: Ratio of Subjective and Objective Indicators in Global Competitiveness Reports

	No. of Indicators	No. of Objective Indicators	Share of Objective Indicators
WEF — Global Competitiveness Index	114	30	26%
WEF — Inclusive Growth and Development Index	12	12	100%
WB — Doing Business	45	45	100%
IMD — World Competitiveness Index	342	226	66%
ACI — Competitiveness Ranking	**102**	**102**	**100%**

Note: No. of objective indicators is based on own calculation.
Source: WEF, IMD, World Bank, ACI.

In measuring competitiveness, the use of objective and reliable data is very important for a non-biased and authentic diagnosis which can be used for designing policies. In this context, the share of objective indicators in the composite indexes is of key importance in our opinion. While WEF — Global Competitiveness Report uses only 30 objective indicators out of the total 114, all of the ACI Competitiveness Ranking's data are objective in its study (Table 1).

The ACI competitiveness framework uses different levels of competitiveness evaluation comprising of 4 environments (with equal weights), 11 sub-environments and overall 102 indicators from different areas. The four pillars to analyse are: Macroeconomic Stability; Government and Institutional Setting; Financial, Businesses and Manpower Conditions; Quality of Life and Infrastructure Development. It is also worth to note that the ACI prepares rankings not just for the composite index, but also for pillars, as well as for several subfields of those.

The results represent robustness of data. The top 5 Chinese regions had almost the same place both in the overall competitiveness ranking and in the 4 environments ranking. The methodology of ACI differs from the method of distance-to-frontier (DTF) used widely by competitiveness reports (WEF, World Bank). While the valuation of ACI shows the performance of economies from the average, the distance-to-frontier method ranks the performance of countries in a scale of 1–7. It would be useful to get a deeper insight into ACI's valuation and better understanding of results between the two methods (ACI's scores from the mean versus DTF). Besides this, as a development opportunity for the future, it would be also worth to compare each regions' performance with that of the neighbouring countries.

In conclusion, ACI Competitiveness Ranking gives accurate information about the competitiveness of the different regions of China. The regional ranking raised attention to the gaps derived from different growth of sub-national economies. ACI highlights the strengths and weaknesses of these regions which can help policymakers in making proper decisions.

Chapter 5

Impact of Real Effective Exchange Rates on Trade in Goods for Mainland China

5.1 Introduction and Motivation

The impact of isolationist "Closed-Door Policies" on Chinese history has been enormous, with such policies and attitudes dominating the foreign policy approaches of successive Chinese governments dating back nearly half a millennium. Barring the relatively isolated instance of broader economic and political outreach defined by the Ming Dynasty Admiral Zheng He's maritime expeditions — which were themselves conceived of as distinctly uneconomical displays of imperial prestige more than anything else — China's engagement with the wider world has been limited indeed (Porter 2016). Deng Xiaoping's announcement of the Chinese Economic Reform, or the "Reform and Opening-up Policy" in 1978 was an event of singularly historic importance, and international trade has correspondingly begun to exert a substantially greater influence on the domestic economy (Lardy 1993). These shifts in policy have brought about enormous change in nearly all aspects of daily life for China's population, and have seemed additionally to have made China's growth rate as sustainable as it has been explosive (Lin *et al.* 2003).

The initial "Opening-up" was followed by a long period of restructuring and reorientation, which culminated in China's accession to the World Trade Organisation (WTO) in 2001. This period of restructuring was broadly comprised of three stages. The early 1980s to July 1986 can be identified as the preparation stage. Following this, the second stage, which was characterized by lively debate over whether China's trade system was to follow the defining paradigm of a planned economy or market economy, took more than half a decade, from February 1987 to October 1992. Detailed bilateral trade negotiations were subsequently conducted between China and other countries, which constituted the third stage, spanning from October 1992 to September 2001. On the 11th of December 2001, the WTO officially announced that China had become its 143rd member.

According to WTO's documents on the event, entitled Accession of the People's Republic of China, China was to liberalise its banking, financial, insurance, telecommunication and services sectors to a considerable extent by allowing for the inflow of foreign investment. Restrictions on retail, wholesale and distribution were also to be removed, and import tariffs were to be lowered.

Even prior to its accession to the WTO, China's importance to global trade had been growing significantly (Ianchovichina and Martin 2001; Chow 2003; Bhattasali *et al.* 2004), and its importance to Global Value Chains was also rising commensurately (Kaplinsky 2000; Cattaneo *et al.* 2010). China's increasing significance in this regard can be attributed to domestic economic reforms which were ongoing at the time. During the 1980s, for example, five Special Economic Zones (SEZs) and 14 Open Coastal Cities (OCCs) were demarcated by Beijing, within which were to be implemented special tax concessions and less restrictive regulations on foreign exchange and land use. These policies were in turn designed to facilitate inflows of foreign capital and technology, which would thus enhance China's position as an exporter (Wei 1995).

As a result of both its accession to the WTO and these aforementioned domestic economic regulations, China's trade surged at the beginning of the 21st century. In terms of exports, China overtook Japan to become Asia's top exporter in 2004, a mere three years after it joined the WTO. China would continue this trend in subsequent years by overtaking the US in 2007 and Germany in 2009 to become the world's single largest exporter (WTO International Trade Statistics 2015).

In 2008, the Global Financial Crisis (GFC) erupted in the US, with its effects radiating across the world over the course of 2009. The world economy was severely affected, and world trade declined significantly. Furthermore, the deleterious effects of the GFC have been persistent and long-lasting, affecting the global economy to the present day. In the midst of this turmoil, China also saw significant drops in both exports and imports, but soon recovered with even higher growth rates in both measures, displaying a notable fortitude in the face of overwhelming economic unrest. In 2015, world energy prices dropped by 45 percent and the growth of world merchandise trade had fallen by more than 10 percent, but China's share of world trade also reached the highest point.

Making preparations for the future, China established the China (Shanghai) Pilot Free Trade Zone (CPFTZ) in 2013 to further strength its trade position. In the same year, President Xi Jinping launched the "Belt and Road Initiative" (BRI), aiming to promote trade in both its coastal areas and its inner provinces, i.e. Western China, which have historically experienced uneven rates of economic development relative to the coastal provinces.

Speaking with specific reference to regional development, the Eastern Coastal Area has consistently been the top contributor for exports. Exports from this region have accounted for between 80 percent and 90 percent of total national exports, peaking at 89.22 percent in 2005. Western China's contribution to China's total exports has also increased relatively steadily over the last two decades. This can be attributed to the China Western Development Strategy led by former President Jiang Zemin in 2000 as well as the more recent developments brought about by the implementation of the BRI.

More closely examining the situation at the provincial level, it can be noted that Guangdong's exports increased almost 10-fold from 1996 to 2015. This can largely be attributed to the fact that three of the eight Special Economic Zones, namely Shenzhen, Zhuhai and Shantou, are all located in Guangdong, which contributes significantly to the province's exports.

Taking this historical background into account, the first objective of this chapter is to study the trade flows of Mainland China by analysing trends and patterns at the national level, regional level and provincial level. The regional- and provincial-level studies in particular facilitate the identification of more specific policy implications, which can in turn be helpful in understanding variations in the trade flows at a disaggregated level. This chapter will also enhance the policy-maker's understanding by not only providing analyses of trade flows in comparison with GDP and world trade statistics but also taking into consideration the latest sectoral and bilateral trade conditions in 2015.

The second objective of this chapter is to study the trade flows — with a particular focus on exports — of 10 coastal provinces of Mainland China by analysing the impact of REER. One may argue, for example, that any large disparity in exports could be related to the various structural, institutional and geographical factors which differ across certain provinces. The ACI competitiveness score is adopted to capture all these factors.

5.2 Trends and Patterns in International Trade in Goods

5.2.1 Data Coverage and Data Sources

A total of 20 years of annual data, ranging from 1996 to 2015, has been utilised for the analysis. This data thus covers 3 periods: (1) the pre-WTO period from 1996 to 2001; (2) the post-WTO and pre-GFC period from 2002 to 2007; and (3) the post-GFC period from 2008 to 2015.

The primary data source is China's National Bureau of Statistics, which reports on exports and imports on an annual basis at both national and provincial levels. It also provides details of sectoral distribution of national exports and imports annually. Another primary data source is the World Bank, which reports annually on global exports and imports, as well as the bilateral shares of export and import *vis-à-vis* China's trading partners.

5.2.2 Trade in Goods at the National Level

As mentioned, China's trade has grown steadily in terms of both exports and imports since the Chinese Economic Reform or Reform and Opening-up led by Deng Xiaoping in 1978. According to the China Statistical Yearbook 2016, aggregate trade increased from $20.64 billion in 1978 to $69.60 billion in 1985, and further increased to $115.44 billion in 1990 — a more than 5-fold increase in 12 years. Growth in this period was driven by many factors, such as early reforms which granted permission to private entrepreneurs to start businesses, the privatisation of some state-owned industries, and most importantly, the establishment of SEZs and OCCs. In July 1979, Shenzhen, Zhuhai, Shantou and Xiamen became the first batch of SEZs in China. Additionally, in 1984, the prior open-policy measures granted OCC status to 14 cities along the Pacific coast, namely Beihai, Tianjin, Shanghai, Dalian, Qinhuangdao, Yantai, Qingdao, Lianyungang, Nantong, Ningbo, Wenzhou, Fuzhou, Guangzhou and Zhanjiang. This initial group of OCCs was joined by 140 more cities in 1988, including provincial capitals like Hangzhou, Nanjing and Shenyang. These regions were associated with exceptional tax concessions and less restrictive regulations on foreign exchange and land use, thereby promoting the inflow of foreign capital and technology, thus facilitating international trade in the 1980s (Wei 1995).

From 1996 to 2015, aggregate trade, exports and imports (Figure 5.1) exhibit very similar trends and patterns. During the period of the Asian Financial Crisis, there was no significant growth for aggregate trade, export and import. Aggregate trade increased from $325.16 billion in 1997 to $360.63 billion in 1999 — around an 11 percent increment. Exports and imports have

Figure 5.1: Aggregate Trade, Export and Import of Mainland China, 1996–2015

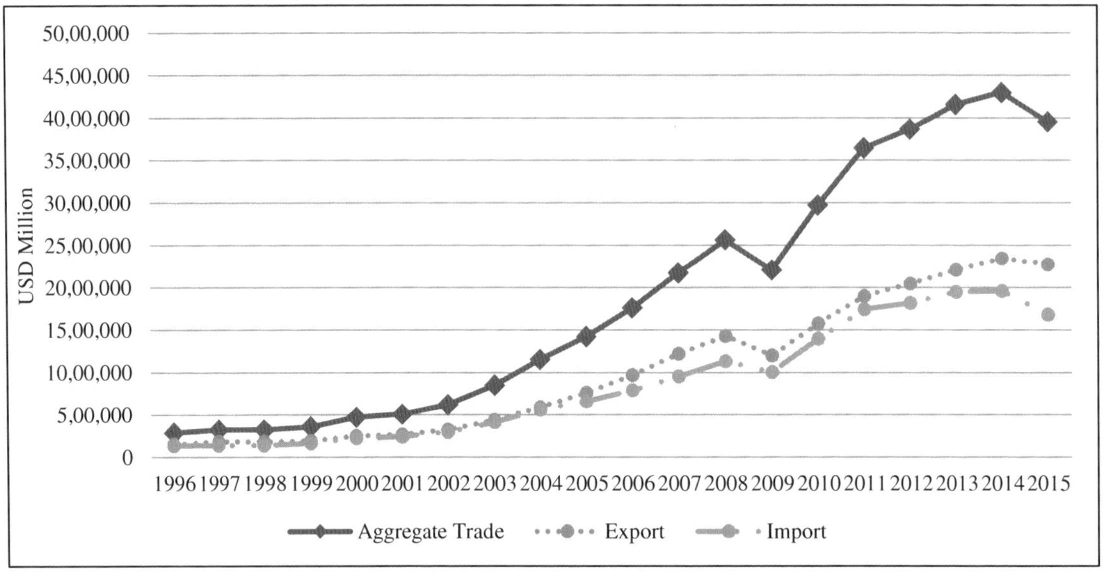

Source: Asia Competitiveness Institute based on information retrieved from National Bureau of Statistics of China.

increased from $182.79 billion to $194.93 billion and from $142.37 billion to $165.70 billion, respectively, with growth rates of 7 percent and 16 percent.

Trade began to surge after 2001, with China's accession to the WTO. With a much greater degree of interaction with global markets, China committed to further liberalising capital markets in order to make progress on commitments made in accordance with rule-based WTO guidelines (Whalley and Xin 2006). Additionally, the number of state-owned enterprises decreased by 48 percent between 2001 and 2004, signalling China's dedication to its obligations as a WTO member (Brandt *et al.* 2008).

As can be noted from Figure 5.1, aggregate trade, exports and imports peaked at $256.32 billion, $143.07 billion and $113.25 billion, respectively, in 2008, prior to the onset of the GFC. Trade values experienced a downturn in the year 2009, but soon rebound in 2010, surpassing their values in 2008. By 2014, aggregate trade, exports and imports reached $430.15 billion, $234.23 billion and $195.92 billion, respectively. China's growth in these fields from 2001 to 2014 is thus 744 percent, 780 percent and 700 percent, respectively.

In 2015, according to the National Bureau of Statistics, the GDP growth rate of China declined to 6.9 percent, the lowest in 25 years. Trade, as one of the important factors contributing to GDP, also fell, as indicated in Figure 5.1.

The following graphs focus on exports as a share of world exports and domestic GDP (Figure 5.2), and imports as a share of world imports and domestic GDP (Figure 5.3). The two graphs exhibit similar trends.

One interesting observation is that China's exports (or imports) as a share of world exports (or imports) has consistently increased, ultimately rising from 2.77 percent (or 2.51 percent) in 1996 to 13.72 percent (or 10.04 percent) in 2015. Despite the Asian Financial Crisis or GFC, China

Figure 5.2: Export (Share of World Export and Percent of GDP) of Mainland China, 1996–2015

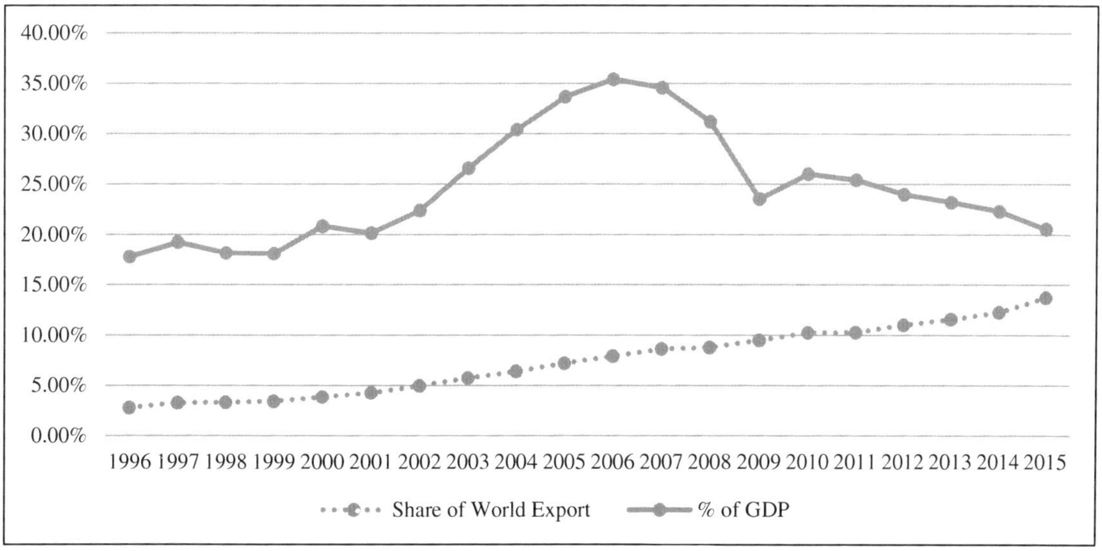

Source: Asia Competitiveness Institute based on information retrieved from National Bureau of Statistics of China and World Bank.

Figure 5.3: Import (Share of World Export and Percent of GDP) of Mainland China, 1996–2015

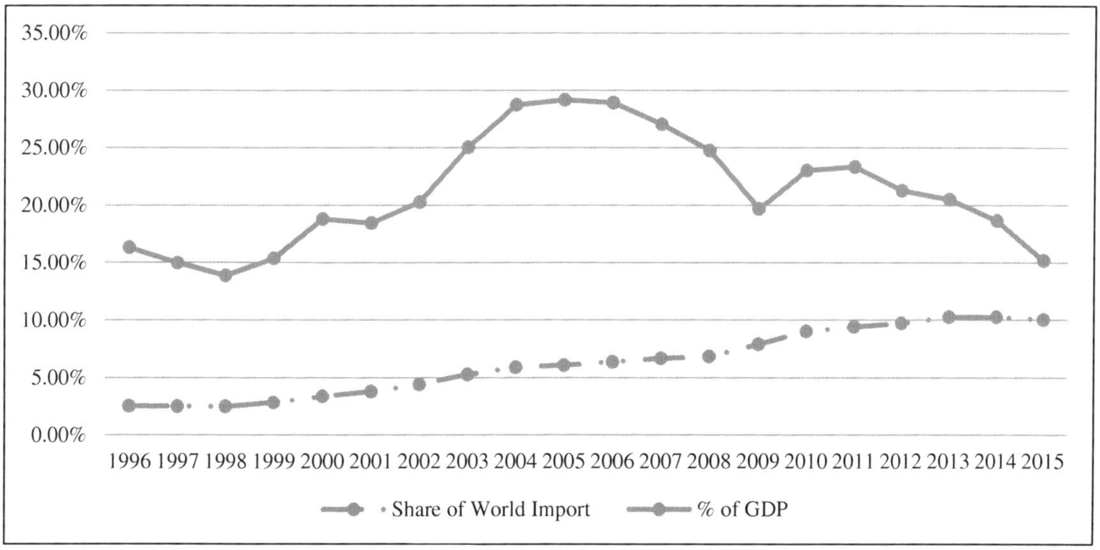

Source: Asia Competitiveness Institute based on information retrieved from National Bureau of Statistics of China and World Bank.

has consistently outperformed the rest of the world's economies in terms of both exports and imports. This is clearly indicative of China's growing importance to global markets.

While the two curves, i.e. exports (or imports) as share of world exports (or imports), are almost linear, both graphs still reflect the fact that 2001 was a watershed moment. The annual increment from 1996 to 2001 (as indicated by the slope of the curve) is relatively consistent at around 0.25 percent and 0.21 percent for export and import share, respectively. However, the annual increment increased to 0.62 percent and 0.40 percent after 2001, reflecting a significant increase in the significance of China to international trade, and vice versa.

Even when considered as a share of world exports (or imports), China's exports (and imports) have grown significantly. They notably assume an inverse U shape when considered as a share of China's GDP. There is also slight fluctuation around the period of the Asian Financial Crisis, which occurred prior to China's entry into the WTO. Prior to 2001, exports contributed from 17 percent to 21 percent of China's GDP, while imports contributed between 13 percent and 19 percent to GDP. After 2001 however, the significance of both exports and imports to the Chinese economy surged, with exports peaking at 35.43 percent in 2006 and imports doing likewise at 29.18 percent in 2005. These astronomical increases in trade volume proportionate to overall economic performance were a driving force contributing to the extremely high rate of GDP growth during that period, which exceeded 10 percent in 2005 and did not fall below that figure until around 2012.

Contrastingly, consumption as a share of GDP fell gradually from 62.85 percent in 2000 to 50.37 percent in 2005.[1] In response, China's Eleventh "Five Year Plan" placed a much greater emphasis on the growth of consumption over trade, implementing policy measures which have seen some success, as can be noted in Figures 5.2 and 5.3. Additionally, as shown in these figures, exports and imports as share of GDP has gradually decreased in recent years, reaching 20.57 percent and 15.21 percent, respectively, by 2015. There was a sharp drop and small recovery during and after the GFC period, but the contributions of both exports and imports to China's GDP has continuously decreased after that.

5.2.3 Trading Partners and Sectoral Distribution of Trade in Goods in Mainland China

This section will begin with a descriptive analysis of Mainland China's trade relationship with its eight largest exporting partners in the years 2000, 2005, 2010 and 2015. This group of economies includes the US, Hong Kong, Japan, South Korea, Germany, Netherland, the United Kingdom and Singapore. Figure 5.4 illustrates a trend towards trade diversification, and the degree to which trade volumes to individual economy have changed or remained stable is notable. For example, the percentage of overall Mainland China's exports to Japan fell from 16.7 percent in 2005 to 5.96 percent in 2015 — signifying a gradual diminishing of Mainland China's dependence on exports to Japan over that decade. Similarly, the share of Mainland China's exports heading to the US also fell significantly from 2005 to 2010, declining from 21.42 percent to 17.99 percent. Contrastingly, however, the proportions of overall export volume which have headed to Mainland China's other export partners have remained relatively steady, barring slight fluctuations for Hong Kong, with which trade volume as percentage of total Mainland China's

[1] Consumption data is from WTO, final consumption expenditure (% of GDP). Accessed from http://data.worldbank.org/indicator/NE.CON.TETC.ZS?locations=CN on 08/06/2017.

Figure 5.4: Major Exporting Partners of Mainland China in 2000, 2005, 2010 and 2015

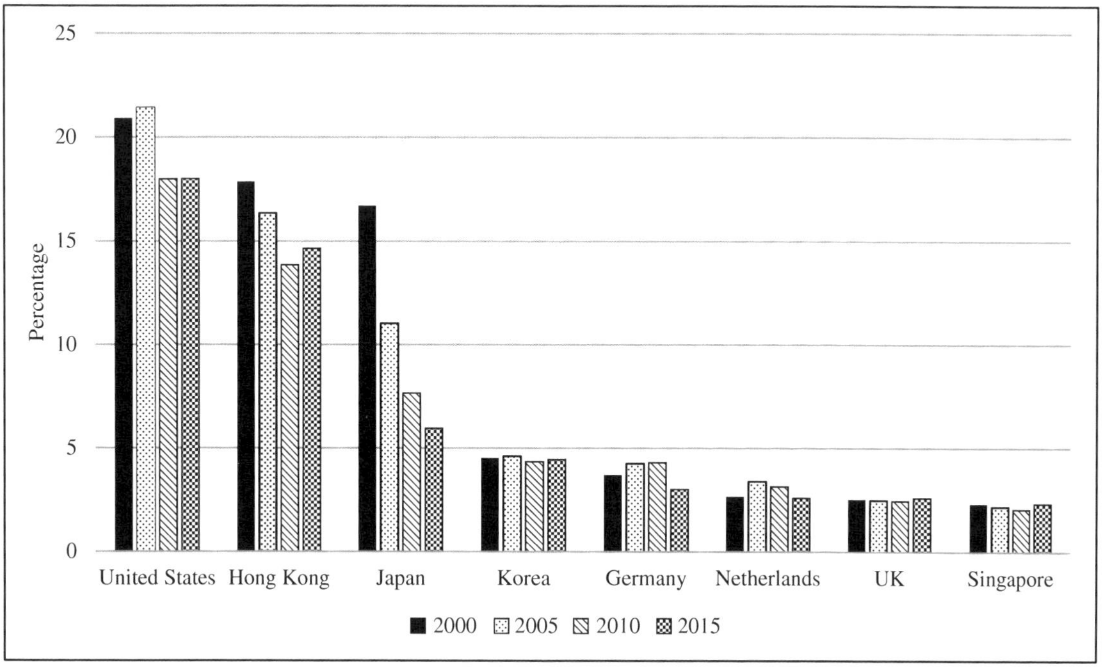

Source: Asia Competitiveness Institute based on information retrieved from the World Bank.

trade decreased from 2000 to 2010, but recovered in 2015. Furthermore, the combined shares of total Mainland China's exports which have headed to these seven economies have also declined sharply from 71.25 percent to 53.64 percent between 2000 and 2015. This is a clear indication that Mainland China's export concentration is decreasing, and that it has been working to diversify its trading options. As Figure 5.5 illustrates that exports to North American countries (e.g. the US) and East Asian countries (e.g. Japan) has decreased over the past 15 years and thus, it can be inferred that the share of exports intended for European, African and Latin American countries must also have increased.

The economies from which Mainland China imports most are Japan, South Korea, the US, Germany, Taiwan, Malaysia, Singapore and Australia (Figure 5.5), in that order. Imports from these eight economies comprise roughly 53 percent of Mainland China's imports across all the years. Similar to the situation with exports, imports from Japan have fallen significantly from comprising 18.44 percent of total Mainland China's imports in 2005, to 8.51 percent by 2015. Correspondingly, while Japan was initially the top importer of goods into China, it has by 2015 become only China's fourth largest import partner by, having been overtaken by South Korea, the US and Taiwan.

Singapore is another country from which China has gradually imported proportionally less goods since 2005, even as it has contrastingly increased its imports from Taiwan. This can likely be attributed to the fact that in 2005, the former Chinese President Hu Jintao and Lien Chan, who

Figure 5.5: Major Importing Partners of Mainland China in 2000, 2005, 2010 and 2015

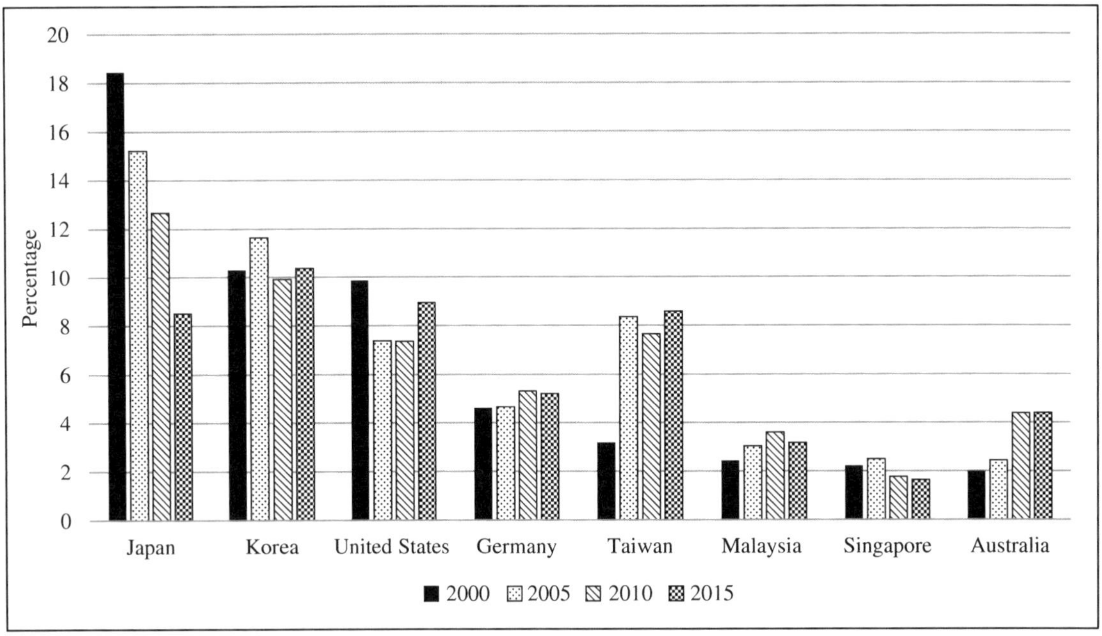

Source: Asia Competitiveness Institute based on information retrieved from the World Bank.

was at the time Chairman of the Taiwanese Kuomintang, met in Beijing to discuss various economic partnerships between Mainland China and Taiwan. During these discussions, they agreed to improve mutual investment and trade, and notably resolved recurrent issues regarding the sale of agricultural products imported from Taiwan to Mainland China.

In addition to the trading partners of Mainland China, it is also important to highlight the sectoral distribution of trade. Figures 5.6 and 5.7 list the sectorial distribution of Mainland China's exports and imports in 2015, based on Primary Goods and Manufactured Goods.[2] There are five categories under each classification. Primary goods include: (1) *Food and Live Animals Used Mainly for Food*; (2) *Beverages and Tobacco*; (3) *Non-edible Raw Materials*; (4) *Mineral Fuels, Lubricants and Related Materials* and (5) *Animal and Vegetable Oils, Fats and Wax*. Manufactured goods include: (1) *Chemicals and Related Products*; (2) *Light Textile Industrial Products, Rubber Products, Minerals and Metallurgical Products*; (3) *Machinery and Transport Equipment*; (4) *Miscellaneous Products* and (5) *Products Not Otherwise Classified*.

It can be observed from Figures 5.6 and 5.7 that *Machinery and Transport Equipment* is a major component of both overall Mainland China's exports and imports, making up 46.59 percent of total exports and 40.63 percent of total imports. This in turn demonstrates that Mainland

[2]This is based on Standard International Trade Classification (SITC).

Figure 5.6: Sectoral Distribution of Export in 2015

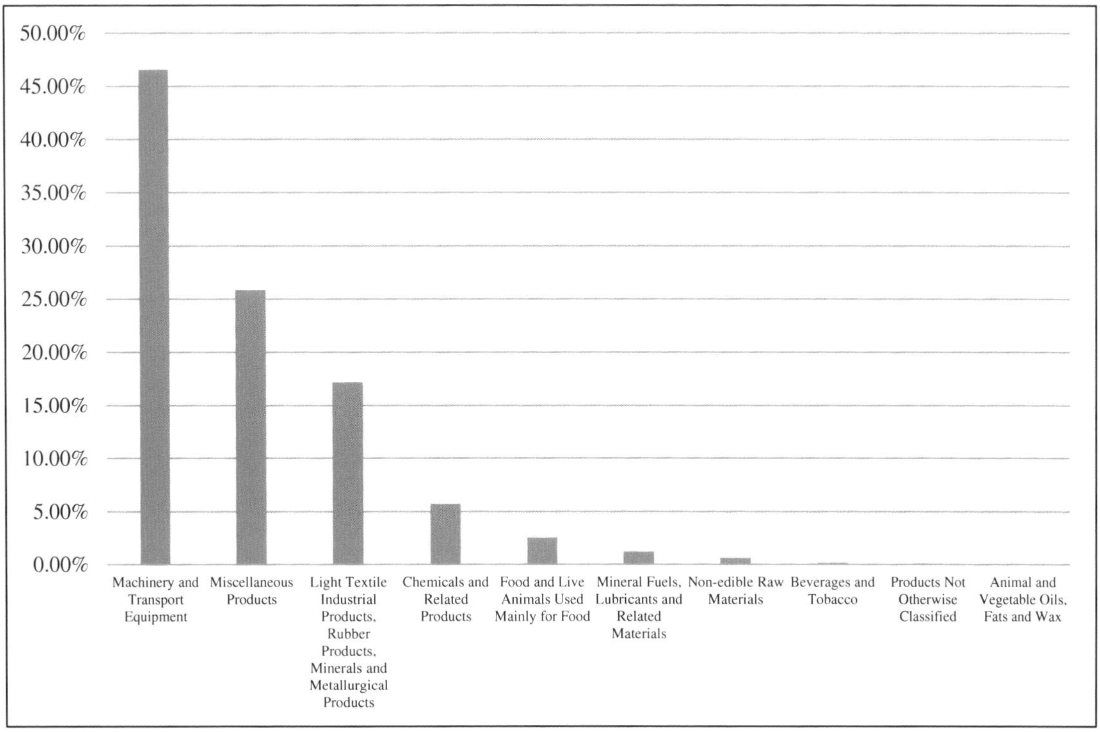

Source: Asia Competitiveness Institute based on information retrieved from National Bureau of Statistics of China.

China is specialised in assembly operations and thus assumes a central role in the Global Value Chain (Kaplinsky 2000; Lemoine and Ünal-Kesenci 2004; Hu and Gang 2005).

Figure 5.6 also illustrates that *Miscellaneous Products* and *Light Textile Industrial Products, Rubber Products, Minerals and Metallurgical Products* are the second and third major components of total Mainland China's exports, accounting for 25.84 percent and 17.20 percent of total exports respectively. The rest of the sectors collectively comprise 10.38 percent of total exports. Mainland China's exports clearly hinge mainly on manufactured products, rather than on primary products.

As Figure 5.7 contrastingly illustrates, *Non-edible Raw Materials* and *Mineral Fuels, Lubricants and Related Materials* are ranked 2nd and 3rd, with shares of 12.49 percent and 11.82 percent respectively. This in turn demonstrates that Mainland China is largely reliant on the import of primary goods. Furthermore, *Chemicals and Related Products*, *Light Textile Industrial Products, Rubber Products, Minerals and Metallurgical Products* and *Products Not Otherwise Classified* all individually comprise from 5.13 percent to 10.20 percent of total imports, indicating that Mainland China's imports are more diversified than its exports.

Figure 5.7: Sectoral Distribution of Import in 2015

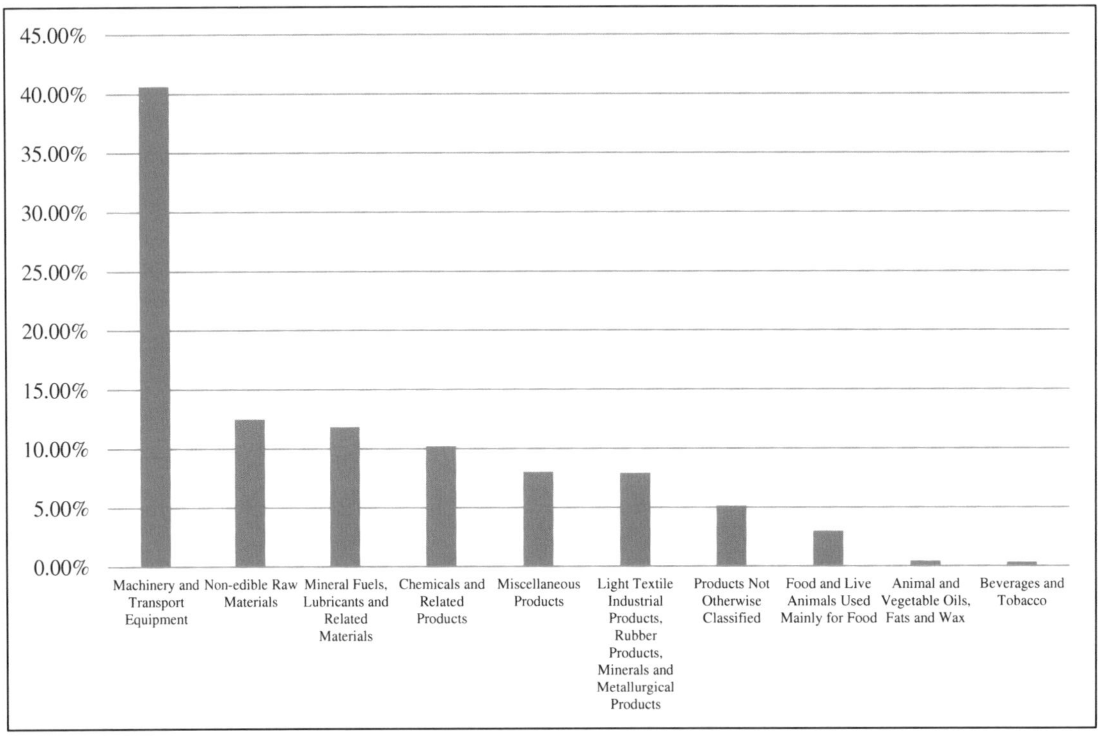

Source: Asia Competitiveness Institute based on information retrieved from National Bureau of Statistics of China.

5.2.4 Trade in Goods at Regional and Provincial Levels

China's National Bureau of Statistics publishes provincial level trade data, covering 31 provinces in Mainland China. First, the trade statistics is studied at the regional level, before proceeding to analysing statistics at the provincial level.

Mainland China can be roughly divided into four regions: The Eastern Coastal Area, Central China, Western China and North-eastern China. The Eastern Coastal Area consists of Beijing, Fujian, Guangdong, Hainan, Hebei, Jiangsu, Shandong, Shanghai, Tianjin and Zhejiang. Central China consists of Anhui, Henan, Hubei, Hunan, Jiangxi and Shanxi. Western China consists of Chongqing, Gansu, Guangxi, Guizhou, Inner Mongolia, Ningxia, Qinghai, Shaanxi, Sichuan, Tibet, Xinjiang and Yunnan. North-eastern China consists of Heilongjiang, Jilin and Liaoning. Regional data is obtained by aggregating provincial level data.

Figures 5.8 and 5.9 illustrate each region's contribution to total national exports and imports. As can be noted from both figures, The Eastern Coastal Area has consistently been the top contributor to both exports and imports from 1996 to 2015. Its exports have accounted for between 80 percent and 90 percent of total national exports, peaking at 89.22 percent in 2005; meanwhile, imports to the region account for between 84.52 percent and

Figure 5.8: Share of Regional Merchandise Export to Mainland China's Export

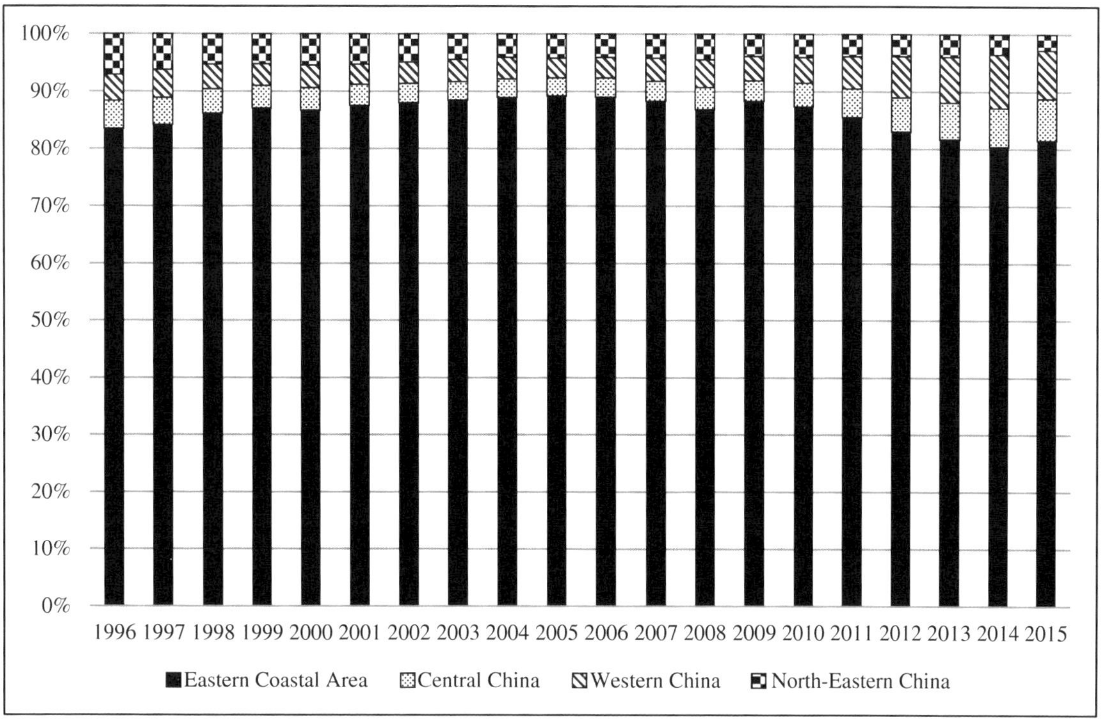

Source: Asia Competitiveness Institute based on information retrieved from National Bureau of Statistics of China.

90.67 percent of total national imports. The Eastern Coastal Area's centrality in this regard can be explained by the fact that it retains the first mover advantage, due to having been supported and positioned by the central government to lead in the implementation of reforms which opened up the Chinese economy. This has created vital institutional advantages and development opportunities for the region when it comes to trade. In fact, all the eight SEZs, including the recently announced Xiong'an New Area, are located within provinces in the Eastern Coastal Area. Furthermore, 2013 saw Shanghai become host to the first CPFTZ, which is intended as a testbed for a number of economic and social reforms. In terms of special trade policies, commodities entering to the zone are not subject to duty and customs clearance. This model was applied to Tianjin, Guangdong and Fujian, three other Eastern Coastal provinces, in 2015.

To further support the Belt and Road Initiative announced in 2013 by President Xi Jinping, the Pilot Free Trade Zone was further expanded to Liaoning (North-eastern Area), Zhejiang (Eastern Coastal Area), Henan, Hubei (Central China), Chongqing, Sichuan and Shaanxi (Western China) in 2017. This is thus a "from point to line, further to surface" process.

With the Belt and Road initiative and the China Western Development Strategy led by former President Jiang Zemin in 2000, improvements are observed in Western China's contributions to

Figure 5.9: Share of Regional Merchandise Import to Mainland China's Import

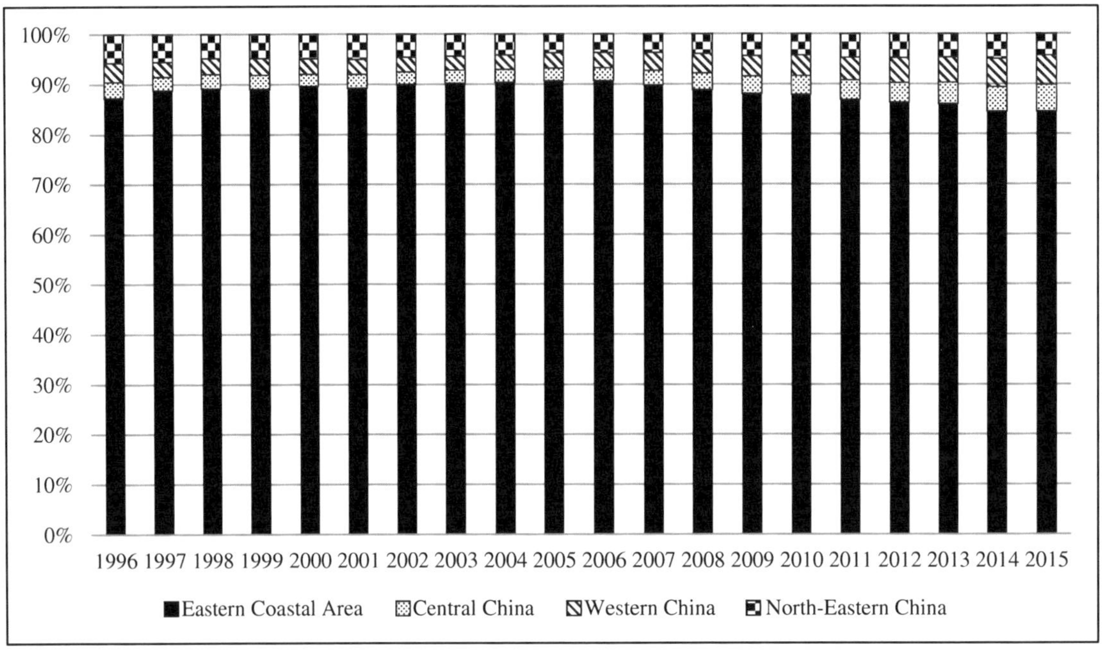

Source: Asia Competitiveness Institute based on information retrieved from National Bureau of Statistics of China.

China's total exports and imports. For example, Western China's contributions to total exports have increased relatively steadily from 1996 to 2015, going from having accounted for 4.58 percent of total exports in 1996 to accounting for 8.43 percent of total exports in 2015 (Figure 5.8). Western China's share of total national imports has similarly risen from 3.82 percent to 5.91 percent (Figure 5.9) in the same period.

Next, provincial data are examined and illustrated in Figures 5.10–5.13, which track the development of China's top seven exporting and importing provinces from 1996 to 2015.

Mainland China's top provinces by exports are Beijing, Fujian, Guangdong, Jiangsu, Shandong, Shanghai and Zhejiang (Figure 5.10). Firstly, Figure 5.10 makes quite clear that China's accession to the WTO in 2001 was a significant boon to exports. Secondly, it is notable that the documented provinces follow exactly the same trend as the national export value, up to and including experiencing similar drops during the GFC in 2009, with the exception of Beijing. This can be attributed to the fact that prior to the 2008 Beijing Olympics, there was a gradual shifting of heavy industries away from Beijing to the neighbouring province of Hebei. Thus, there were no significant changes to Beijing's exports after 2008.

Guangdong's exports have risen tremendously from 493.37 billion Yuan in 1996 to 4005.93 billion Yuan in 2015, an almost 10-fold increase. Guangdong province is a coastal province located on China's south-eastern coast. It is also home to the Pearl River delta, an economic powerhouse that was one of the drivers of China's development in the earlier years of its

Figure 5.10: Top 7 Exporting Provinces in Mainland China

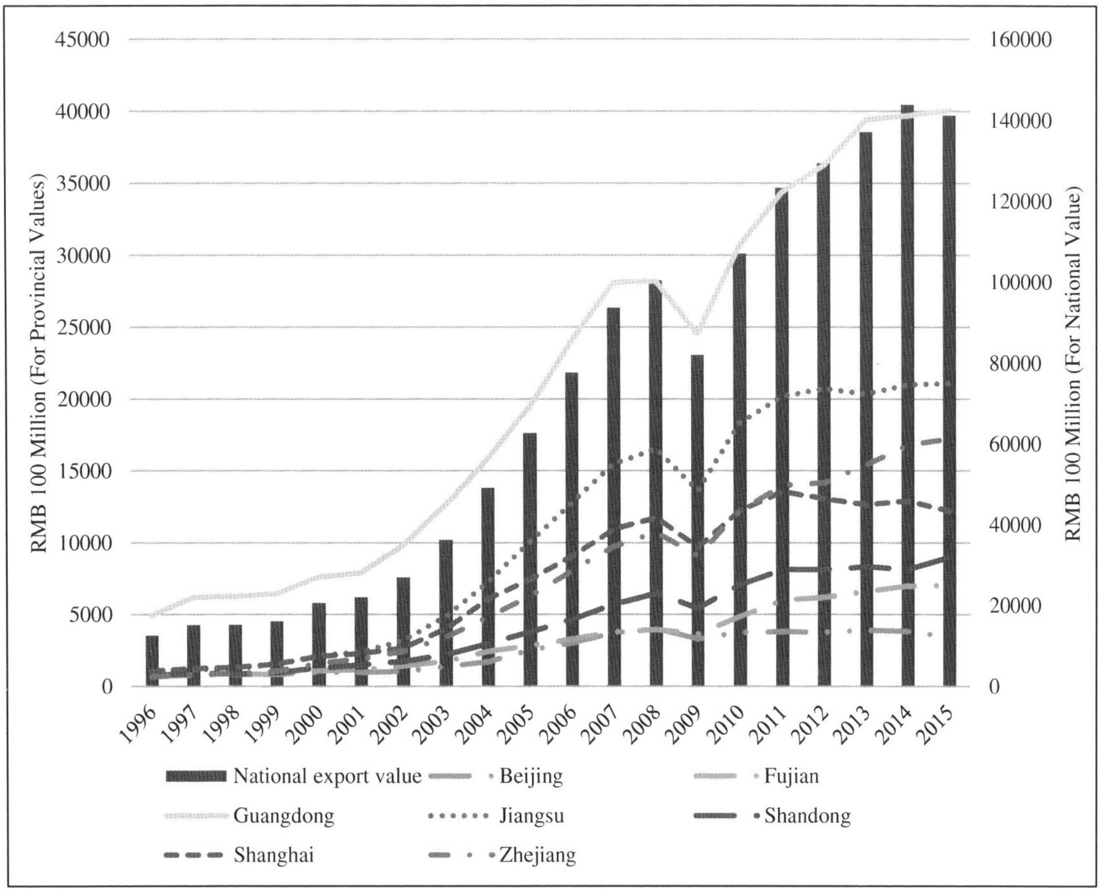

Source: Asia Competitiveness Institute based on information retrieved from National Bureau of Statistics of China.

liberalisation. The fact that three out of the eight currently operational SEZs, namely Shenzhen, Zhuhai and Shantou are all located in Guangdong contributes significantly to the province's exports. Guangdong's booming economy correspondingly accounts for a significant share of China's total national exports.

Over this same two-decade period, Jiangsu, Zhejiang and Shanghai have also experienced twenty two-fold, twenty six-fold and eleven-fold increases in export volumes respectively, with exports reaching 2109.21 billion Yuan, 1721.11 billion Yuan and 1220.23 billion Yuan in 2015. A clear growth slowdown can be observed after the GFC in 2009, with export value in absolute terms flattening for Jiangsu. There is even a decrease in the volume of Shanghai's exports, which resulted in the city being overtaken by neighbouring Zhejiang, which continued to experience reasonable growth after the GFC.

Shandong and Fujian provinces underwent a slow but steady improvement in exports over the same two decades.

Figure 5.11: Export (Percentage of GRDP) of Top 7 Provinces from Mainland China

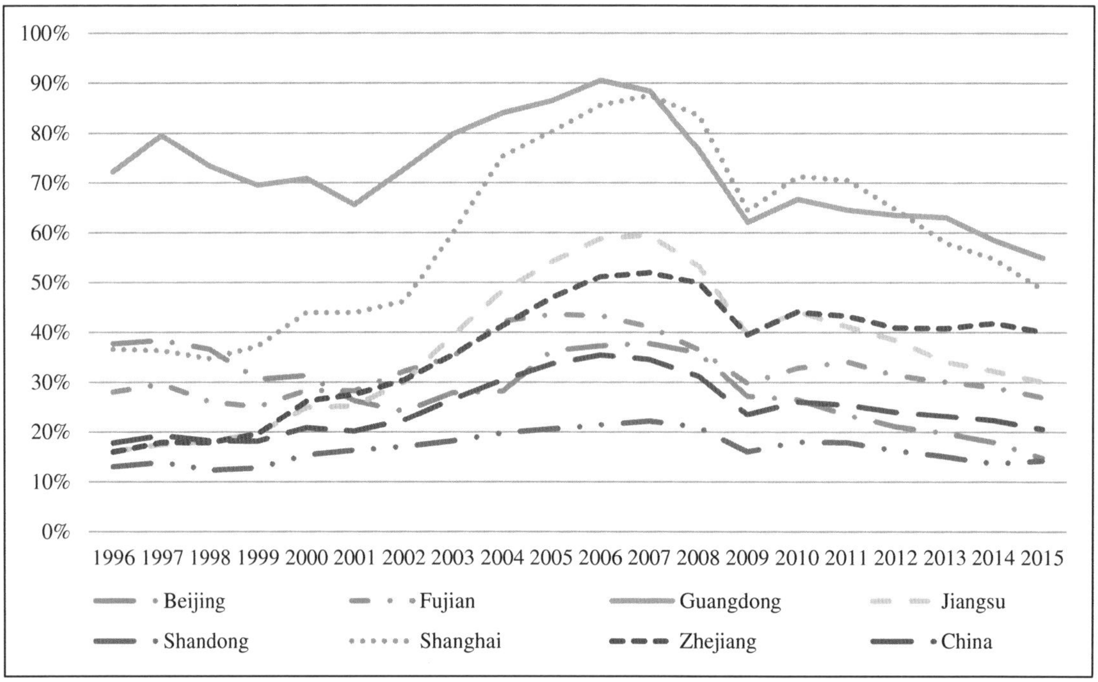

Source: Asia Competitiveness Institute based on information retrieved from National Bureau of Statistics of China.

Figure 5.11 reflects exports as a share of Gross Regional Domestic Product (GRDP) for the top seven provinces, in comparison with Mainland China's aggregate exports as share of GDP. It is obvious that there was a boom immediately following China's accession to the WTO in 2001, with the share peaking around 2006, followed by a gradual decrease which continues to persist. The provincial trend is very similar to the national trend, indicating a high correlation. The specific movements of these trends can be explained by referring to the Eleventh "Five-Year Plan", which saw the central government begin to emphasise consumption over trade.

The share of exports for Guangdong, Shanghai, Shandong, Jiangsu and Zhejiang are consistently above the national average, after the WTO accession. These five provinces are the top export-oriented provinces in Mainland China, with this being especially relevant to Guangdong and Shanghai, where exports contributed to 90.53 percent of GRDP in 2006 and 87.55 percent of GRDP in 2007 respectively. The SEZs in Guangdong and Shanghai have consistently made significant contributions to exports, however, the establishment of the CPFTZ in Shanghai in 2013 did not increase its export share, which is a clear indication that as a financial centre, Shanghai's development is leaning more towards its financial services sectors and less towards manufacturing.

Figure 5.12: Top 7 Importing Provinces in Mainland China

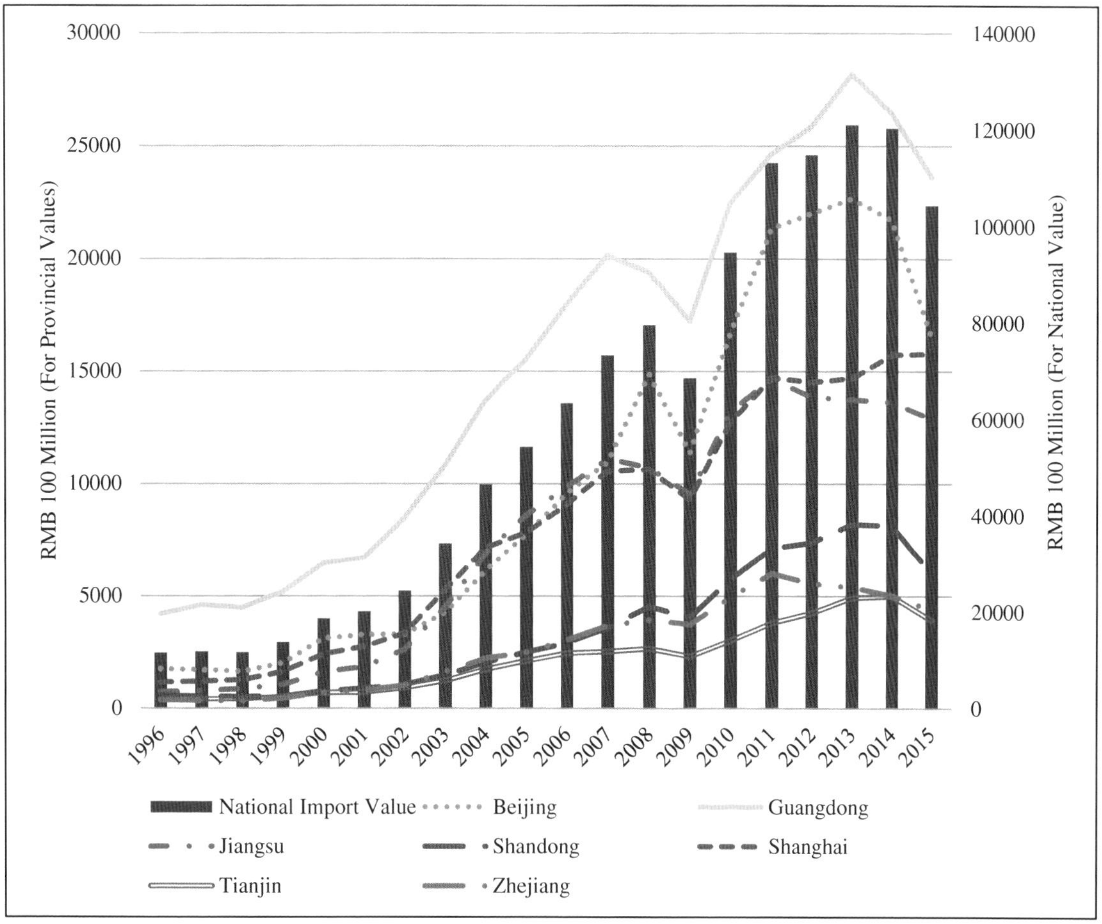

Source: Asia Competitiveness Institute based on information retrieved from National Bureau of Statistics of China.

The list of Mainland China's top seven importing provinces is nearly identical to the list of top seven exporting provinces, except for the fact that Fujian is replaced by Tianjin (Figure 5.12). As Figure 5.12 illustrates, the import trend is similar to the export trend visible in Figure 5.10, except that there is a noticeable drop in imports from 2013 to 2015. The fact that prices of energy, minerals and non-ferrous metals decreased since 2013, while prices for food and beverage, manufactured unit value and agricultural raw material remained relatively stable at 2012 levels (WTO International Trade Statistics 2015), accounts for the decrease in import value for most of the provinces examined above.

In terms of imports as share of GRDP in Figure 5.13, Beijing is far and away the leader, with imports hitting 134 percent of the provinces GRDP in year 2008. Even though the world economy was hit by the GFC during and after 2008, the success of the Beijing Olympic Games

Figure 5.13: Import (Percentage of GRDP) of Top 7 Provinces from Mainland China

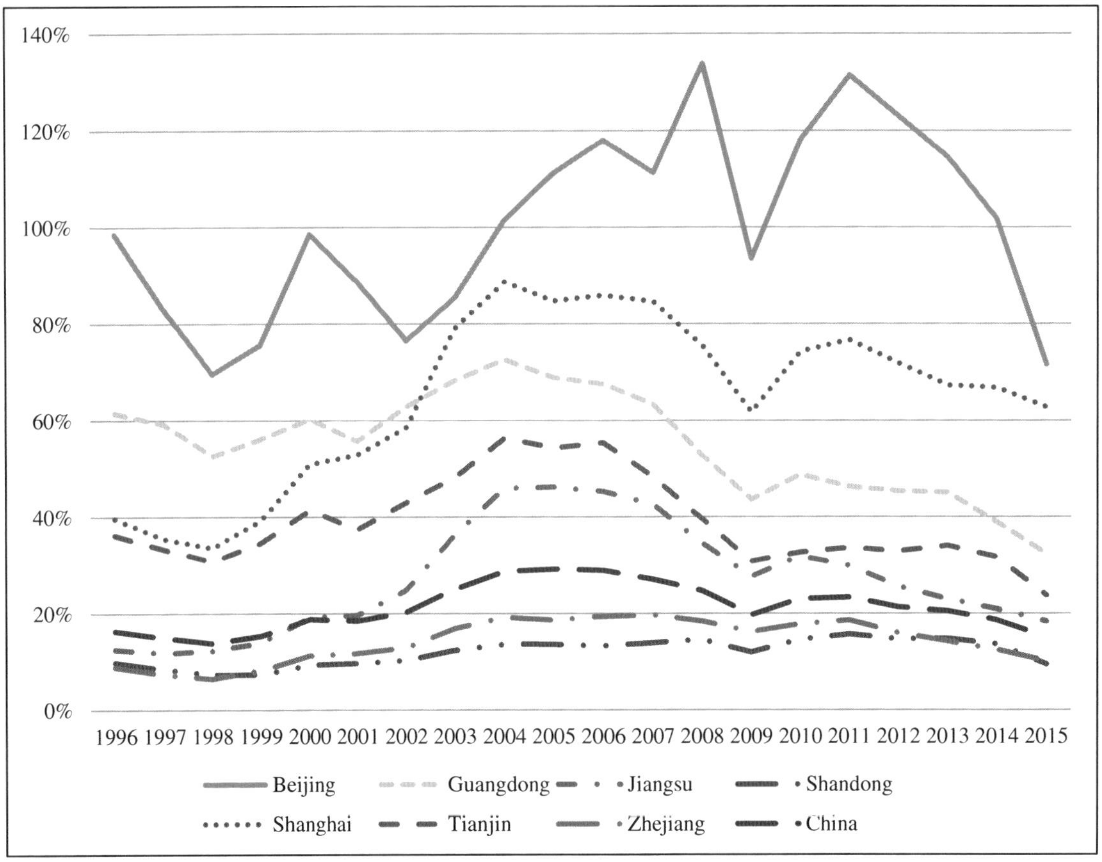

Source: Asia Competitiveness Institute based on information retrieved from National Bureau of Statistics of China.

greatly affected the import values for the year. Nevertheless, with populations having soared by 2015 to 21.71 million and 24.15 million for Beijing and Shanghai respectively (National Bureau of Statistics of China), imports have constituted more than 60 percent of their respective GRDPs since 2001.

With the announcement of establishing the Xiong'an New Area with the aims of curbing urban sprawl, bridging growth disparity and protecting the ecology, the non-capital functions of Beijing will be transferred there. With such measures, Beijing's population will undoubtedly decline slightly, and imports as a share of GRDP will likewise fall in the future.

This paper also studies the correlation between provincial trade and their respective GRDP over the period of 1996 to 2015 (Tables 5.1 and 5.2). There are strong, positive correlations between both exports and imports and GRDP, with an average of 0.951 and 0.945 respectively. For exports (Table 5.1), Zhejiang has the highest correlation of 0.987, while Beijing's

Table 5.1: Bi-variate Correlation between Export and GRDP for Top 7 Provinces

Bi-variate Correlation	Beijing	Fujian	Guangdong	Jiangsu	Shandong	Shanghai	Zhejiang
1996–2015	0.872	0.978	0.974	0.938	0.969	0.936	0.987
1996–2001	0.903	0.947	0.966	0.984	0.961	0.977	0.983
2002–2007	0.993	0.979	0.998	0.998	1.000	0.997	0.998
2008–2015	–0.085	0.965	0.954	0.855	0.890	0.543	0.975

Source: Asia Competitiveness Institute based on information retrieved from National Bureau of Statistics of China.

Table 5.2: Bi-variate Correlation between Import and GRDP for Top 7 Provinces

Bi-variate Correlation	Beijing	Guangdong	Jiangsu	Shandong	Shanghai	Tianjin	Zhejiang
1996–2015	0.949	0.942	0.895	0.968	0.976	0.956	0.931
1996–2001	0.919	0.965	0.962	0.855	0.950	0.945	0.928
2002–2007	0.990	0.986	0.971	0.995	0.981	0.970	0.993
2008–2015	0.605	0.770	0.649	0.752	0.918	0.880	0.473

Source: Asia Competitiveness Institute based on information retrieved from National Bureau of Statistics of China.

correlation is 0.872, the lowest among the top seven exporting provinces, over the two decades. For imports (Table 5.2), Shanghai achieves the highest correlation of 0.976, while Jiangsu is lowest, at 0.895.

This correlation was further studied by breaking the two decades into three phases: (1) 1996–2001 the pre-WTO phase; (2) 2002–2007 the pre-GFC phase and (3) 2008–2015 the post-GFC phase.

The first important observation is that after China's accession to the WTO, the correlation becomes higher for all the top seven provinces for both exports and imports, indicating that the link between trade and GRDP has been strengthened. This correlation can clearly be seen to drop significantly during and after the GFC. For Beijing's exports, the correlation even drops to negative values, the reason for this being, as noted above, that the movement of many heavy industries out of Beijing due to the Beijing 2008 Olympic Games had a significant impact on its exports. This, when taken in conjunction with the GFC, and the consequently diminishing demand from abroad, resulted in greatly reduced export opportunities.

The correlation between imports and GRDP also reduced significantly, i.e. all but Shanghai and Tianjin are below 0.8. What could account for this may be the fact that China recovered faster from the GFC, while the rest of the world's economies were still suffering from the aftereffects. This could have resulted in a relatively lower import prices, and thus the lowering of import values.

5.3 Literature Review[3]

5.3.1 Overview of the Theory

There has been a long debate within theoretical literature regarding the impact on exports of REER, both in terms of levels and volatility.

In terms of REER level, theory tends to agree that depreciation will lead to higher exports, through a direct competitiveness effect. The export price decreases, thus increasing the quantity demanded abroad (Mussa 1984; Dornbusch 1996; Bernard and Jensen 2004; Frieden *et al.* 2006; Staiger and Sykes 2010). However, the positive effects of this may be dampened by other factors. First, if firms are unable to fully adjust the price of the exported goods in the destination country (Goldberg and Knetter 1997). Second, if a majority of the country's exports are processing exports or value-added exports, an increase in the import price will increase the cost of production, thus dampening the price competitiveness effect from depreciation (Zhao and Xing 2006; Powers and Riker 2013).

In terms of the impact of REER volatility on exports, the consensus reached within the theoretical literature is that higher REER volatility will deter exports through two effects (Ethier 1973; Cushman 1983; Peree and Steinherr 1989; Arize *et al.* 2000; Huchet-Bourdon and Korinek 2011). First is direct effect, whereby higher uncertainty of revenues from exports are associated with higher risk. Second is the cost effect, whereby transaction cost becomes higher with higher volatility. However, there are also factors that will dampen this negative effect. Sunk costs that firms incur will make them less responsive to REER volatility (Dixit 1989; Krugman 1989; Franke 1991). Such circumstances tend to encourage "wait-and-see" attitudes, making firms reluctant to withdraw from the market due to all the investment incurred. In addition, the presence of financial instruments makes hedging possible (Aghion *et al.* 2009). If the only source of uncertainty is linked to exchange rate fluctuations, perfect forward markets neutralise the effects of exchange rate volatility on the volume of trade (Baron 1976).

5.3.2 Empirical Literature Review

Existing empirical literature on the impact of REER levels on exports in general are in line with theory. The host country's currency depreciation encourages exports, but the associated exchange rate volatility has an offsetting effect (Fang *et al.* 2006). The effect is higher for existing exporters rather than new entrant exporters (Bernard and Jensen 2004). Freund and Pierola (2012), and Haddad and Pancaro (2010) argue that the effect is more important for developing countries. More recent studies have focused on the effects of the GFC. Kang (2016) has shown that the

[3]This section is based on the paper Tan *et al.* (2018).

impact of real exchange rate on export has decreased in the post-GFC era compared with the situation as it stood, prior to the GFC.

REER volatility has ambiguous effects on trade, depending on the specification of the estimation technique and the measure of volatility (Hooper and Kohlhagen 1978; Carter *et al.* 1984; McKenzie 1999; Taglioni 2002; Ozturk 2006). Dell'Ariccia (1999), Rose (2000) and Anderton and Skudelny (2001) show that higher REER volatility will decrease exports, although the effect is small and the results are not entirely robust to changes in specification. Sauer and Bohara (2001) demonstrate that the negative relationship between REER volatility and exports are significant for least developed countries (LDCs) in Latin America and Africa. However, they do not find such a relationship for Asian LDCs or industrialised countries.

Empirical literature focusing on China at the aggregate or national level tends to confirm the theoretical findings, similarly concluding that REER depreciation will lead to higher exports and higher REER volatility will discourage exports. Saang Joon (2008) studied China–US bilateral trade using quarterly data from 1995 to 2006 through an error correction model. Yang and Gu (2016) studied bilateral trade between China and Singapore using monthly data from 1993 to 2013 through gravity models. Marquez and Schindler (2007) and Zhang (1999) used monthly data from the 1990s to the 2000s in time series models, while Shaikh and Ouyang (2015) and Nishimura and Kenjiro (2013) studied the topic using annual data from 1980 to 2013 and daily data from 2002 to 2011, respectively. There are also papers using panel fixed-effect models to address the impact of REER on China's exports to its trading partners with annual data from the 1980s to the 2000s (Wang *et al.* 2012; Hua 2008; Chit 2008). However, there does not appear to be any empirical paper focused on the impact of REER on exports at the provincial level. Hua (2011) and Yan *et al.* (2016) focus on the impact of exchange rate on economic growth at the provincial level. They show that exports are an important factor for growth, and exchange rate has a negative impact on exports. Park and Prime (1997), Sun and Parikh (2001) and Yao (2006) focus on the relationship between exports and economic growth at the provincial level and argue that exports play an important role in GDP growth. Wu (2007) studied the determinants of exports at the provincial and regional levels and concluded that foreign direct investment (FDI), government spending and infrastructure development affect provincial exports positively. He also demonstrated that the Eastern Coastal Area performs better in terms of exports than the non-coastal regions.

In summary, this study's value addition is in contributing to the corpus of literature which analyses the impact of REER level and volatility on Mainland China's exports at the provincial level, with specific focus on the provinces of the Eastern Coastal Area, with the most recent data available, i.e. from 2000 to 2015. A summary of the empirical literature review has been summarised in Table 5.3.

Table 5.3: Summary of Empirical Literature Review

No.	Citation	Unit of Analysis	Countries/ Provinces Studied	Methodology	Period of Study	Dependent Variable	Independent Variable	Findings
1	Hua, Ping, and Clermont Université. 2011. "The Economic and Social Effects of Real Exchange Rate — Evidence from the Chinese Provinces." 51.	Country	29 provinces of China	GMM system estimation approach and panel data	1987–2008	Per capita real GDP	Real exchange rate; capital intensity; employment ratio; education; exports; industry; FDI; public investments; level of a real GDP per capita lagged one period; a dummy variable for coastal provinces and its interaction term with the real exchange rate; provincial fixed effect; period effect	Real exchange rate appreciation had a negative effect on the economic growth, higher in coastal than in inland provinces, contributing to a minimising of the gap of GDP per capita between the two kinds of provinces.
2	Yan, Guo, Sheng Li, Yaqi Lin, and Jie Li. 2016. "Real Effective Exchange Rate and Regional Economic Growth in China: Evidence from Provincial Data." *China & World Economy* 24: 43–63.	Country	30 China provinces	GMM system estimation approach and panel data	2000–2011	Real GDP growth	Provincial REER, fixed investment to GDP, FDI to GDP, ratio of total import and export volume to GDP, total government consumption, high school enrolment rate	Depreciation promotes net exports, which then promotes growth. The benefit from REER depreciation is smaller for the growth in coastal provinces than non-coastal provinces.
3	Saang Joon, Baak. 2008. "The Bilateral Real Exchange Rates and Trade Between China and the U.S." *China Economic Review* 19: 117–127.	Country	China and US	Estimate cointegrating equations (Error correction model)	1995Q1–2006Q2	Real exports	Real GDP; real bilateral exchange rate; real exchange rate volatility	1% depreciation of the renminbi raises the Chinese exports to the US by 1.7%, while 1% depreciation of the US dollar raises the US exports to China by around 0.4%.

4	Marquez, Jaime, and John Schindler. 2007. "Exchange-Rate Effects on China's Trade*." *Review of International Economics* 15: 837–853.	Country	China	Time-series	Late 1990s to mid-2000s	Export share to the rest of world	Real effective exchange rate; China's economic activity (level of China's industrial production index); the stock of foreign direct investment in China	Real appreciation of real effective exchange rate of RMB has significant negative impact on China's aggregate export.
5	Chou, W. L. 2000. "Exchange Rate Variability and China's Exports." *Journal of Comparative Economics* (Elsevier BV) 28: 61–79.	Country	China	Time-series	Q1 1981 to Q4 1996	Export share to the rest of world	Real effective exchange rate; China's economic activity (level of China's industrial production index); the stock of foreign direct investment in China	Real appreciation of real effective exchange rate of RMB has a significant negative impact on China's aggregate export.
6	Zhang, Zhaoyong. 1999. "Foreign Exchange Rate Reform, the Balance of Trade and Economic Growth: An Empirical Analysis for China." *Journal of Economic Development* 24.	Country	China	Time-series	Jan 1992 to Jan 1997	Real exports	Real foreign income; relative prices; exchange rate variability	Exchange rate volatility has a long-run negative effect on aggregate exports.
7	Mendoza, Enrique. 1995. "The Terms of Trade, the Real Exchange Rate, and Economic Fluctuations." *International Economic Review* 36: 101–137.	Country	G-7 countries and 23 developing countries	Compares numerical solutions of the competitive equilibrium of a dynamic stochastic model of a small open economy with actual business cycles. Study also uses HP filter method	—	Autocorrelation of terms of trade	Correlation between trade balance and terms of trade, gross domestic product (GDP), private consumption (C), fixed investment (I), and the real effective exchange rate (RER)	Terms-of-trade shocks account for nearly half of the actual GDP variability; terms-of-trade shocks cause real appreciations and positive interest differentials, although productivity shocks have opposite effect.

(*Continued*)

Table 5.3: *(Continued)*

No.	Citation	Unit of Analysis	Countries/ Provinces Studied	Methodology	Period of Study	Dependent Variable	Independent Variable	Findings
8	Yang, Guangpu, and Qingyang Gu. 2016. "Effects of Exchange Rate Variations on Bilateral Trade with a Vehicle Currency: Evidence from China and Singapore." *Journal of International Money and Finance* 68: 50–73.	Country	China and Singapore	Gravity model	Jan 1993 to Dec 2013	Real export	Exchange rate level and volatility between China and US, as well as Singapore–US, CPI of both countries, WTO dummy, 2005 China exchange rate reform dummy, GDP of both countries, FTA dummy	In the short run, export volume from China to Singapore is negatively affected by Singapore–US exchange rate. Volatility effect is insignificant but negative.
9	Wang, Chun-Hsuan, Chun-Hung A. Lin, and Chih-Hai Yang. 2012. "Short-Run and Long-Run Effects of Exchange Rate Change on Trade Balance: Evidence from China and its Trading Partners." *Japan and the World Economy* 24: 266–273.	Country	China and 18 trading partners	Panel model	2005–2009	Trade balance	Domestic GDP, foreign GDP, bilateral exchange rate	Real appreciation of RMB has significant positive impact on trade balance for five trading partners. Significant negative impact on trade balance for three trading partners. No significant impact for the rest of the 10 trading partners.
10	Shaikh, Sarfaraz, and Ouyang Hongbing. 2015. "Exchange Rate Volatility and Trade Flows: Evidence from China, Pakistan and India." *International Journal of Economics and Finance* 7: 121.	Country	China, Pakistan and India	Time-series, ARDL model	1980–2013	Real export	Relative price, real world GDP, exchange volatility	Exchange rate volatility is negatively associated with Chinese exports in the short run while it is positively associated in the long run.

11	Hua, Ping. 2008. "Real Exchange Rates and China's Bilateral Exports Towards Industrialized Countries." *Journal of Chinese Economic and Business Studies* 6: 241–259.	Country	China and 11 industrialised countries	GMM system estimation	—	Bilateral export	Foreign GDP, bilateral REER, REER of other countries in terms of RMB, REER of the importer in terms of competitors	Regress all the three REER measures in one equation and find negative and significant impact of exchange rate on real bilateral export.
12	Nishimura, Yusaku, and Kenjiro Hirayama. 2013. "Does Exchange Rate Volatility Deter Japan-China Trade? Evidence from Pre- and Post-Exchange Rate Reform in China." *Japan and the World Economy* 25–26: 90–101.	Country	China and Japan	Time-series, ARDL model	Jan 2002 to Dec 2011	China–Japan bilateral export	Real income in Japan, bilateral exchange volatility, real exchange rate	REER volatility negatively affects China's exports to Japan during the reform period in 2005. The level of the exchange rate also has a significant impact on Chinese exports.
13	Chit, Myint Moe. 2008. "Exchange Rate Volatility and Exports: Evidence from the ASEAN-China Free Trade Area." *Journal of Chinese Economic and Business Studies* 6: 261–277.	Country	China, Indonesia, Malaysia, Phillipines, Thailand	Panel model	1982–2005	Bilateral export	Real GDP of foreign country, relative price, real bilateral exchange rate, volatility of bilateral exchange rate, border dummy, free trade agreement dummy	Bilateral real exchange rate volatility has a significant negative impact on the bilateral exports of the five countries. But bilateral real exchange rate has significant positive effect. The result is consistent, if considering the pre-1997 and post-1997 Asia financial crisis periods separately.

5.4 Data Description, Statistical Computation and Sources

The REER data was obtained from both Bank for International Settlements (BIS) and Bruegel. In fact, the correlation of these two data sets is 0.9989, as shown in Figure 5.14 below. BIS data was used for the baseline studies, while Bruegel data was used for robustness check.

The world demand data is from the World Bank. The world GDP was used as a proxy for world demand. Santos-Paulino and Thirlwall (2004) argued that world GDP should be calculated to exclude the GDP of the exporting country; however, Mainland China presents a particularly special case. China plays a very important role in the GVC, and processing exports and value-added exports attract greater attention than exports alone. However, these two sets of data are not available at the provincial level. Thus, China's GDP, which is a measure of domestic demand that includes goods imported, was used as a proxy for the value-added study. Hence, China's GDP was included into world GDP for the baseline model, while was excluded it for the robustness check.

Real exports and the indicators for the ACI Competitiveness Index are derived from provincial-level data. The sources include the World Bank, the United Nations, official government statistics from the National Bureau of Statistics of China and various statistical bureaus at the provincial level.

Competitiveness is defined in the context of the ACI Competitiveness Index, which is introduced in Chapter 2. However, there is a caveat in this chapter as the dependent variable is export, and indicators 1.2.01 Trade Balance, 1.2.02 International Merchandise Export, 1.2.03 International Merchandise Import and 1.2.04 Openness to Trade are dropped to avoid endogeneity in the regression. Therefore, only 98 indicators are used for the Competitiveness Index computation. The summary of data sources used is shown in Table 5.4 below.

The data coverage is from 2000 to 2015, except in the case of competitiveness data, which covers 2000–2014. The focus will be on the 10 provinces of Mainland China's Eastern Coastal

Figure 5.14: Real Effective Exchange Rate

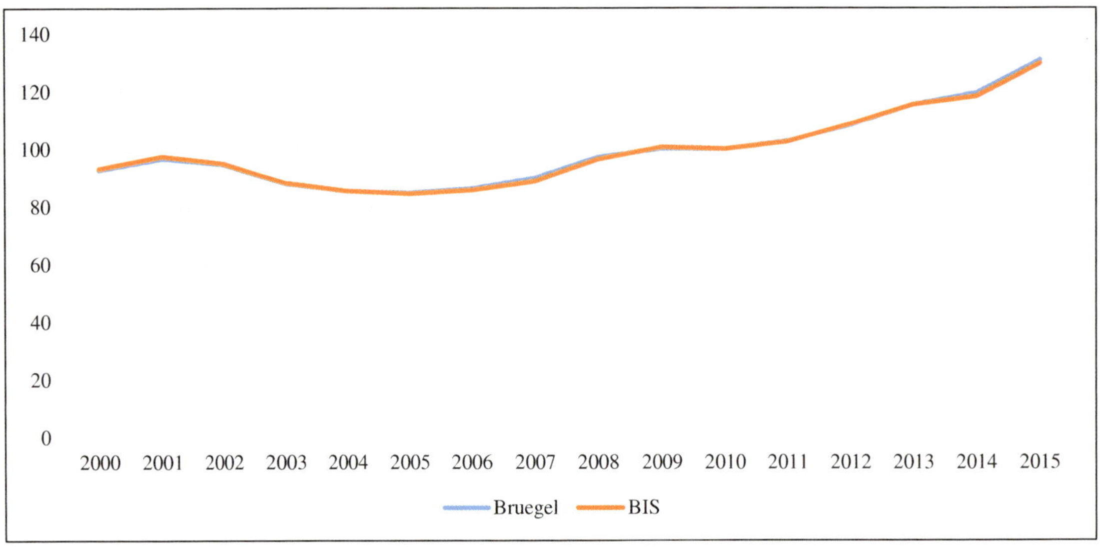

Source: Asia Competitiveness Institute based on information retrieved from BIS and Bruegel.

Table 5.4: Sources and Definitions of Key Variables

Variable	**Unit**	**Definition**	**Sources**
REER	Index	Monthly Average	BIS
REER Volatility (SD)	Monthly Standard Deviation	Monthly Standard Deviation	BIS
Exports of Merchandise Goods	Yuan	Provincial exports for merchandise goods	China Data Online
World GDP	USD	GDP of the world	World Bank
ACI Competitiveness Score	Index	By using 98 indicators, under 4 environments, covering **Macroeconomic Stability, Government and Institutional Setting, Financial, Businesses and Manpower Conditions,** and **Quality of Life and Infrastructure Development**. It measures the relative performance of the provinces.	ACI Calculation

Source: Asia Competitiveness Institute.

Figure 5.15: Average of Real Exports vs. Average of ACI Competitiveness Score (2000–2014)

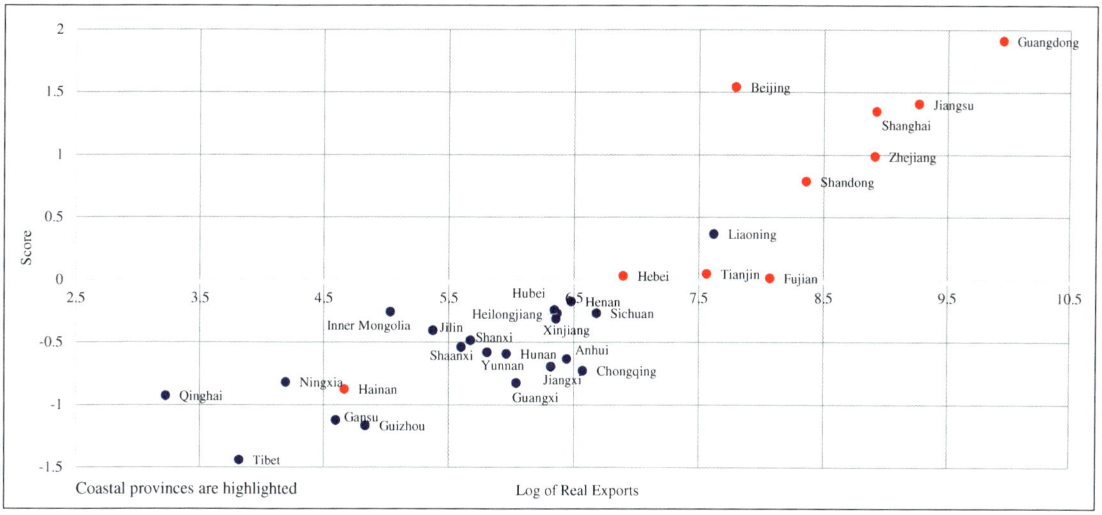

Source: Asia Competitiveness Institute.

Area, as they constitute more than 80 percent of national exports during this period.[4] As previously noted, this is primarily due to the Reform and Opening-up, which was followed by the setup of Special Economic Zones and Open Coastal Cities in the provinces in question.

The 10 coastal provinces are also at the top in the ACI Competitiveness ranking, except for Hainan which lags behind. The scatter plot in Figure 5.15 shows a clear positive correlation

[4] The four economic zones in Mainland China are defined in Section 5.2.4.

Table 5.5: China's Eastern Coastal and Overall Competitiveness Ranking

Provinces	ACI Overall Competitiveness Ranking	Exports Ranking
Guangdong	1	1
Beijing	2	9
Jiangsu	3	2
Shanghai	4	4
Zhejiang	5	3
Shandong	6	5
Tianjin	8	8
Hebei	9	10
Fujian	10	6
Hainan	26	26

Source: Asia Competitiveness Institute.

Table 5.6: Descriptive Statistics

Variable	Mean	Between Std. Dev.	Within Std. Dev.	Min	Max	Observations	Number of Provinces
Ln Real Exports	7.94	1.46	0.54	4.18	10.34	160	10
Ln World GDP	29.16	0	0.45	28.44	29.82	160	10
Ln REER	4.59	0	0.12	4.44	4.87	160	10
Ln REER Volatility (SD)	2.12	0	1.22	0.74	4.46	160	10
ACI Competitiveness Score	0.7096	0.8615	0.2241	–0.9511	2.3052	150	10

Source: Asia Competitiveness Institute.

between each province's real exports and competitiveness score. Table 5.5, meanwhile, shows the exact ranking.

Thus, for the empirical exercise, the focus will be on the 10 Eastern Coastal Provinces. For robustness checks, 9 coastal provinces will be considered, excluding Hainan. The summary statistics are shown in Table 5.6.

5.5 Empirical Methodology

The export demand function has been adopted from extant literature, for example Santos-Paulino and Thirlwall (2004) and IMF (2016). A standard export demand function depends on world demand, which is a measure of world income, and relative price competitiveness, which is measured by REER in this case. If the price and income elasticities of demand are constant, the standard Cobb–Douglas function can be applied as follows:

$$Y_t = A(X_t)^{\alpha}(W_t)^{\beta}$$

where Y_t is the export of the domestic country at time t; A is a constant; X_t is the relative price competitiveness between the domestic country and foreign countries at time t; W_t is the world demand at time t; α is the price elasticity of demand and β is the income elasticity of demand.

By taking logs, the basic model for regression is obtained as

$$lnY_t = a_0 + \alpha lnX_t + \beta lnW_t + \varepsilon_t$$

where ε_t is the error term. Two modifications are made to this basic model. First, this study focuses on 31 provinces in Mainland China, thus a panel data framework is adopted. Hence, province indicator i and provincial fixed effect u_i are added into the equation to give

$$lnY_{i,t} = a_0 + \alpha lnX_{i,t} + \beta lnW_{i,t} + u_i + \varepsilon_{i,t}$$

Second, a provincial-level control variable is introduced into the equation. Fugazza (2008) has studied the determinants of export demand and split them into internal and external components. He argues that external factors are related to foreign demand conditions, including trade tariffs, transportation cost, physical infrastructure, etc., while internal factors refer to the supply side, such as access to raw materials, resources, labour, capital, technology, and so on.

Chen (2012), Mendoza (1995), Marquez and Schindler (2007) and Hua (2011) use investment-related variables to study the export regression. Caballero and Corbo (1989) use CPI as a control for inflation. Hua (2011) controls for employment; Gala (2008) controls for education and infrastructure; Chen (2012) considers population growth rate; and Cushman (1983) and Mendoza (1995) control for private consumption.

There is no consensus in the literature on which control variable to use. In this chapter, the ACI Competitiveness Index is introduced. ACI's methodology measures competitiveness at the following levels: (1) Overall Competitiveness, (2) Four Environments, (3) 11 Sub-environments and (4) 98 Indicators. It is comprehensive, and essentially encompasses all the information available, including investment-related, education-related, and infrastructure-related variables, among others. With this score, the possible factors which affect export have been taken into account. This also serves as a control variable at the provincial level. Thus, the estimation equation becomes

$$lnY_{i,t} = a_0 + \alpha lnX_{i,t} + \beta lnW_{i,t} + \gamma(ACI\ Score_{i,t}) + u_i + \varepsilon_{i,t} \qquad (1)$$

For the relative price competitiveness measure, $X_{i,t}$, both REER level and REER volatility will be utilised. The former is defined as the monthly average of the REER for each year. The latter has two measures, (1) the standard deviation of monthly REER and (2) the coefficient of variation of monthly REER.

5.6 Empirical Results

5.6.1 Baseline Results

This section begins with a panel fixed-effect model for Equation (1) with 10 coastal provinces. Table 5.7 column 1 shows the relationship between real export and world demand. Column 2 includes the price competitiveness effect, i.e. REER level and volatility. Column 3 further introduces REER volatility and the ACI competitiveness score.

World demand and relative price competitiveness are indeed important factors leading to real export growth, which confirms the theory of export demand function. It is found that REER volatility is insignificant in affecting real exports, while ACI competitiveness score, which essentially encompasses all the control variables used in the literature, has a significant positive effect on real exports.

The results in Table 5.7 take the GVC context into consideration, i.e. China's GDP is included in the world GDP. It can be predicted that a 1 percent increase in the world demand will increase real export by 1.35 percent. A 1 percent depreciation, i.e. a 1 percent increase in the price competitiveness, will correspondingly lead to a 2.36 percent increase in real exports. If a given province increases its overall competitiveness by 1 standard deviation, the real export of that province will increase by 57.1 percent.

Before the switch of exchange rate regime in 2005, Chinese Yuan was rather stable in the foreign exchange market. This is primarily due to its being pegged to the US dollar. After the

Table 5.7: Main Results (World GDP Including China)

Ln(Real Exports)	**(1) Baseline**	**(2) Model 1**	**(3) Model 2**
Ln(World GDP including China)	**1.071*****	**1.589*****	**1.345*****
	(0.0751)	(0.131)	(0.140)
Ln(REER)		**–2.478*****	**–2.360*****
		(0.374)	(0.415)
REER Volatility (s.d.)		–0.00675	–0.00661
		(0.00544)	(0.00690)
ACI Competitiveness Score			**0.571*****
			(0.158)
Constant	–23.27***	–26.99***	–20.85***
	(2.189)	(2.501)	(2.599)
Observations	160	160	150
R-squared	0.782	0.912	0.938
Number of code	10	10	10

Notes: Robust standard errors in parentheses. ***$p < 0.01$, **$p < 0.05$, *$p < 0.1$.
Source: Asia Competitiveness Institute.

change of regime, the currency would be set with reference to a basket of other currencies. Figure 5.14 shows continuous currency appreciation after the year 2005. The exchange rate curves for both BIS and Bruegel are smooth over the period of study. With rational expectations on changes in exchange rates, REER volatility does not play a significant role in affecting real exports.

5.6.2 *What-if* Simulation

Besides the rich information the ACI competitiveness score contains, there is another advantage for including this value into our estimation equation. We are able to perform "*What-if*" simulations to improve the bottom performing indicators of a particular province, so that the score improvement for the province requires no assumptions. The detailed methodology is introduced in Chapter 2.

Table 5.8 below shows the score improvement for each province after performing this exercise. The highlighted column shows the corresponding prediction for real export growth. The expected growth follows the following formula:

$$lny^{new} = lny^{old} + \gamma(ACI\ Score\ Improvement)$$

$$Expected\,Growth \equiv \frac{y^{new} - y^{old}}{y^{old}} = e^{\gamma(ACI\ Score\ Improvement)} - 1$$

Table 5.8: ACI Competitiveness Score Before and After *What-if* Simulation

Provinces	ACI Competitiveness Score 2014			Expected Growth of Real Exports
	Before *What-if* Simulation	After *What-if* Simulation	Score Improvement	
Beijing	1.8157	2.0702	0.2545	21.1%
Fujian	0.1645	0.4225	0.2580	21.4%
Guangdong	2.2891	2.5436	0.2545	21.1%
Hainan	–0.8399	–0.3548	0.4851	44.0%
Hebei	–0.0090	0.3565	0.3655	31.6%
Jiangsu	1.9049	2.1716	0.2667	22.2%
Shandong	0.8129	1.1931	0.3802	33.0%
Shanghai	1.4235	1.8337	0.4102	36.1%
Tianjin	–0.0931	0.3300	0.4231	37.4%
Zhejiang	1.3245	1.5845	0.2600	21.6%

Source: Asia Competitiveness Institute.

Taking Zhejiang province as an example, the competitiveness score would be increased by 0.2600, from 1.3245 to 1.5846, which implies that the real exports will increase by 21.6 percent.

We are also able to target specific indicators. If we focus on the Physical Infrastructure, improving the Length of Railways in Operation (from 2347 km to 3349 km) and Length of Highways (from 116,367 km to 133,493 km) to the level of the national average, Zhejiang will increase its competitiveness score by 0.01, from 1.3245 to 1.3345, which implies that real exports will increase by 0.8 percent.

5.7 Robustness Checks

The following section presents the robustness checks that have been performed to ascertain the consistency of the findings. The world demand and ACI competitiveness score both remain significantly positive, and the REER level is still significantly negative, when (1) China's GDP is excluded from world GDP; (2) an alternative measure of REER volatility is used, i.e. coefficient of variation instead of standard deviation; (3) Bruegel data is used instead of BIS data series and (4) 9 coastal provinces are considered, excluding Hainan.

Table 5.9 shows the first robustness check results by excluding China's GDP from the world. The coefficient for world demand is 5.195, significantly larger than 1.345, which is the value when including China's GDP as shown in Table 5.7. The influence on real exports is much

Table 5.9: Robustness Check (World GDP Excluding China)

Ln(Real Exports)	**(1) Baseline**	**(2) Model 1**	**(3) Model 2**
Ln(World GDP excluding China)	**4.754*****	**6.217*****	**5.195*****
	(0.328)	(0.504)	(0.493)
Ln(REER)		**–1.785*****	**–1.569*****
		(0.324)	(0.338)
REER Volatility (s.d.)		0.00941	–0.00289
		(0.00652)	(0.00706)
ACI Competitiveness Score			**0.615*****
			(0.145)
Constant	–76.94***	–94.88***	–78.06***
	(5.848)	(7.853)	(7.645)
Observations	160	160	150
R-squared	0.838	0.919	0.951
Number of code	10	10	10

Notes: Robust standard errors in parentheses. ***$p < 0.01$, **$p < 0.05$, *$p < 0.1$.
Source: Asia Competitiveness Institute.

stronger when the processing exports and the value-added in exports are not controlled. Export growth rate will be reduced by 3.8 percent if the imported components are controlled. This shows that processing exports is the major component of exports in China, and China's position in the GVC is relatively low-ended.

The rest of the robustness check results are presented in Tables 5.10 and 5.11. The results are consistent with the baseline model. The impact of world demand on real exports is positive and significant. A 1 percent increase in world demand will lead to around 1.4 percent increase in real exports. The effect of the ACI competitiveness score also remains significantly positive.

For the price competitiveness variables, depreciation will significantly raise real exports by about 2.4 percent, while REER volatility is still insignificant.

Table 5.10: Robustness Check (Alternative Data and Measures of REER Volatility)

Ln(Real Exports)	**(1) Robustness 1**	**(2) Robustness 2**	**(3) Robustness 3**
Ln(World GDP)	**1.345*** **	**1.370*** **	**1.371*** **
	(0.140)	(0.146)	(0.146)
lnREERbis	**–2.360*** **		
	(0.415)		
REERVcvbis	–0.00661		
	(0.00690)		
lnREERbru		**–2.467*** **	**–2.440*** **
		(0.444)	(0.426)
REERVbru		0.0104	
		(0.00886)	
REERVcvbru			0.946
			(1.040)
ACI Competitiveness Score	**0.571*** **	**0.561*** **	**0.561*** **
	(0.158)	(0.160)	(0.160)
Constant	–20.85***	–20.87***	–21.00***
	(2.599)	(2.595)	(2.670)
Observations	150	150	150
R-squared	0.938	0.934	0.934
Number of code	10	10	10

Notes: Robust standard errors in parentheses. ***$p < 0.01$, **$p < 0.05$, *$p < 0.1$.
Source: Asia Competitiveness Institute.

Table 5.11: Robustness Check (9 Coastal Provinces)

Ln(Real Exports)	(1) **Baseline**	(2) **Model 1**	(3) **Robustness 1**
Ln(World GDP)	**1.109*****	**1.690*****	**1.491*****
	(0.0718)	(0.0931)	(0.0681)
Ln(REER)		**–2.782*****	**–2.745*****
		(0.240)	(0.204)
REER Volatility (s.d.)		–0.00216	0.000267
		(0.00319)	(0.00299)
ACI Competitiveness Score			**0.423*****
			(0.102)
Constant	–24.04***	–28.18***	–22.95***
	(2.094)	(2.183)	(2.009)
Observations	144	144	135
R-squared	0.789	0.942	0.959
Number of code	9	9	9

Notes: Robust standard errors in parentheses. ***$p < 0.01$, **$p < 0.05$, *$p < 0.1$.
Source: Asia Competitiveness Institute.

5.8 Concluding Notes and Policy Implications

There are two key events in China's recent history which have had particularly significant impacts on exchange rate and exports — China's accession to the WTO in 2001 and the change in the exchange regime in 2005. China's trade as a share of GDP and exports as a share of GDP peaked at 66 percent and 33 percent, respectively, after accession to the WTO, and started to decline after the exchange regime change, being measured at 40 percent and 19 percent, respectively in 2015. It should also be noted that China's exports as a share of world exports has consistently increased at a significant rate, except during the slowdown brought about by the GFC. This demonstrated the resilience of Chinese economy in the face of economically undesirable circumstances around the world. The economic shutdown of China in 2015 also very clearly affected the world trade position (World Trade Statistical Review 2016), which was at the time dampening China's trade performance. These forces reinforced each other, leading to drops in both exports and imports.

China is getting more involved with the GVC over the last two decades, and this can explain the increase in the share of total exports occupied by items classified as Machinery and Transport Equipment from 23 percent to 47 percent. This also demonstrates that China is specialised in assembly operations and thus assumes a central role in the GVC. China's exports clearly hinge mainly on manufacturing products, rather than on primary products, and thus exports like mineral fuels have decreased to 3 percent. For manufacturing products, the highest growth detected after the GFC was in the category of light textile industrial products, whereas the highest growth after the entry to WTO was in Chemicals and Related Products.

There is also a clear trend towards trade diversification. All of Mainland China's major trading partners, e.g. the US, Hong Kong and Japan, have experienced a drop in their export shares *vis-à-vis* China over the 16 years spanning from 2000 to 2015. For example, the percentage of Mainland China's total exports intended for Japan has diminished over time, falling from 16.7 percent in 2000 to 6.0 percent in 2015. This in turn demonstrates that there is a gradual diminishing of Mainland China's dependence on exports to Japan over that decade. The exporting share to "other countries" — that is to say, countries other than the aforementioned major trading partners — increased from 29 percent in 2000 to 46 percent in 2015. This is a clear indication that Mainland China's export concentration is decreasing.

Regional-level studies furthermore indicate that the Eastern Coastal Area has been the cornerstone performer in Mainland China in terms of trade flows, while the other regions are significantly lagging behind, primarily due to their less strategic locations and the implementation of opening-up policies, especially with regard to the SEZs and CPFTZs in the coastal regions. However, recent trends indicate that Western China is gradually improving, with its exports accounting for 8.43 percent of total exports and its imports accounting for 5.91 percent of total imports in 2015. With the China Western Development Strategy and the Belt and Road Initiative, the foundations have been set for Western China to become a new engine for trade growth. However, North-eastern China performed poorly in recent years, largely due the scandal that erupted when it was revealed that Liaoning province had been fabricating key statistical data to inflate its economic performance.

At the provincial level, Guangdong has led both exports and imports in absolute terms over the last two decades. When taken as a share of GRDP, however, exports have decreased since 2007, with imports likewise having declined since 2005. This demonstrates that the major contributors to Guangdong's GRDP are shifting. A similar trend can be observed for all the top seven provinces. Since the Eleventh "Five-Year Plan", all the provinces have been undergoing structural economic reforms, which have switched the emphasis from trade to domestic consumption.

With the empirical analysis on impact of exchange rate on exports by deploying panel fixed-effect model, it can be observed that there is a strong negative correlation between the REER levels and exports of 10 provinces in Mainland China's Eastern Coastal Area, while REER volatility remained negative but had an insignificant impact.

World demand has a positive and significant effect on exports, which explains the slowdown, if not decrease, of export growth for the 10 coastal provinces, after the GFC. ACI competitiveness score, which encompasses all the relevant factors affecting export, shows a significant positive impact on performance of provincial exports. Higher competitiveness at domestic levels in turn reflects higher exporting advantages.

As China's position in the GVC becomes more and more important, it is relevant to study exports in the context of the GVC. However, due to limitations of data, processing export and value-added export data are not available at the provincial level. Therefore, China's GDP had to be used to proxy the import component of exports, which is a drawback of this study. This would be improved in future work.

In conclusion, China has experienced dramatic improvements in terms of trade in the 30 years that have passed since the proclamation of the and Reform Opening-up policy in 1978. After its accession to the WTO, China has come to play an important role in the global market, becoming the top exporter in the world. Unexpected events such as the GFC have had a significant negative impact on China's trade, but China has quickly bounced back. With the outbreak of the US–China trade war in 2018, how will China's trade position in the global market be affected? This topic is further discussed in Chapter 6 of this book.

References

Aghion, Philippe, Philippe Bacchetta, and Romain Ranciere. 2009. "Exchange Rate Volatility and Productivity Growth: The Role of Financial Development." 44.

Anderton, R., and Frauke Skudelny. 2001. "Exchange Rate Volatility and Euro Area Imports." Working Paper, Quebec a Montreal — Recherche en gestion. https://econpapers.repec.org/paper/fthuqamge/64.htm.

Arize, Augustine C., Thomas Osang, and Daniel J. Slottje. 2000. "Exchange-Rate Volatility and Foreign Trade: Evidence From Thirteen LDC's." *Journal of Business & Economic Statistics* 18: 10–17. doi: 10.1080/07350015.2000.10524843.

Baron, David P. 1976. "Fluctuating Exchange Rates and the Pricing of Exports." *Economic Inquiry* 14: 425–38. https://econpapers.repec.org/article/oupecinqu/v_3a14_3ay_3a1976_3ai_3a3_3ap_3a425-38.htm.

Bernard, Andrew B., and J. Bradford Jensen. 2004. "Why Some Firms Export." *The Review of Economics and Statistics* 86: 561–569. http://www.jstor.org/stable/3211647.

Bhattasali, Deepak, Shantong Li, and Will Martin. 2004. "China and the WTO: Accession, Policy Reform and Poverty Reduction Strategies." Tech. rep., The World Bank, 1–352. http://documents.worldbank.org/curated/en/578141468770462057/China-and-the-WTO-accession-policy-reform-and-poverty-reduction-strategies.

Brandt, Loren, Thomas G. Rawski, and John Sutton. 2008. "Chinas Industrial Development." In *Chinas Great Economic Transformation*, edited by Loren Brandt and Thomas G. Rawski, 569–632. Cambridge University Press. doi:10.1017/cbo9780511754234.016.

Caballero, Ricardo J., and Vittorio Corbo. 1989. "The Effect of Real Exchange Rate Uncertainty on Exports: Empirical Evidence." *World Bank Economic Review* 3: 263–278. doi:10.1093/wber/3.2.263.

Carter, Jennie Lee. 1984. "Exchange Rate Volatility and World Trade." https://www.elibrary.imf.org/abstract/IMF084/02200-9781557750655/02200-9781557750655/front.xml?rskey=IC97Cb&result=9&redirect=true.

Cattaneo, Olivier, Gary Gereffi, and Cornelia Staritz. 2010. "Global Value Chains in a Postcrisis World: A Development Perspective." Tech. rep., The World Bank, 1-0. http://documents.worldbank.org/curated/en/432691468332065846/Global-value-chains-in-a-postcrisis-world-a-development-perspective.

Chen, Jinzhao. 2012. "Real Exchange Rate and Economic Growth: Evidence from Chinese Provincial Data (1992–2008)." 29.

Chit, Myint Moe. 2008. "Exchange Rate Volatility and Exports: Evidence from the ASEAN-China Free Trade Area." *Journal of Chinese Economic and Business Studies* 6: 261–277. doi:10.1080/14765280802283543.

Chou, W. L. 2000. "Exchange Rate Variability and China's Exports." *Journal of Comparative Economics* (Elsevier BV) 28: 61–79. doi:10.1006/jcec.1999.1625.

Chow, Gregory C. 2003. "Impact of Joining the WTO on China's Economic, Legal and Political Institutions." *Pacific Economic Review* 8: 105–115. doi:10.1111/j.1468-0106.2003.00213.x.

Cushman, David. 1983. "The Effects of Real Exchange Rate Risk on International Trade." *Journal of International Economics* 15: 45–63. https://econpapers.repec.org/article/eeeinecon/v_3a15_3ay_3a1983_3ai_3a1-2_3ap_3a45-63.htm.

Dell'Ariccia, Giovanni. 1999. "Exchange Rate Fluctuations and Trade Flows: Evidence from the European Union." *IMF Staff Papers* 46: 315–334. https://www.jstor.org/stable/3867646.

Dixit, Avinash. 1989. "Entry and Exit Decisions under Uncertainty." *The Journal of Political Economy* 97: 620–638. http://www.jstor.org/stable/1830458.

Dornbusch, Rüdiger. 1996. "The World Economy In 1996." 2. https://www.project-syndicate.org/commentary/the-world-economy-in-1996.

Ethier, Wilfred. 1973. "International Trade and the Forward Exchange Market." *American Economic Review* 63: 494–503. https://econpapers.repec.org/article/aeaaecrev/v_3a63_3ay_3a1973_3ai_3a3_3ap_3a494-503.htm.

Fang, WenShwo, YiHao Lai, and Stephen Miller. 2006. "Export Promotion through Exchange Rate Changes: Exchange Rate Depreciation or Stabilization." *Southern Economic Journal* 72: 611–626. https://econpapers.repec.org/article/sejancoec/v_3a72_3a3_3ay_3a2006_3ap_3a611-626.htm.

Franke, Günter. 1991. "Exchange Rate Volatility and International Trading Strategy." *Journal of International Money and Finance* 10: 292–307. https://econpapers.repec.org/article/eeejimfin/v_3a10_3ay_3a1991_3ai_3a2_3ap_3a292-307.htm.

Freund, Caroline, and Martha Denisse Pierola. 2012. "Export Surges." *Journal of Development Economics* 97: 387–395. https://econpapers.repec.org/article/eeedeveco/v_3a97_3ay_3a2012_3ai_3a2_3ap_3a387-395.htm.

Frieden, J. A. 2006. *Global Capitalism: Its Fall and Rise in the Twentieth Century.* W.W. Norton. https://books.google.com.sg/books?id=Yc3SngEACAAJ.

Fugazza, Macro. 2008. "Export Performance and Its Determinants: Supply and Demand Constraints." https://ssrn-com.libproxy1.nus.edu.sg/abstract=1281486.

Gala, Paulo. 2008. "Real Exchange Rate Levels and Economic Development: Theoretical Analysis and Empirical Evidence."

Goldberg, Pinelopi Koujianou, and Michael M. Knetter. 1997. "Causes and Consequences of the Export Enhancement Program for Wheat." In *The Effects of U.S. Trade Protection and Promotion Policies* 273–296. University of Chicago Press. http://www.nber.org/chapters/c0316.

Haddad, Mona, and Cosimo Pancaro. 2010. "Can Real Exchange Rate Undervaluation Boost Exports and Growth in Developing Countries? Yes, But Not for Long." 5.

Hooper, Peter, and Steven W. Kohlhagen. 1978. "The Effect of Exchange Rate Uncertainty on the Prices and Volume of International Trade." *Journal of International Economics* 8: 483–511. https://econpapers.repec.org/article/eeeinecon/v_3a8_3ay_3a1978_3ai_3a4_3ap_3a483-511.htm.

Hu, W. E. N., and Z. E. N. G. Gang. 2005. "Study of Global Value Chain Governance and Local Industrial Network Upgrading — Case of Pudong Integrated Circuit Industrial Network." *China Industrial Economy* 7: 20–27.

Hua, Ping. 2008. "Real Exchange Rates and China's Bilateral Exports Towards Industrialized Countries." *Journal of Chinese Economic and Business Studies* 6: 241–259. doi:10.1080/14765280802283493.

Hua, Ping, and Clermont Université. 2011. "The Economic and Social Effects of Real Exchange Rate Evidence from the Chinese Provinces." 51.

Huchet-Bourdon, Marilyne, and Jane Korinek. 2011. "To What Extent Do Exchange Rates and their Volatility Affect Trade?" OECD Trade Policy Paper, OECD Publishing. https://econpapers.repec.org/paper/oectraaab/119-en.htm.

Ianchovichina, Elena, and Will Martin. 2001. "Trade Liberalization in China's Accession to the World Trade Organization." Policy Research Working Paper Series, The World Bank. https://econpapers.repec.org/paper/wbkwbrwps/2623.htm.

IMF. 2016. *World Economic Outlook.* International Monetary Fund. https://www.ebook.de/de/product/28140703/imf_world_economic_outlook_october_2016.html.

Kang, Jong. 2016. "International Trade and Exchange Rate." SSRN Scholarly Paper, Social Science Research Network, Rochester, NY. https://papers.ssrn.com/abstract=2856296.

Kaplinsky, R. 2000. "Globalisation and Unequalisation: What Can Be Learned from Value Chain Analysis?" *Journal of Development Studies* 37: 117–146. https://econpapers.repec.org/article/tafjdevst/v_3a37_3ay_3a2000_3ai_3a2_3ap_3a117-146.htm.

Krugman, Paul. 1989. "Differences in Income Elasticities and Trends in Real Exchange Rates." *European Economic Review* 33: 1031–1046. https://econpapers.repec.org/article/eeeeecrev/v_3a33_3ay_3a1989_3ai_3a5_3ap_3a1031-1046.htm.

Lardy, N. R. 1993. *Foreign Trade and Economic Reform in China.* Cambridge University Press. https://books.google.com.sg/books?id=01fzPp11Q0QC.

Lemoine, Francoise, and Deniz Ünal-Kesenci. 2004. "Assembly Trade and Technology Transfer: The Case of China." *World Development* 32: 829–850. https://econpapers.repec.org/article/eeewdevel/v_3a32_3ay_3a2004_3ai_3a5_3ap_3a829-850.htm.

Lin, Justin Yifu, Fang Cai, and Zhou Li. 2003. *The China Miracle: Development Strategy and Economic Reform.* Hong Kong: Chinese University Press.

Marquez, Jaime, and John Schindler. 2007. "Exchange-Rate Effects on China's Trade*." *Review of International Economics* 15: 837–853. doi:10.1111/j.1467-9396.2007.00700.x.

McKenzie, Michael D. 1999. "The Impact of Exchange Rate Volatility on International Trade Flows." *Journal of Economic Surveys.* https://onlinelibrary.wiley.com/doi/abs/10.1111/1467-6419.00075.

Mendoza, Enrique. 1995. "The Terms of Trade, the Real Exchange Rate, and Economic Fluctuations." *International Economic Review* 36: 101–37. https://econpapers.repec.org/article/ieriecrev/v_3a36_3ay_3a1995_3ai_3a1_3ap_3a101-37.htm.

Mussa, Michael. 1984. "The Theory of Exchange Rate Determination." NBER Chapters, National Bureau of Economic Research, Inc., 13–78. https://econpapers.repec.org/bookchap/nbrnberch/6829.htm.

Nishimura, Yusaku, and Kenjiro Hirayama. 2013. "Does Exchange Rate Volatility Deter Japan-China trade? Evidence from Pre- and Post-Exchange Rate Reform in China." *Japan and the World Economy* 25–26: 90–101. https://econpapers.repec.org/article/eeejapwor/v_3a25-26_3ay_3a2013_3ai_3a_3ap_3a90-101.htm.

Ozturk, Ilhan. 2006. "Exchange Rate Volatility and Trade: A Literature Survey." *International Journal of Applied Econometrics and Quantitative Studies* 3: 85–102. https://econpapers.repec.org/article/eaaijaeqs/v_3a3_3ay2006_3ai_3a1_5f5.htm.

Park, Jong H., and Penelope B. Prime. 1997. "Export Performance and Growth in China: A Cross-Provincial Analysis." *Applied Economics* 29: 1353–1363. doi:10.1080/00036849700000026.

Peree, Eric, and Alfred Steinherr. 1989. "Exchange Rate Uncertainty and Foreign Trade." *European Economic Review* 33: 1241–1264. https://econpapers.repec.org/article/eeeeecrev/v_3a33_3ay_3a1989_3ai_3a6_3ap_3a1241-1264.htm.

Porter, J. 2016. *Imperial China, 1350–1900.* Rowman & Littlefield. https://books.google.com.sg/books?id=RzwmjgEACAAJ.

Powers, William, and David Riker. n.d. "Exchange Rate Pass-through in Global Value Chains: The Effects of Upstream Suppliers." 22.

Rose, Andrew. 2000. "One Money, One Market: Estimating the Effect of Common Currencies on Trade." Tech. rep., National Bureau of Economic Research, Cambridge, MA. doi:10.3386/w7432.

Saang Joon, Baak. 2008. "The Bilateral Real Exchange Rates and Trade Between China and the U.S." *China Economic Review* 19: 117–127. doi:10.1016/j.chieco.2008.02.003.

Santos-Paulino, Amelia, and Anthony Thirlwall. 2004. "The Impact of Trade Liberalisation on Exports, Imports and the Balance of Payments of Developing Countries." *Economic Journal* 114: F50–F72. https://econpapers.repec.org/article/ecjeconjl/v_3a114_3ay_3a2004_3ai_3a493_3ap_3af50-f72.htm.

Sauer, Christine, and Alok Bohara. 2001. "Exchange Rate Volatility and Exports: Regional Differences between Developing and Industrialized Countries." *Review of International Economics* 9: 133–152. https://econpapers.repec.org/article/blareviec/v_3a9_3ay_3a2001_3ai_3a1_3ap_3a133-52.htm.

Shaikh, Sarfaraz, and Ouyang Hongbing. 2015. "Exchange Rate Volatility and Trade Flows: Evidence from China, Pakistan and India." *International Journal of Economics and Finance* 7: 121. doi:10.5539/ijef.v7n11p121.

Staiger, Robert, and Alan O. Sykes. 2010. "Currency Manipulation and World Trade." *World Trade Review* 9: 583–627. https://econpapers.repec.org/article/cupwotrrv/v_3a9_3ay_3a2010_3ai_3a04_3ap_3a583-627_5f00.htm.

Sun, Haishun, and Ashok Parikh. 2001. "Exports, Inward Foreign Direct Investment (FDI) and Regional Economic Growth in China." *Regional Studies* 35: 187–196. doi:10.1080/713693805.

Taglioni, Daria. 2002. "Exchange Rate Volatility as a Barrier to Trade: New Methodologies and Recent Evidence." *Economie Internationale* 227–259. https://econpapers.repec.org/article/ciicepiei/2002-1t-2th.htm.

Tan, Khee Giap, Xuyao Zhang, and Diamanta Vania Lavi. 2018. "Impact of Real Effective Exchange Rate Movements on Exports by Mainland China Provinces." Working Paper.

Wang, Chun-Hsuan, Chun-Hung A. Lin, and Chih-Hai Yang. 2012. "Short-Run and Long-Run Effects of Exchange Rate Change on Trade Balance: Evidence from China and its Trading Partners." *Japan and the World Economy* 24: 266–273. https://econpapers.repec.org/article/eeejapwor/v_3a24_3ay_3a2012_3ai_3a4_3ap_3a266-273.htm.

Wei, Shang-Jin. 1995. *The Open Door Policy and China's Rapid Growth: Evidence from City-Level Data.* Vol. 4, in *Growth Theories in Light of the East Asian Experience, NBER-EASE*, 73–104. National Bureau of Economic Research, Inc. https://EconPapers.repec.org/RePEc:nbr:nberch:8545.

Whalley, John, and Xian Xin. 2006. "China's FDI and Non-FDI Economies and the Sustainability of Future High Chinese Growth." Working Paper, National Bureau of Economic Research. doi:10.3386/w12249.

Wu, Yanrui. 2007. "Export Performance in China's Regional Economies." *Applied Economics* 39: 1283–1293. https://econpapers.repec.org/article/tafapplec/v_3a39_3ay_3a2007_3ai_3a10_3ap_3a1283-1293.htm.

World Trade Organisation. 2015. *Intenational Trade Statistics 2015*. WTO.https://www.ebook.de/de/product/24181053/world_tourism_organization_international_trade_statistics_2015.html.

World Trade Organisation. 2016. *World Trade Statistics Review.* WTO. Doi:10.30875/489e720b-en.

Yan, Guo, Sheng Li, Yaqi Lin, and Jie Li. 2016. "Real Effective Exchange Rate and Regional Economic Growth in China: Evidence from Provincial Data." *China & World Economy* 24: 43–63. doi:10.1111/cwe.12180.

Yang, Guangpu, and Qingyang Gu. 2016. "Effects of Exchange Rate Variations on Bilateral Trade with a Vehicle Currency: Evidence from China and Singapore." *Journal of International Money and Finance* 68: 50–73. doi:10.1016/j.jimonfin.2016.06.010.

Yao, Shujie. 2006. "On Economic Growth, FDI and Exports in China." *Applied Economics* 38: 339–351. https://econpapers.repec.org/article/tafapplec/v_3a38_3ay_3a2006_3ai_3a3_3ap_3a339-351.htm.

Zhang, Zhaoyong. 1999. "Foreign Exchange Rate Reform, the Balance of Trade and Economic Growth: An Empirical Analysis for China." *Journal of Economic Development* 24.

Zhao, Laixun, and Yuqing Xing. 2006. "Global Production and Currency Devaluation." *Review of International Economics* 14: 202–211. doi:10.1111/j.1467-9396.2006.00570.x.

Discussant Notes

Comments on "Impact of Real Effective Exchange Rates on Trade in Mainland China Provinces"

Dr Luo Hairong

Research Fellow, Institute of World Economy, Shanghai Academy of Social Sciences

Since China's accession to the World Trade Organization at the end of 2001, China has experienced a long and remarkable growth in its economic performance with a large increase in its external trade volume. China is now the largest exporter and second largest importer of the world. There are many stories to tell when it comes to the success of China's trade development, and there is already plenty of literature and studies done on China's trade success. However, most research only looks at China's economy as a whole and the relationship it has with total trade, partly because of the shortage of trade and other related data. In other words, most studies simply analyse China's trade development at the macro level. But it is also worth going further and looking deeper into the details of both trade structures and trade patterns. As far as I know, there is very limited research that looks into trade issues at the subnational level. In contrast, the research conducted by the Asia Competitiveness Institute (ACI), Lee Kuan Yew School of Public Policy, National University of Singapore, makes an outstanding contribution to academia as a substantial supplement for trade theories and practices. As a result of China's unbalanced development strategy, economic and trade development varies vastly between different regions and provinces. By examining China's trade structure at the provincial level, this study helps to provide a rather new angle as well as a better and more detailed understanding of China's trade development. That is to say, firstly, this study is a crucial endeavour that aims to break the traditional underestimation of China's provincial trade structure.

Secondly, I notice that the result of this study builds upon ACI's persistent efforts on developing the empirical model. As far as I know, ACI has been upgrading and updating the model as well as its competitiveness indices over a long period of time. Its continuous effort not only makes its empirical model more sophisticated and more convincing, but also serves as an outstanding benchmark that may help decision makers to perform better, with the consistent time-series observation of competitiveness data. The model in this study now covers provincial data which is likely to bring more information to the subnational governments. This is a sound improvement because local governors would play more and more important roles on the ground as governments became more and more decentralized. In the case of Shanghai, the local government is now dedicating all available resources and efforts to making the city become one of the international metropolises. ACI's competitiveness index can serve as a good reference for Shanghai's governor to better manage the city and devise better development plans.

Thirdly, the world trade structure as well as trade patterns are now faced with the new trend of global value chains. Nowadays, transnational corporations are no longer operating merely as goods exporters or factory investors. With the support of information technology, supply chain management skills and processing trade policies, transnational corporations are setting up factories all over the world as a production chain in which intermediate goods are flowing from border to border. Take the Apple Corporation as an example. Apple products are assembled as the final product in China, whereas different parts and components of the products are imported in from other economies such as Japan, Korea, and Germany. In order words, it is worth studying the trade theory via the perspective of global value chains. Of course, the data for the value addition of trade is still far from satisfactory due to various factors, but still I would rather recommend putting more effort in exploring the new trade structure and trade patterns, which may bring some interesting results.

In addition to the previous comments on the study, I would like to address some brief issues on the topic. The first point I would like to make is that a stable exchange rate regime is one of the most important factors to ensure China's success in trade development. By reviewing China's currency exchange regime reform since its opening-up policy in late 1980s, we can tell that the government was very cautious on the exchange rate regime through its implementation of incremental reforms. The reforms not only brought more transparency and marketization in the exchange system, but also kept the exchange rate comparatively stable. In this way, both traders and investors have great confidence in China's exchange regime and thus contribute to the success of China's FDI inflows and trade development.

The second point is that by looking at the provincial external trade structure, we will find that most trade flows come from the east coast. This is not only because of better economic development in the eastern part of China, but also because of trade costs. Thanks to the low cost of transportation, over 55 percent of imports come via the sea, and over 60 percent of exports leave via the sea. Other trade transportation methods are comparatively smaller due to high costs and geographic restrictions. That is to say, the east coast region in China benefits more from trade development. It is hence still necessary to help other regions, especially landlocked provinces, to lower trade costs for further trade development.

Last but not least, China's trade development is benefiting greatly from the globalization process. By looking at trade modes, we find that processing trade is one of the most important trade modes for China. This is mainly due to China's success in integrating into the global production chain. With a stable currency and friendly investment environment, foreign manufacturers are willing to invest in China, leading to huge growth of trade volumes. Since China's accession to WTO, foreign-owned companies have been playing an important role in China's import and export activities. More than half of China's export volume could be attributed to those companies, while their import volume is only slightly smaller than the amount of import from domestic companies. In other words, China's stable currency exchange regime as well as China's accession to globalization contributes greatly to China's success in trade development.

Chapter 6

Concluding Remarks and Directions for Future Research

6.1 US Faces Credibility Trap as China Looks a Century Ahead[1]

The US has been a benign and generous superpower. It is still a superpower but it has become less benign and generous. Its unilateral actions in many areas have caused hurt. China is an emerging power. It is bumping into the US but the US will not let its supremacy be strategically challenged. The two worlds are colliding — there will be disruption, collateral damage. And grief. This may come across as apocalyptic but I will share why I've come to the conclusion the question is no longer when the collision will take place but what form it will take.

Some years ago when the US announced its policy pivot to Asia, containing China through a chain of military bases, commentators and analysts warned of the Thucydides trap. Basically, this means an incumbent power and a rising power cannot avoid conflict. Most believed the Thucydides trap was not inevitable. I was one of them. My reasoning was China had gone out of its way to declare its rise will be peaceful. Then-US President Barack Obama sought to cooperate, to have China as a stakeholder in major global initiatives like the Paris climate accord and the Iran nuclear deal. Such accords encouraged China to act responsibly and observe international norms.

The US accepted China's accession to the WTO as a non-market economy even knowing its state enterprises were economic players. The US and China also benefited from increasing trade and economic interdependence. Meanwhile, China simply lacked the military power to challenge the US. As events unfold, I have turned pessimistic.

Pessimism

My primary reason is the US is resetting its relations with China and the rest of the world. Its new foreign policy is America first. In its execution, it seems to be America only. US President Donald Trump is applauded by both sides of American politics for standing up to China. This is not just an American president using China as a whipping boy to win the November congressional elections. Mr Trump is also tapping into the deep vein of fear in the country over the perceived long-term threat posed by China.

At the World Economic Forum Davos meeting in January, a top concern was the clash of major powers. Ninety-three per cent of those surveyed expected relations between major powers — read US and China — to worsen. Mr Trump is acting on his campaign slogan of America First. He has pulled the US out of the Paris Climate Change Accord. He has withdrawn the country from the Trans-Pacific Partnership, which was ready for signing. He

[1] This section includes the opening address by Singapore's former Prime Minister and now Emeritus Senior Minister Goh Chok Tong at ANZ's Finance and Treasury Forum in Singapore, reprinted with permission.

re-negotiated NAFTA. He wants NATO to spend more on defence and not expect the US to protect Europe with an American budget. He says US military exercises with South Korea are a waste of money. He has threatened to pull the US out of the WTO. In short, he is pulling the carpet from under the feet of the multilateral world order which the US has helped to create. This is disruptive diplomacy unfolding before our eyes.

John Bolton, Mr Trump's National Security Advisor, said in 2000 if he was "redoing the UN Security Council today, I would have one permanent member, the US, because that's a real reflection of the distribution of power in the world". It seems the US has abandoned its "prosper thy neighbour" policy of multilateralism, replacing it with a "beggar thy neighbour" policy of unilateralism. In practical terms, unilateralism means the strong extracting benefits from the weak. It is like a top rank Yokozuna sumo wrestler grappling with an opponent several ranks down below. The match is unequal. Nor are allies and friends spared.

Besides unilateralism versus multilateralism there is another ideological conflict: between market capitalism and state capitalism. It is short-term benefits or profits for companies versus long-term strategic interests of the state. This is not a level playing field for free market players. The US is trying to level it by redefining the rules of free trade through bilateral negotiation. But China is not Mexico or Canada. It will resist. It thinks, as a late economic player in a global marketplace, a state-driven industrial policy is the way to overcome an unequal contest.

The Trump administration sees relations with China as a competitive, zero-sum game. Analysts say "Trump and his advisers have come to view China as a malign power and direct competitor and adversary whose expanding influence must be blunted through extreme countermeasures". They label China as the "revisionist power" — whatever that means. To me, it is the Thucydides trap.

Balance

China's quick rise as the world's second biggest economy and with its huge trade surpluses, have thrown the US off-balance. Its rapid technological advancement sets off alarm bells. Its actions in the South China Sea and militarisation of islands there threaten US security interests in Asia.

The country's "Made in China 2025" industrial policy only heightens US fears. China aims to dominate the next 10 future industries, like artificial intelligence, robotics, biotech and aerospace. While this declaration is partly propaganda for domestic consumption, the US sees it as China waving a red flag. The US will not cede any technological advantage to China. It has accused China of intellectual property theft and forced transfer of technology from companies investing in China. Now, someone in the US has even suggested not granting visas to students from the People's Republic of China. Students learning at the best universities in the US is now feared as "stealing knowledge".

China's Belt-and-Road Initiative is China's strategic answer to the US containment strategy. China has claimed the whole of the South China Sea and has militarised many islands there. It is building up a modern naval force. It cannot challenge the US's maritime power but can deny the US Navy moving freely in the South China Sea and Taiwan Straits with asymmetrical capabilities. China was never a maritime power but it will be one regionally.

China is showing its model of political and economic governance is viable. As democracy flounders in many Western countries, its socialist capitalism with Chinese characteristics may prove to be an attractive alternative to liberal Western democracy. Lastly, China is seen to be ruled by one strong authoritarian man with a vision to realise his China dream — that is, Make China Great Again.

Weapons

Military conflict is not imminent between the US and China. The Chinese do not want it, nor can the US justify it. So the US has chosen economic weapons, starting with trade tariffs. Trade tariffs are being imposed on the grounds of national security. The World Trade Organisation is being ignored. The argument is tariffs will not just protect US jobs and industries but also slow down China's growth and damage its economy. Initially, Chinese officials called it "economic terrorism". Now, they change it to "economic bullying". A better term may be "economic containment".

Yes, tariffs are being enforced, ostensibly against everyone who has huge trade surpluses with the US, but the big target is China. Smaller countries like Mexico, Canada and South Korea will bend to the US's will — but not China. It is not just because China is huge. It is also because it's humiliation by foreign powers in the last century is deeply etched in its memory.

President Trump's arithmetic is simple: if you export three times more to me than I export to you, I can hurt you more than you can hurt me. I will surely win in an all-out trade war. And indeed, China is more vulnerable than America in a tariff tit-for-tat. But, as Martin Wolf wrote in The Financial Times, "the President's demands on tariffs and imports are ridiculous. No sovereign state could accept them". He concluded "this may be a decisive moment for the relations between the world's two greatest powers".

From trade, it could move into other economic and non-economic areas like education, currency manipulation and technology and increased sales of arms to Taiwan. Expect the two countries to lock horns for a long time. President Trump needs the political gain but President Xi cannot lose political face.

The Chinese are worried about President Trump. They do not think he is erratic or impulsive. They look at the people he has picked for his Administration, they see Mr Trump has acted on his election rhetoric. He is the first president to bash China on three fronts — trade, ideology and military.

How is China responding? So far China has responded with restraint, with a statesmanlike manner. It is not looking for a fight but it cannot just turn the other cheek. China is reacting to the US trade tariffs on its products and levying the same rate of tariffs on American imports up to the same value. At the same time, it is signalling the dispute can be resolved with negotiation — but not with a gun pointed to its head.

China tries to occupy the high moral ground. At Davos earlier this year, Xi Jinping championed the cause of free trade and multilateralism. A few months later, he confirmed China's position in Bo'ao. China's Foreign Minister Wang Yi said: "China and US can compete but need not be rivals, if anything, we need to be partners".

One People's Liberation Army general proclaimed China will not enter into an arms race. China's defence expenditure is about 1.3 per cent of GDP, while the US and Russia have consistently kept theirs at above 3 per cent. Nevertheless, at the 19th Party Congress last October, President Xi Jinping said "China will complete the modernisation of its armed forces by 2035 and achieve a world-class military by 2050 that could fight and win wars". This bravado will only reinforce American views that a strategic battle against China must begin now.

Thomas Friedman wrote in The New York Times that US and European government officials and business leaders had made it crystal clear to him what's going on right now is nothing less than a struggle to redefine the rules governing the economic and power relations of the world's oldest and newest superpowers. This is not just a trade tiff. Ruan Zongze, Executive Vice-President of the Chinese Foreign Ministry's research institute concurs: "This is a defining moment for US–China relations; it is about a lot more than trade and tariffs, this is about the future."

According to Mr Friedman, the trade hardliners in the Trump administration believe this is a fight worth having now, before it is too late, before China gets too big. But is it just the trade hardliners? What about the military hardliners? The battle is joined. The US is pursuing its trade tariffs aggressively, while China is responding calmly. On the surface anyway.

Implication

What are the implications for Asia? I will just flag two: one, Asian countries may be forced to take sides. Other than Japan and South Korea, which are allies of the US, they will not want to. Two, if tariffs imposed by the US on China remain, there will be a shift in the present global supply chain. Countries with cheaper cost production will benefit more. Overall, all countries will suffer collateral damage from trade protectionism and slower global economic growth.

Asian countries are anxious but reacting sensibly. They want the rules-based multilateral trading system to remain. Japan took the lead, to conclude a comprehensive Trans-Pacific Partnership after the US pulled out of the PPP. ASEAN is working hard to conclude the Regional Comprehensive Economic Partnership. China and India, amongst others, are members. The US is not.

What is the impact on Singapore? Singapore will surely be impacted by the trade war. Trade is three times the size of our GDP. Singapore is also a significant player in the global supply chain. The impact will be at three levels: first, the impact of a generalised slow-down is applicable to all countries. Second, the impact arising from the disruptions to the global supply chains. And third, the impact from slower global economic growth. However, the Ministry of Trade and Industry has concluded the net impact is likely to be modest. This is in the near term. Where will it all end?

In the Financial Times, Mr Wolf wrote this "is more likely to be the beginning of the end of the rules-governed multilateral trading order that the US itself has created". US trade representative Robert Lighthizer has said allowing China into the WTO in 2001 was a "mistake". Furthermore, President Trump has reiterated "the agreement establishing the (WTO) was the single worst trade deal ever". He has threatened to pull out of the WTO "if it does not treat the United States better".

French President Emmanuel Macron warned Europe could no longer rely on the US to look out for its security. He wanted to launch an exhaustive review of security, with all partners, and Russia. The US has remained in the Asia-Pacific. All countries in the region, including China, want the US here. Its presence is essential to the geopolitical stability of the region. Despite the global shift, the US will still be the bigger power for a long time to come, but China will gain weight and influence.

I surmise China's leaders are convinced the US is out to contain it. Two senior figures I met in Hong Kong last month told me that too. China thinks decades ahead. I sat in a meeting between Deng Xiaoping and Lee Kuan Yew in 1978. Mr Deng gave a historical sweep of China's past travails and his vision for China in the next 100 years. In contrast, US Presidents think one election at a time. So China will wait out Trump — two, perhaps six, years. Meanwhile, it will upgrade its economy, invest in technology and modernise its armed forces.

The US has been a benign and generous superpower. It is still a superpower but it has become less benign and generous. Its unilateral actions in many areas have hurt allies, friends and rivals alike. Credibility, reliability, trust and respect are essential for a superpower if it is to be a global leader. America First is diminishing the global stature, moral leadership and influence of the US. Ironically, the foreign policy of America First — to Make America Great Again — may actually diminish America's greatness on a world stage. Ironically again, the incumbent power, in trying to curb the rise of an emerging power, may end up accelerating it.

China will press in with renewed energy to break out of any US stranglehold. It will not trust the US as the sole policeman of the world. The US is flexing its muscles, showing might is right. That surely, is not an example the world wants China to emulate. Whatever happens we have to adjust to a new balance of power in the future — at least in Asia.

6.2 The Validity and Effectiveness of the Accusation of China Violating Intellectual Property Rights

On 22nd March 2018, the US released an investigation report and deemed China's violation of its intellectual property (IP) rights. To punish such behaviour, the White House imposed unilateral tariffs on China and subsequently triggered the US–China trade disputes (The White House 2018). A key accusation raised in the investigation report is that China violated IP rights of US companies through the practices of government-forced technology transfers. As documented in the report, such practices distorted regular business activities, created an unfair competition environment, and thus undermined the competency of US businesses (Office of the United States Trade Representative 2018). China, indeed, has a business environment unfavourable to foreign capitals. According to China's *Foreign Investment Catalogue*, industries can be categorised into four groups as shown in Table 6.1.

Typically, industries featured with intensive research and development spending, including manufacturing whole automobiles, manufacturing commercial aircraft, telecommunication services and medical institutions, are listed under the "restricted" group. Also, the catalogue states that Chinese companies need to have controlling interest when forming JVs, undeniably providing Chinese companies natural advantages over foreign ones when negotiating technology transfers (National Development and Reform Commission 2017).

Table 6.1: The Categorisations of China's *Foreign Investment Catalogue*

Group	Explanation
"Encouraged"	Foreign investors who seek to enter the "encouraged" industries will be subjected to preferential policy favouring them.
"Restricted"	Foreign investors who seek to enter the "restricted" industries need to form Joint Ventures (JVs) with domestic enterprises to gain market access.
"Prohibited"	Foreign investors are not allowed to invest in "prohibited" industries.
"Permitted"	Foreign companies are allowed to enter the "permitted" industries and will be subjected to the same treatment as domestic ones will be. All industries not included in the catalogue are deemed "permitted".

Source: Asia Competitiveness Institute based on information retrieved from the National Development and Reform Commission.

As government may add industries to or remove them from the list at its discretion, the external environment is unfriendly for foreign companies since they could lose existing policy support and even be confined to new restrictions at any time. In fact, restrictions on manufacturing whole automobiles were strengthened in the past decade. Policymakers "encouraged" manufacturing of whole automobiles until 2010, removed this industry from the catalogue from 2011 to 2014, and have put it under the "restricted" group since 2015 (National Development and Reform Commission 2007, 2011, 2015, 2017).

In such an environment, it comes as no surprise that Chinese companies would leverage the policy advantages to acquire technological innovations crucial to their products. Moreover, policymakers encourage domestic companies to acquire foreign technologies actively. According to the medium- and long-term national technology development plan, Chinese companies should not acquire technologies that the domestic market could provide, but rather focus on those that are only available overseas. Subsequently, local companies should digest, absorb and thereafter improve upon those technologies to develop indigenous products that are competitive globally (State Council 2006).

China's market environment and government policies rendered concerns among American companies. Figure 6.1 illustrates some survey responses from AmCham China and the US–China Business Council (USCBC). According to the 2013 and 2014 AmCham China Business Climate Survey, at least 30 percent of the surveyed companies worried about *de facto* technology transfers when seeking accession to the Chinese market by forming JVs. Further, according to the 2017 Member Survey done by USCBC, 19 percent of respondents said that they were asked directly for technology transfers during negotiations, while some of the requests were reportedly from government entities.

Notwithstanding the popularity of concerns from the US and the unfairness of the business environment in China, there is a lack of hard evidence on whether any transfers were forced by either the central or the local government. The investigation report also confirmed this fact. As documented in the Office of United States Trade Representative (2018), China ceased to support mandatory technology transfers since its accession into WTO, although the Chinese government may still perform forced technology transfers "behind closed doors". In this regard, the accusation seems only valid to the extent that policies favouring only Chinese companies facilitate

Figure 6.1: Some Responses from 2013 to 2014 China Business Climate Survey Report and USCBC 2017 Member Survey

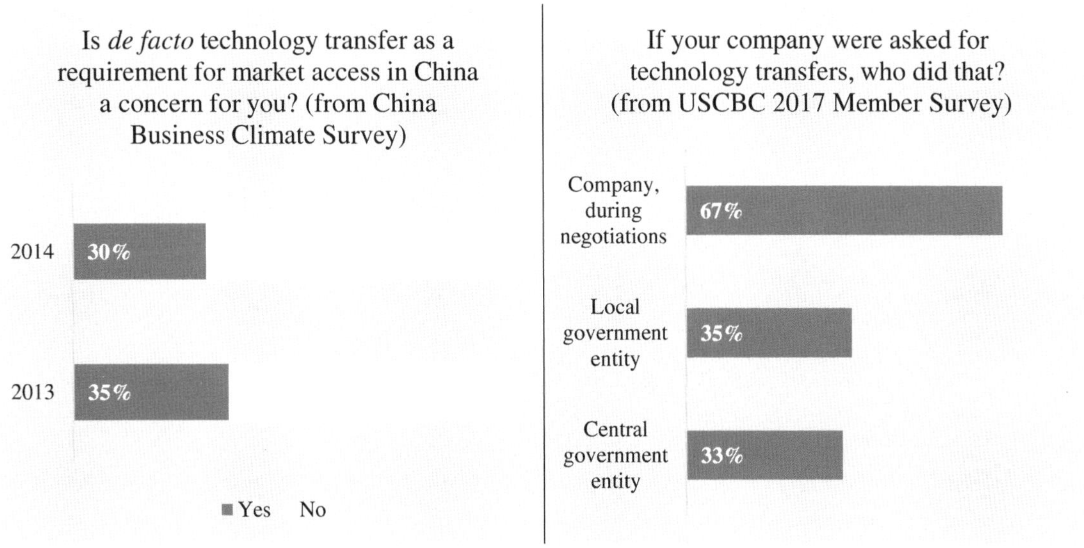

Source: Asia Competitiveness Institute based on information retrieved from AmCham China and USCBC.

unfairness in competition between domestic and foreign entities. On the other hand, the accusation appears to overstate the unfairness by labelling many practices of technology transfers as government-driven activities.

Generally speaking, the scepticism suggests that companies in the US are unsatisfied with the technology transfer regime due to the risk of potential imitation done by Chinese competitors. Although China's protections on intellectual properties should be strengthened, it is still unclear whether or not this accusation will bring forth a new regime of IP rights protections in China.

In the first place, the government may be reluctant to strengthen the protection because such practice is likely to grant monopolistic positions to foreign firms in technology-intensive industries (Braga *et al.* 2000). For example, Qualcomm, a US-based smartphone chip producer, was investigated under China's Anti-Monopoly Law in 2013 because of its unfair cross-licensing terms. As a result of this investigation, the firm was fined USD 975 million for its anti-competitive conducts. Besides, empirical research in the literature suggested that strong IP protection has a weak effect on the economic growth in developing countries or economies with highly protected markets (Gould and Gruben 1996; Schneider 2005). Therefore, as China is still growing and its market is not fully liberalised, policymakers may have less incentive to prioritise IP protections.

Another concern is that the accusation and succeeding trade sanctions are coercive and may not yield any constructive result. Coercion usually provokes a retaliatory response instead of a compromise. For instance, not long after the US announced the trade sanctions on China, the latter imposed its counter tariffs on 2nd April 2018. Moreover, trade disputes started due to similar circumstances (IP infringement) that happened in 1992, 1995 and 1996, three times in history.[2] Amid the

[2] For more information about the three historical disputes between the US and China, see Yu (2000) and Bird (2006).

Figure 6.2: The Retaliation Cycle between China and the US (Begins from the Top-Right Quadrant)

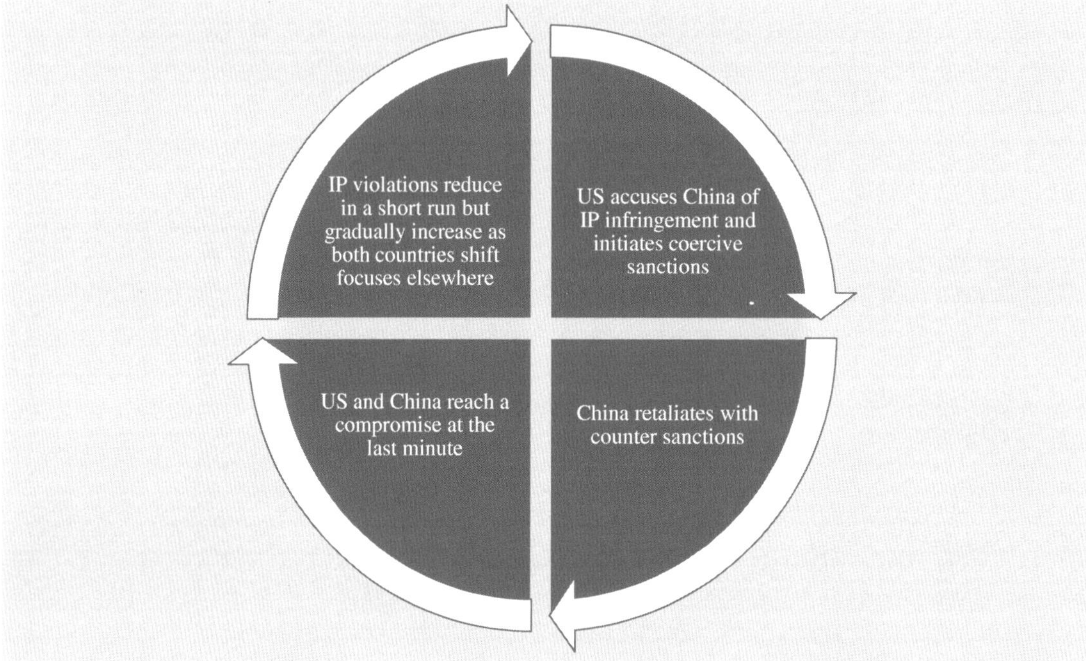

Source: Asia Competitiveness Institute based on information retrieved and reproduced from Bird (2006).

1996 trade dispute, China even responded to the sanctions in a hostile manner by turning away from the US company Boeing and signing an order with the European company Airbus (Yu 2000). In view of all three disputes, scholars abstracted a "retaliation cycle", as shown in Figure 6.2, out of the reciprocation between the US and China. The cycle outlines the unproductive nature of these disputes because each time the coercion from the US only produced short-term results, but not long-term strong enforcement of IP protection in China (Yu 2000; Bird 2006).

For China to accept stronger IP protection, challenges come from two aspects. One is the conflict between protecting domestic companies or foreign patentees; another is the lack of leniency in the unilateral and coercive approach adopted by the US. Despite these challenges, China is changing gradually. On the one hand, a *Foreign Investment Law* has been submitted to the National People's Congress; the new law strictly prohibited government-forced technology transfers to restrict government interference in regular business activities (Standing Committee of the National People's Congress 2019).

For the first time, China will impose legal controls on technology transfers for better protection on the interest of foreign companies. On the other hand, as depicted in Figure 6.3, China was the third largest purchasers of IP in 2017. What's more, it achieved a 178 percent decadal growth in payments for IP, standing out of all other countries in the same period. The rapid growth in payments indicates a rising public awareness of IP protections in China and provides the basis for implementing stronger IP protection rules.

Simply accusing China's violation of IP rights seems not to be a constructive idea since the accusation ignores efforts that China has made to strengthen IP protection. The accusation from

Figure 6.3: Top Five Countries in Payments for the Use of Intellectual Property (2017)

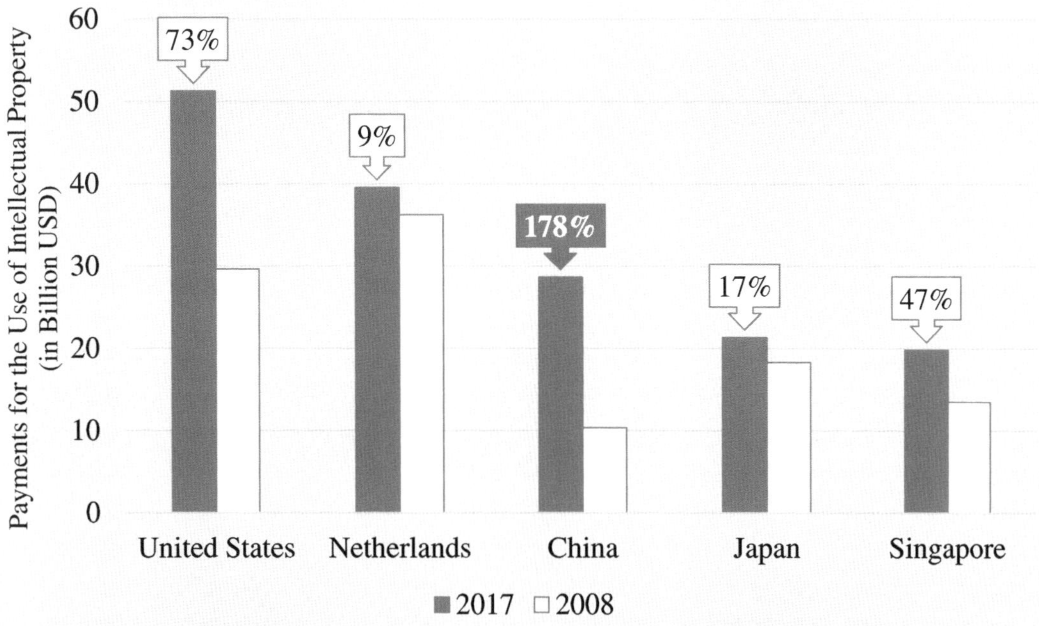

Source: Asia Competitiveness Institute based on information retrieved from the World Bank.

the US is also a prelude to trade sanctions, which may give rise to retaliatory approaches instead of any compromise from China. In light of the increasing awareness of the general public, the Chinese government should continue to improve IP protections. With better protection, domestic companies in China may devote more resources for research and development, which would eventually feed into the growth of China's economy.

6.3 US, China and WTO Rules

Founded in 1995, WTO is one of the youngest international organisations. Its primary function is to ensure that trade flows as "smoothly, predictably and freely as possible".[3] However, even among its member countries, expectations differ significantly. For instance, some argue that the WTO should "mainly function as a forum for international cooperation" through removing trade barriers and resolving conflicts, while some find that the WTO should not only focus on the arbitration of commercial interests, but also real developmental issues, such as the alleviation of world poverty (Elsig 2013).

Although WTO has both legislative and judicial channels for achieving its objectives, the judicial channel is the one consequently functioning as the focus for action, with the number of cases for dispute settlement increasing rapidly since the turn of the century. In its 24 years of existence, the Dispute Settlement System (DSS) has handled over 500 cases.[4]

---

[3] For more information, see https://www.wto.org/english/thewto_e/whatis_e/inbrief_e/inbr_e.pdf.

[4] For more information, see https://www.wto.org/english/tratop_e/dispu_e/dispu_e.htm.

The Dispute Settlement Mechanism (DSM) of WTO

A dispute arises when a member state (the complainant state) claims that another member state (the respondent state) has violated an agreement or commitment that it has made in the WTO. The complainant state may call for consultations with the respondent state. If the dispute is not resolved within 60 days, a panel is set up to consider arguments from the sides, and a ruling is issued. The report issued by the Panel is *defacto* adopted by all the members unless there's a consensus against it within 60 days of issuance of the report. This "negative consensus" is what makes the DSS unique and effective as it prevents states from blocking rulings and stalling the process. After the ruling has been adopted, each party has the right to appeal to the standing Appellate Body. However, this is restricted to matters regarding legal interpretations and law formulated under the purview of the panel. If adjudged to be in favour of the complainant state, the WTO gives it the right to impose retaliatory restrictions for a specific period of time over the respondent state (Shedd *et al.* 2015). It also mandates the respondent to repeal those specific restrictions and conform to WTO standards.

However, the effectiveness of the dispute resolution at the WTO has been questioned. One argument is that WTO retaliation rules are skewed against developing countries and that WTO retaliation rules impair the utility of WTO dispute settlement for these countries (Nottage 2010). An assertion commonly used to support this argument is that the major founding powers, such as the US, manipulate the system to their advantage, as seen for instance through the enactment of veto power by the Trump administration in the prevention of the replacement of four judges in the Appellate Body (Brennan 2019). Such moves have been deemed to deal great damage to the organisation, rendering WTO's resolution system ineffective (Brennan 2019). This, in turn, creates an environment lacking the presence of an established third party, such that bilateral solutions dominate — more often to the advantage of the bigger party (Brennan 2019). Other critiques lambasting the effectiveness of dispute resolution at the WTO argue that this ineffectiveness is based on the acceptance of certain countries as members into the WTO. Those members may not share common values, such as the "belief in the rule of law", which is fundamental for the successful functioning of the dispute settlement mechanism, but WTO lacks specific effective methods to force its members to share the same values and to comply with the rules.[5]

Nonetheless, given the alternatives and the constraints that the WTO has to work within, WTO's dispute resolution mechanism should be considered successful. Several scholars have observed the trend of high voluntary compliance rates to WTO report rulings, even in cases where the smaller party may not be able to retaliate (Nottage 2010). As pointed out by the same article, retaliation has also been observed to be the "exception rather than the rule": out of the 60 WTO disputes where retaliation was possible, the complainant pursued and gained retaliation rights from the WTO Dispute Settlement Body (DSB) in only nine of those disputes, with retaliatory measures being imposed in only five of them. In a study conducted by Davis (2008) on trade cases involving the US, it was found that disputes under the purview of WTO's DSS have shorter durations compared to those not directed to the WTO adjudication (Agon and Shany 2014). Established larger defendant member states are also observed to oppose the conduct

[5] For more information, see this interview https://www.jri.co.jp/MediaLibrary/file/report/WuJunhua/pdf/10774.pdf.

inconsistent with WTO law, presumably because they subscribe to preserving the legitimacy of the legal system as they may need it for their purposes, and in part due to the "shaming pressure" from other members in support of the WTO system (Nottage 2010). Quantitative research by Maton and Maton (2007) also demonstrates how the actual practices of the WTO DSS, in general, underpin its objectives of "independence and impartiality", as shown for instance through the release of several reports that did actually run counter to the interests of "powerful members" (Agon and Shany 2014). Most scholars generally support this view.[6]

The data furthermore reflect that developing countries have requested authorisation from the DSB to retaliate and pursued their requests at least as frequently as developed countries have done, thereby contradicting the belief that developing countries regard WTO retaliatory regulations as useless (Nottage 2010).

Additionally, developing countries are not defenceless — they do, for instance, possess the ability to "cross-retaliate" in areas of intellectual property rights and services (Nottage 2010). Insofar as the defendant voluntarily provides compliance, developing countries thereby have sufficient grounds to view the WTO DSS as an effective policy towards the removal of "illegal trade barriers" enacted by other WTO countries (Nottage 2010). This view has also been corroborated in a qualitative study conducted by Conti (2009), which showed that countries with low retaliation capacity recognise the legitimacy of the DSS, as it offers important opportunities to them, thereby levelling the playing field (Agon and Shany 2014).[7]

US–China Disputes at WTO

Although the WTO DSS could be regarded as effective for most of the countries, opinions as to whether the WTO has been effective in resolving disputes between the US and China vary widely, depending on the benchmarks used. Recent trade-associated tensions between the two countries demonstrated, for instance, how the Trump administration disregarded WTO regulations by adopting a unilateral approach of threatening suspension of concessions instead of a traditional approach of forming negotiations under WTO rules. This move was argued to have triggered China to respond correspondingly, resulting in a situation where the two largest members of the trading system disregard the rules (Ha and Posen 2018).

In the timeframe from China's accession into the WTO till 2016, trade disputes between China and the US were predominantly approached using the regulations instituted in WTO rules and China's accession protocols, through the utilisation of "quiet diplomacy, bilateral dialogues,

[6] See for instance Howse and Esserman (2006).

[7] The author nevertheless highlights that this should not detract from the fact that the dispute resolution system is "not yet fully satisfactory for developing countries", a complaint rooted in how "most developing members have not yet participated in the DSS either as a party or third party", that "empirical studies reveal inequalities among WTO member states that hinder the developing members' ability to use the DSS and effectively defend their economic interests through the formal mechanisms it provides", that "complaints brought by smaller, less-developed countries are more likely to languish in the DSS". To be lamented is also "the lack of legal capacity among developing states, which limits their ability to settle disputes advantageously during the consultations stage — the stage in which the majority of WTO cases end, and where most of the fullest concessions by the defendants are attained".

the WTO DSS, and domestic trade remedies" (Agon and Shany 2014). As of the time of the preparation of this book, China has been the single member country receiving the most complaints (23 cases) from the US — nearly three times more than the single member country receiving the next highest number of complaints from the US, and forming 19 percent of its total cases as defendant.[8] In the same period, China has only filed 15 complaints against the US, although it has to be noted that the US forms a significantly higher percentage of the cases as a defendant against China, at 68 percent.[9]

The alleged factors contributing to the bulk of the complaints brought by the US against China can be classified into the three categories: China's failure to fully embrace market-oriented policies; the enactment of protectionist measures, such as the government ownership and control of key market players and the deployment of "massive market-distorting subsidies"; and all kinds of unreasonable policies and practices that undermine the US's intellectual property rights, innovation and technological development (Office of the United States Trade Representative 2018). It is, however, predominantly the third category which the US has chosen and can pursue under the auspices of the WTO. Specifically, it is claimed that US firms have been deprived of the ability to set market-based terms in licensing by China, and thus they are unable to be paid legally on market terms for their technologies (Ha and Posen 2018). This claim rests on the basis that the practices violate the Agreement on Trade-Related Aspects of Intellectual Property Rights (TRIPS), which prevent members treating foreign and domestic firms unequally (Ha and Posen 2018).

The areas of dissatisfaction experienced by China towards the US tend to focus on the following topics: (1) the strict high-tech export control prohibiting the export of a great range of competitive US high-tech products to China, (2) criticising China for encouraging independent innovation, (3) lack of "equal treatment" by the US towards China after the reform of the US export control system in 2010, specifically through the continuation of the arms embargo against China, (4) the lack of equal treatment to Chinese investors in the national security review of mergers and acquisitions, (5) the abuse of Trade Remedy Measures by the US, for instance through the use of alternative state, separate rates, public institutions, external benchmarks and other unfair approaches, with the intention to impose abnormally high tax rates on Chinese products (Ministry of Commerce 2017). Further complaints include that the imposition of measures by the US enables protectionism, hindering the functioning of the Appellate Body; the inadequate response of the US towards the Appellate Body report pertaining to anti-dumping proceedings involving China; and the double standards that the US is the only WTO Member which fails to implement the DSB's rulings and recommendations under the TRIPS Agreement (Ministry of Commerce 2018, 2019).

However, if one were to take a longer period in consideration, specifically from the period when China officially became a WTO member, the effectiveness of the WTO DSM could be

[8] Namely, Canada at 8 complaints. The total number of cases filed by the US is 123. For more information, see https://www.wto.org/english/tratop_e/dispu_e/dispu_maps_e.htm?country_selected=USA&sense=e.

[9] The total number of cases filed by China is 22. For more information, see https://www.wto.org/english/tratop_e/dispu_e/dispu_maps_e.htm?country_selected=CHN&sense=e.

regarded as significant. Insofar as the assertion that China has utilised the WTO DSM to resolve critical issues about its domestic industries is accurate. According to Zeng (2013), the increasing resort to DSM may have helped to direct conflicts from bilateral trade relationship to the multilateral forum and to avoid any influence from other pressure groups hampering the US–China trade relations, thereby preventing the intensification of the strained bilateral trade relations. This sentiment was echoed by the then US trade representative Ambassador Susan C. Schwab, that the cases brought against China should be viewed as a form of engagement rather than a failure in trade relations. Those cases convey the information that these two countries have worked to resolve disputes about obligations through neutral and legal methods, which were aimed at preventing trade wars but not fuelling them (Malawer 2007).

Evaluating the Extent to Which China Follows WTO Rules

Regarding the contentions the US has towards China, in particular the protection of intellectual property rights (IPR) mentioned in Section 6.3.2, China has argued that it "takes its commitments under the TRIPS agreement seriously", for instance through the establishment of a more comprehensive legal system for intellectual property protection and "intellectual property courts", the intensification of clamping down related crimes and the setting up of a "National Leading Group for Combating IPR Infringement and Counterfeits" led by the State Council for promoting a long-term mechanism (Ministry of Commerce 2017, 2019).

Although China's refutation of this issue seems valid, the main point of its argument only focuses on the existence of IPR protection framework but provides no grounds for the effectiveness of it. As the TRIPS agreement is only one of many WTO multilateral agreements, China's insufficient answer to the US allegation could open up discussions on the extent to which China follows WTO rules. One method to evaluate that is through the number and type of complaints brought against China through WTO's dispute settlement mechanism. As of the time of preparation of this book, China has had a total of 43 cases brought against it, the majority (74 percent) originating from the US and the EU.[10]

Aside from the IPR issues, the majority of the disputes brought against China tend to concentrate on issues involving WTO subsidy disciplines when Chinese State-Owned Enterprises (SOEs) are subsidy recipients. These types of problems mainly concern whether Chinese SOEs should be treated as public entities and whether benefits not in the form of financial contributions provided by SOEs can be viewed as subsidies (Li and Tu 2018). In this respect, WTO rulings were at that point ambiguous. On the one hand, SOEs cannot be automatically categorised as "public bodies" based on state ownership and need to be analysed case by case. On the other hand, it was left open whether the provision of benefits by a "public body" constitutes a financial contribution.

It has also been argued that in providing state subsidies to certain industries, China is essentially adopting economic strategies similar to that of other developed nations such as the US and

[10]The total number of cases filed by the US and the EU against China is 32. For more information, see https://www.wto.org/english/tratop_e/dispu_e/dispu_maps_e.htm?country_selected=CHN&sense=e.

Germany, the latter of which has mostly not been deemed problematic thus far, at least by the developed countries. For instance, 11.8 percent of the shares and one-fifth of the voting rights of the world's largest car maker, Volkswagen belong to the state of Lower Saxony. Two of the largest finance businesses in the US, Freddie Mac and Fannie Mae, jointly managing portfolios over USD five trillion, are both mainly government-owned (Edwards 2018). These inconsistencies further obfuscate the murkiness of the extent to which China can be deemed as playing by the rules of the game.

Further factors complicating the assessment of the extent to which China actually is compliant to WTO rules hinge on two main factors: (1) the non-recognition by the major powers of China's Market Economy Status (MES) and (2) that China was subject to unusually stringent conditions to qualify for membership in the WTO.

First, even though many countries have already recognised the MES of China bilaterally, the major powers in the WTO, including the US, the EU and Japan persist in not allowing China MES, instead of continuing the "surrogate country" methodology in anti-dumping cases against China (Li and Tu 2018). This has been argued to enable the enactment of higher anti-dumping duties against Chinese products (Li and Tu 2018; Zeng 2013). In particular, the non-market economy (NME) status have resulted in an imposition of a "double remedy" (i.e. both countervailing and anti-dumping duties) on the same Chinese products. Although China attempted to challenge the USDOC's approach of using the NME methodology as the basis for calculation, the panel and Appellate Body still largely depend on the NME clause in their rulings (Zeng 2013). Yet, this can potentially be understood through factors that go beyond purely economic rationale — the considerable trade surplus that China has with the US and the relevant political and economic power disparity associated with this phenomenon could partially account for the differential treatment (specifically the awarding of MES) of other Eastern European economies arguably similar in political and economic structures to China, but which do not possess the same trade surplus disparity with the US (Li and Tu 2018).

Second, multiple scholars have argued that China has been subject to unusually strict regulations not expected of other member states, for instance the "WTO-plus obligations and the WTO-minus rights", including the prevention of China from seeking "special and different (S&D)" treatment as do other developing members when joining the WTO, the obligation to provide national treatment to both foreign "products and persons", whereas normal WTO national treatment clauses only involve products; and the enactment of "alternative benchmark" methodology in countervailing duty cases against China (Li and Tu 2018; Garnaut *et al.* 2018). China has thus asserted that this designation has resulted in unfair treatment by the major WTO powers towards itself (Ministry of Commerce 2017), thereby calling into question the extent to which it is possible to evaluate Chinese compliance to WTO rulings objectively.

Role and Ambitions of China in the WTO

The acceptance of China as a WTO member in 2001 and China's interactions with the WTO in the years after has been argued to have several implications, both for the institution itself as well as for developing countries. The current WTO system has been accused of being insufficiently capable of responding to the needs and situations of transitional economies, a group which has characteristics of both market and non-market economies and to which several developing countries belong to (Li and Tu 2018). China's accession has specifically been asserted to have established a prominent example for the WTO to embrace developing countries, in particular those transitional economies, for instance, Vietnam and Russia. Meanwhile, China's case also provides strong support for the legitimate positions of the least developed countries in WTO negotiations (Li and Tu 2018). In doing so, China has not only contributed to making the system more inclusive and universal but has also arguably reshaped the power structure of the WTO. The existence of China has changed the power balance between developed and developing countries in the decision-making process of the WTO, challenging the dominance of the US and other major players and thus creating a multipolar system (Li and Tu 2018). In this new system, China has also been increasingly perceived as taking on a potential leadership role to promote multilateralism in the WTO (Li and Tu 2018). One possible implication of this phenomenon is the designing of measures to adapt to the needs of different members. For instance, improving incentives for members to pursue plurilaterals in the WTO would provide a mechanism for them to acknowledge diversified preferences and priorities across the membership (Hoekman and Mavroidis 2015).

A key area in which China could take the lead in paving the way forward for other developing countries is with the WTO Agreement on Government Procurement Agreement (GPA). The GPA is a plurilateral agreement within the framework of the WTO to mutually open government procurement markets among its parties.[11] It comprises to date 47 WTO members. China currently possesses only observer status but is in the process of acceding to become a member, after having submitted six offers to become part of the GPA, ever since negotiations began officially in 2007. China's absence as a member has been noticeable, especially since the country, as one of the largest developing and transitional economies with the largest public sector, would potentially bring substantial market opportunities for international trade (Li and Tu 2018). These factors, together with China's attempts in previous years to bridge the gaps to meet the criteria set out for being a member, speak for its potential in opening paths for the accession of similar developing economies into the GPA.

Another possibility for China as a force for change in the WTO lies in the enactment of institutional regulations. A complement to the hard-law approach (typically taken by the WTO) would be the inclusion of the soft-law approach, a trait deemed characteristic of both Chinese and Asian political dealings, specifically through informal institutional arrangements, which provide members leeway in implementing measures with consideration of the specific characteristics of their economies, also emphasising the importance of the principle of consensus (Li and Tu 2018). The soft-law approach as practised by China during its G20 presidency in 2016 has been observed to be relatively successful, predominantly in facilitating cooperation among both developing and developed countries as well as in supporting the long-run existence of a multilateral trading system (Li and Tu 2018).

[11] For more information, see https://www.wto.org/english/tratop_e/gproc_e/gp_gpa_e.htm.

6.4 Will Fundamentals of China's Economy Be Altered and Policy Reform Measures Be Deepened as the Result of the US–China Trade War?

Recently, the deadline for imposing tariffs between the US and China has been extended as talks continue between officials from both the countries. Since the content of these negotiations remains undisclosed, policymakers in other nations can only speculate on the outcomes of these talks.

Based on our sources and recent developments, China is likely to agree to the following concessions after the first rounds of negotiations:

a. Joint mutual tariff reduction to a low of 5% and eventually towards zero, albeit with a few exceptions, and potentially a proposition for a US–China free trade agreement;
b. An agreement to develop informal protections on intellectual properties (IP) while also working with the US towards creating a formal mechanism for IP protections that is agreeable to both countries within the next three years;
c. Agreeing to treat foreign enterprises similar to Chinese state-owned enterprises in terms of operation space, taxation, grants and subsidies;
d. Creating a timetable for the reduction of Chinese trade surplus to the US by a fixed percentage for a year for five years through escalating the purchase of US goods and services;
e. Liberalisation of trade in technology, especially in non-military technology cooperation, and the mutual liberalisation of trade in technology within three years;
f. A further liberalisation in China's financial sector through allowing greater participation by foreign enterprises for industries including banking, insurance and securities services;
g. To eventually establish an RMB exchange rate regime that is driven entirely by the market, which would have China peg the RMB exchange rate to the USD for five years.

As discussed, the impacts and ramifications of the US–China trade war should not be taken lightly. The currently mounting external pressures exerted by the Western economic powers could however be a blessing in disguise for China: These pressures potentially aid China in combatting strong domestic resistance from vested-interest quarters usually associated with the undertaking of hard policy measures, for instance in the instituting of new rules and regulations to deepen economic reforms which could ultimately mitigate the adverse impacts brought about by the trade war.

First, the trade war has effectively hindered China's access to foreign technology. China's firms remain reliant on foreign technology as it constantly imports essential parts and components required for the assembling of domestically produced goods. One such component is the semiconductor chip. In 2017, approximately one-third of China's exports was electronic goods powered by semiconductor chips. The demand for such components is therefore tremendous, and when domestic production cannot support such demand, imports will have to step in to fill the gap. Data from the US International Trade Commission shows that China is the second largest export destination for US semiconductors in 2017 (Semiconductor Industry Association 2018).

Restricting access to such components will therefore hurt China's economy. Consequently, it is essential for China to not only press on with the "Made in China 2025 Initiative" (MIC2025) but to accelerate its execution as well. MIC2025, inspired by Germany's Industry 4.0, is essentially a strategic plan by China to modernise its industrial capabilities. The initiative focuses heavily on 10 strategic sectors which will help to secure China's position as a global powerhouse in high-tech industries. Through replacing its reliance on foreign technology with its own innovation, China will be able to achieve both self-sufficiency as well as transit from a low-cost manufacturer into a high-end producer of goods strong enough to compete with countries such as Germany, South Korea and Japan. In order for MIC2025 to work, it is critical for China to recruit and gather top foreign researchers and scientists for further advancement in research and development.

Second, the trade war has also resulted in exchange rate volatility. This negatively impacts domestic firms and foreign investors' confidence. Volatile exchange rates heighten the risks investors face as their investments may progressively diminish in value. Therefore, investors are likely to prefer allocating their investments somewhere else. This in turn translates to capital flight and loss of FDI. Domestic firms will also see their profits diminishing as they trade internationally. China will therefore need to step up the internationalisation of the RMB and facilitate non-USD invoicing, trading and investments. While these may not necessarily eliminate the volatility of its exchange rate, it helps to mitigate the effect by minimising the reliance on it. Domestic firms will be able to trade exclusively using RMB which will eliminate the risks of currency mismatch and therefore reduce its transactional costs. This has the effect of helping Chinese firms to expand and grow domestically and internationally (Zhang and Tao 2014).

Internationalisation of the RMB will also increase the demand for RMB. This will eventually lead to the appreciation of the RMB, thereby bringing in more capital. While this may hurt its exports, the appreciation of RMB will also bring in cheaper imports, in turn facilitating the acceleration of the MIC2025 initiative. Furthermore, financial institutes will now be able to gain access to more funds as they can issue bonds at lower interest rates. The Chinese government will also have access to these funds, which will allow it to sustain a higher fiscal deficit, in other words enabling higher government spending. However, the internationalisation of RMB is not without costs. It can bring along with it a higher probability of asset bubbles and financial instability. It is therefore essential for China to also improve its financial regulatory system to avoid systemic risks and crises.

Third, the potential loss of exports caused by the ensuing US–China trade war should not be underestimated. As a result, China should be looking to shift its exports to other regions, especially Asia. This can be done by building and improving the geopolitical relations with ASEAN, India, Japan and South Korea. China can do so by fine-tuning its strategies on its Belt and Road Initiative and by avoiding set to debt traps. Essentially, the BRI is a development strategy that aims to boost trade and stimulate economic growth across Asia, achieved through the building of a massive amount of infrastructure connecting approximately 80 countries together. This is a massive project for China as it covers one-third of global GDP and one-quarter of total global trade in goods and services.

However, the fear of excessive debt, as exemplified by Sri Lanka, has resulted in many countries (including Pakistan, Malaysia, Myanmar and Bangladesh) scaling down or scrapping their projects which were part of the Belt and Road Initiative. In order to ease such fears, China could work with Singapore — which has a competitive advantage as Asia's Infrastructure Hub — to develop, evaluate, finance and invest in its infrastructure projects. Ultimately, China will have to reassure these countries that China is committed to working together with them and that the BRI is beneficial for everyone. A successful BRI will also help to promote the internationalisation of the RMB.

Fourth, a trade war could potentially intensify competition among domestic firms. As mentioned, US tariffs will lower China's exports. This will eventually translate to excess domestic supply, which will then increase competition among domestic firms, resulting in a drop in prices and profits. According to data from the National Bureau of Statistics, the total annual profit by industrial enterprises fell from approximately RMB 7.5 trillion in 2017 to just RMB 6.6 trillion for 2018. While sourcing for new export markets is essential, it is also vital to promote the privatisation and consolidation of SOEs under mixed ownership in order for firms to increase their efficiency and profits.

Finally, the trade war is accelerating a manufacturing shift towards Southeast Asia as firms try to avoid getting hit by US tariffs. These in turn take jobs and exports away from China, potentially harming its economy. China should therefore continue with its economic restructuring and the expansion of its tertiary sectors, particularly its service sector. This will also help in catering to the increasing domestic demand triggered by the rising middle class.

The US–China trade war is unlikely to end, at least in the medium term. The magnitude of the resulting adverse impacts is causing uncertainty, thus delaying or disrupting potential investment, both domestically and externally, in the Chinese economy. This could pose severe repercussions for China. It is therefore crucial for China to eliminate, or at the very least mitigate these adverse impacts, in order to continue restructuring its economy from the over-dependence on the export production-driven strategy towards the current innovation-driven production and domestic consumption-led, high value-added services-oriented economy.

6.5 Confronting the Production Shifts, Identifying China's Growth Momentum in the Aftermath of the Trade Tension

According to UNCTAD (2019), the US–China trade disputes have laid heavy burden on the manufacturing sectors of both countries. US imposed tariffs targeting imports worth about USD 250 billion and nearly all affected goods are from the manufacturing sector. China imposed USD 110 billion worth of tariffs on its imports, of which about USD 50 billion related to intermediate manufacturing products. Certainly, the huge tariff burden will make overseas procurement of raw materials and processing goods more expensive for companies located in China.

Moreover, it is worth the attention that the rise of manufacturing cost could be an existing trend further exacerbated by the trade disputes. As shown in Figure 6.4, China's minimum wage growth from 2005 to 2013 reached 90%, much higher than the figures of several developing and developed economies. As a result of this increase, companies, in particular low-cost manufacturing ones, would have to incur higher labour cost for their production. According to ILO, the

Figure 6.4: Growth of Minimum Wage for Selected Economies between 2005 and 2013

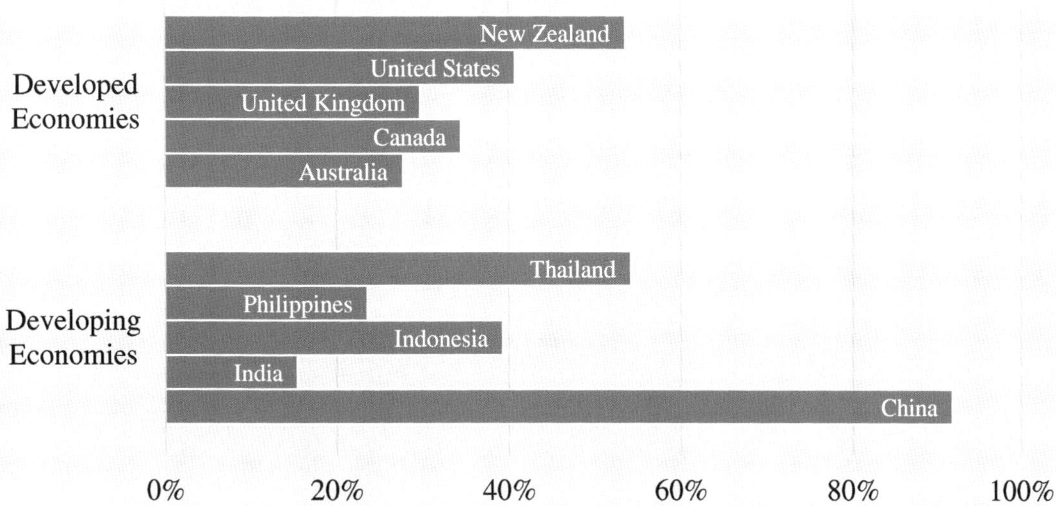

Note: Calculations are based on PPP USD constant price in 2011.
Source: Asia Competitiveness Institute based on information retrieved from ILO.

minimum wage level of China in 2013 was PPP USD 395. India, Indonesia, Philippines and Thailand reached USD 179, USD 351, USD 677 and USD 629, respectively.

Due to the rising manufacturing cost, China would probably be a less attractive option than other developing countries for multinational corporations (MNCs) building new plants and factories. More seriously, China may bear a risk of domestic MNCs shifting their productions out of its domain. However, although moving upward in the global value chain (GVC) may prevent China from direct competition with economies at the lower end, the country may still suffer from direct competitions against economies with high productivity and high-skill innovations. If China fails to compete with those economies at the higher end of the GVC, it may fall into a pitfall of growth slowdown. Therefore, to mitigate those impacts to the manufacturing sector and be prepared for other potential consequences, China should discover new sources for its economic growth.

Interestingly, the country may find what it needs domestically. With the synergies yielded by regional cooperation, three emerging megalopolises, Guangdong–Hong Kong–Macau Greater Bay Area (GBA), Yangtze River Delta (YRD) and Beijing–Tianjin–HeBei (BTH), may bring forth unique characteristics to the growth of China's economy. In order to identify these characteristics and growth momentums brought by them, the following sections will provide dedicated discussion for each of these regions.

6.5.1 Guangdong–Hong Kong–Macau Greater Bay Area

The GBA (Figure 6.5) was first mentioned in the BRI initiative, in which the government portrayed the crucial positions of Shenzhen, Guangzhou, Zhuhai and Fujian in facilitating opening-up of China's economy and cooperation with Hong Kong, Macau, Taiwan and other economies

Figure 6.5: Map of Guangdong–Hong Kong–Macau Greater Bay Area

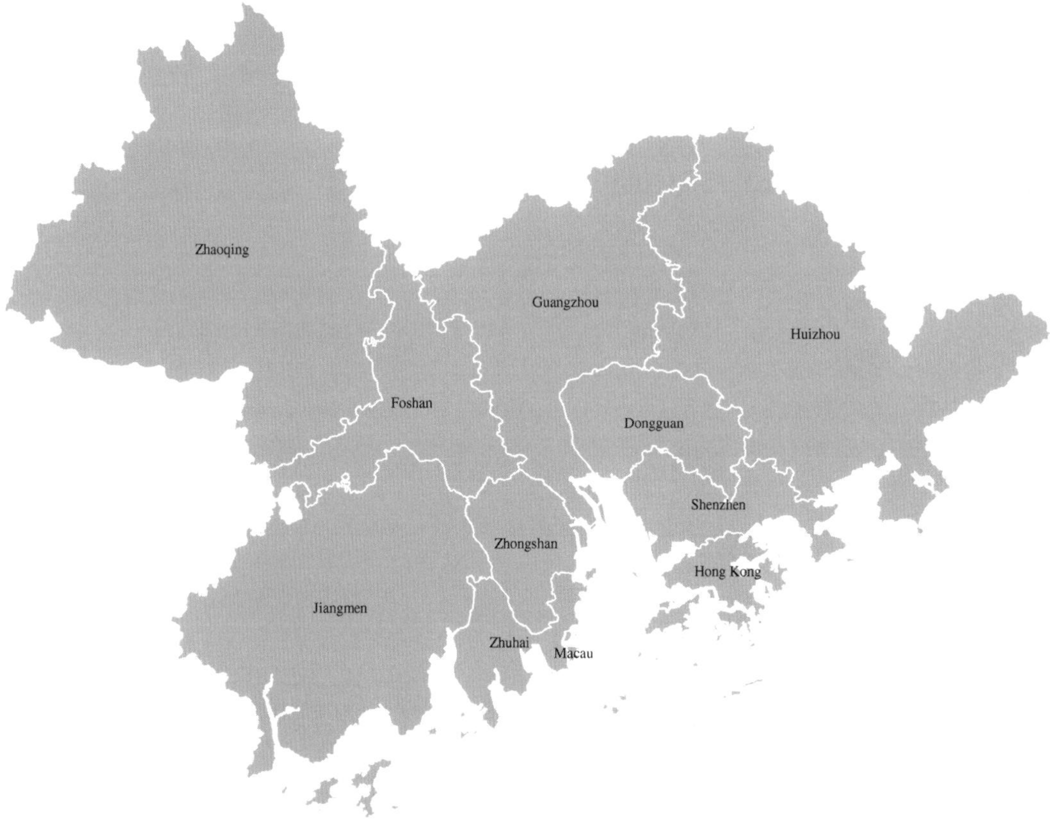

Source: Asia Competitiveness Institute based on information retrieved from National Geomatics Centre of China.

along the Maritime Silk Road (National Development and Reform Commission, Ministry of Foreign Affairs, and Ministry of Commerce 2015).

The plan fully materialised on 1st July 2017, when the National Development and Reform Commission and government officials from Guangdong, Hong Kong and Macau jointly signed the framework agreement for deepening their cooperation. As mentioned in this agreement, this cooperation could leverage unique strengths in the GBA, creating economic vibrancy for the entire area. Cities of Guangdong, such as Shenzhen, could serve as the technology and innovation hub; Hong Kong, underpinned by its competitiveness in finance and trade, could further attract global investors and push the internationalisation of RMB; Macau is famous for its tourism and entertainment industries and would be a platform for pulling FDI from Portuguese-speaking countries (National Development and Reform Commission *et al.* 2017).

Building upon the agreement, the central government initiated another strategic plan on 18th February 2019 detailing the priorities of development for the GBA. As pointed out by this plan, the development of the GBA should focus on cultivating innovation, improving transport connectivity both domestically and internationally, enhancing livability of cities and facilitating market openness. Through the implementation of supporting policies, governments will also be playing an important role in the development process (State Council 2019).

The development opportunities of the GBA, as underscored by the policies and plans, attribute to its two primary advantages: technology advancement and trade openness, which stem from the growth of two economies, Shenzhen and Hong Kong, respectively. Technology advancement in Shenzhen cannot be separated from the contribution of domestic companies such as Huawei, ZTE and Tencent. These companies are highly integrated in Shenzhen's economy, and thus their influence should be taken into serious consideration. In 2016, the top 20 firms in terms of GDP contribution amounted to 26.5 percent of the aggregate volume of the city (Government of Shenzhen 2017). Among these firms, Huawei, ZTE and Tencent reportedly ranked first, second and fifth, underlining their values and close relationship to the economy of Shenzhen.

According to the 2017 annual reports, ZTE spent RMB 12.96 billion on research and development (R&D). Tencent, in the same year, reported RMB 17.46 billion under that account. Huawei, as the highest GDP contributor, devoted even more resources into R&D, registering a spending of RMB 89.69 billion.[12] As shown in Figure 6.6, their spending in R&D in 2017 are even higher than those of many provinces; Huawei outperformed 25 provinces, while ZTE and Tencent defeated eight and 13 provinces, respectively. With the involvement of these firms and their strong commitment to crafting innovation, technology development would be integrated into Shenzhen's economy. Either directly or indirectly, Shenzhen would benefit from the efficiency and productivity improvement from technologies. Additionally, the GBA would inherit possible economic benefits from Shenzhen and could leverage them in its growth.

Figure 6.6: Comparing Research and Development Spending of Huawei, ZTE and Tencent with Provincial Figures (2017)

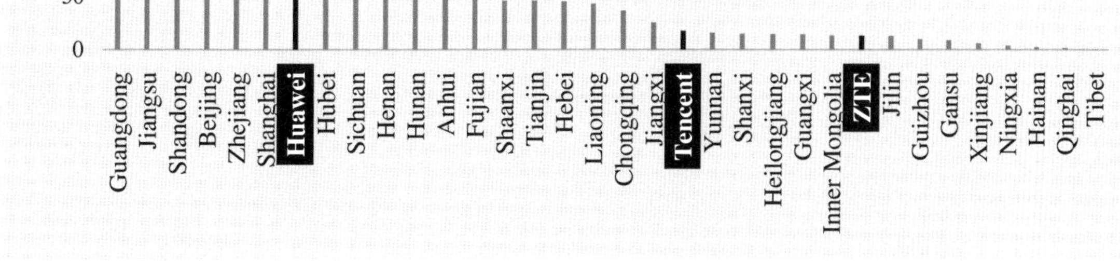

Source: Asia Competitiveness Institute based on information retrieved from National Bureau of Statistics of China.

[12] For more information about these companies, see their annual reports at: https://www.tencent.com/en-us/articles/17000391523362601.pdf (Tencent); https://res-www.zte.com.cn/mediares/zte/Investor/20180326/E1.pdf (ZTE); https://www-file.huawei.com/-/media/corporate/pdf/annual-report/annual_report2017_en.pdf?la=en (Huawei).

Beyond the existing benefits, other possible opportunities may be identified in Shenzhen's ongoing technology development. For instance, the deployment of 5G network may contribute to the economy in two different ways. One direct contribution of that is likely to be the increase of infrastructure investment due to the needs for upgrading existing or constructing new network infrastructure. As a side effect, the proliferation of infrastructure projects may also increase job opportunities.

Another indirect benefit could be the increase of communication efficiency. The 5G network, compared with 4G, further reduces communication latency. This improvement might be crucial to many service industries requiring consistent and reliable tracking of system performances. For instance, hospitals may implement remote patient monitoring on the basis of the ultra-low latency of 5G network (Campbell *et al.* 2017). With numerous possible applications, the 5G value chain is estimated to generate economic output worth about USD 3.5 trillion globally. In particular, China could enjoy USD 984 billion, almost 30 percent of the total value (Campbell *et al.* 2017). As the headquarters of Huawei and ZTE, Shenzhen, as well as the GBA, could embrace this opportunity better than any other region. According to IPlytics, Huawei and ZTE in 2019 ranked second and third among all firms in terms of the ownership of 5G Standard-Essential Patents.[13]

Besides the presence and potential of technology advancement, the importance of trade openness, another primary advantage of the GBA, should also be highlighted. The increase in import or export volume could promote economic growth through a number of ways such as technology transfers, economies of scale and comparative advantages (Yanikkaya 2003). In the GBA, Hong Kong is the key to vitalising trade activities. Even the location of Hong Kong could be crucial since this area is along major sea routes and directly coordinates the trade between Mainland China and global partners. The strategic position of Hong Kong is further underpinned by the fact that it ranked as the sixth busiest container port by World Shipping Council in 2016.

Aside from the geographical advantages, customs policies in Hong Kong also favour trade activities. Hong Kong is a Free Economic Zone and its restriction on import is limited to the extent that only four types of goods are subjected to excise duties, namely, tobacco, hydrocarbon oil, alcoholic beverages and methyl alcohol. For other types of goods, Hong Kong does not levy any customs tariffs or any form of tax (General Administration of Customs n.d.). Such regime indicates a direct cost saving for import and export companies.

On the other hand, the efficiency of customs clearance in Hong Kong is recognised globally. According to World Economic Forum (2018), Hong Kong ranked ninth among 140 economies. Highly efficient customs services suggest that trade companies could save delivery time, and thus indirectly reduce shipping and handling cost or other opportunity costs due to unmet customer expectations of delivery time. As a result, cost savings would incentivise international companies choosing Hong Kong as the platform for trading with Mainland China.

---

[13] Standard-essential patents (SEPs) are patents setting technical standards for the industry. Once approved, they would become almost irreplaceable for future inventions. Thus, companies with more SEPs would have greater leverage in the industry. For more information about SEPs, see Bosworth *et al.* (2018).

In addition to the established advantages, strong policy supports from governments of the GBA would offer Hong Kong or even the whole area greater attractiveness to global exporters. For example, Hong Kong, together with Guangdong, launched the Single E-lock Scheme (SELS) on 28 March 2016. As described in the scheme, an "e-lock" will be applied to the shipment of goods when it is crossing the customs boarder. This lock will be accredited by both customs authorities, thus reducing duplicate inspection on the same shipment and expediting the flow of cargoes.

Since January 2019, the coverage of the SELS in the GBA (Mainland) has been extended to 51 clearance points. With 12 clearance points in Hong Kong, the SELS has provided 612 routes for shipment in between customs (Customs and Excise Department of Hong Kong 2019). Moreover, governments in the GBA have implemented several infrastructure projects to improve the cross-boundary transportation network. Guangzhou–Shenzhen–Hong Kong Express Rail Link was opened in September 2018; Hong Kong–Zhuhai–Macau Bridge was opened later in October of the same year; the Second Humen Bridge is scheduled to commence operation in the first half of 2019; and Shenzhen–Zhongshan Bridge will commence operation in 2024. In summary, it is obvious that the SELS and these facilities will improve the connectivity between Hong Kong and rest of the cities of the GBA, reduce the transportation time between buyers and ports, and motivate companies exporting to this megalopolis.

As China is moving away from a quantitative economic growth towards a high-quality economic growth, trade openness and technology advancement could be two catalysts facilitating a smooth transition. That being said, government highlighting the development of GBA could be justified. With advantages on trade and technology, the GBA would be a great leverage for China to rely on and could play an important role in China's economy at the next stage.

6.5.2 Yangtze River Delta

The development of YRD megalopolis (Figure 6.7) was first proposed in May 2010. At that time, cities in the YRD region already owned a complete urban system, with more than 60 percent of the urbanisation rate in major cities. With the sound urban foundation and economic strength, the YRD was chosen to be an important "gateway" for connecting domestic and international markets. Shanghai, with the strongest economic performance in the YRD, was portrayed as the core city of this development plan (National Development and Reform Commission 2010).

The development of YRD was further emphasised on 12th September 2014. According to the guidance from the State Council, cities in the YRD should leverage the geographical advantages and coordinate constructions of regional railways and highways with the existing Yangtze River waterway, eventually building this area into a transportation hub (State Council 2014). The strategic position of the YRD became critical after the release of BRI. On 1st June 2016, the National Development and Reform Commission drafted a new development plan for the YRD region. Shanghai was again in the central position of this development (National Development and Reform Commission 2016).

The primary advantage of the YRD is its geographical location, since the BRI sea route intersects with this place. Shanghai, as a starting point of the 21st Century Maritime Silk Road, would

Figure 6.7: Map of Yangtze River Delta

Source: Asia Competitiveness Institute based on information retrieved from National Geomatics Centre of China.

carry important functions of connecting foreign investors with the domestic market. Although the level of market liberalisation would be crucial to the success of this connection, reaching a fully liberalised status may not be immediately probable for the whole YRD. Unlike the GBA, the YRD still has many cities lacking basic economic infrastructure. However, despite that the region still needs to improve; Shanghai, as the core of this region, could already contribute to the regional economy in the form of attracting foreign investment. The unique advantage of Shanghai lies upon its well-established free trade zone, which could further bring economic opportunities to the YRD area.

China (Shanghai) Pilot Free Trade Zone (SPFTZ) has more functions than just providing a platform for trade activities. As the first free trade zone in China, SPFTZ adopted a concept of full liberalisation, acting as a piloting test zone for China's new policy practices and approaches. For example, before the country declared increasing liberalisation of the finance sector in 2018, SPFTZ had already embraced such practices since 2015 (State Council 2015).

SPFTZ is also characterised by the multidimensionality of the port functions. According to Wan *et al.* (2014), functions of the port comprise industrial production, port logistics, shipping services, financial services, trade services and community services, all of which are supported by preferential policies of the zone. This seamless integration, together with the absence of customs duty, could give rise to an increase of cross-border e-commerce businesses, because companies in the SPFTZ could rapidly respond to variations in market demand with low cost. For instance, an e-commerce platform called "Buyeasi" is established in the SPFTZ, with an aim of selling international products to Chinese customers (Wan *et al.* 2014). In this regard, SPFTZ could provide an environment fostering the vibrancy of businesses.

Another economic opportunity could attribute to the reduction on currency controls. According to Yao and Whalley (2015), both organisations and individuals could open "free trade accounts" at financial institutions in SPFTZ. Under this account, RMB and foreign currencies would be regulated by the same set of rules. Even cross-border capital transactions, which are highly restricted outside SPFTZ, could be directly settled by this account. Further, the central bank also encouraged institutions such as China Foreign Exchange Trade Center to provide cross-border RMB transactions in the SPFTZ. All these efforts enable a different currency regime, in which companies conducting cross-border transactions would suffer less from the volatility of on- and off-shore RMB spreads. The reduction of risk exposure would encourage firms to use RMB as the currency for settlement. In the long run, this practice may also help promote China's advocacy of the internationalisation of RMB.

Nevertheless, even if the YRD could rely on Shanghai driving the regional development, the lack of regional cooperation may still hinder the realisation of benefits that Shanghai could create for the regional economy. This problem was also pointed out by the 2016 development plan. Therefore, for the YRD to assume more responsibilities on China's economy, regional economic integration should certainly be put on a higher priority.

6.5.3 Beijing–Tianjin–Hebei

In March 2014, the government working report first highlighted the importance of regional cooperation in the development of Beijing, Tianjin and Hebei (Li 2014). On 30th April 2015, the "Beijing–Tianjin–Hebei Coordinated Development Plan" was released. This plan clarified the roles of Beijing, Tianjin and Hebei in development of the BTH (Figure 6.8) and determined the short-term, midterm and long-term targets for it. As documented in the plan, Beijing would phase out its non-capital functions, such as general manufacturing industries, regional logistics bases and wholesale markets, while these functions will be reclaimed by Tianjin and Hebei. The plan aims at rebalancing the functions of the BTH so that the regional economic structure would be optimised (Central Politburo of the Communist Party of China 2015).

Besides rebalancing the regional development, the plan also emphasised improving connectivity in the BTH. While the effect of the rebalancing of urban functions have not yet been unveiled, the connectivity improvement could already be observed. On 20th September 2015, the inter-city railway between Beijing and Tianjin completed its extension to Yujiapu station, connecting Beijing and Tianjin Binhai New Area. On 28th December 2015, Jinbao Railway commenced operation and the travelling time from Tianjin to Baoding was reduced to about an hour.

On 23rd December 2016, the Pinggu line, the first regional express between Hebei and Beijing, started its construction; the construction is scheduled to be completed in 2020 (Xinhua News Agency 2016). In August 2018, the last two broken highways in the BTH were cleared and opened for operation (Beijing Daily 2018). The improvement of regional connection could bring economic

Figure 6.8: Map of Beijing–Tianjin–Hebei

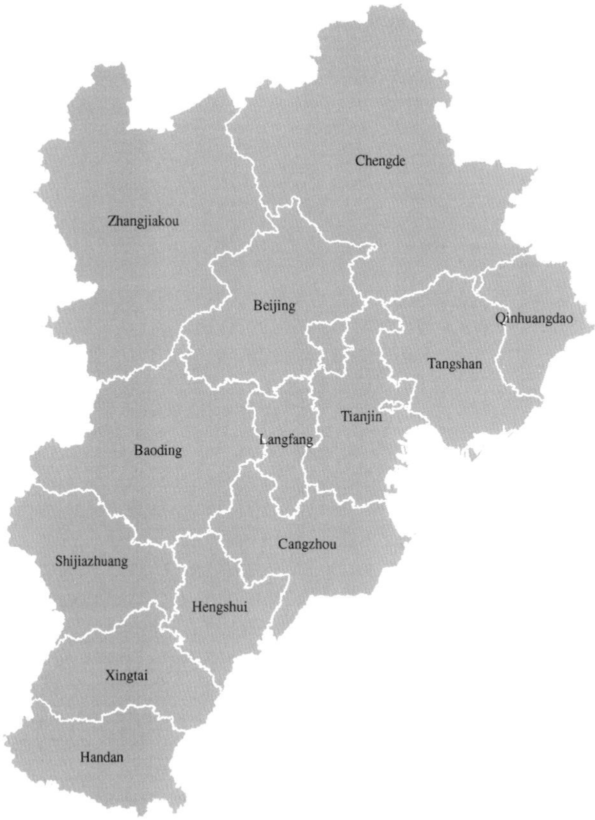

Source: Asia Competitiveness Institute based on information retrieved from National Geomatics Centre of China.

benefits to the BTH. If the rebalancing of functions among Beijing, Tianjin and Hebei succeeded, their industries and economies would be complementary to each other. If the BTH is strongly connected, then it could benefit from the economies of scale, saving costs but increasing outputs.

However, unlike the GBA and YRD, the development of BTH is highly intervened by the central government. The lack of market mechanism may be a risk for this region to cultivate future growth on the basis of high connectivity. In addition, the effectiveness of the rebalancing is yet to materialise.

6.5.4 Singapore Involving in China's Regional Development

As the previous rotating chairman of ASEAN, Singapore has put huge efforts into strengthening regional cooperation. The country was one of the founders of Trans-Pacific Partnership (TPP) and has been continuously pushing for regional free trade agreements (FTAs), such as the Comprehensive and Progressive Agreement for Trans-Pacific Partnership (CPTPP).

In view of Singapore's efforts for economic integration among countries, it would be no surprise that China could borrow Singapore's experience into its development of megalopolises.

In fact, Singapore could participate in China's regional economic development by offering constructive suggestions in three aspects.

First, most of the Chinese regions are still subjected to strong policy restrictions on trade. Although the flourish of trade might be a driver for regional economic development, the stringent restrictions could discourage global companies and thus limit China's integration into the global market. Leveraging on the experience in forming FTAs with different countries, Singapore could be the bridge between China and other economies and help the country solidify the trade relationship with its partners. This bridge might be particularly crucial for megalopolises relying on trade, such as the GBA and YRD.

Second, Singapore has risen to be one of the most competitive financial centres, together with London, New York and Hong Kong. Therefore, Singapore could be the infrastructure evaluation, arbitration, investment and financing hub in Asia. By cooperating with Singapore, China could not only widely disseminate information about the internationalisation of RMB but also speed up fostering the BRI, which is the key to its high-quality economic development. The infrastructure development in China's megalopolises may also benefit from the investment inflows brought by Singapore.

Third, while cities in these megalopolises are experiencing rapid urbanisation, their urban middle-class population, with high consumption ability, would also expand. To cater to this rising demand, these megalopolises should provide an attractive modern lifestyle to their people. China, especially these regions, could be worth referring to Singapore's practices in bolstering e-commerce, digitalisation and livability. Singapore's experience in providing smart urban solutions might be what China can learn from.

In summary, the development of the GBA, YRD and BTH could be challenged due to the lack of experience in regional cooperation. Singapore could support the growth of these regions with its expertise and resources. As such, the integration of Singapore into China's regional development plan might offer China opportunities for a more vibrant economy.

6.6 Agenda for Future Research: Welfare Spending and Fiscal Sustainability for Mainland China

According to the International Monetary Fund (IMF) studies, the sustainable debt-to-GDP ratio for a developed country is 60 percent, while this ratio drops to 40 percent for a developing or emerging economy (International Monetary Fund 2002; Clements *et al.* 2010). As shown in Figure 6.9, China's central government debt has already passed the sustainable 40 percent level, reaching 47.6 percent in 2017. With the clear increasing trend, debt problem deserves attention from policymakers.

There are two obvious turning points in this debt-to-GDP ratio trend. The first one is in 1995, as the new Budget Law strengthened the distribution and supervisory function of budget and improved the budget management. The second one is in 2008, due to the Chinese Economic Stimulus Plan, under which the central government announced an RMB four trillion stimulus to minimise the impact of the Global Financial Crisis.

Figure 6.9: The Central Government Debt-to-GDP Ratio

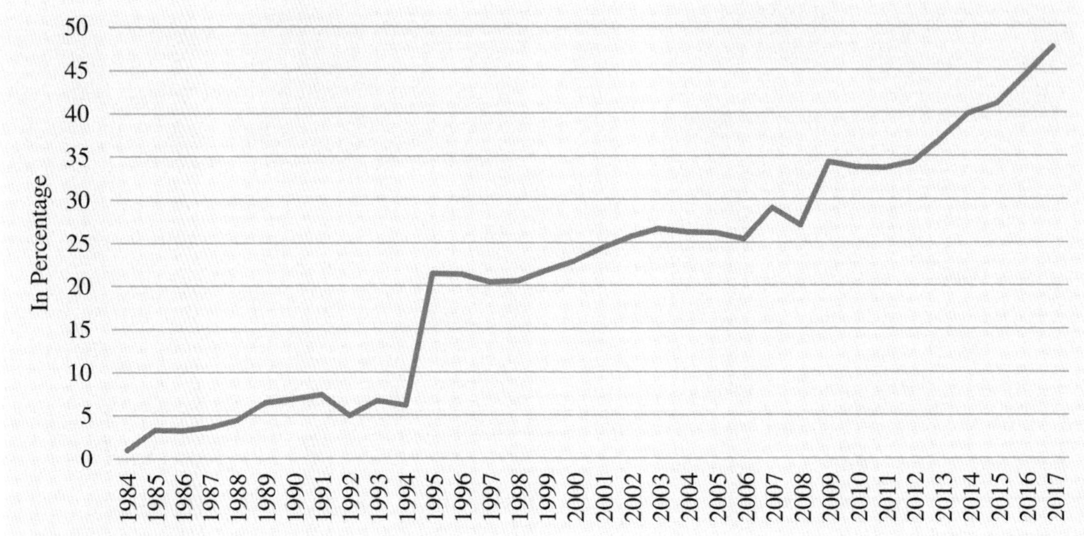

Source: Asia Competitiveness Institute based on information retrieved from the World Bank.

In terms of local government debt-to-GDP ratio, as demonstrated in Figure 6.10, all the provinces experienced a significant growth from 2000 to 2015. Notably, Guizhou province was the highest among all the provinces, reaching almost 100 percent in 2015. On average, the provincial debt-to-GDP ratio has increased from 29 percent in 2000 to 46 percent in 2015, exceeding the sustainable level defined by IMF.

There are two solutions to the unsustainably growing debt problem. One is to raise government revenue and the other is to reduce government expenditure. Tax revenue is the major source of government revenue. However, the tax rate is relatively fixed over a period of time. Thus, to solve the debt crisis, most of the governments would choose an austerity budget to cut their expenditure.

In general, government expenditure consists of essential government expenditure, such as infrastructure, and non-essential government expenditure, such as social welfare expenditure. On the one hand, essential government expenditure is crucial for the national development, which is clearly outlined in the national development plan. Thus, it is not feasible for a government to cut or reduce these expenditures in the short run.

On the other hand, a government does have the choice on the amount of non-essential expenditure. However, policymakers are also aware of the difficulty in reducing the social welfare expenditure. Once welfare system is established, any cut in citizen's social benefits may lead to political instability. Therefore, policymakers should plan the social welfare expenditure wisely, to avoid unsustainable accumulation of debt.

More recently, in the 19th National Congress of the Communist Party of China held from 18th to 24th October 2017 in Beijing, President Xi Jinping emphasised the importance of investing more in education, healthcare and welfare benefits in order to map out the goal of tackling imbalances in social and economic development.

Figure 6.10: 2000 and 2015 Local Government Debt-to-GDP Ratios

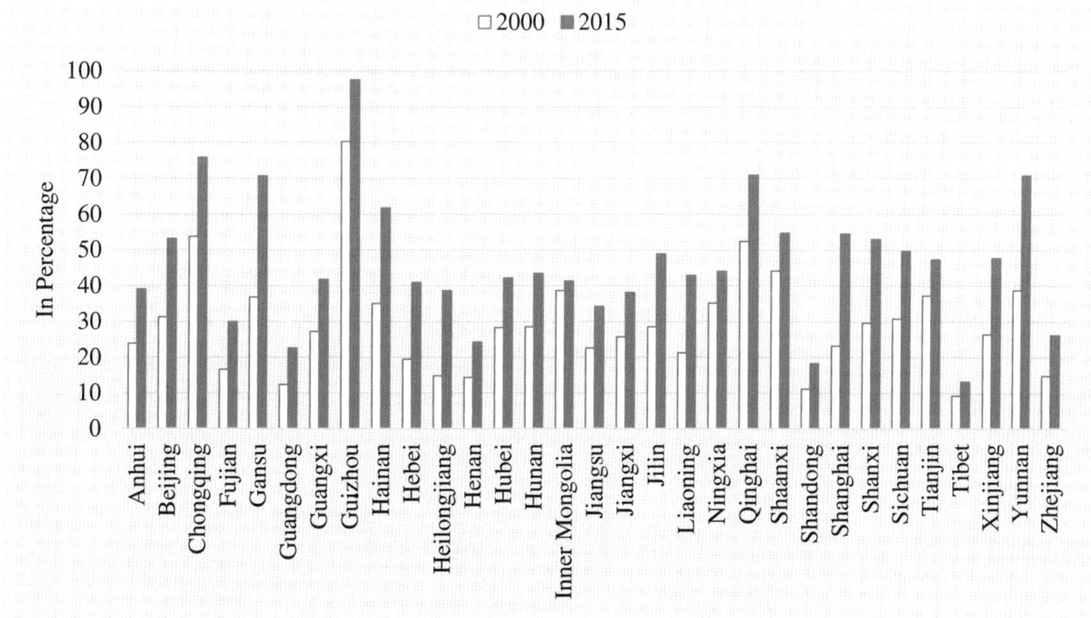

Source: Asia Competitiveness Institute based on information retrieved from National Bureau of Statistics of China.

For education policy, China has emphasised to solve the "Oversized Class" problem for primary and secondary schools since 2016.[14] The aim is to eliminate all the big classes by 2020. According to the Ministry of Education of China, there were still about 368,000 big classes by the end of 2017, accounting for 10.1 percent of the total number of primary and secondary school classes. There is a significant drop of 56,000 compared to the number in 2016. Such policy requires the government to invest in both education infrastructure and human capital.

As for healthcare policy, China has announced the "Healthy China 2030" blueprint in October 2016, aiming to provide universal health security for all Chinese citizens by 2030. The government also issued the 13th Five-Year Plan for medical reform in 2017, setting forth the goals, policy directions and strategic priorities for healthcare reforms in the following five years.

As far as pension reforms are concerned, there were some notable policy developments in June 2017. First, the State Council decided to expedite the implementation of the pilot tax-deferred pension plan, which would essentially shift part of the tax burden from pensioners to the government. In addition, the Chinese government also took initiatives to promote elderly endowment insurance with customised services for elderly customers (KPMG 2017). Notwithstanding the intention of the establishment of such programmes to improve social welfare, the affordability and better services rendered for pensioners could come at the cost of a substantially higher social expenditure for the Chinese government given the ageing population in the Chinese society.

[14] A class with more than 56 students is deemed "oversized".

The future research in the next book will exactly address the question that whether the ever-increasing welfare expenditure will lead to a serious debt crisis. After controlling the revenue and essential government expenditure, the study would be able to predict the annual growth rate of debt. If the number is positive, government must pay attention to its expenditure. The study will serve as an early warning to the government, that if such an expenditure pattern persists, the government will be facing the danger of bankruptcy.

The study will not only give a broad picture on how Mainland China performs at the country level, but also focuses on sub-national economies. Given the diversity and inequality of Mainland China provinces, with different government budget conditions and social expenditure levels, the policy recommendation will also be tailor-made for each individual province.

References

Agon, Sivan Shlomo, and Yuval Shany. 2014. "The WTO Dispute Settlement System." In *Assessing the Effectiveness of International Courts*, 189–222. Oxford University Press. doi:10.1093/acprof:oso/9780199643295.003.0009.

AmCham China. 2013. "China Business Climate Survey Report 2013." Resreport, American Chamber of Commerce in the People's Republic of China. https://media.npr.org/documents/2013/may/AmChamSurvey.pdf.

AmCham China. 2014. "China Business Climate Survey Report 2014." Resreport, American Chamber of Commerce in the People's Republic of China. https://media.npr.org/documents/2013/may/AmChamSurvey.pdf.

Beijing Daily. 2018. "京津冀最后两条高速" "断头路" 将于 8 月正式通车 The Last Two "Broken Highways" in Beijing-Tianjin-Hebei to Commence Operation in August (in Chinese)." 8. http://www.beijing.gov.cn/bmfw/jtcx/ggts/t1556710.htm.

Bird, Robert C. 2006. "Defending Intellectual Property Rights in the BRIC Economies." *American Business Law Journal* (Wiley) 43: 317–363. doi:10.1111/j.1744-1714.2006.00019.x.

Bosworth, D. Scott, Russell W. Mangum, and Eric C. Matolo. 2018. "FRAND Commitments and Royalties for Standard Essential Patents." In Complications and Quandaries in the ICT Sector: Standard Essential Patents and Competition Issues, edited by Ashish Bharadwaj, Vishwas H. Devaiah and Indranath Gupta, 19–36. Singapore: Springer Singapore. doi:10.1007/978-981-10-6011-3_2.

Braga, Carlos A. Primo, Carsten Fink, and Claudia Paz Sepulveda. 2000. Intellectual Property Rights and Economic Development. The World Bank. doi:10.1596/0-8213-4708-x.

Brennan, Peter. 2019. "US, China Trade Rivals Spar as WTO's Future Hangs in Balance."

Campbell, Karen, Jim Diffley, Bob Flanagan, Bill Morelli, Brendan O'Neil, and Francis Sideco. 2017. "The 5G economy: How 5G technology will contribute to the global economy." IHS Economics and IHS Technology (Qualcomm Technologies) 4: 16. https://cdn.ihs.com/www/pdf/IHS-Technology-5G-Economic-Impact-Study.pdf.

Central Politburo of the Communist Party of China. 2015. "京津冀协同发展规划纲要 Beijing-Tianjin-Hebei Coordinated Development Plan (in Chinese)." 4.

Clements, Benedict, R. Juan Toro, and Victoria Perry. 2010. From Stimulus to Consolidation: Revenue and Expenditure Policies in Advanced and Emerging Economies. Vol. 10. International Monetary Fund. doi:http://dx.doi.org/10.5089/9781616350420.087.

Conti, J. A. 2009. "Producing Legitimacy at the World Trade Organization: The Role of Expertise and Legal Capacity." Socio-Economic Review (Oxford University Press (OUP)) 8: 131–155. doi:10.1093/ser/mwp023.

Customs, and Excise Deparment of Hong Kong. 2019. "跨境一锁计划内容 The Content of SELS (in Chinese)." https://www.customs.gov.hk/sc/trade_facilitation/sels/content/index.html#clearance.

Davis, C. L. 2008. "The Effectiveness of WTO Dispute Settlement: An Evaluation of Negotiation Versus Adjudication Strategies."

Edwards, John. 2018. "Economic Conflict between America and China: A truce Declared, the Talks Begin." resreport, Lowy Institute. http://www.lowyinstitute.org/sites/default/files/Edwards_Economic%20conflict%20between%20America%20and%20China_WEB_0.pdf.

Elsig, Manfred. 2013. "Functioning of the WTO: Mapping the Challenges and Asking the Hard Questions." 12. http://e15initiative.org/publications/functioning-of-the-wto-mapping-the-challenges-and-asking-the-hard-questions/.

Garnaut, Ross, Ligang Song, and Cai Fang. 2018. China's 40 Years of Reform and Development: 1978–2018. ANU Press. http://www.jstor.org/stable/j.ctv5cgbnk.

General Administration of Customs. n.d. "香港进出口货物通关须知 Notice on Customs Clearance in Hong Kong (in Chinese)." http://www.customs.gov.cn/customs/302427/302446/302451/zymyhbhgt-gjs/xg/399706/index.html.

Gould, David M., and William C. Gruben. 1996. "The Role of Intellectual Property in Economic Growth." *Journal of Development Economics* (Elsevier BV) 48: 323–350. doi:10.1016/0304-3878(95)00039-9.

Government of Shenzhen. 2017. "深圳 GDP" "大蛋糕" 20 强企业贡献 26% Top 20 Companies Contributeing 26% to Shenzhen's GDP (in Chinese)." 3. http://www.sz.gov.cn/cn/xxgk/zfxxgj/zwdt/201703/t20170322_6083571.htm.

Ha, Jiming, and Adam S. Posen. 2018. "US–China Economic Relations: From Conflict to Solutions." resreport, Peterson Institute for International Economics. https://piie.com/file/18297/download?token=3K7ntg2I.

Hoekman, Bernard M., and Petros C. Mavroidis. 2015. "Embracing Diversity: Plurilateral Agreements and the Trading System." World Trade Review (Cambridge University Press (CUP)) 14: 101–116. doi:10.1017/s1474745614000378.

Howse, Robert, and Susan Esserman. 2006. "The Appellate Body, the WTO Dispute Settlement System, and the Politics of Multilateralism." In The WTO at Ten: The Contribution of the Dispute Settlement System, 61–80. Cambridge University Press.

International Monetary Fund. 2002. "Assessing Sustainability." (International Monetary Fund). https://www.imf.org/external/np/pdr/sus/2002/eng/052802.htm.

KPMG. 2017. "China pensions outlook: Evolution, Diversification and Convergence." Techreport, KPMG. https://assets.kpmg/content/dam/kpmg/cn/pdf/en/2017/12/china-pension-outlook.pdf.

Li, Keqiang. 2014. "政府工作报告 (2014 年 3 月 5 日第十二届全国人民代表大会第二次会议） Government Working Report, Presented at the Second Meeting of the 12th National People's Congress on 5 Mar 2014 (in Chinese)." National People's Congress, 3. http://www.gov.cn/guowuyuan/2014-03/14/content_2638989.htm.

Li, Siqi, and Xinquan Tu. 2018. "Impact of Chinese Characteristics on the World Trade Organization: Challenges and Strategies." *China & World Economy* (Wiley) 26: 107–126. doi:10.1111/cwe.12239.

Malawer, Stuart S. 2007. "United States-China Trade Litigation in the WTO." Virgiina Lawyer 28. https://ssrn.com/abstract=1169450.

Maton, J., and C. Maton. 2007. "Independence Under Fire: Extra-legal Pressures and Coalition Building in WTO Dispute Settlement." *Journal of International Economic Law* (Oxford University Press (OUP)) 10: 317–334. doi:10.1093/jiel/jgm008.

Ministry of Commerce. 2017. "Research Report on China–US Economic and Trade Relations." Resreport, Ministry of Commerce. http://images.mofcom.gov.cn/www/201705/20170525093626470.pdf.

———. 2018. "Statement by H.E. Ambassador Zhang Xiangchen of China at the 14th Trade Policy Review of the United States." http://wto2.mofcom.gov.cn/article/chinaviewpoins/201812/20181202817631.shtml.

———. 2019. "Statement by China at the DSB Meeting." http://wto2.mofcom.gov.cn/article/chinaviewpoins/201903/20190302840377.shtml.

Ministry of Education. 2018. "教育部就消除义务教育超大班额工作约谈个别省市负责人 The Ministry of Education Interviewed Serveral Governors of Provinces and Cities on Eliminating the Problem of Overcrowding in Classes (in Chinese)." 7. http://www.moe.gov.cn/jyb_xwfb/gzdt_gzdt/s5987/201807/t20180713_342942.html.

National Development and Reform Commission. 2007. "外商投资产业指导目录（2007 年修订） Foreign Investment Catalogue (2007) (in Chinese)." 10. http://www.ndrc.gov.cn/fzgggz/flfg/flgz/201507/t20150701_710512.html.

———. 2010. "长江三角洲地区区域规划 The Regional Planning of Yangtze River Delta (in Chinese)." 5. http://www.ndrc.gov.cn/zcfb/zcfbghwb/201006/t20100622_585472.html.

———. 2011. "外商投资产业指导目录（2011 年修订） Foreign Investment Catalogue (2011) (in Chinese)." 12. http://wzs.ndrc.gov.cn/zcfg/201405/t20140507_671017.html.

———. 2016. "长江三角洲城市群发展规划 The Regional Development Plan for Cities in Yangtze River Delta (in Chinese)." 6. http://www.ndrc.gov.cn/zcfb/zcfbghwb/201606/t20160603_806390.html.

———. 2015. "外商投资产业指导目录（2015 年修订） Foreign Investment Catalogue (2015) (in Chinese)." 3. http://www.ndrc.gov.cn/zcfb/zcfbl/201503/t20150313_667332.html.

———. 2017. "外商投资产业指导目录（2017 年修订） Foreign Investment Catalogue (2017) (in Chinese)." 6. http://www.ndrc.gov.cn/zcfb/zcfbl/201706/t20170628_852857.html.

National Development and Reform Commission, Government of Guangdong, Government of Hong Kong, and Government of Macau. 2017. "深化粤港澳合作 推进大湾区建设框架协议 Deepening the Cooperation among Guangdong, Hong Kong and Macau, and Promoting the Construction of the Greater Bay Area Framework Agreement (in Chinese)." 7. http://www.ndrc.gov.cn/gzdt/201707/W020170704333479293820.pdf.

National Development and Reform Commission, Ministry of Foreign Affairs, and Ministry of Commerce. 2015. "Vision and Actions on Jointly Building Silk Road Economic Belt and 21st-century Maritime Silk Road." http://www.ndrc.gov.cn/gzdt/201503/t20150330_669392.html.

Nottage, Hunter. 2010. "Evaluating the Criticism that WTO Retaliation Rules Undermine the Utility of WTO Dispute Settlement for Developing Countries." In The Law, Economics and Politics of Retaliation in WTO Dispute Settlement, edited by Chad P. Bown and Joost Pauwelyn, 319–338. Cambridge University Press. doi:10.1017/cbo9780511674594.016.

Office of the United States Trade Representative. 2018. "Findings of the Investigation into China's Acts, Policies, and Practices Related to Technology Transfer, Intellectual Property, and Innovation under Section 301 of the Trade Act of 1974." Resreport, Office of the United States Trade Representative. https://ustr.gov/sites/default/files/enforcement/301Investigations/301%20Report%20Update.pdf.

Schneider, Patricia Higino. 2005. "International Trade, Economic Growth and Intellectual Property Rights: A Panel Data Study of Developed and Developing Countries." *Journal of Development Economics* (Elsevier BV) 78: 529-547. doi:10.1016/j.jdeveco.2004.09.001.

Semiconductor Industry Association. 2018. "Proposed Determination of Action Pursuant to Section 301: China's Acts, Policies, and Practices Related to Technology Transfer, Intellectual Property, and Innovation." Tech. rep., Semiconductor Industry Association. https://www.semiconductors.org/wp-content/uploads/2018/08/Final-_SIA_Submission_on_301_Tariffs.pdf.

Shedd, Daniel T., Brandon J. Murrill, and Jane M. Smith. 2015. "Dispute Settlement in the World Trade Organization (WTO): An Overview." Dispute Settlement in the World Trade Organization 19.

Standing Committee of the National People's Congress. 2019. "关于《中华人民共和国外商投资法 (草案)》的说明 Explanation of the 'People's Republic of China Foreign Investment Law (Draft)' (in Chinese)." 3. http://www.xinhuanet.com/politics/2019-03/09/c_1124211684.htm.

State Council. 2006. "实施《国家中长期科学和技术发展规划纲要 (2006–2020 年)》的若干配套政策 Several Supporting Policies for Implementing the 'National Medium- and Long-Term Science and Technology Development Plan Outline (2006–2020)' (in Chinese)." 2. http://www.gov.cn/gongbao/content/2006/content_240246.htm.

———. 2014. "国务院关于依托黄金水道推动长江经济带发展的指导意见 Guidance of the State Coucil: Utilising the Golden Waterway to Promote Development of Yangtze River Economic Belt (in Chinese)." 9. http://www.gov.cn/zhengce/content/2014-09/25/content_9092.htm.

———. 2015. "进一步推进中国（上海）自由贸易试验区金融开放创新试点 加快上海国际金融中心建设方案 Promoting the Financial Openness and Innovation in China (Shanghai) Pilot Free Trade Zone and Accelerating the Transformation of Shanghai into an International Financial Center (in Chinese)." 10. http://www.china-shftz.gov.cn/PublicInformation.aspx?GID=7b2fe462-1bcb-4fb6-afd6-5c45328ef29f&CID=953a259a-1544-4d72-be6a-264677089690&MenuType=1&navType=null.

———. 2019. "粤港澳大湾区发展规划纲要 Outline Development Plan for the Guangdong-Hong Kong-Macao Greater Bay Area (in Chinese)." 2. http://www.gov.cn/zhengce/2019-02/18/content_5366593.htm#1.

The White House. 2018. "Presidential Memorandum on the Actions by the United States Related to the Section 301 Investigation." https://www.whitehouse.gov/presidential-actions/presidential-memorandum-actions-united-states-related-section-301-investigation/.

UNCTAD. 2019. Key Statistics and Trends in Trade Policy 2018: Trade Tensions, Implications for Developing Countries. Tech. rep., United Nations Conference on Trade and Development. https://unctad.org/en/pages/PublicationWebflyer.aspx?publicationid=2345.

US–China Business Council. 2017. "US–China Business Council 2017 Member Survey." resreport, US–China Business Council. https://www.uschina.org/sites/default/files/2017_uscbc_member_survey_1.pdf.

Wan, Zheng, Yang Zhang, Xuefeng Wang, and Jihong Chen. 2014. "Policy and Politics Behind Shanghai's Free Trade Zone Program." *Journal of Transport Geography* (Elsevier BV) 34: 1–6. doi:10.1016/j.jtrangeo.2013.10.015.

World Economic Forum. 2018. "The Global Competitiveness Report 2018." Tech. rep., Geneva: World Economic Forum. http://www3.weforum.org/docs/GCR2018/05FullReport/TheGlobalCompetitivenessReport2018.pdf.

Xinhua News Agency. 2016. "北京首条延伸至河北的轨道平谷线开工建设 Pinggu Line, Beijing's Regional Express to Hebei Started Construction (in Chinese)." 12. http://www.gov.cn/xinwen/2016-12/23/content_5151992.htm.

Yanikkaya, Halit. 2003. "Trade Openness and Economic Growth: A Cross-country Empirical Investigation." *Journal of Development Economics* (Elsevier BV) 72: 57–89. doi:10.1016/s0304-3878(03)00068-3.

Yao, Daqing, and John Whalley. 2015. "The China (Shanghai) Pilot Free Trade Zone: Background, Developments and Preliminary Assessment of Initial Impacts." *The World Economy* (Wiley) 39: 2–15. doi:10.1111/twec.12364.

Yu, Peter K. 2000. "From Pirates to Partners: Protecting Intellectual Property in China in the Twenty-First Century." *SSRN Electronic Journal* (Elsevier BV). doi:10.2139/ssrn.245548.

Zeng, K. 2012. "High Stakes: United States-China Trade Disputes under the World Trade Organization." International Relations of the Asia-Pacific (Oxford University Press (OUP)) 13: 33–63. doi:10.1093/irap/lcs014.

Zhang, Liqing, and Kunyu Tao. 2014. "The Benefits and Costs of Renminbi Internationalization." Tech. rep., ADB Institute, 29.

Appendix 1

Provincial-Level Economies' Competitiveness Analysis — List of Indicators

No.	Indicator	Unit	Reversed Indicator
1	MACROECONOMIC STABILITY		
1.1	***Regional Economic Vibrancy***		
1.1.01	Gross Regional Product	100 Million Yuan, Constant Prices at 2000	
1.1.02	Real GRP Growth	Percentage Change per Annum	
1.1.03	GRP Per Capita	Yuan per person, Constant Prices at 2000	
1.1.04	Primary Industry	100 Million Yuan, Constant Prices at 2000	
1.1.05	Secondary Industry	100 Million Yuan, Constant Prices at 2000	
1.1.06	Tertiary Industry	100 Million Yuan, Constant Prices at 2000	
1.1.07	Gross Capital Formation (percent)	Percentage of GRP	
1.1.08	Inflation Rate (Consumer Price Index)	Percentage Change per Annum	R
1.1.09	Inflation Rate (Retail Price Index)	Percentage Change per Annum	R
1.1.10	Net Regional Trade	100 Million Yuan, Constant Prices at 2000	
1.1.11	Regional Tourist Arrivals	10,000 Person-Times	
1.1.12	Regional Tourism Receipts	100 Million Yuan, Constant Prices at 2000	
1.1.13	Planned Regional Investment	100 Million Yuan, Constant Prices at 2000	
1.1.14	Realised Regional Investment	100 Million Yuan, Constant Prices at 2000	
1.1.15	Industry Gross Output Value	100 Million Yuan, Constant Prices at 2000	
1.2	***Openness to Trade and Services***		
1.2.01	Trade Balance (percent)	Percentage of GRP	
1.2.02	International Merchandise Exports	100 Million Yuan, Constant Prices at 2000	
1.2.03	International Merchandise Imports	100 Million Yuan, Constant Prices at 2000	
1.2.04	Openness to Trade	Ratio	
1.2.05	International Visitor Arrivals	10,000 Person-Times	
1.2.06	International Tourism Receipts	100 Million Yuan, Constant Prices at 2000	
1.3	***Attractiveness to Foreign Investors***		
1.3.01	Planned Foreign Direct Investment (Excl. Regional Investment)	100 Million Yuan, Constant Prices at 2000	
1.3.02	Realised Foreign Direct Investment (Excl. Regional Investment)	100 Million Yuan, Constant Prices at 2000	

(Continued)

(Continued)

No.	Indicator	Unit	Reversed Indicator
1.3.03	Foreign Funded Enterprises (percent) (Industrial Enterprises Above Designated Size)	Percentage of Total Enterprises	
1.3.04	Total Taxes on Foreign Funded Companies	10,000 Yuan, Constant Prices at 2000	
2	**GOVERNMENT AND INSTITUTIONAL SETTING**		
2.1	***Government Policies and Fiscal Sustainability***		
2.1.01	Government Revenue	100 Million Yuan, Constant Prices at 2000	
2.1.02	Tax Revenue	100 Million Yuan, Constant Prices at 2000	
2.1.03	Tax Revenue/Government Revenue	Percentage of Government Revenue	
2.1.04	Government Consumption Expenditure	Percentage of GRP	
2.1.05	Budget Balance	Percentage of GRP	
2.2	***Institutions, Governance and Leadership***		
2.2.01	Domestic-Funded Enterprises (Industrial Enterprises Above Designated Size)	Number	
2.2.02	State-Owned Enterprises (Industrial Enterprises Above Designated Size)	Percentage of Total Enterprises	R
2.2.03	Collective-Owned Enterprises (Industrial Enterprises Above Designated Size)	Percentage of Total Enterprises	R
2.2.04	Limited Liability Corporations (Industrial Enterprises Above Designated Size)	Percentage of Total Enterprises	
2.2.05	Joint-Stock Companies (Industrial Enterprises Above Designated Size)	Percentage of Total Enterprises	
2.2.06	Private Enterprises (Industrial Enterprises Above Designated Size)	Percentage of Total Enterprises	
2.2.07	Foreign-Funded Enterprises (Industrial Enterprises Above Designated Size)	Number	
3	**FINANCIAL, BUSINESSES AND MANPOWER CONDITIONS**		
3.1	***Financial Deepening and Business Efficiency***		
3.1.01	Household Savings Deposits	100 Million Yuan, Constant Prices at 2000	
3.1.02	Total Deposits	100 Million Yuan, Constant Prices at 2000	
3.1.03	Total Loans	100 Million Yuan, Constant Prices at 2000	
3.2	***Labour Market Flexibility***		
3.2.01	Total Employed Persons	10,000 persons	
3.2.02	Self-Employed Persons (Urban Area)	Percentage of Total Employment	
3.2.03	Unemployment Rate (Urban Area)	Percentage	R
3.2.04	Secondary & Tertiary Staff Workers (percent)	Percentage of Total Employment	

(Continued)

No.	Indicator	Unit	Reversed Indicator
3.2.05	Average Annual Wage of Staff and Workers	Yuan, Constant Prices at 2000	
3.2.06	Total Wages Bill of Employed Persons in Urban Units	100 Million Yuan, Constant Prices at 2000	
3.2.07	Wages Paid Out by State-Owned Units	Percentage of Total Wages	R
3.2.08	Wages Paid Out by Urban Collective Units	Percentage of Total Wages	R
3.2.09	Wages Paid Out by Other Units	Percentage of Total Wages	
3.3	***Productivity Performance***		
3.3.01	Overall Labour Productivity	Yuan per Person-Year, Constant Prices at 2000	
3.3.02	Primary Industry, Value-Added per Worker	Yuan per Person-Year, Constant Prices at 2000	
3.3.03	Secondary Industry, Value-Added per Worker	Yuan per Person-Year, Constant Prices at 2000	
3.3.04	Tertiary Industry, Value-Added per Worker	Yuan per Person-Year, Constant Prices at 2000	
3.3.05	Investment in Fixed Assets	100 Million Yuan, Constant Prices at 2000	
4	**QUALITY OF LIFE AND INFRASTRUCTURE DEVELOPMENT**		
4.1	***Physical Infrastructure***		
4.1.01	Population	10,000 Persons, Year-end	
4.1.02	Urban Population	Percentage of Total Population	
4.1.03	Population Density	Persons per Square km	R
4.1.04	Length of Railways in Operation	Km	
4.1.05	Length of Highways	Km	
4.1.06	Length of Navigable Inland Waterways	Km	
4.1.07	Passenger Distance of Railways in Operation	100 Million Person-km	
4.1.08	Passenger Distance of Highways	100 Million Person-km	
4.1.09	Passenger Distance of Navigable Inland Waterways	100 Million Person-km	
4.1.10	Passenger Distance of Total Civil Aviation Routes	100 Million Person-km	
4.1.11	Motor Vehicles per km of Highways	Per km	R
4.1.12	Coal	10,000 Tonnes	
4.1.13	Oil	Tonne	
4.1.14	Electric Hydropower	100 Million kWh	
4.1.15	Crude Steel	10,000 Tonnes	
4.1.16	Pig Iron	10,000 Tonnes	

(Continued)

(*Continued*)

No.	Indicator	Unit	Reversed Indicator
4.1.17	Steel Products	10,000 Tonnes	
4.1.18	Cement	10,000 Tonnes	
4.1.19	Total Land Area	Square km	
4.1.20	Cultivated Land	1,000 Ha	
4.2	***Technological Infrastructure***		
4.2.01	Persons per Fixed Telephone Subscriber	Per Fixed Telephone Subscriber	R
4.2.02	Internet Penetration	Percentage of Total Population	
4.2.03	Personal Computer	Per 100 Urban Households	
4.2.04	High Technology Expenditure	Percentage of Total Government Expenditure	
4.2.05	Persons per Mobile Telephone Subscriber	Per Mobile Telephone Subscriber	R
4.2.06	Urban Television Sets	Units per 100 Households	
4.2.07	Rural Television Sets	Units per 100 Households	
4.2.08	Expenditure on Science and Technology	Percentage of GRP	
4.2.09	Number of Scientific and Technical Journal Publications	Number	
4.2.10	Patents Granted	Number	
4.3	***Standard of Living, Education and Social Stability***		
4.3.01	Illiteracy Rate	Percentage of Population Age 15 and Above	R
4.3.02	Number of Educational Institutions	Total Units	
4.3.03	Disparity between Primary and Secondary Institutions	Percentage	R
4.3.04	Tertiary Institutions	Percentage of Total Institutions	
4.3.05	Student–Teacher Ratio (Primary)	Ratio	R
4.3.06	Student–Teacher Ratio (Secondary)	Ratio	R
4.3.07	Student–Teacher Ratio (Tertiary)	Ratio	R
4.3.08	Health Expenditure	Percentage of Total Government Expenditure	
4.3.09	Urban Population Growth	Percentage Change per Annum	
4.3.10	Air Pollution	milligram/cu.m	R
4.3.11	Ageing Profile	Percentage of Population Over 65 years	R
4.3.12	Old Age Dependency Ratio	Ratio	R
4.3.13	Motor Vehicles per Person	Per Person	
4.3.14	Death Rate	Per 1,000 Persons	R
4.3.15	Adequacy of Hospitals	10,000 Persons per Hospital	R
4.3.16	Population per Hospital Bed	10,000 Persons per Hospital Bed	R
4.3.17	Population per Medical Personnel	10,000 Persons per Medical Personnel	R
4.3.18	Per Capita Annual Urban Household Income	Yuan, Constant Prices at 2000	

Appendix 2

Regional Competitiveness Analysis — List of Indicators and Notes on Data Aggregation Method

No.	Indicator^	Unit	Reversed Indicator	Aggregation Method*
1	MACROECONOMIC STABILITY			
1.1	***Regional Economic Vibrancy***			
1.1.01	Gross Regional Product	100 Million Yuan, Constant Prices at 2000		Method 1
1.1.02	Real GRP Growth	Percentage Change per Annum		Method 2
1.1.03	GRP Per Capita	Yuan per person, Constant Prices at 2000		Method 3
1.1.04	Primary Industry	100 Million Yuan, Constant Prices at 2000		Method 1
1.1.05	Secondary Industry	100 Million Yuan, Constant Prices at 2000		Method 1
1.1.06	Tertiary Industry	100 Million Yuan, Constant Prices at 2000		Method 1
1.1.07	Gross Capital Formation (percent)	Percentage of GRP		Method 3
1.1.08	Inflation Rate (Consumer Price Index)	Percentage Change per Annum	R	Method 4a
1.1.09	Inflation Rate (Retail Price Index)	Percentage Change per Annum	R	Method 4a
1.1.10	Industry Gross Output Value	100 Million Yuan, Constant Prices at 2000		Method 1
1.2	***Openness to Trade and Services***			
1.2.01	Trade Balance (percent)	Percentage of GRP		Method 3
1.2.02	International Merchandise Exports	100 Million Yuan, Constant Prices at 2000		Method 1
1.2.03	International Merchandise Imports	100 Million Yuan, Constant Prices at 2000		Method 1
1.2.04	Openness to Trade	Ratio		Method 3
1.2.05	International Visitor Arrivals	10,000 Person-Times		Method 1
1.2.06	International Tourism Receipts	100 Million Yuan, Constant Prices at 2000		Method 1
1.3	***Attractiveness to Foreign Investors***			
1.3.01	Planned Foreign Direct Investment (Excl. Regional Investment)	100 Million Yuan, Constant Prices at 2000		Method 1
1.3.02	Realised Foreign Direct Investment (Excl. Regional Investment)	100 Million Yuan, Constant Prices at 2000		Method 1
1.3.03	Foreign Funded Enterprises (percent) (Industrial Enterprises Above Designated Size)	Percentage of Total Enterprises		Method 3
1.3.04	Total Taxes on Foreign Funded Companies	10,000 Yuan, Constant Prices at 2000		Method 1

(Continued)

(*Continued*)

No.	Indicator^	Unit	Reversed Indicator	Aggregation Method*
2	**GOVERNMENT AND INSTITUTIONAL SETTING**			
2.1	***Government Policies and Fiscal Sustainability***			
2.1.01	Government Revenue	100 Million Yuan, Constant Prices at 2000		Method 1
2.1.02	Tax Revenue	100 Million Yuan, Constant Prices at 2000		Method 1
2.1.03	Tax Revenue/Government Revenue	Percentage of Government Revenue		Method 3
2.1.04	Government Consumption Expenditure	Percentage of GRP		Method 3
2.1.05	Budget Balance	Percentage of GRP		Method 3
2.2	***Institutions, Governance and Leadership***			
2.2.01	Domestic-Funded Enterprises (Industrial Enterprises Above Designated Size)	Number		Method 1
2.2.02	State-Owned Enterprises (Industrial Enterprises Above Designated Size)	Percentage of Total Enterprises	R	Method 3
2.2.03	Collective-Owned Enterprises (Industrial Enterprises Above Designated Size)	Percentage of Total Enterprises	R	Method 3
2.2.04	Limited Liability Corporations (Industrial Enterprises Above Designated Size)	Percentage of Total Enterprises		Method 3
2.2.05	Joint-Stock Companies (Industrial Enterprises Above Designated Size)	Percentage of Total Enterprises		Method 3
2.2.06	Private Enterprises (Industrial Enterprises Above Designated Size)	Percentage of Total Enterprises		Method 3
2.2.07	Foreign-Funded Enterprises (Industrial Enterprises Above Designated Size)	Number		Method 1
3	**FINANCIAL, BUSINESSES AND MANPOWER CONDITIONS**			
3.1	***Financial Deepening and Business Efficiency***			
3.1.01	Household Savings Deposits	100 Million Yuan, Constant Prices at 2000		Method 1
3.1.02	Total Deposits	100 Million Yuan, Constant Prices at 2000		Method 1
3.1.03	Total Loans	100 Million Yuan, Constant Prices at 2000		Method 1
3.2	***Labour Market Flexibility***			
3.2.01	Total Employed Persons	10,000 persons		Method 1
3.2.02	Self-Employed Persons (Urban Area)	Percentage of Total Employment		Method 3

(*Continued*)

No.	Indicator^	Unit	Reversed Indicator	Aggregation Method*
3.2.03	Unemployment Rate (Urban Area)	Percentage	R	Method 3
3.2.04	Secondary & Tertiary Staff Workers (percent)	Percentage of Total Employment		Method 3
3.2.05	Average Annual Wage of Staff and Workers	Yuan, Constant Prices at 2000		Method 4a
3.2.06	Total Wages Bill of Employed Persons in Urban Units	100 Million Yuan, Constant Prices at 2000		Method 1
3.2.07	Wages Paid Out by State-Owned Units	Percentage of Total Wages	R	Method 3
3.2.08	Wages Paid Out by Urban Collective Units	Percentage of Total Wages	R	Method 3
3.2.09	Wages Paid Out by Other Units	Percentage of Total Wages		Method 3
3.3	***Productivity Performance***			
3.3.01	Overall Labour Productivity	Yuan per Person-Year, Constant Prices at 2000		Method 3
3.3.02	Primary Industry, Value-Added per Worker	Yuan per Person-Year, Constant Prices at 2000		Method 3
3.3.03	Secondary Industry, Value-Added per Worker	Yuan per Person-Year, Constant Prices at 2000		Method 3
3.3.04	Tertiary Industry, Value-Added per Worker	Yuan per Person-Year, Constant Prices at 2000		Method 3
3.3.05	Investment in Fixed Assets	100 Million Yuan, Constant Prices at 2000		Method 1
4	**QUALITY OF LIFE AND INFRASTRUCTURE DEVELOPMENT**			
4.1	***Physical Infrastructure***			
4.1.01	Population	10,000 Persons, Year-end		Method 1
4.1.02	Urban Population	Percentage of Total Population		Method 3
4.1.03	Population Density	Persons per Square km	R	Method 3
4.1.04	Length of Railways in Operation	Km		Method 1
4.1.05	Length of Highways	Km		Method 1
4.1.06	Length of Navigable Inland Waterways	Km		Method 1
4.1.07	Passenger Distance of Railways in Operation	100 Million Person-km		Method 1
4.1.08	Passenger Distance of Highways	100 Million Person-km		Method 1
4.1.09	Passenger Distance of Navigable Inland Waterways	100 Million Person-km		Method 1
4.1.10	Passenger Distance of Total Civil Aviation Routes	100 Million Person-km		Method 1

(*Continued*)

(Continued)

No.	Indicator^	Unit	Reversed Indicator	Aggregation Method*
4.1.11	Motor Vehicles per km of Highways	Per km	R	Method 3
4.1.12	Coal	10,000 Tonnes		Method 1
4.1.13	Oil	Tonne		Method 1
4.1.14	Electric Hydropower	100 Million kWh		Method 1
4.1.15	Crude Steel	10,000 Tonnes		Method 1
4.1.16	Pig Iron	10,000 Tonnes		Method 1
4.1.17	Steel Products	10,000 Tonnes		Method 1
4.1.18	Cement	10,000 Tonnes		Method 1
4.1.19	Total Land Area	Square km		Method 1
4.1.20	Cultivated Land	1,000 Ha		Method 1
4.2	***Technological Infrastructure***			
4.2.01	Persons per Fixed Telephone Subscriber	Per Fixed Telephone Subscriber	R	Method 3
4.2.02	Internet Penetration	Percentage of Total Population		Method 3
4.2.03	Personal Computer	Per 100 Urban Households		Method 4a
4.2.04	High Technology Expenditure	Percentage of Total Government Expenditure		Method 3
4.2.05	Persons per Mobile Telephone Subscriber	Per Mobile Telephone Subscriber	R	Method 3
4.2.06	Urban Television Sets	Units per 100 Households		Method 4a
4.2.07	Rural Television Sets	Units per 100 Households		Method 4a
4.2.08	Expenditure on Science and Technology	Percentage of GRP		Method 3
4.2.09	Number of Scientific and Technical Journal Publications	Number		Method 1
4.2.10	Patents Granted	Number		Method 1
4.3	***Standard of Living, Education and Social Stability***			
4.3.01	Illiteracy Rate	Percentage of Population Age 15 and Above	R	Method 3
4.3.02	Number of Educational Institutions	Total Units		Method 1
4.3.03	Disparity between Primary and Secondary Institutions	Percentage	R	Method 4a
4.3.04	Tertiary Institutions	Percentage of Total Institutions		Method 3
4.3.05	Student–Teacher Ratio (Primary)	Ratio	R	Method 4a
4.3.06	Student–Teacher Ratio (Secondary)	Ratio	R	Method 4a
4.3.07	Student–Teacher Ratio (Tertiary)	Ratio	R	Method 4a
4.3.08	Health Expenditure	Percentage of Total Government Expenditure		Method 3

(Continued)

No.	Indicator^	Unit	Reversed Indicator	Aggregation Method*
4.3.09	Urban Population Growth	Percentage Change per Annum		Method 3
4.3.10	Air Pollution	milligram/cu.m	R	Method 4b
4.3.11	Ageing Profile	Percentage of Population Over 65 years	R	Method 3
4.3.12	Old Age Dependency Ratio	Ratio	R	Method 3
4.3.13	Motor Vehicles per Person	Per Person		Method 3
4.3.14	Death Rate	Per 1,000 Persons	R	Method 3
4.3.15	Adequacy of Hospitals	10,000 Persons per Hospital	R	Method 3
4.3.16	Population per Hospital Bed	10,000 Persons per Hospital Bed	R	Method 3
4.3.17	Population per Medical Personnel	10,000 Persons per Medical Personnel	R	Method 3
4.3.18	Per Capita Annual Urban Household Income	Yuan, Constant Prices at 2000		Method 4a

Note: ^The five indicators, namely 1.1.10 Net Regional Trade, 1.1.11 Regional Tourist Arrivals, 1.1.12 Regional Tourism Receipts, 1.1.13 Planned Regional Investment and 1.1.14 Realised Regional Investment, are used for the competitiveness ranking analysis by economy, but they are not used for the competitiveness ranking analysis by region. This is due to the nature of their definition, which renders it impossible to use sub-regional data alone to derive the regional data and also due to unavailability of relevant data published on the regions.

***Method 1: Since it is based on absolute quantity, we can get the regional value by summing across all the economies within this region.**

Example for Method 1: Gross Regional Domestic Product (GRDP); Unit: 100 million yuan, Constant Prices at 2000

For Region A with n economies at time t,

$$GRDP_{A,t} = \sum_{i=1}^{n} GRDP_{i,t}$$

Method 2: Once we have computed the aggregated data for each region across the years according to Method 1, it is straightforward to calculate, say for example, growth rate of that particular data by region according to its definition.

Example for Method 2: GRDP Growth; Unit: Percentage Change Per Annum

For Region A with n economies at time t,

$$GRDP\,Growth_{A,t} = \frac{GRDP_{A,t} - GRDP_{A,t-1}}{GRDP_{A,t-1}}$$

Method 3: Since both the numerator and denominator are absolute quantities, we aggregate them across all the economies within the region to get the regional values, from which we compute the ratio, hence arriving at the regional value for indicator.

Example for Method 3: Gross Capital Formation; Unit: Percentage of GRDP

For Region A with n economies at time t,

$$Gross\,Capital\,Formation_{A,t} = \frac{\sum_{i=1}^{n} Gross\,Capital\,Formation_{i,t}}{\sum_{i=1}^{n} GRDP_{i,t}}$$

Method 4: Since the economy-level data is in the form of ratio or percentage that cannot be easily disaggregated into the numerator and denominator, the regional value for the indicator is obtained by taking the weighted average of the

economy-level data. We can either take the weighted average based on population (Method 4a) or weighted average based on land size (Method 4b), depending on the nature of the indicator.

Example for Method 4: Inflation Rate (Consumer Price Index); Unit: Percentage Change per Annum

For Region A with n economies at time t,

$$Inflation\,Rate_{A,t} = \frac{\sum_{i=1}^{n}(Population_{i,t} \times Inflation\ Rate_{i,t})}{\sum_{i=1}^{n} Population_{i,t}}$$

Appendix 3

Competitiveness Analysis — The Algorithm

A step-by-step description of the ranking process is described below for *N* economies, *M* practical indicators and *C* environments, with each environment comprising *S* sub-environments.

(1) Compute the mean value of practical indicator *j* ($j = 1, ..., M$),

$$\bar{X}_j = \frac{1}{N}\sum_{i=1}^{N} X_{ij}$$

where X_{ij} represents the value that economy *i* ($i = 1, ..., N$) takes for practical indicator *j*.

(2) For each practical indicator *j* ($j = 1, ..., M$), calculate its standard deviation (SD),

$$SD_j = \sqrt{\frac{1}{N}\sum_{i=1}^{N}\left(X_{ij} - \bar{X}_j\right)^2}$$

(3) Compute the standardised value of indicator (SVI) that each economy *i* ($i = 1, ..., N$) takes under each of the practical indicators *j* ($j = 1, ..., M$),

$$SVI_{ij} = \frac{X_{ij} - \bar{X}_j}{SD_j}$$

(4) Compute the "ranked" standardised value of indicator (RSVI) that each economy *i* ($i = 1, ..., N$) takes under each of the practical indicators *j* ($j = 1, ..., M$),

$$RSVI_{ij} = \begin{cases} SVI_{ij}, & \textit{if a higher value is better} \\ -SVI_{ij}, & \textit{if a lower value is better} \end{cases}$$

(5) For each of the practical indicators *j* ($j = 1, ..., M$), a ranking can be obtained for economies: economies with a higher value of RSVI for indicator *j* are ranked ahead of those with a lower value.

(6) For each economy *i* ($i = 1, ..., N$), calculate the RSVI for each sub-environment *k* ($k = 1, ..., S$) belonging to environment *l* ($l = 1, ..., C$),

$$Raw\_RSVI_{i,lk} = \frac{1}{y_{lk}}\sum_{p=1}^{y_{lk}} RSVI_{i,j_{lk,p}}$$

$$Mean\_RSVI_{lk} = \frac{1}{N}\sum_{i=1}^{N} Raw\_RSVI_{i,lk}$$

$$SD\_RSVI_{lk} = \sqrt{\frac{1}{N}\sum_{i=1}^{N}\left(Raw\_RSVI_{i,lk} - Mean\_RSVI_{lk}\right)^2}$$

$$RSVI_{i,lk} = \frac{Raw\_RSVI_{i,lk} - Mean\_RSVI_{lk}}{SD\_RSVI_{lk}}$$

where y_{lk} is the total number of practical indicators under sub-environment k of environment l and $(RSVI_{i,j_{lk,1}},\ldots,RSVI_{i,j_{lk,y_{lk}}})$ are the RSVIs for economy i that make up sub-environment k of environment l.

(7) For each economy i ($i = 1, ..., N$), calculate the RSVI for each environment l ($l = 1, ..., C$),

$$Raw\_RSVI_{i,l} = \frac{1}{S_l}\sum_{k=1}^{S_l} RSVI_{i,lk}$$

$$Mean\_RSVI_l = \frac{1}{N}\sum_{i=1}^{N} Raw\_RSVI_{i,l}$$

$$SD\_RSVI_l = \sqrt{\frac{1}{N}\sum_{i=1}^{N}\left(Raw\_RSVI_{i,l} - Mean\_RSVI_l\right)^2}$$

$$RSVI_{i,l} = \frac{Raw\_RSVI_{i,l} - Mean\_RSVI_l}{SD\_RSVI_l}$$

where $(RSVI_{i,l1},\ldots, RSVI_{i,lS})$ are the RSVIs for the S sub-environments under each environment l.

(8) Overall rank score of economy i ($i = 1, ..., N$),

$$Raw\_R_i = \frac{1}{C}\sum_{l=1}^{C} RSVI_{i,l}$$

$$Mean\_R = \frac{1}{N}\sum_{i=1}^{N} Raw\_R_i$$

$$SD\_R = \sqrt{\frac{1}{N}\sum_{i=1}^{N}\left(Raw\_R_i - Mean\_R\right)^2}$$

$$R_i = \frac{Raw\_R_i - Mean\_R}{SD\_R}$$

Economies with a higher R_i are ranked ahead of those with lower value of R_i, and the economy with the highest R_i is the most competitive economy.

Step (5) provides the ranking of each economy for each individual practical indicator. To achieve this ranking, Step (4) adjusts the value of the SVIs so that a higher value will lead to a better ranking in terms of "competitiveness". Depending on the nature of the indicator in question, a higher or lower value may reflect a more "competitive" economy. Take for instance the practical indicators "Gross Regional Product (GRP)" and "Unemployment Rate (Urban Area)". A higher GRP but a lower unemployment rate suggests better economic performance which makes an economy more competitive. In most cases where a higher value is better (e.g. GRP), the SVIs of economies are considered, and those with a higher SVI value will have a better ranking. However, for indicators where the inverse is true (e.g. Unemployment Rate (Urban Area)), the "negative SVI" values are compared between economies and a lower SVI value will lead to a better ranking. Step (4) thus seeks to make all standardised values of all practical indicators consistent for ranking purposes.

Step (6) determines the sub-environment rankings of each economy. The average RSVI of all the indicators in the sub-environment is calculated, re-standardised across all the economies and compared to other economies. Economies with a higher average RSVI rank better in the sub-environment.

To arrive at the ranking for each environment, the RSVIs of the sub-environments are averaged and re-standardised across all the economies as detailed by Step (7). Finally, Step (8) requires the RSVI values of each environment to be averaged and re-standardised across all the economies to determine the overall ranking of the economy. Economies with a higher RSVI are ranked ahead of those with a lower RSVI.

Although the number of sub-environments and indicators varies for each main environment, the aggregate score for each main environment is given an equivalent weighting: 25 percent of the Greater China Overall Competitiveness Index. Identical weights are assigned to each environment as they represent equivalent significance to the computation of the Index. This method is repeated and applied consistently across all the economies to ensure precision of the rankings. Mathematically, this can be illustrated as follows:

Greater China Overall Competitiveness Index:

$$\begin{aligned} = & \ 25 \text{ percent} \times (\text{Macroeconomic Stability}) \\ & + 25 \text{ percent} \times (\text{Government and Institutional Setting}) \\ & + 25 \text{ percent} \times (\text{Financial, Businesses and Manpower Conditions}) \\ & + 25 \text{ percent} \times (\text{Quality of Life and Infrastructure Development}) \end{aligned}$$

Appendix 4

Shapley Weightage

We will present the "Bottom-up" approach in this appendix. We start with indicator-level computation, then sub-environment- and environment-level computation, and finally the index construction.

1 Indicator Level

For each indicator $i \in I$ and each economy $e \in E$, the standardised value (or z-score) is

$$SV_{ei} = \frac{X_{ei} - \overline{X_i}}{SD_i} \tag{1}$$

where X_{ei} is the data input for economy e in indicator i, $\overline{X_i} = \frac{1}{E}\Sigma_{e=1}^{E} X_{ei}$ is the mean value of the indicator i, and $SD_i = \sqrt{\frac{1}{E}\Sigma_{e=1}^{E}(X_{ei} - \overline{X}_i)^2}$ is the standard deviation of the indicator i.

Now, let v^I be the characteristic function of the indicators, where v^I: $2^I \to \mathbb{R}$. Then for each indicator $i \in I$, $v^I(i)$: $\mathbb{R}^E \to \mathbb{R}$, which reflects that the value of indicator i is derived from X_{ei} for all $e \in E$. As we involve large number of indicators in our case studies, for the ease of numerical computation, we simply define that

$$v^I(i) = \sum_{e=1}^{E} |SV_{ei}| \tag{2}$$

The absolute value is used, as (1) it guarantees the positiveness of $v(i)$ which is required by the definition of Shapley value; and (2) the simple sum of the z-scores is zero, i.e. $\Sigma_{e=1}^{E} SV_{ei} = 0$.

We further assume the Additivity of the characteristic function v^I, i.e.

$$v^I(i \cup j) = v^I(i) + v^I(j) \text{ for any indicator } i, j \in I. \tag{3}$$

With all these defined, we are able to proceed with the computation of the Shapley value Φ_i^I of indicator $i \in I$.

$$\Phi_i^I = \sum_{\mathbb{I} \subseteq I \setminus \{i\}} \frac{|\mathbb{I}|!(I - |\mathbb{I}| - 1)!}{I!} (v^I(\mathbb{I} \cup i) - v^I(\mathbb{I})) \quad \text{for all } i \in I \tag{4}$$

With the assumption of Additivity, equation (4) can be simplified as

$$\Phi_i^I = \sum_{\mathbb{I}\subseteq I\setminus\{i\}} \frac{|\mathbb{I}|\,!(I-|\mathbb{I}|-1)!}{I!}(v^I(\mathbb{I}\cup i)-v^I(\mathbb{I}))$$

$$= \sum_{\mathbb{I}\subseteq I\setminus\{i\}} \frac{|\mathbb{I}|\,!(I-|\mathbb{I}|-1)!}{I!}v^I(i) = v^I(i) \tag{4*}$$

Then the indicator weight w_i^I based on Shapley value is simply

$$w_i^I = \frac{\Phi_i^I}{\sum_{j=1}^{I}\Phi_j^I} = \frac{v^I(i)}{\sum_{j=1}^{I}v^I(j)} \tag{5}$$

Economically, the Shapley value of each indicator i, Φ_i^I, measures the inequality among all the economies. The higher the Φ_i^I of an indicator i, the more divergent the performance across different economies. More weight, w_i^I, will thus be assigned to i. If a government has the aim of reducing inequality, it should implement policies to improve the indicators with more weight.

2 Sub-Environment Level and Environment Level

For each economy $e \in E$, the computed data of any sub-environment $s \in S$ is determined by the indicators comprised, i.e. I_s. Equation (5) has determined the weight of each indicator, and let w_i^{Is} be the weight of indicator $i \in I_s$. Thus, formally, the computed data of any sub-environment $s \in S$ for any economy $e \in E$ is

$$X_{es} = \sum_{i=1}^{I_s} w_i^{Is} SV_{ei} \tag{6}$$

Similar to the indicator-level analysis, we have the standardised score for sub-environment $s \in S$ is SV_{es}.

Let $v^S : 2^S \to \mathbb{R}$ be the characteristic function for the sub-environments. Then for each sub-environment $s \in S$, $v^S(s) : \mathbb{R}^S \to \mathbb{R}$ represents that the value of sub-environment s is derived from X_{es} for all $e \in E$. We have

$$v^S(s) = \sum_{e=1}^{E} |SV_{es}| \tag{7}$$

By the Additivity assumption, the Shapley value of each sub-environment $s \in S$ is

$$\Phi_s^S = v^S(s) \tag{8}$$

and the weight of each sub-environment is

$$w_s^S = \frac{\Phi_s^S}{\sum_{j=1}^{S} \Phi_j^S} = \frac{v^S(s)}{\sum_{j=1}^{S} v^S(j)} \tag{9}$$

The construction of Shapley value and the weight associated with each environment is similar to the analysis above and thus is omitted. Let $v^N : 2^N \to \mathbb{R}$ be the characteristic function for the environments. The Shapley value of each environment $n \in N$ is

$$\Phi_n^N = v^N(n) \tag{10}$$

and the weight of each environment is

$$w_n^N = \frac{\Phi_n^N}{\sum_{j=1}^{N} \Phi_j^N} = \frac{v^N(n)}{\sum_{j=1}^{N} v^N(j)} \tag{11}$$

The economic interpretation of Φ_s^S and Φ_n^N are the same as the indicators'. They capture the inequality across all the economies at the sub-environment level and environment level, respectively. The higher the weight w_s^S and w_n^N, the more divergent the performance across different economies. Thus, government attention should be drawn to such a sub-environment and environment.

3 Index Construction

In order for us to construct the final index to rank all the economies, first, we find the final computed score for each economy $e \in E$, i.e.

$$F_e = \sum_{n=1}^{N} w_n^N SV_{en} \tag{12}$$

where SV_{en} is the standardised value for economy e under environment n.

Then, we standardise the final computed score,

$$R_e = \frac{F_e - \bar{F}}{SD_F} \tag{13}$$

where $\bar{F} = \frac{1}{E}\Sigma_{e=1}^{E} F_e$ and $SD_F = \sqrt{\frac{1}{E}\Sigma_{e=1}^{E}(F_e - \bar{F})^2}$

All the economies, $e \in E$, will be ranked according to the value R_e, which is also the index score for each economy.

Asia Competitiveness Institute - World Scientific Series

(Continued from page vi)

2017 Impact Estimation of Exchange Rate on Foreign Direct Investment Inflows and Annual Update of Competitiveness Analysis for 34 Greater China Economies
by Tan Khee Giap, Zhang Xuyao, Leong Puey Ei & Tan Yang En Isaac (Lee Kuan Yew School of Public Policy, NUS, Singapore)

2017 Annual Competitiveness Analysis and Impact of Exchange Rates on Foreign Direct Investment Inflows to Sub-National Economies of India
by Tan Khee Giap, Sasidaran Gopalan, Jigyasa Sharma & Leong Puey Ei (Lee Kuan Yew School of Public Policy, NUS, Singapore)

2017 Annual Competitiveness Analysis and Impact of Exchange Rates on Foreign Direct Investment Inflows to Sub-National Economies of Indonesia
by Tan Khee Giap, Mulya Amri, Nursyahida Ahmad & Diamanta Vania Lavi (Lee Kuan Yew School of Public Policy, NUS, Singapore)

2016

2016 Annual Competitiveness Analysis and Growth Slowdown Analysis for ASEAN-10
by Tan Khee Giap, Nguyen Le Phuong Anh & Luu Nguyen Trieu Duong (Lee Kuan Yew School of Public Policy, NUS, Singapore)

2016 Growth Slowdown Analysis by Income Thresholds and Annual Update of Competitiveness Analysis for 34 Greater China Economies
by Tan Khee Giap, Wang Peng & Xie Teleixi (Lee Kuan Yew School of Public Policy, NUS, Singapore)

Inaugural 2016 Ease of Doing Business Index on Attractiveness to Investors, Business Friendliness and Competitive Policies (EDB Index ABC) for 21 Sub-National Economies of India
by Tan Khee Giap, Sasidaran Gopalan, Jigyasa Sharma & Tan Kong Yam (Lee Kuan Yew School of Public Policy, NUS, Singapore)

2016 Annual Competitiveness and Growth Slowdown Analysis for Sub-National Economies of India
by Tan Khee Giap, Sasidaran Gopalan, Anuja Tandon & Tan Kong Yam (Lee Kuan Yew School of Public Policy, NUS, Singapore)

2016 Growth Slowdown Analysis, Ease of Doing Business Index, and Annual Competitiveness Studies of Indonesia's Sub-National Economies
by Tan Khee Giap, Mulya Amri, Nursyahida Ahmad & Tan Kong Yam (Lee Kuan Yew School of Public Policy, NUS, Singapore)

2016 Annual Competitiveness Analysis and Development Strategies for Indonesian Provinces
by Tan Khee Giap, Mulya Amri & Nursyahida Ahmad (Lee Kuan Yew School of Public Policy, NUS, Singapore)

2015

2015 Annual Competitiveness Analysis, Agricultural Productivity and Development Vision for ASEAN-10
by Tan Khee Giap, Nguyen Le Phuong Anh, Sasidaran Gopalan & Luu Nguyen Trieu Duong (Lee Kuan Yew School of Public Policy, NUS, Singapore)

2015 Estimation of Agricultural Productivity and Annual Update of Competitiveness Analysis for Greater China: Optimising Agricultural Productivity and Promoting Innovation Driven Growth
by Tan Khee Giap, Yuan Randong & Xie Teleixi (Lee Kuan Yew School of Public Policy, NUS, Singapore)

2015 Agricultural Total Factor Productivity and Competitiveness Analysis for States and Federal Territories and Five Regions of India: Annual Competitiveness Update and Evidence on the Agricultural Development Models for Selected Indian States
by Tan Khee Giap, Sasidaran Gopalan & Anuja Tandon (Lee Kuan Yew School of Public Policy, NUS, Singapore)

2015 Agricultural Productivity, Decentralisation, and Competitiveness Analysis for Provinces and Regions of Indonesia
by Tan Khee Giap, Nurina Merdikawati, Mulya Amri & Tan Kong Yam (Lee Kuan Yew School of Public Policy, NUS, Singapore)

2015 Annual Competitiveness Analysis and Development Strategies for Indonesian Provinces
by Tan Khee Giap, Mulya Amri, Nurina Merdikawati & Nursyahida Ahmad (Lee Kuan Yew School of Public Policy, NUS, Singapore)

2014

2014 Annual Competitiveness Ranking and Simulation Study for ASEAN-10 and Development Strategies to Enhance Asia Economic Connectivity
by Tan Khee Giap, Sangiita Yoong Wei Cher, Sasidaran Gopalan & Nguyen Le Phuong Anh (Lee Kuan Yew School of Public Policy, NUS, Singapore)

2014 Annual Provincial and Regional Competitiveness Analysis for Greater China Economies: Development Strategies under the New Normal
by Tan Khee Giap, Yuan Randong & Sangiita Yoong Wei Cher (Lee Kuan Yew School of Public Policy, NUS, Singapore)

2014 Regional Competitiveness Analysis and a Master Plan on Regional Development Strategies for India: Annual Competitiveness Update and Evidence on Economic Development Model for Selected States of India
by Tan Khee Giap, Linda Low, Kartik Rao & Tan Kong Yam (Lee Kuan Yew School of Public Policy, NUS, Singapore)

2014 Provincial and Inaugural Regional Competitiveness Analysis: Safeguarding Indonesia's Growth Momentum
by Tan Khee Giap, Nurina Merdikawati, Mulya Amri & Tan Kong Yam (Lee Kuan Yew School of Public Policy, NUS, Singapore)

2014 Annual Competitiveness Analysis and Development Strategies for Indonesian Provinces
by Tan Khee Giap, Nurina Merdikawati, Mulya Amri & Blake Harley Berger (Lee Kuan Yew School of Public Policy, NUS, Singapore)

2013

Annual Analysis of Competitiveness, Simulation Studies and Development Perspective for 34 Greater China Economies: 2000–2010
by Tan Khee Giap, Yuan Randong, Sangiita Yoong Wei Cher & Yang Mu (Lee Kuan Yew School of Public Policy, NUS, Singapore)

Annual Analysis of Competitiveness, Simulation Studies and Development Perspective for 35 States and Federal Territories of India: 2000–2010
by Tan Khee Giap, Linda Low, Tan Kong Yam & Kartik Rao (Lee Kuan Yew School of Public Policy, NUS, Singapore)

Competitiveness Analysis and Development Strategies for 33 Indonesian Provinces
by Tan Khee Giap, Mulya Amri, Linda Low & Tan Kong Yam (Lee Kuan Yew School of Public Policy, NUS, Singapore)